Constitutional Law in Switzerland

Constitutional Law in Switzerland

Second Edition

Alexander Misic
Nicole Töpperwien

This book was originally published as a monograph in the International Encyclopaedia of Laws/Constitutional Law.

Founding Editor: Roger Blanpain
General Editor: Frank Hendrickx
Volume Editors: André Alen & David Haljan

Stämpfli Publishers

Wolters Kluwer

Published by:
Kluwer Law International B.V.
PO Box 316
2400 AH Alphen aan den Rijn
The Netherlands
E-mail: international-sales@wolterskluwer.com
Website: lrus.wolterskluwer.com

Sold and distributed in North, Central and South America by:
Wolters Kluwer Legal & Regulatory U.S.
7201 McKinney Circle
Frederick, MD 21704
United States of America
Email: customer.service@wolterskluwer.com

Sold and Distributed in Switzerland by:
Stämpfli Publishers Ltd.
Wölflistr. 1, P.O. Box 5662
CH-3001 Berne
Switzerland
E-mail: verlag@staempfli.com
Phone: +41 31 300 66 44
Website: www.staempfliverlag.com

Sold and distributed in all other countries by:
Air Business Subscriptions
Rockwood House
Haywards Heath
West Sussex
RH16 3DH
United Kingdom
Email: international-customerservice@wolterskluwer.com

ISBN 978-90-411-9613-2 (Kluwer)
ISBN 978-3-7272-2581-9 (Stämpfli)

e-Book: ISBN 978-90-411-9614-9
web-PDF: ISBN 978-90-411-9615-6

The Authors

Alexander Misic studied law at the University of Fribourg (Switzerland) and the Catholic University of Leuven (Belgium). He received a master's degree (LLM) from Cornell Law School (USA) and a doctorate degree (Dr.iur., PhD) from the University of Zurich. He is currently working as a lawyer at the European Court of Human Rights in Strasbourg. In his previous position as a registrar (*Gerichtsschreiber*) at the Swiss Federal Supreme Court he predominantly dealt with cases regarding constitutional, administrative and criminal law. Before, he was an assistant lawyer at the European Court of Human Rights and a registrar at the Swiss Federal Administrative Court in St. Gallen (with main focus on mutual administrative assistance in tax matters between the USA and Switzerland; task force 'UBS cases'). He publishes in the fields of constitutional litigation, human rights, criminal procedure, administrative law and federalism.

Nicole Töpperwien studied law at the University of Fribourg (Switzerland), she received a master's degree from Benjamin N. Cardozo School of Law (New York, USA) and a doctorate (Dr.iur.) from the University of Fribourg. As a co-founder of a Swiss consultancy company, she provides expertise on constitution-making and a range of power-sharing issues, including federalism, decentralization and the inclusion of non-majority groups, with a focus on conflict affected contexts. She regularly supports constitution-making and legislative processes, conducts political analysis, assessments and evaluations, organizes governance study-visits to Switzerland and provides trainings and policy-oriented research. From March 2012 to March 2013 she served as Senior Power-sharing Expert in the Standby team of Mediation Experts for the Mediation Support Unit, Department of Political Affairs of the UN.

Table of Contents

Table of Contents

List of Abbreviations

Glossary

AG	Aargau (Swiss canton)
AI	Appenzell Innerrhoden (Swiss half-canton)
AJP/PJA	*Aktuelle Juristische Praxis/Pratique juridique actuelle* (law review)
AR	Appenzell Ausserrhoden (Swiss half-canton)
AS	Chronological Compilation of Federal Legislation
BBl	Bundesblatt = Federal Gazette (http://www.admin.ch/ch/d/ff/index.html)
BE	Berne (Swiss canton)
BGE	Entscheidungen des Schweizerischen Bundesgerichts = Decision of the Federal Supreme Court (for an explanation of the citing system *see* Part I, Chapter VII, §2)
BGG	Bundesgesetz vom 17. Juni 2005 über das Bundesgericht (Bundesgerichtsgesetz, SR 173.110) = Federal Supreme Court Act
BL	Basel-Land (Swiss half-canton)
BS	Basel-City (Swiss half-canton)
BV	Bundesverfassung der Schweizerischen Eidgenossenschaft vom 18. April 1999 (SR 101) = Constitution of the Swiss Confederation
CCPR	U.N. Covenant on Civil and Political Rights of 16 December 1966 (UN Pact II; SR 0.103.2)
CHF	Swiss Franc(s)
Constitution	Constitution of the Swiss Confederation of 18 April 1999 (SR 101)
ECHR	European Convention for the Protection on Human Rights and Fundamental Freedoms of 4 November 1950 (SR 0.101)
EFTA	European Free Trade Association
EU	European Union
FR	Fribourg (Swiss canton)
GE	Geneva (Swiss canton)
GL	Glarus (Swiss canton)

GR	Grisons (Swiss canton)
JU	Jura (Swiss canton)
LU	Lucerne (Swiss canton)
NE	Neuchâtel (Swiss canton)
NGO	Non-Governmental Organization
NW	Nidwalden (Swiss half-canton)
NZZ	*Neue Zürcher Zeitung* (newspaper)
OW	Obwalden (Swiss half-canton)
recht	*Zeitschrift für juristische Ausbildung und Praxis* (law review)
SG	St. Gallen (Swiss canton)
SH	Schaffhausen (Swiss canton)
SJZ	*Schweizerische Juristen-Zeitung* (law review)
SO	Solothurn (Swiss canton)
SR	Systematic Compilation of Federal Legislation
SZ	Schwyz (Swiss canton)
TG	Thurgau (Swiss canton)
TI	Ticino (Swiss canton)
UN	United Nations
UNO	United Nations Organization
UR	Uri (Swiss canton)
VAT	Value Added Tax
VD	Vaud (Swiss canton)
VPB	Verwaltungspraxis der Bundesbehörden = Administrative Practice of Federal Agencies (http://www.vpb.admin.ch)
VS	Valais (Swiss canton)
ZBl	Schweizerisches Zentralblatt für Staats- und Verwaltungsrecht (law review)
ZG	Zug (Swiss canton)
ZH	Zurich (Swiss canton)
ZSR	*Zeitschrift für Schweizerisches Recht* (law review)

Preface to the Second Edition

In the past six years – since the publication of this book[1] – there have been several amendments to the Swiss Constitution. In 2012, in order to protect and preserve landscapes mainly in the Alpine regions of Switzerland, the People approved stricter limits on the construction of second homes (Article 75b of the Constitution). The popular initiative 'Against rip-off salaries' was accepted in 2013, introducing considerable requirements for Swiss stock companies listed in Switzerland or abroad (Article 95(3) of the Constitution). One year later, the majority of the People and the cantons adopted Article 121a of the Constitution regarding the control of immigration (popular initiative 'Against mass immigration'), as well as Article 123c of the Constitution according to which convicted paedophiles shall permanently lose the right to carry on a profession or voluntary activity involving minors or dependent persons. As some of these initiatives do not seem to be easily reconcilable with fundamental rights and Switzerland's international obligations, the debate regarding the relationship between domestic and international law has gained new impetus. Furthermore, the Constitution and the relevant legislation have been amended within short notice in the field of asylum and immigration law. Finally, the case law of the European Court of Human Rights has occasionally provoked hash reactions in the political and legal sphere, namely concerning the right to private and family life (Article 8 of the Convention).

Faithful to our goal to present a concise overview of Swiss constitutional law we have thoroughly revised the monograph and rewritten several parts:

- Alexander Misic was responsible for the General Introduction, Part I (Sources of Constitutional Law), Part II, Chapter 5 (Organisation of the Judiciary, especially the Federal Courts), Part IV, Chapter 2 (Fundamental Rights), Part IV, Chapter 5 (Judicial Control of Administrative Action) and Part V (Specific Problems). He is grateful to Aisling Ní Riain (BSc University of Glasgow) for proofreading his texts and for her excellent linguistic input. The views set out in this publication are those of the author and do not reflect any official opinion.
- Nicole Töpperwien revised Part II, Chapters 1–4 (State Organization), Part III (Federalism), Part IV, Chapter 1 (Rules Concerning Citizenship and Relevance of Citizenship), Part IV, Chapter 3 (Constitutional Problems of Minorities) and Part IV, Chapter 4 (Legal Position of Aliens).

1. The first edition of this book was published in 2005 under a different title ('Swiss Constitutional Law'). Later on, in order to take into account publications on constitutional law from other countries, the publisher decided to harmonize the title of the series ('Constitutional Law in … '). Hence, according to the way of counting, the present monograph is the second edition of the new series, or the third edition of the book on Swiss Constitutional Law written by the authors.

Preface to the Second Edition

To our regret, Professor Thomas Fleiner has decided to retire from this book. We would like to express our sincere gratitude to our former teacher for providing inspiration and support, for bringing this project to fruition and for his contribution to the success of this book.

Finally, we would like to thank the editors and the publishers for their patience and our friends and colleagues for their invaluable help. We are grateful to the Swiss Federal Chancellery for the authorization to use and modify the English translation of the text of the Federal Constitution.

The Authors
1 September 2017
Lausanne/Berne

General Introduction

Chapter 1. A Short Outline of Swiss Constitutional History

Selected Bibliography: *Historisches Lexikon der Schweiz/Dictionnaire historique de la Suisse/Dizionario storico della Svizzera.* Volumes 1–13 (each in German, French and Italian [two volumes in Rumantsch Grischun]). Basel: Schwabe Verlag, 2002–2014 (online version on: www.hls-dhs-dss.ch); Aubert Jean-François. *Petite histoire constitutionnelle de la Suisse.* 3rd ed. Berne: Francke, 1979; Belser Eva Maria. Basler Kommentar, Einleitung; Biaggini Giovanni. 'Entwicklungen und Spannungen im Verfassungsrecht: Versuch einer Standortbestimmung zehn Jahre nach Inkrafttreten der Bundesverfassung vom 18. April 1999'. In *Schweizerisches Zentralblatt für Staats- und Verwaltungsrecht [ZBl].* 2010, 1 et seq.; Giovanni Biaggini. 'Grundlagen und Grundzüge staatlichen Verfassungsrechts: Schweiz'. In *Handbuch Ius Publicum Europaeum (IPE), vol. I: Grundlagen und Grundzüge staatlichen Verfassungsrechts*, edited by Armin von Bogdandy, Pedro Cruz Villalón & Peter M. Huber. Heidelberg: C.F. Müller, 2007, 565–623; Biaggini Giovanni. 'Switzerland'. In *How Constitutions Change*, edited by Dawn Oliver & Carlo Fusaro. Chapter 14. Oxford: Hart Publishing. 2011; Church Clive H. & Head Randolph C. *A Concise History of Switzerland.* Cambridge University Press, 2016; Egli. 7 et seq.; Fleiner & Giacometti, 1 et seq.; Haller. *Swiss Constitution*, 7 et seq.; Häfelin, Haller, Keller & Thurnherr, §2; Kley Andreas. St. Galler Kommentar, Geschichtliche Einleitung; Kölz Alfred. 'Geschichtliche Grundlagen'. In Thürer et al., 111–127 (with further references); Kölz Alfred. *Neuere schweizerische Verfassungsgeschichte – Ihre Grundlinien vom Ende der Alten Eidgenossenschaft bis 1848.* Zurich: Stämpfli, 1992; Kölz Alfred. *Neuere schweizerische Verfassungsgeschichte – Ihre Grundlinien in Bund und Kantonen seit 1848.* Zurich: Stämpfli, 2004; Maissen Thomas. *Geschichte der Schweiz.* Baden: hier & jetzt, 2010; Rhinow René. 'Zur Aktualisierung der Bundesverfassung, oder: Nachführung ist mehr als Nachführung'. In Sitter-Liver, 563–572; Steinberg, 8 et seq.; Tschannen, §2.

§1. Introduction

1. Switzerland is a country with a population of approximately 8.4 million inhabitants. Its neighbouring territories are Austria, France, Germany, Italy and Liechtenstein. Although situated at the centre of Europe, it is not a member of the European Union (EU). Switzerland has four national languages – German, French, Italian and Romansh – as well as a population that mainly consists of Protestant and

Catholic religious denominations. The borders between these linguistic and religious groups do not overlap but instead intersect each other. Centuries before the creation of the Swiss Confederation in 1848, the cantons and municipalities of the country had been developing their own political identities and traditions. This cultural legacy is still reflected nowadays in the country's cultural diversity, especially in its diversity of political decision-making procedures and of cantonal and communal organizational structures.

2. From the perspective of comparative constitutional law, Switzerland presents an interesting and unique case insofar as it did not follow a similar path as most other European countries: Switzerland never attempted to homogenize its population nor did it divide the territory along linguistic, religious or cultural borders in order to align with Germany, France, Italy and Austria. Primarily through federalism and democracy, Switzerland managed to create and preserve institutions that respected the existing diversity while also unifying to a certain extent the Swiss population. This Swiss model of peaceful coexistence will be elaborated upon in Part II and Part III of this monograph. The Swiss experience and possible lessons to be drawn from for other multi-ethnic societies (especially in the process of nation-building after conflicts) have raised the attention of political actors and scholars from all over the world. Anyone who has the intention of understanding Swiss constitutional law will have to take into consideration the vastly different situations Switzerland has encountered throughout its history. Therefore, it is justified to start this outline with the historical background of the country prior to the creation of the Swiss federal state in 1848 (*infra* §2 of this chapter) and then to focus on the historical evolution of the three Federal Constitutions of 1848, 1874 and 1999 (*infra* §3 of this chapter).

§2. Historical Background Before the Creation of the Confederation (1291–1847)

3. Descriptions of Swiss constitutional history usually begins with the period of the Old Swiss Confederacy (*Alte Eidgenossenschaft*). With the construction of new and faster trade routes through the Alps, which before had almost insurmountably separated Central Europe from Italy, the territory of Central Switzerland around Lake Lucerne gained great strategic importance (which lasts to this day: the Gotthard Tunnel still is the quickest passage through the Alps). As a reward for their support in military campaigns in Italy, Friedrich II of the Holy Roman Empire declared that the valleys of Uri (1231) and Schwyz (1240) fell under the king's exclusive jurisdiction (exempting them therefore from the jurisdiction of any other counts and dukes).

4. However, after the death of his successor, Rudolf von Habsburg, in the year 1291, however, the situation grew unstable. The counts of Habsburg, whose ancestral seat in today's Canton of Aargau, was less than 100 kilometres away tried to regain control and influence on these territories. Uri, Schwyz and Unterwalden feared that they might lose their prerogatives. As a consequence they signed the Swiss Charter of Confederation on August 1291 (*Bundesbrief*) creating a treaty-based defence alliance combined with a system of arbitration for conflicts among themselves. The founding myth claims that on 1 August 1291 representatives of Uri, Schwyz and Unterwalden met in a meadow on the western shore of Lake Lucerne and swore in the famous Oath of Rütli (*Rütlischwur*) to help each other fend off anybody who might try to suppress them as well as not to fight against each other. For this reason, the 1 August is celebrated as Switzerland's national holiday (Article 110(3) of the Constitution). The alliance was directed at the reeves of the Count of Habsburg, but it did not aim to secede from the Holy Roman Empire. The main objectives of the alliance were to regain and to renew old autonomy rights, to prevent the predominance of neighbouring powers ('*no foreign judges*') and to guarantee an internal balance of power.

5. Gradually, other cantons – then called *Orte* – joined the alliance by subsequent treaties, thereby developing a treaty-based confederation. While safeguarding the sovereignty of the Member States, the purpose of the alliance was to facilitate as much cooperation as necessary to defend the independence of its members. Therefore, in order to preserve diversity, the Member States accepted unification to a certain extent. Up to the end of the eighteenth century the different entities that formed Switzerland were not equal, making their status dependent on the treaty which linked them to the union. Status was negotiable. For example, when Fribourg and Solothurn requested entrance into the confederation, they had to accept fewer rights than most other entities in order to avoid a predominance of cities over rural Member States (*Stanser Verkommnis* of 1481, mediated by the hermit and ascetic Niklaus von Flüe of Obwalden, the patron saint of Switzerland), whereas other areas were subject territories, such as the Vaud, which was under the control of Berne.

6. The only common institution was the *Diet (Tagsatzung)*, a non-permanent conference of the Member States with legislative and executive authority. The representatives were strictly bound by the instructions from their Member States. In order to preserve the continuation of their own sovereignty, it was the intention of the Member States not to create a strong and flexible organ. Consequently, the Diet lacked substantial competences. Decisions had to be taken unanimously. This allowed the Member States to develop their own political regimes. Most Member States had patrician oligarchic systems (Berne, Fribourg or Solothurn), which allowed only members of a small number of families to vote. Other Member States relied on the guild's system (Zurich, Basel, Schaffhausen). For many decisions, the mountainous and rural regions relied on the so-called *Landsgemeinde*, an assembly of all the male citizens who usually gathered after Sunday mass in an open-air meeting and voted on legislative matters through direct democracy (of course, without the secrecy of the ballot, which is one of the main reason why Switzerland has not ratified the Additional Protocol No. 1 to the European Convention on Human Rights (ECHR) yet). Nevertheless, inhabitants of the areas under control of the cities (e.g., Zurich, Berne, Lucerne and Basel) as well as the peasants of the subject territories under common administration by all Member States of the old Swiss Confederation (Aargau, Thurgau, Vaud), were deprived of all political rights.

7. During the Reformation period, the power and corrupted state of the Roman church were being condemned in Switzerland by several reformers, most prominently by John Calvin and Guillaume Farel (in Geneva) and by Huldrych Zwingli (in Zurich). As a religious renewal movement, the Reformation quickly spread from Zurich to the eastern and northern parts of the country. Central Switzerland resisted the reformed beliefs and remained firmly Catholic region. Based on several peace treaties (*Kappeller*

Landfrieden in 1531, later reaffirmed in the *Aargauer Friede* of 1812) the principle of '*cuius regio eius religio*' was established namely for the cantons and in special cases even for municipalities. Thus, Switzerland became a patchwork of different Catholic and Protestant communities. Zwingli's reforms in particular included a very strong political component, which significantly contributed to the democratization of the church and the state in Switzerland. His reforms also inspired the English Reformation of Henry VIII. In addition, Zwingli's theory of an alliance between God and the believers (*Bundestheologie*) inspired the philosophy of Althusius, which ultimately strongly influenced the development of federalism in the United States. Rising tensions between the (more democratic) progressive and commercial cities and the (more conservative) rural areas of Central Switzerland resulted in a division which developed into a critical issue of political conflict.

8. The Thirty Years' War on the European Continent (1618–1648) strengthened these divisions and threatened the unity of the country. Switzerland's leaders quickly realized that only neutrality as a foreign policy strategy would allow them to be excluded from the international wars waged between the European countries, thereby maintaining internal peace between the different religious groups within the country. Towards the end of the war, the Swiss even managed to organize a common Protestant and Catholic defence against intrusion from the outside (*Wiler Defensionale*; 1647). The formal independence from the German Empire and the sovereignty of Switzerland was recognized in the Westphalian Peace Treaty of 1648.

9. By the end of the eighteenth century, modernization in neighbouring countries, industrialization and the professionalization of armies, along with the ideas of the French Revolution, triggered demands for a stronger centralization and modernization of Switzerland. In 1798, Napoleon Bonaparte invaded Switzerland and founded the *Helvetic Republic*, a centralized state in accordance with the French prototype. The Swiss territory was then transformed into equal, though purely administrative, units called *cantons*. However, Switzerland soon proved to be ungovernable as a centralized state due to the several *coups d'état* carried out between 1800 and 1802. Nevertheless, the ideas of the French Revolution fell on fertile soil and began to spread out, such as the idea of democratic institutions, the guarantee of fundamental rights, equality and the doctrine of separation of powers). Through the Mediation Act of 19 February 1803, Napoleon reintroduced nineteen autonomous cantons as main and equal power holders with different official languages, but Switzerland remained a French protectorate.

10. After Napoleon's defeat, Switzerland opted again for a loose Confederation, but the equal status of the cantons remained (Confederate Treaty of 7 August 1815). At the Vienna Congress in 1815, fearing that the neighbouring Great Powers might split up the territory of Switzerland among themselves, Tsar Alexander I of Russia (whose tutor, friend and secretary was Frédéric-César de la Harpe , a Swiss politician and intellectual) insisted on the international recognition of the borders and the perpetual neutrality of Switzerland. On 20 November 1815, Switzerland's perpetual neutrality was internationally recognized and guaranteed by the Paris Charter. Swiss neutrality was reconfirmed multiple times, such as in the Treaty of Versailles on 28 June 1919, in the aftermath of World War I and in the London Declaration of 13 February 1920.

11. The formerly subjected territories and the predominantly liberal (mostly Protestant) cantons adopted a progressive democracy. In the primarily Catholic cantons the old influential families regained power and introduced conservative structures. In order to resist the pressure for centralization and democratization from the liberal cantons, the conservative cantons (Lucerne, Uri, Schwyz, Unterwalden, Zug, Fribourg and Valais) formed a secret union (*Sonderbund*) that violated provision 6 of the Confederate Treaty. When the union was revealed in June 1846 and the conservatives refused to dissolve it, the liberal cantons dissolved the *Sonderbund* by force. The year of 1847 entered in Swiss history as the year of civil war (*Sonderbund* War). The civil war began on 3 November 1847, with attacks from the *Sonderbund* alliance. Due to the actions of Guillaume Henri Dufour from Geneva, the general of the federal troops and later co-founder of the International Committee of the Red Cross, the *Sonderbund* war was over after twenty-seven days (with 86 dead and 500 wounded soldiers). In 1848, the first Swiss Federal Constitution was adopted, which was a compromise between the victors and the defeated of the civil war.

§3. Switzerland as a Federal State

I. The Creation of the First Federal State in Europe: The Federal Constitution of 1848

12. The Confederate Treaty of 1815 had been accompanied by an ever denser web of treaties concluded between the cantons leading to closer cooperation. In 1848, the supporters for a federal state were able to capitalize the fact that most of the neighbouring European countries were absorbed with revolutions and their own political and socio-economic problems. The conservative powers in Switzerland were heavily divided and in a weakened state. The moment for the creation of a federal state had come. Shortly after the end of the *Sonderbund* war, a reform commission began working on a constitutional draft which was presented to the Diet on 8 April 1848 and adopted with minor alterations on 27 June 1848. The Diet decided – against the provisions of the Confederate Treaty – that the Confederate Treaty would be replaced by the Federal Constitution, if the Constitution were approved by the majority of the cantons. The constitutional text was subsequently submitted to the cantons. Fifteen cantons and one half-canton approved the Constitution, six cantons and one half-canton decided against. On 6 November 1848, both chambers of the Federal Assembly sat for the first time in Berne.

13. Thus, the first European federation was founded. Switzerland retained its official name *Confoederatio Helvetica.* The Constitution was named: Federal Constitution of the Swiss Confederation – despite the obvious paradoxical nature of the name. With the new Federal Constitution of 1848, Switzerland took an important step towards modernity whilst also combining the experience and the achievements of the cantons with the ideas from the French Revolution and with some institutional elements of the American Constitution. It became a federal state based on a constitutionally guaranteed balance of self and shared rule. The Constitution introduced a moderate centralization in areas for which more cooperation was deemed necessary (such as foreign policy, customs, the postal sector, currency). However, it did not assign any taxing powers to the federal level, nor did it establish a unified Swiss army. All powers not explicitly attributed to the federal level remained with the cantons. The Constitution guaranteed a stable institutional setup through the introduction of a bicameral parliament system according to the American model and the creation of the Federal Council modelled after the *directoire* of revolutionary France. The political institutions were shaped so as to balance the interests of Switzerland and that of the cantons. The Constitution also included certain fundamental rights and liberties such as the equality before the law, the freedom of establishment, the freedom of religion (for Catholics and Protestants only, however) and the liberty of the press. From the 1860s onward, a further democratization of the cantons was carried out. Many of the direct democratic instruments within the cantons were introduced between 1860 and 1874.

II. One Army, One Market, One Law: The Federal Constitution of 1874

14. The autonomy of the cantons, e.g., in the area of police, education, private and criminal law, the judiciary, healthcare, work, commerce and banking, but also fiscal sovereignty, was one reason for the relatively swift reconciliation between the former enemies of the *Sonderbund* war. Gradually, during the German-French War in 1870 in particular, demands for a new constitutional framework with stronger centralization grew exponentially. After several failed attempts for a constitutional revision, a new federal constitution was adopted by a fairly clear margin by the People and the cantons in the referendum of 19 April 1874. It came into force on 29 May 1874. The new Federal Constitution of 1874 did not decisively change the organizational structure of the federal state. However, it did introduce a far stronger centralization of the country and – as a counterbalance – strengthened the democratic rights of the citizens.

15. The centralization included new federal powers for the unification of the law, especially in the field of private and criminal law (Article 64 of the Federal Constitution of 1874). Furthermore, the Constitution provided for a single economic market, a stronger federal judiciary in the form a permanent Federal Supreme Court,[2] and a unified army.

16. Furthermore, the Federal Constitution introduced the right of the citizens to demand a referendum on federal statutes. In 1891, the popular initiative for the

---

2. The official name of the Court is *Bundesgericht* (in German), *Tribunal fédéral* (in French), *Tribunale federale* (in Italian) and *Tribunal federal* (in Rumantsch). This denomination – the correct English translation being 'Federal Court' – has historical reasons. Until recently – before the creation of lower federal courts – there existed only two federal courts in the Swiss Confederation: The Federal Court in Lausanne and the Federal Insurance Court in Lucerne (with the reform of the judiciary, the latter was integrated into the Federal Court in 2006). Since then, more federal courts have been established: the Federal Criminal Court started to operate in 2004, the Federal Administrative Court in 2007 and the Federal Patent Court in 2011. Thus, the use of the term 'Federal Court' may become increasingly misleading for foreign readers attempting to understand the Swiss system of the federal judiciary. For reasons of clarity, the term 'Federal Supreme Court' is used throughout this monograph in order to denominate 'the highest judicial authority of the Confederation' (Art. 188(1) of the Constitution).

partial amendment of the Constitution was added. However, democratic rights were limited to men. Women were not allowed to vote on the federal level before 1971 (after attempts to introduce their right to vote failed in 1959).

17. The Federal Constitution of 1874 introduced further fundamental rights, such as economic freedom, the right to free primary school education, the right to marry, the extension of the scope of application of the right of establishment and the freedom of belief and conscience to members of all confessions. A systematic Bill of Rights was still lacking, but lacunae in the field of the protection of fundamental rights were gradually filled by the case law of the Federal Supreme Court (e.g., the judicial recognition of the right to property as an implied fundamental right in 1959, which was integrated into the Constitution in 1969, *see infra* Part IV, Chapter 2, §1 I C and §4 VII) and by the accession of Switzerland to the ECHR in 1974.

18. By creating a permanent Federal Supreme Court with substantive jurisdiction, the Federal Constitution of 1874 entrusted the Court, *inter alia*, with the task of protecting the constitutional rights of the citizens (*see infra* Part IV, Chapter 2, §1 I) as well as judging appeals of individuals regarding violations of concordats and state treaties (Article 113 of the Federal Constitution of 1874). For this purpose, the Public Law Appeal (*staatsrechtliche Beschwerde*) served as a specific legal remedy before the Federal Supreme Court against unconstitutional statutes and decisions of the cantons. Taking into consideration the vast powers of the cantons, this form of constitutional review was a revolutionary innovation at that time period in constitutional history. However, as far as the constitutional review of *federal laws* by the Federal Supreme Court was concerned, Article 113(3) of the Federal Constitution of 1874 contained an important (and still valid) restriction on that matter. According to this provision, federal laws as well as those international treaties recognized by the Federal Assembly must be applied by the Federal Supreme Court (*even if* the Court holds the federal law or certain provisions thereof to be unconstitutional). Due to the older federal legislature being discriminatory especially against women, this part of the population suffered the most from the lack of constitutional review of federal laws. The details of this constitutional 'immunization of federal laws' (Biaggini) from judicial review will be discussed *infra* in Part IV, Chapter 2, §7 of this monograph.

19. Although the Swiss Constitution is one of the most frequently amended constitutions, Switzerland has one of the most stable political systems in the world. At first glance this might appear paradoxical, but the system's stability may be due to a viable system of direct democracy, which encourages the citizens to participate actively in matters they want (or do not want) to be regulated. Consequently, between 1874 and 1999, there were approximately 150 partial revisions of the Federal Constitution. In addition to the ones already mentioned the most important partial amendments of the Federal Constitution of 1874 concerned the creation of a new canton, the Canton of Jura (in 1979) and the introduction of a national social security system in 1890 and in 1925. In spite of those numerous constitutional revisions, the overall constitutional design regarding the organization of the federal institutions and authorities, first adopted in 1848, remains in substance almost the same today.

III. A New Design: The Federal Constitution of 1999 and the Subsequent Reform Steps

20. The drawback of those numerous partial amendments of the Federal Constitution of 1874 was that the constitutional text soon became confusing and, in parts, a barely decipherable patchwork of provisions. The constitutional charter was also incomplete because it did not mirror all constitutional changes (e.g., excepting the right to property, none of the other implied fundamental rights recognized by the Federal Supreme Court were formally anchored into the Constitution). Although multiple attempts for a complete amendment of the Federal Constitution of 1874 were being made, a total of 125 years would elapse before the People and the cantons adopted a new federal constitution. The motivation for creating a new federal constitution was mainly led by the desire for a systematic, comprehensive and formally appealing constitutional text ('constitutional update'; *Nachführung, mise à jour*). In addition, there were proposals for further reforms in the areas of federalism, democracy and the *Rechtsstaat* (including institutional questions). However, the proponents of these reforms agreed not to include them in the constitutional draft in order to avoid opposition. Instead, it was decided to introduce them later through partial amendments once the new constitution had been adopted. One hundred and fifty years after the establishment of the federal state, the Federal Assembly passed the new Federal Constitution in December of 1998, the anniversary year. The mandatory referendum scheduled for 18 April 1999 brought a rather narrow, albeit positive, result in favour of the new federal constitution which entered into force on 1 January 2000.

21. In the years following the adoption of the Federal Constitution of 1999 three major and substantial reform packages were presented to the People and the cantons: The subsequent reform steps contained the reform of the judiciary (approved by the People in 2000), People's democratic rights (approved in 2003) and the reform of fiscal federalism (approved in 2004).

Chapter 2. The Pillars of the Swiss Constitution

§1. The Classic Pillars of the Constitution and the Emergence of Further Structural Principles

Selected Bibliography: Auer, Malinverni & Hottelier. Vol. I, 490 et seq.; Biaggini. Kommentar, Einleitung; Eichenberger Kurt. Kommentar BV 1874. Verfassungsrechtliche Einleitung; Egli, 23 et seq.; Häfelin, Haller, Keller & Thurnherr, § 4; Haller. *Swiss Constitution*, 27 et seq.; Haller, Kölz & Gächter, §§ 9, 16, 17 and 19; Mastronardi Philippe. 'Strukturprinzipien in der Verfassung?'. In *Beihefte zur Zeitschrift für Schweizerisches Recht [ZSR]* no. 7. Basel 1988; Rhinow, Schefer & Uebersax, 31 et seq.; Tschannen, §6.

22. Which structural principles essentially hold the Swiss constitutional order together? The attentive reader will not find the answer directly in the constitutional text (compared to Article 20(1) of the German Basic Law). The framers of the Constitution were reluctant to anchor a constitutional provision solemnly declaring that Switzerland is a federal and democratic state based upon the rule of law and social justice. Since structural principles as such are not justiciable norms, the drafters rather preferred a pragmatic approach leaving ontological questions unanswered. Although the exact number of structural principles permeating the Constitution is unclear, there is a certain consensus among constitutional scholars that the following four classic structural principles are the essential pillars, without which the Swiss constitutional system would be barely functional: Semi-direct democracy, federalism and the federal state (*Bundesstaat*), liberty and the *Rechtsstaat*, and the welfare state (*Sozialstaat*). As shall be elaborated upon in this chapter, these pillars or structural principles of the federal constitution are closely intertwined. The use of the word 'pillar' shall not imply that the structural principles are – like Giacomettian sculptures – standing somehow isolated in the constitutional landscape.

23. In addition to these established structural principles Rhinow, Schefer and Uebersax as well as Auer, Malinverni and Hottelier observe the emergence of further (mostly written) structural principles in the new federal constitution. In their view, today's Swiss constitutional order is also characterized by a free economy oriented towards competition, the principle of subsidiarity (Article 5a of the Constitution) and sustainable development (Article 73 of the Constitution). They further propose that Switzerland's integration into the international community and openness towards the world (*kooperativer und weltoffener Verfassungsstaat*) constitutes another structural principle.

24. It should be noted that neutrality is not a structural principle of the Constitution. This might come as a surprise to some foreign readers because in an international context, Switzerland is very often closely associated with neutrality. However, from a strictly constitutional law perspective, neutrality is not deemed to have the status of a structural principle. Article 54(2) of the Constitution carefully avoids the mention of neutrality as a goal of Swiss foreign policy and prefers a more general wording, i.e., safeguard of the independence of Switzerland and its welfare, assistance in the alleviation of need and poverty in the world, promotion of respect for human rights and democracy, the peaceful coexistence between the peoples as well as the conservation of natural resources. As explained by Walter Haller (note 71), in Switzerland, neutrality is understood more as a concept of international public law and as an instrument of Swiss foreign policy, rather than as a pillar of the Swiss Constitution. Neutrality, often a topic of vivid political debate, shall be discussed in detail in Part V, Chapter 1, §1 of this monograph.

§2. Semi-direct Democracy (Referendum Democracy)

Selected Bibliography: Auer, Malinverni & Hottelier. Vol. l, 197 et seq.; Auer Andreas. 'Problèmes fondamentaux de la démocratie Suisse'. *In Zeitschrift für Schweizerisches Recht [ZSR].* 1984 II, 1 et seq.; Egli, 60 et seq.; Fossedal Gregory A. *Direct Democracy in Switzerland.* New Brunswick 2002; Frey Bruno, S. 'Direct Democracy'. In *American Economic Review* 84 (1994): 338–348; Grisel Etienne. *Initiative et référendum populaires – Traité de la démocratie semi-directe en droit suisse.* 3rd ed. Berne: Stämpfli, 2004; Haller. *Swiss Constitution,* 28 et seq.; Hangartner Yvo & Kley Andreas. *Die demokratischen Rechte in Bund und Kantonen der Schweizerischen Eidgenossenschaft.* Zurich: Schulthess, 2000; Kiener Regina et al., 'Bedeutungswandel des Rechtsstaats und die Folgen für die (direkte) Demokratie am Beispiel völkerrechtswidriger Volksinitiativen'. In *Schweizerisches Zentralblatt für Staats- und Verwaltungsrecht [ZBl].* 2009, 237 et seq.; Kriesi Hanspeter/Trechsel Alexander. The Politics of Switzerland. Continuity and Change in a Consensus Democracy. Cambridge University Press 2008; Linder. *Swiss Democracy,* passim; Mastronardi Philippe. 'Der Zweck der Eidgenossenschaft als Demokratie'. In *Zeitschrift für Schweizerisches Recht [ZSR].* 1998 II, 317 et seq.; Müller Jörg Paul. *Demokratische Gerechtigkeit.* Munich, 1993; Rhinow René. 'Grundprobleme der schweizerischen Demokratie'. In *Zeitschrift für Schweizerisches Recht [ZSR].* 1984 II, 111 et seq.; Rhinow Schefer & Uebersax, §2/193 et seq.; Tanquerel Thierry. 'Les fondements démocratiques de la Constitution'. In Thürer et al., §18; Tschannen, §6 II; Vatter Adrian. *Das politische System der Schweiz.* 2nd ed. Baden-Baden: Nomos, 2016.

25. By having the distinction of being one of the oldest democracies in the world, Switzerland has managed to slowly transform and democratize previously oligarchic forms of government and to pragmatically develop a diverse set of flexible and locally anchored democratic institutions. Having been surrounded by monarchies and aristocracies for several centuries, the belief in the specificity of Swiss democracy establishes an essential part of the Swiss identity, which is characterized by the broad recognition of a *political* Switzerland. Surprisingly, the democratic principle, though absolutely fundamental, is not mentioned in the Constitution. It is, however, indirectly embodied in it through diverse provisions. Evidence of the importance of the democratic principle is set out in Article 148(1) of the Constitution, according to which the Federal Parliament is the highest authority of the Confederation *subject to the rights of the People and the cantons.* Additionally, the Constitution sets minimum requirements for the democratic organization of the cantons. According to Article 51 of the Constitution, every canton shall adopt a democratic constitution, which must be approved by the cantonal People and must be subjected to amendments, if required by a majority of the cantonal People. The cantonal constitutions must be approved by the Confederation to assure their conformity with federal laws (Article 51(2) of the Constitution, *infra* Part III, Chapter 2, §1 II B).

26. As shall be discussed in this monograph, the Swiss concept of the so-called semi-direct democracy relies on a parliament with representatives elected by the People (representative system; *infra* Part II, Chapter 2, §2), conferring to the People powerful instruments of direct participation and intervention against almost every decision made by the Parliament ('referendum democracy'; *infra* Part II, Chapter 2, §3 and §4). Not surprisingly, this concept forms the state at all levels into a specific political model (consensus-oriented democracy), which cannot easily be compared with other governmental systems. The influence of political parties is strongly diminished compared to other democracies based on the Westminster model. In an open democratic discourse prior to a referendum, all the weak points of any proposed legislation will be challenged and attacked. Therefore, a statute which caters only to the interests of one party is unlikely to pass the referendum. The political elite must always bear this in mind, thus making the *prevention of a referendum* the main aim of Swiss politics. Only legislation that convincingly promotes the public interest is likely to receive the final approval of the People. The Swiss experience also shows that the People are well able to distinguish populist proposals that conceal special interests from proposals in the common interest.

27. The constant pursuit for consensus also attracts the criticism that in a consensus-oriented democracy the real political debate between interested parties takes place behind closed doors and out of public view. In a campaign to win the citizens' support, the People cannot decide on real alternatives, but rather are forced to either accept a predetermined compromise or, as a consequence of a negative vote, to bear responsibility for the shattered remains of the carefully negotiated proposal. Indeed, the permanent search for consensus compels all state authorities to a constant levelling of their policy. The pressure to respect and to reflect Switzerland's inherent diversity is great. The idea of a simple majority rule is consequently largely foreign to the concept of semi-direct democracy. Rather, the permanent search for a fair and just compromise, which ideally comes as close as possible to unanimity, has given rise to a different political culture in which compromise is regarded as a strength and not as a weakness.

28. Of course, the political system a semi-direct democracy has its well-known neuralgic points, especially the absolutization of the democratic principle. As recently observed by Walter Haller in his book on the Swiss Constitution (note 61), '[t]here is a clear tendency to regard the will of the people, as expressed in the results of votes, as almost sacrosanct, even when its compatibility with international law appears to be questionable' (*see* Articles 72(3), 123a, 123b of the Constitution). In order to deal with such situations more appropriately the Federal Council started providing proposals with the aim of making the incompatibility of the initiative with international law more apparent at an earlier stage of the initiative process. Consequently, the Federal Council proposes a substantive (but non-binding) preliminary control of the text of an initiative by the Federal Chancellery before the signatures are collected. If an incompatibility is confirmed, the Federal Council recommends writing this result on each signature sheet. With this information, the citizen (rarely an expert in international law) has a better idea of what she/he is signing. Not surprisingly, the proposal of the Federal Council is debated.

29. Furthermore, especially in the political discourse regarding the introduction of constitutional review of federal laws, the so-called primacy or supremacy of the democratic principle over the *Rechtsstaat* principle is sometimes over-exaggerated by certain political actors. Of course, the 'primacy' of the democratic principle could be deduced from Article 190 of the Constitution, according to which the Federal Supreme Court and all other law-applying authorities must apply federal statutes even if they are unconstitutional (*infra*, Part IV, Chapter 2, §7). But to claim that there is 'primacy' because the democratic legitimacy of Parliament is deemed to be higher than the legitimacy of the Court does accurately represent today's constitutional order. Democracy – at least in the form practised nowadays in Switzerland – is scarcely imaginable without the guarantees of the *Rechtsstaat*, such as the protection of fundamental rights, the separation of powers, and effective judicial process and *vice versa*. In other words: The relationship between democracy and the *Rechtsstaat* is one of intertwinement and reciprocity rather than one of subordination.

§3. Federalism and Federal State

Selected Bibliography: Auer, Malinverni & Hottelier. Vol. 1, 315 et seq. (with further references); Biaggini. Kommentar, Vorbemerkungen Articles 42–135; Egli, 35 et seq.; Fleiner & Basta Fleiner. *Constitutional Democracy*, 593 et seq.; Fleiner & Misic. 'Föderalismus als Ordnungsprinzip der Verfassung'. In Thürer et al., §27; Häfelin, Haller, Keller & Thurnherr, 48, 291 et seq.; Haller. *Swiss Constitution*, 31 et seq.; Hangartner Yvo. *Die Kompetenzverteilung zwischen Bund und Kantonen.* Berne: Lang, 1974; Hänni Peter (ed.). *Schweizerischer Föderalismus und europäische Integration.* Zurich: Schulthess, 2000; Kägi-Diener Regula. 'Zweck und Aufgaben der Eidgenossenschaft aus bundesstaatlicher Sicht'. In *Zeitschrift für Schweizerisches Recht [ZSR].* 1998 II, 49 et seq.; Koller Heinrich. 'Der Preis des Föderalismus aus juristischer Sicht'. In *Festschrift Thomas Fleiner*, 109 et seq.; Saladin Peter. 'Bund und Kantone – Autonomie und Zusammenwirken im schweizerischen Bundesstaat'. In *Zeitschrift für Schweizerisches Recht [ZSR].* 1984 II, 431 et seq.; Schweizer Rainer J. St. Galler Kommentar, Vorbemerkungen Articles 42–135; Rhinow, Schefer & Uebersax, §§5 5 et seq.; Tschannen, §§ 15 et seq.

30. Federalism denies the entitlement of the majority of the nation to be the only legitimate basis of popular sovereignty. The federal state (*Bundesstaat*) replaces absolute sovereignty by diffusing the distribution of powers between the federation, the federal units and sometimes even municipalities. Therefore, the federal principle can be generally understood as a constitutionally guaranteed balance between self-rule and shared rule.

31. Switzerland is a federal state based on a double legitimacy, stemming from the federal principle and Article 1 of the Constitution, which proclaims that the Swiss People *and* the cantons form the Swiss Confederation (for more details *see* Part III).

Again, unlike other federal constitutions (e.g., the German Basic Law or the Belgian Constitution) and due to historical reasons, the Swiss Constitution does not explicitly denominate Switzerland as a federal state. Rather, federalism seems to be taken for granted because Switzerland is founded historically and traditionally upon strong cantonal identities and upon a democratic integration, which, in terms of constitution-making as well as with regard to the decentralization of state powers to cantons and municipalities, recognizes and fosters diversity as well as cantonal and local loyalties. In Switzerland, federalism is neither a correction nor a complement to democracy (in the sense of the Madisonian concept of federalism), but is instead a structural foundation for a consensus-oriented democracy (federalized democracy). The Swiss form of substantial legitimacy not only reconciles federalism and democracy, but it builds upon the view that these two structural principles of the Constitution are and should be integrally related. Thus, the communal character of the Swiss democracy serves to better articulate and protect the interests of structural minorities. Of course, this is not free of criticism. In 2007, the average number of voters represented per seat in the National Council (the democratic chamber of Parliament) was generally (more or less) balanced in contrast to the average number of voters per seat at the Council of States (the federal chamber of Parliament). In the latter, the weight of a vote from the Canton of Appenzell Innerrhoden was almost thirty-nine times higher in comparison to a vote from the Canton of Zurich.

32. Switzerland is composed of three governmental levels (federal, cantonal and municipal), each of which has its own powers. The three-level polity is mirrored in the concept of a threefold citizenship (federal, cantonal and municipal citizenship). The Constitution transfers certain powers to the federal level, while residuary powers lie with the cantons (Articles 3 and 42 of the Constitution). The federal level can only act in the area of expressly enumerated powers. The cantons usually confer considerable autonomy to the municipalities. The federal constitution protects the autonomy of the municipalities only within the limits fixed by the cantonal constitutions (Article 50(1) of the Constitution; *see also infra* Part III, Chapter 3, §1 II).

33. The Constitution provides for the distribution of powers and determines therefore the areas of self-rule. As already shown in the historical introduction of this monograph, the self-rule principle used to be the predominant one in the concept of Swiss federalism. The Constitution, however, provides for shared rule, for instance, through the representation of the cantons in a second chamber of the Parliament (*infra* Part II, Chapter 3) and through the participatory rights of the cantons at the federal level (e.g., the amendment of the Constitution, participation in the preliminary law-making procedure; *infra* Part I, Chapter 3, §2; Part III, Chapter 1, §2 II). Due to the political and financial interdependence between the Confederation and the cantons, there has scarcely remained an area in which the cantons can be completely and absolutely autonomous. In the Federal Constitution of 1999, the element of cooperation, embodied, *inter alia*, in the shared rule principle, was an attempt to compensate for the diminished cantonal autonomy. – Regrettably, it appears that federalism is slowly shifting away from people's minds. In a recent survey of 2017, one-third of the interviewed persons declared federalism to be a 'rather vague' concept to them. Fifty per cent do not feel or do not feel at all committed to federalism.

§4. Freedom and the Rechtsstaat

Selected Bibliography: Auer, Malinverni & Hottelier. Vol. II, 467 et seq.; Egli, 24 et seq.; Fleiner & Basta Fleiner. *Constitutional Democracy*, 221 et seq.; Häfelin, Haller, Keller & Thurnherr, 45 et seq.; Haller. *Swiss Constitution*, 27–28; Benjamin Schindler. St. Galler Kommentar, Article 5 (with further references); Kohler Georg. 'Philosophische Grundlagen der liberalen Rechtsstaatsidee'. In Thürer et al., §15; Müller Jörg Paul & Biaggini Giovanni. 'Die Verfassungsidee angesichts der Gefahr eines Demokratieabsolutimus'. In *Schweizerisches Zentralblatt für Staats- und Verwaltungsrecht [ZBl]*. 2015, 235 et seq. Moor Pierre. 'Principes de l'activité étatique et responsabilité de l'Etat'. In Thürer et al., §16; Schmid Gerhard & Uhlmann Felix. 'Idee und Ausgestaltung des Rechtsstaates'. In Thürer et al., §13 (with further references); Rhinow, Schefer & Uebersax, §2/193 et seq.; Tschannen, §6 III.

34. That men should not be ruled by men, but instead by laws derives from the experience that human dignity and freedom are prime values which must be carefully protected from arbitrariness and the abuse of power. The idea that the positive embodiment of the state legal order must always adhere to the fundamental formal and substantive principles of law and justice was developed primarily within the Anglo-Saxon legal tradition. The Anglo-Saxon notion of the Rule of Law however encapsulates the basic and fundamental principle according to which political might and power is always limited and controlled by the law in the sense of pre-state and pre-positive law. The German notion of *Rechtsstaat* however is an expression of the requirement that all authorities and institutions *created under the constitution of a state* must comply with the positive law (principle of legality).

35. The *Rechtsstaat* principle is mentioned in the Constitution of 1999. According to Article 5(1) of the Constitution, all state activity shall be based on and limited by the law. The Federal Supreme Court usually distinguishes between the formal and substantive *Rechtsstaat* principle. The content and function of the formal *Rechtsstaat* principle is set out in Article 5 of the Constitution (principle of legality, respect of international law), in Articles 29–32 (procedural due process, right to substantive review by an impartial court, *see also* Article 191c of the Constitution) and the principle of separation of powers. The substantive *Rechtsstaat* principle is based upon the idea that all state activity must be in the public interest and proportionate to the goals pursued (Article 5(3) of the Constitution) and respect fundamental rights.

36. The *Rechtsstaat* principle is not completely implemented in the field of constitutional and administrative review. Until the early 1980s, due to the belief in the superiority of (semi-direct) democracy, the Swiss *Rechtsstaat* was underdeveloped. This was particularly the case in fields such as administrative law, in which citizens did not always have the right to an impartial court. Since Switzerland's accession to the ECHR in 1974, the situation has changed considerably. The Federal Supreme Court has made extensive efforts to create harmony in its interpretation of fundamental rights guaranteed in the Convention and the Constitution of 1874. These decisions had a concrete impact on the new Swiss Federal Constitution of 1999 (*see* the extensive catalogue of fundamental rights with a set of justiciable procedural guarantees in the second part of the Constitution [Articles 7–36 of the Constitution]; *infra* Part IV,

Chapter 2). Full constitutional review of federal laws, however, is still not granted (Article 190 of the Constitution; *see infra* Part IV, Chapter 2, §7).

37. The People and the cantons agreed on a constitutional reform of the judiciary on 12 March 2000. The constitutional provisions as well as the majority of the relevant federal acts, especially the Federal Supreme Court Act, entered into force 1 January 2007. In essence, the reform contains the following innovations (*see* for further details *infra* Part II, Chapter 5 and Part IV, Chapter 5, §3):

(1) In legal disputes, every person shall have the fundamental right to a decision by a *judicial* authority (access to justice; Article 29a of the Constitution).
(2) The power to unify civil and criminal procedure law – formerly a traditional domain of the cantons – is delegated to the federal level (Articles 122–123 of the Constitution). On 1 January 2011, the federal rules of civil and criminal procedure entered into force.
(3) The substantive jurisdiction of the Federal Supreme Court is extended over federal elections and voting (Article 189(1)(f) of the Constitution).
(4) In an attempt to reduce the heavy workload of the Federal Supreme Court was made by the creation of the Federal Criminal Court and the Federal Administrative Court (Article 191a of the Constitution) as well as by the creation of additional cantonal judicial authorities (Article 191b of the Constitution). The Federal Patent Court as the Confederation's court of first instance ruling on civil law disputes regarding patents (Article 191a(3) of the Constitution) began to operate in St. Gallen in 2012.
(5) Finally, the Constitution guarantees the independence of the judge as an institutional principle (Article 191c of the Constitution).

38. For various historical and ideological reasons, the 'primacy' of the democratic principle over the *Rechtsstaat* principle has led to a model excluding the full constitutional review of federal laws (*see* Part IV, Chapter 2, §7). But it appears that in Parliament a certain paradigm shift has been going on and that the idea of a full constitutional review of federal laws is not entirely inconceivable anymore. The proposal of the Law Commission of the National Council to simply eliminate Article 190 from the Constitution is at first sight intriguing, but it must be thoroughly examined especially regarding the practical consequences it may have on for the federal and cantonal judiciary and, of course, for all other law-applying authorities.

§5. Welfare State (Social Justice)

Selected Bibliography: Gächter Thomas & Werder Gregori. Basler Kommentar, Article 41 (with further references); Mader Luzius. 'Die Sozial- und Umweltverfassung'. In *Aktuelle Juristische Praxis [AJP]*. 1999, 698 et seq.; Meyer-Blaser Ulrich & Gächter Thomas. 'Der Sozialstaatsgedanke'. In Thürer et al., §34 (with further references); Müller Jörg Paul. *Soziale Grundrechte in der Verfassung?*. 2nd ed. Basel: Helbing & Lichtenhahn, 1981; Tschannen, §6 IV; Tschudi Hans Peter. *Die Sozialverfassung der Schweiz (Der Sozialstaat)*. Berne: Schriftenreihe des Gewerkschaftsbundes, 1986.

39. By quoting a famous sentence of the Swiss writer Adolf Muschg the Preamble of the Constitution points out that the strength of the people is measured by the well-being of its weakest members. Furthermore, Article 2 of the Constitution defines the promotion of common welfare and the equality of opportunity as a goal of the Swiss Confederation. Nevertheless, the Constitution does not designate Switzerland as a welfare state (*Sozialstaat*). Rather than outlining an abstract model of social justice, the Constitution creates a social safety net through various social insurances, and it contains several social fundamental rights and social goals.

40. The Swiss social security system has grown organically and gradually over the course of the twentieth century. Based on the three pillars, namely through the federal old-age, survivors' and invalidity insurance, the occupational pension scheme and private pension schemes, the Confederation took measures to ensure adequate financial provision for the elderly, surviving spouses and children, and persons with disabilities (Articles 111 and 112 of the Constitution). Additionally, the Confederation and cantons shall pay supplementary benefits to people whose basic living expenses are not covered by benefits from the old-age, survivors and invalidity insurance (Article 112a of the Constitution). The Confederation encourages the rehabilitation of people eligible for invalidity benefits by providing cash and non-cash benefits (Article 112b of the Constitution). Home care programmes for the elderly and people with disabilities are provided for by the cantons (Article 112c of the Constitution). Furthermore, the Confederation has legislated in the fields of occupational pension schemes (Article 113 of the Constitution), unemployment insurance (Article 114 of the Constitution), child allowances and maternity insurance (Article 116 of the Constitution) as well as health and accident insurances (Article 117 of the Constitution). Finally, persons in need shall be supported by the canons of their residence (Article 115 of the Constitution).

41. The catalogue of fundamental rights of the Constitution contains so-called social fundamental rights (*Sozialgrundrechte*), which are enforceable before a court: Article 12 of the Constitution provides that persons in need and unable to provide for themselves have the right to assistance and care and to the financial means required for a decent standard of living, while Article 19 of the Constitution guarantees the right to an adequate and free primary school education (*infra* Part IV, Chapter 2, §5). Of great practical importance is the right to free legal assistance and free legal counsel. According to Article 29(3) of the Constitution, anyone who lacks sufficient means may invoke this fundamental right, unless their case appears to have no prospect of success. If it is necessary in order to safeguard their rights, they also have the right to free legal representation in court (*infra* Part IV, Chapter 2, §6 I C). Furthermore, the Constitution enumerates in Article 41 several social objectives (*Sozialziele*), which are of objective-programmatic nature and do not confer rights to state benefits. As a complement to personal responsibility and private initiative, the Confederation and the cantons shall endeavour to ensure that:

- everyone has access to social security;
- everyone has access to the health care that they require;
- families are protected and encouraged as communities of adults and children;
- everyone who is fit to work can earn their living by working under fair conditions;

- anyone seeking accommodation for themselves and their family can find suitable accommodation on reasonable terms;
- children and young people as well as persons of employable age can obtain an education and undergo basic and advanced training in accordance with their abilities;
- children and young people are encouraged to develop into independent and socially responsible people and are supported in their social, cultural and political integration.

Chapter 3. State Territory

§1. Overall Territory

42. Switzerland covers an area of 41,285 square kilometres, approximately two hundred times smaller than the territory of the United States of America. Since 40% of the territory is uninhabitable (mountains, glaciers, etc.) the population is concentrated mainly in the flat and arable areas between the Alps and the Jura mountains (called *Mittelland*).

§2. Cantons

43. The Swiss territory, as enumerated in Article 1 of the Constitution, is divided into twenty-three cantons: Zurich, Berne, Lucerne, Uri, Schwyz, Unterwalden, Glarus, Zug, Fribourg, Solothurn, Basel, Schaffhausen, Appenzell, St. Gallen, Grisons, Aargau, Thurgau, Ticino, Vaud, Valais, Neuchâtel, Geneva and Jura. The Canton of Jura was created in 1978 as a result of a secession from the Canton of Berne (*infra* Part III: Chapter 2, II). The Constitution of 1999 no longer lists the cantons Unterwalden, Basel and Appenzell, but enumerates the half-cantons Nidwalden and Obwalden, Basel-City and Basel-Land, Appenzell Innerrhoden and Appenzell Ausserrhoden.

44. The mountainous Canton of Grisons is the largest territory with 7,105 square kilometres, whereas the Canton of Basel-City is the smallest with 37 square kilometres.

Cantonal Territories

Canton	*Territory in square km*	*Canton*	*Territory in square km*
1. Grisons	7,105	14. Jura	837
2. Berne	5,961	15. Neuchâtel	803
3. Valais	5,225	16. Solothurn	791
4. Vaud	3,212	17. Glarus	685
5. Ticino	2,812	18. Basel-Land	517
6. St. Gallen	2,026	19. Obwalden	491
7. Zurich	1,729	20. Schaffhausen	299
8. Fribourg	1,671	21. Geneva	282
9. Luzern	1,493	22. Nidwalden	276
10. Aargau	1,404	23. Appenzell Ausserrhoden	243
11. Uri	1,077	24. Zug	239
12. Thurgau	991	25. Appenzell Innerrhoden	173
13. Schwyz	909	26. Basel-City	37

45. Three of the twenty-three cantons are divided into so-called *half-cantons*. In the Middle Ages, the Canton of Unterwalden decided to separate into two half-cantons, Obwalden and Nidwalden. For mainly territorial reasons, the geographical location made the cooperation between the two parts of the canton difficult. The division of the Canton of Appenzell into Appenzell Innerrhoden and Appenzell Ausserrhoden was a result of the counter-reformation. The canton was split into a Catholic and a Protestant part in 1597.

46. In 1832–1833, the Canton of Basel divided into Basel-City and Basel-Land due to a dispute between the city of Basel and the countryside, which essentially felt dominated by the city. When a referendum on the separation of the two territories failed, the canton expelled all municipalities that had not voted to remain with the Canton of Basel. These municipalities then formed the half-canton of Basel-Land, which was later joined by other municipalities. The Diet (the governing institution in Switzerland at that time), however, denied both cantons the right to a full vote each. Like the half-cantons of Appenzell Innerrhoden and Ausserrhoden, and Nidwalden and Obwalden, they had to share a common vote in the Diet. Today, the half-cantons each have only one seat in the Council of States, while the other cantons dispose over two seats each (*infra* Part II, Chapter 3, §1 II and III). With minor exceptions, the half-cantons' status is very similar to that of ordinary cantons. Due to this similarity of status, one can often find the statement that there are twenty-six cantons or twenty-six cantonal regimes, even though there are officially only twenty 'ordinary' cantons and six half-cantons. Whether there are twenty-three or twenty-six federal subdivisions depends on the way of counting.

§3. Municipalities

47. Each canton decides on the organization of its own territory, which is divided into municipalities. The municipalities, which have considerable autonomy, namely in fiscal, construction or zoning matters, are usually called *Gemeinde, commune* (French), *commune* (Italian). In the Canton of Appenzell Innerrhoden the lowest level of government is called *Bezirk* instead of *Gemeinde*. On an average, each Swiss municipality has 2,100 inhabitants. However, 45% of the Swiss municipalities have less than 500 inhabitants, and more than 200 municipalities have less than 100 inhabitants. At the other extreme, the City of Zurich, which also forms a municipality, has about 400,000 inhabitants. Overall, in 2016, Switzerland had approximately 2,300 political municipalities compared to the 3,021 municipalities in 1999. Their numbers are constantly decreasing, largely due to mergers.

48. In 1998, the Canton of Fribourg consisted of a total of 246 municipalities. Of these, 192 had less than 1,000 inhabitants. In 1998, the average number of inhabitants per municipality throughout Switzerland was 940. Therefore, the average community in the Canton of Fribourg was noticeably smaller than the average Swiss one. For socio-economic reasons, the administration of Fribourg created an incentive system for mergers, which was widely used (forty-one mergers between 2000 and 2006). As of 2017, the Canton of Fribourg consists of 136 municipalities. So far, the policy of merging municipalities has had more success in the French, Italian and Romansh-speaking areas than in the German-speaking ones (for a recent case regarding an initiative in the Canton of Ticino to merge 17 municipalities with the city of Locarno and 16 municipalities with the city of Bellinzona without prior consultation of the concerned municipalities *see* the Decision of the Federal Supreme Court BGE 142 I 216. The Court held that the cantonal initiative violated international law, *in casu* the European Charter of Local Self-Government of 15 October 1985, and declared the initiative null and void).

§4. Districts

49. Seventeen Cantons additionally divide their territory into districts (*Bezirke*). While the municipalities have a relatively significant degree of autonomy, these districts are in most cases purely administrative units. The head of the district can be compared to *préfet* in the French system. Only the Cantons of Schwyz and the Canton of Grisons confer to their districts (*Bezirke* or *Kreise*) autonomy and an independent public law status, thereby introducing an additional level in the federal system.

§5. Regions

50. For strategic planning purposes, the Federal government divided Switzerland into regions. So far, these regions remain artificial entities and their importance in the state structure is minimal.

§6. Capital

51. The capital of Switzerland is Berne and the City of Berne is part of the territory of the Canton of Berne. The City of Berne has approximately 142,000 inhabitants as of 2016. Unlike to the capitals of the United States or Mexico, the federal institutions of the Swiss Confederation do not form a distinct federal district.

Chapter 4. Population (Demographic Data)

§1. Overall Population

52. At the end of 2015, Switzerland had 8,327,126 permanent residents, with a density of 203 persons living per square kilometres. Between 1932–2015, the population has doubled from 4.1 million to 8.3 million. In 2015, 25% of the overall population were foreigners (1910: 14.7%). (Note: The demographical data is taken from the Swiss Federal Statistical Office at www.statistik.admin.ch.)

§2. Cantonal Populations

53. The Canton of Zurich has the largest number of inhabitants (1,466,424 in 2015), whereas the half-canton of Appenzell Innerrhoden has the lowest population total with 15,974 inhabitants (in 2015).

Cantonal Populations in 2015

Canton	*Population*	*Canton*	*Population*
1. Zurich	1,466,424	14. Grisons	196,610
2. Berne	1,017,483	15. Basel-City	191,817
3. Vaud	773,407	16. Neuchâtel	178,107
4. Aargau	653,675	17. Schwyz	154,093
5. St. Gallen	499,065	18. Zug	122,134
6. Geneva	484,736	19. Schaffhausen	79,836
7. Lucerne	398,762	20. Jura	72,782
8. Ticino	351,946	21. Appenzell Ausserrhoden	54,543
9. Valais	335,696	22. Nidwalden	42,420
10. Fribourg	307,461	23. Glarus	40,028
11. Basel-Land	283,231	24. Obwalden	37,076
12. Thurgau	267,429	25. Uri	35,973
13. Solothurn	266,418	26. Appenzell Innerrhoden	15,974

§3. Languages

54. Of the languages spoken in the country, 66.1% of the population is Swiss-German or German-speaking, 18.4% French-speaking, 11% Italian-speaking and 0.8% Romansh-speaking, while 9.4% speaks other languages (all data from 2000). Note that Rhaeto-Romanic is a general name for several related dialects of the Romance group of the Italic subfamily of the Indo-European family of languages. The principal Rhaeto-Romanic dialects are Romansh (with several sub-families in the Canton of Grisons: Surselvan, Sutsilvan-Surmeir and Puter), Ladin (Italian Tyrol) and Friulian (Northeastern Italy). Furthermore, Swiss-German (*Schwiizerdütsch*) is a generic term for all Alemanic dialects spoken in the German-speaking part of Switzerland which can be divided into Low, High and Highest Alemanic. However, each dialect is again separated into an impressive variety of local subdialects. It is not uncommon that a person from the Low or High Alemanic region (Basel or Zurich) has problems to fully understand somebody speaking a Highest Alemanic dialect (Valais). Swiss-German is the *spoken* everyday language. In contrast to other Alemanic regions outside Switzerland (e.g., Alsace in France) Swiss-German is very popular (regardless of the social level of the speaker) and dominates daily life not only in the countryside but also in the urban areas. Most importantly, it should not be confused with Swiss Standard German (*Schweizer Hochdeutsch; Schriftdeutsch*) which is the official *written* language in German-speaking Switzerland. It is mostly *spoken* as a sign of politeness and respect in the presence of non-Alemanic speakers and (usually) during lectures or in news broadcasts. Most people from other German-speaking countries hardly understand Swiss-German (a reason why Swiss dialect movies or TV series broadcasted in Germany or Austria must be synchronized or subtitled), but have no difficulty in reading or understanding Swiss Standard German. Swiss children learn Swiss Standard German, which is often perceived by them as a foreign language, at primary school. The following figures, Figures 1 and 2, show the linguistic situation in Switzerland (reprint from the 2017 edition of 'The Swiss Confederation – Brief Guide', with kind permission of the Federal Chancellery) and in the Canton of Grisons (reprint from Jachen C. Arquindt et al., *Die viersprachige Schweiz*. Einsiedeln: Benziger Verlag, 1982, with kind permission of the Museum Fram Archive in Einsiedeln).

Figure 1 Linguistic Situation in Switzerland

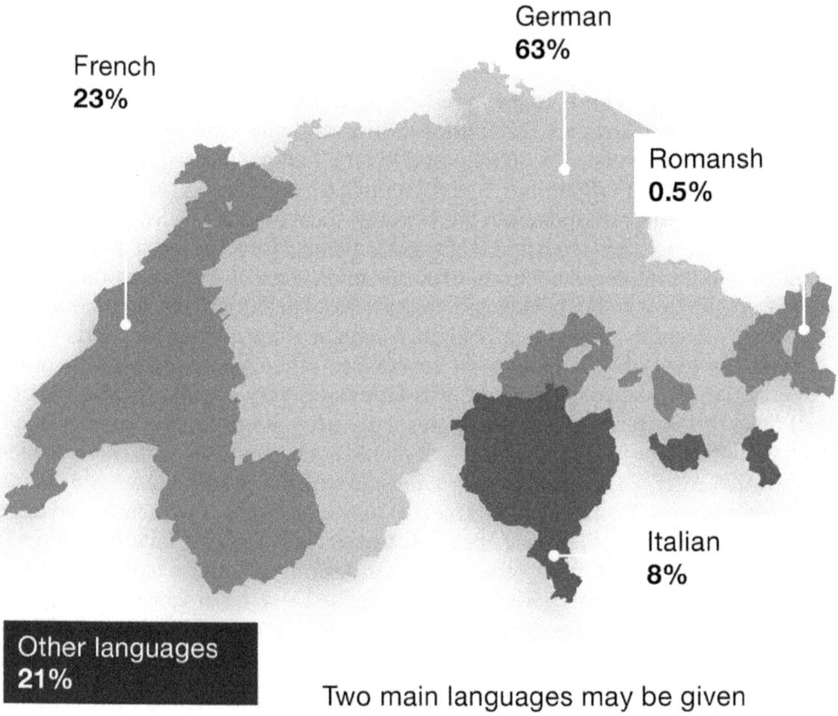

Figure 2 Linguistic Situation in the Canton of Grisons

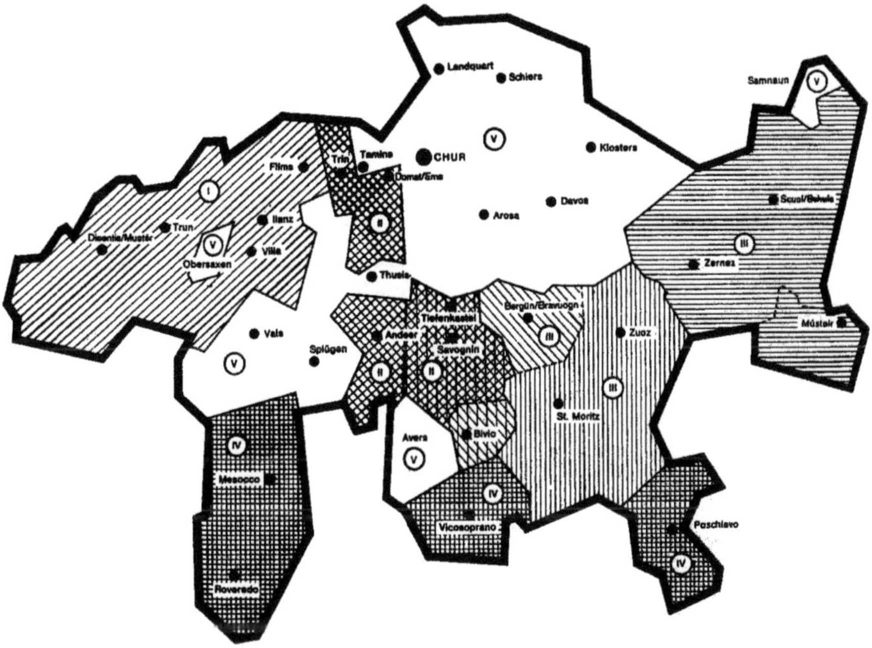

Note: I. = Sursilvan, II. = Sutsilvan-Surmeir, III. = Putér, IV. = Italian, V. = Swiss-German/German.

§4. Religion

55. In 2016, 38% of the population were Roman Catholic, 26.2% Protestant, 5% Muslim, 2.2% Christian Orthodox, 0.2% Jewish and 22.2% did not adhere to a religious group.

§5. Cities

56. In 2015, the six most populated cities were Zurich (396,027), Geneva (194,565), Basel (168,620), Berne (140,634), Lausanne (135,629) and Winterthur (106,778). Other larger cities in Switzerland are St. Gallen, Lucerne, Biel (Bienne), Thun, Köniz, La Chaux-de-Fonds, Schaffhausen, Fribourg (Freiburg) and Neuchâtel (Neuenburg).

§6. Unemployment

57. In 2016, there was an unemployment rate of 3.7% with the highest unemployed segments being foreigners, women and people in the average age group of 15–24 years old.

§7. Foreigners

58. In 2015, 2,049,000 foreigners were living in Switzerland (25% of the population). They mainly originated from Italy (311,742), Germany (300,691), Portugal (267,474), France (122,970), Kosovo (106,879), Spain (82,334), Serbia (71,260), Turkey (69,215), Macedonia (64,448) and the United Kingdom (41,766). In 2015, 39,523 persons requested asylum; to 6,377 persons were granted asylum. In 2015, Swiss citizenship was granted to 40,689 persons.

Part I. Sources of Constitutional Law

Chapter 1. Treaties

Selected Bibliography: Aubert Jean-François. 'Notions et fonctions de la Constitution'. In Thürer et al., § 1; Auer, Malinverni & Hottelier. Vol. I, 443 et seq.; Biaggini Giovanni. 'Das Verhältnis der Schweiz zur internationalen Gemeinschaft'. In *Aktuelle Juristische Praxis [AJP]*. 1999, 722 et seq.; Cottier Thomas et al. (eds), *Der Staatsvertrag im schweizerischen Verfassungsrecht: Beiträge zu Verhältnis und methodischer Angleichung von Völkerrecht und Bundesrecht.* Berne, 2001; Cottier Thomas & Hertig Maya. 'Das Völkerrecht in der neuen Bundesverfassung: Stellung und Auswirkungen'. In Zimmerli et al., 1 et seq.; Cottier Thomas et al., *Die sektoriellen Abkommen Schweiz – EG, Ausgewählte Fragen zur Rezeption und Umsetzung der Verträge vom 21. Juni 1999 im schweizerischen Recht.* Berne: Stämpfli, 2002; Egli, 13 et seq.; Häfelin, Haller, Keller & Thurnherr, § 63; Haller. *Swiss Constitution*, 249 et seq.; Kälin Walter et al., *Völkerrecht.* 4th ed. Berne: Stämpfli, 2016; Keller Helen. *Rezeption des Völkerrechts.* Berlin: Springer, etc. 2003; Mahon. Vol. I, 59 et seq.; Müller Georg. 'Rechtssetzung und Staatsverträge'. In Thürer et al., §70; Müller Jörg Paul & Wildhaber Luzius. *Praxis des Völkerrechts.* 3rd ed. Berne: Stämpfli, 2001; Rhinow, Schefer & Uebersax, §38; Tschannen, §9; Villiger Markus E. *Commentary on the 1969 Vienna Convention on the Law of Treaties.* Leiden/Boston: Martinus Nijhoff Publishing. 2009.

§1. In General

59. International treaties are usually defined as written or unwritten, synallagmatic or concludent agreements between two states or other subjects of international law, governed by international law, obliging the contracting parties to do, tolerate or omit something (*see* Decision of the Federal Administrative Court BVGE 2010/7 paragraph 3.3.1, and the definition in Article 2(1)(a) of the Vienna Convention of 23 May 1969 on the Law of Treaties [SR 0.111], which however only applies to treaties between states). For Switzerland, international treaties are of utmost importance, particularly due to its small geographical size and its non-integration into the EU. This led not only to the conclusion of a series of bilateral treaties between Switzerland and the EU but also to a very dense web of treaties with countries all around the world (e.g., in the area of free trade, double taxation conventions, etc.). The details regarding the treaty-making procedure as prescribed by the Constitution will be discussed *infra* in Part V, Chapter 1, §3 of this monograph.

§2. Monistic System

60. Although the Constitution does not mention it Switzerland relies on a monistic system. International treaties, duly entered into force (*infra*, Part V, Chapter 1, §2), are regarded as an integral part of the national legal system. Since Switzerland has adopted the monistic system, further transformation of a treaty within the national statutory system is not required (Decisions of the Federal Supreme Court BGE 127 II 177, 181 and BGE 120 Ib 360, 366). Nevertheless, the treaty remains an international treaty, and the interpretation of it is governed by the Vienna Convention. As a general rule, international treaties must first be published in the Official Compilation of Federal Legislation (Article 2 of the Federal Publication Act; SR 170.512) and, subsequently, in Section Zero of the Systematical Compilation of Federal Legislation. Upon publication, the self-executing provisions of the international treaty gain binding force for the individual (Article 10 of the Federal Publication Act). The Federal Supreme Court has affirmed the self-executing character of international treaty provisions under two conditions: (1) the provision must directly regulate rights and duties of the individual, *and* (2) the provision must be sufficiently concretized in order to establish an appropriate legal basis for authoritative adjudication (Decisions of the Federal Supreme Court BGE 120 Ia 1, 11 and BGE 124 III 90, 91).

§3. The Relationship Between Treaties and National Law

Selected Bibliography: Biaggini. Kommentar, Article 5 (note 26 et seq.); Häfelin, Haller, Keller & Thurnherr. §63 IV; Haller. *Swiss Constitution*, 253 et seq.; Helen Keller et al., 'Anspruch und Realität der 'Selbstbestimmungsinitiative'. In *Aktuelle Juristische Praxis [AJP/PJA]*. 2016, 712 et seq., 867 et seq., 1007 et seq.; Schindler Diedrich. 'Der Vorrang des Völkerrechts und des Völkerrechts vor dem nationalen Recht als Problem der demokratischen Legitimation des Rechts'. In *'Rechtskollisionen', Festschrift für Anton Heini.* Zurich, 1995, 321 et seq.; Michel Nicolas. 'L'imprégnation du droit étatique par l'ordre juridique international'. In Thürer et al., §4; Rhinow, Schefer & Uebersax, §38 IV; Thürer Daniel. 'Verfassungsrecht und Völkerrecht'. In Thürer et al., §11; Thürer Daniel. 'Bundesverfassung und Völkerrecht'. Kommentar BV 1874, note 13 et seq.; Tschannen, §9.

61. The relationship between treaties and national law is one of the most challenging and most debated questions in Swiss constitutional law and politics. It can be only outlined here in the most rudimentary way. According to Article 5(4) of the Constitution, the Confederation and the cantons shall respect international law. Note the ambiguity of the formulation by the use of the term 'respect' in the constitutional text. Thus, although the state is bound to act in good faith according to Article 5(3) of the Constitution (*pacta sunt servanda*), it is not apparent if this provision may be considered as the constitutional basis for the supremacy of international law over national law. In order to reduce the complexity of the relationship between international treaties and national law, the Federal Supreme Court and constitutional scholars have identified three basic patterns and proposed the following solutions to remedy (with more or less success) the normative conflicts.

62. First, the relationship between international treaties and constitutional provisions is unclear. The Constitution does not provide a concrete answer. However it is commonly agreed upon that *ius cogens* (in the narrow sense as defined by international law) takes precedence over constitutional law (*see also* Article 139(2) of the Constitution). With respect to other international law provisions, a balancing test is applied in order to give precedence to the more important norm, such as fundamental rights over purely international administrative agreements. Since the provisions regarding fundamental rights of the new Swiss Constitution and the provisions of the ECHR and the UN-Pacts I and II do not essentially differ from each other (*see* Part IV, Chapter 2, §1), the Federal Supreme Court has put them (from a procedural perspective) on equal footing.

63. Second, the relationship between international treaties and federal acts (*Bundesgesetze*) has led to a complex case law of the Federal Supreme Court. As a general rule, international law takes precedence over federal statutory law. However there are two important exceptions regarding:

(1) the relationship of international law to prior federal statutory law; and
(2) the relationship of federal statutory law to prior international law.

64. Ad (1): The Court maintains that newly adopted international law takes precedence over *prior* federal statutory law (the *lex posterior* rule). *Ad* (2): In a series of important cases, namely in *Schubert* (Decision of the Federal Supreme Court BGE 99 Ib 39), the Court clarified to a certain extent the relationship between a newly adopted federal statute in contrast to a prior international treaty provisions. In the cited case, the Court decided that the new federal statutory provision prevails if the Federal Parliament intentionally deviated from international law. The *Schubert* doctrine was widely criticized and partially overruled in *Propaganda Material PKK* (Decision of the Federal Supreme Court BGE 125 II 417). The Court has emphasized in *PKK* that conflicts shall be – to the extent possible – avoided through the interpretation of federal statutory law in conformity with constitutional and international law (*verfassungskonforme Auslegung*). Furthermore, if the normative conflict cannot be resolved through constitutional interpretation, the Court affirmed that international law would always prevail at least in cases of a conflict between international human rights and newly adopted federal statutory law (no *lex posterior* rule; *see* Decision of the Federal Supreme Court BGE 122 II 485, 487). However, parts of the ruling in *Schubert*, according to which newly adopted federal statutory provision would prevail over international law *if Parliament intentionally deviated from international law*, are still good law (Decisions of the Federal Supreme Court BGE 112 II 1, 13 and BGE 118 Ib 277, 281, reaffirming *Schubert*). But *PKK* clarified, that *Schubert* laws are intrinsically void if they violate *ius cogens* or international human rights.

65. Third, it is acknowledged that international law always takes precedence over federal ordinances and contrary cantonal law.

66. On 12 August 2016, the Swiss Popular Party (SVP) handed in the signatures collected for its federal popular initiative 'Swiss law instead of foreign judges (Self-determination initiative)' at the Federal Chancellery. The initiative's goal is to add to Article 5(1) of the Constitution a second sentence declaring the Federal Constitution to be 'the ultimate source of law'. Subject to peremptory norms under international law (*ius cogens*), the Federal Constitution shall rank above international law and take precedence over it (new Article 5(4) second sentence of the Constitution). The Confederation and the cantons shall not create obligations under international law which are in contradiction with the Federal Constitution (new Article 56a(1) of the Constitution). In case of contradiction between the Federal Constitution and international law, the Confederation and the cantons agree to amend those obligations under international law to suit the Federal Constitution; if necessary, subject to peremptory norms under international law, the respective treaties are to be terminated (new Article 56a(2) and (3) of the Constitution). Federal acts and international law that have been approved by referendum are binding on the Federal Supreme Court and other law-applying authorities (new Article 190 of the Constitution). – It is noteworthy that in the current public debate, predominantly weighing the pros and cons of leaving the ECHR and a fiery jeremiad against the judicial activism as allegedly practised by the European Court for Human Rights, the economic effects of and the loss of reputation through the initiative remain – at least so far – rather unevaluated. This is insofar surprising as Switzerland is earning every second Swiss franc abroad and is therefore intertwined in a dense web of international treaties. The question of whether the unclear wording and the rigid rules of the proposed initiative will allow Switzerland to remain a reliable treaty party or not must be left open for the time being. The Federal Council delivered a report in July 2017 and took as expected a critical stance not only on the various issues set out above. The popular vote is set for the end of 2018/beginning of 2019.

§4. Important Treaties

67. Important international treaties are: The ECHR of 4 November 1950 (in force in Switzerland since 1974; SR 0.101), the International Covenant on Economic, Social and Cultural Rights (UN-Pact I; SR 0.103.1), the International Covenant on Civil and Political Rights (UN-Pact II; SR 0.103.2) (in force in Switzerland since 1992), and the Bilateral Agreements I between the Swiss Confederation and the EU (in force since June 2002). The Bilateral Agreements I regulate the economic relationship with the EU in areas such as personal freedom of movement, air and land traffic, reduction of technical trade barriers and research. The Bilateral Agreements II mainly deal with the 'left-overs' of the Bilateral Agreements I, such as education, agriculture, services and pensions, media and environment. However, the Bilateral Agreements II also focuses on rigid topics such as the closer cooperation in the fields of police, justice, asylum, migration (Dublin/Schengen) and taxation. Furthermore, a very dense web of international treaties concluded between Switzerland and other states all around the globe and international organizations cover other important areas, namely taxation (double taxation treaties), energy, traffic, public procurement, health, finances and economy, etc.

Chapter 2. Constitution

68. Switzerland has a written federal constitution and twenty-six written cantonal constitutions.

§1. Federal Constitution

69. The Federal Constitution of 1999 is the supreme law of Switzerland. The Constitution of 1874 has been completely amended to enhance the structure and the readability of the constitutional text (so-called *Nachführung*). Hence, the amendment did not bring forth any fundamental contextual changes (*see* already General Introduction, Chapter 1, §3 III).

I. System

70. The Federal Constitution is divided into titles, chapters, sections and articles. The division into titles and chapters is the following:

Title 1: General Provisions

Title 2: Fundamental Rights, Civil Rights, and Social Objectives

Chapter 1: Fundamental Rights

Chapter 2: Citizenship and Political Rights

Chapter 3: Social Objectives

Title 3: Confederation, Cantons, and Municipalities

Chapter 1: Relationship between the Confederation and the Cantons

Chapter 2: Powers

Chapter 3: Finances

Title 4: People and Cantons

Chapter 1: General Provisions

Chapter 2: Initiative and Referendum

Title 5: Federal Authorities

Chapter 1: General Provisions

Chapter 2: Federal Parliament

Chapter 3: Federal Council and Federal Administration

Chapter 4: Federal Supreme Court and Other Judicial Authorities

Title 6: Revision of the Federal Constitution and Transitory Provisions

Chapter 1: Amendment of the Constitution

Chapter 2: Transitory Provisions

II. Constitutional Amendments

Selected Bibliography: Aubert & Mahon. commentaire, Articles 192–195; Biaggini Giovanni. 'Switzerland'. In *How Constitutions Change*, Dawn Oliver & Carlo Fusaro (eds). Chapter 14. Oxford: Hart Publishing. 2011; Biaggini. Kommentar, Articles 192–195; Egli, 67 et seq.; Epiney Astrid & Diezig Stefan. Basler Kommentar BV, Articles 192–194; Haller. Swiss Constitution, 232 et seq.; Häfelin, Haller, Keller & Thurnherr, §60; Hangartner Yvo & Bernhard Ehrenzeller. St. Galler Kommentar, Articles 193 and 194; Müller Reto Patrick. St. Galler Kommentar, Article 195; Rhinow, Schefer & Uebersax, 523 et seq.; Tschannen, §44.

71. The Swiss Federal Constitution can be amended *completely* or *in part* at any time (Article 192(1) of the Constitution). However, the mandatory provisions of international law (*ius cogens*) may not be violated (Article 193(4) of the Constitution).

72. A *total amendment* of the Constitution can be proposed by the People by means of the constitutional initiative (*infra* Part II, Chapter 2, §3 I), by one of the Chambers of Parliament or by the Federal Assembly. If the initiative emanates from the People or if the two Chambers of Parliament disagree on the total amendment, the People will decide in a popular vote if a total amendment should be undertaken. Should the popular vote be successful, both Chambers of Parliament are to be newly elected (Article 193 of the Constitution). With respect to the Constitution of 1999, both Chambers agreed upon the project of a total amendment. Therefore, *no popular vote on the question regarding* the *necessity to amend* was needed. As a consequence, it became superfluous to newly elect two Parliamentary Chambers.

73. A *partial amendment* of the Federal Constitution may be proposed through a constitutional initiative or by the Federal Parliament (Article 194(1) of the Constitution).

74. The Constitution, amended in total or in part, enters into force only after acceptance by both the People and the cantons through popular vote (Article 195 of the Constitution).

§2. Cantonal Constitutions

Selected Bibliography: Auer Andreas. *Staatsrecht der schweizerischen Kantone*. Berne: Stämpfli 2016; Auer, Malinverni & Hottelier. Vol. I, 580 et seq.; Biaggini. Kommentar, Article 51; Buser. Kantonales Staatsrecht, passim; Eichenberger Kurt. *Verfassung des Kantons Aargau.* Aarau, etc.: Sauerländer, 1986; Ehrenzeller Bernhard. 'Reformprozesse im Verfassungsrecht von Bund und Kantonen'. In Thürer et al., §12; Ehrenzeller Bernhard & Nobs Roger. 'Gemeinsamkeiten und Unterschiede der totalrevidierten Kantonsverfassungen'. In *Schweizerisches Zentralblatt für Staats- und Verwaltungsrecht [ZBl].* 2009, 1 et seq.; Rhinow, Schefer & Uebersax, §10; Tschannen, §18.

75. The cantons as 'small states or republics' give themselves their own democratic constitution organize the three branches of cantonal government and checks and balances between them, and regulate the political rights of their citizens including referendum and initiative of the people. Article 51(1) of the Constitution only requires that the cantonal constitutions must be 'democratic'. Hence, the cantonal constitutions differ significantly from each other depending on the cantonal traditions and the time of their adoption. Since the entry into force of the new federal constitution in the year 2000 several cantons amended their constitutions as well (the so-called renaissance of cantonal constitutions).

Cantonal Constitutions

Constitution of the Canton	*Date of Adoption*	*Constitution of the Canton*	*Date of Adoption*
Zurich	2005	Schaffhausen	2002
Berne	1993	Appenzell Ausserrhoden	1995
Lucerne	2007	Appenzell Innerrhoden	1872
Uri	1984	St. Gallen	2001
Schwyz	2010	Grisons	2003
Obwalden	1968	Aargau	1980
Nidwalden	1965	Thurgau	1987
Glarus	1988	Ticino	1997
Zug	1894	Vaud	2003
Fribourg	2004	Valais	1907
Solothurn	1986	Neuchâtel	2000
Basel-City	2005	Geneva	2012
Basel-Land	1984	Jura	1977

Chapter 3. Legislation

§1. Forms of Legislation

Selected Bibliography: *See inter alia,* Auer, Malinverni & Hottelier, 514 et seq.; Biaggini. Kommentar, Article 164; Häfelin, Haller, Keller & Thurnherr, §61; Haller. *Swiss Constitution*, 242 et seq.; Müller Georg. 'Rechtssetzung und Staatsverträge'. In Thürer et al., §70, 1006–1112; Müller Georg & Uhlmann Felix, *Elemente einer Rechtssetzungslehre.* 3rd ed. Zurich: Schulthess 2013; Rhinow, Schefer & Uebersax, §27; Tschannen, §45.

76. In order to protect the political rights of the People and of the cantons (e.g., to allow the People to initiate a referendum), all important provisions establishing legal rules must be enacted in the form of *federal statutes* or *federal acts* (both terms are used inter-changeably in this monograph). Apart from this requirement, legislative powers may be delegated by federal act unless this is prohibited by the federal constitution (Article 164(2) of the Constitution). Thus, important legislative provisions may not be delegated to another branch of the government.

77. This raises the question what exactly is meant by the term 'important provisions'. Article 164(1) of the Constitution tries to clarify by listing some examples, such as:

- the exercise of political rights;
- restrictions of constitutional rights;
- the rights and obligations of individuals;
- the subject, the object and the calculation of taxes;
- the duties and services of the Confederation;
- the obligations of the cantons in implementing and executing federal laws, as well as the organization and structure of federal authorities.

78. This monograph mainly focuses on the following federal acts:

- The Federal Act of 16 December 2005 on Foreign Nationals (SR 142.20).
- The Federal Asylum Act of 26 June 1998 (SR 142.31).
- The Federal Act of 17 December 2004 on Freedom of Information in the Administration (SR 152.3).
- The Federal Act of 17 December 1976 on Political Rights (SR 161.1).
- The Federal Act of 13 December 2002 on the Federal Assembly (Parliament Act; SR 171.10).
- The Federal Act Regarding the Organization of the Government and the Administration (SR 172.010).
- The Federal Act of 20 December 1968 on Administrative Procedure (Federal Administrative Procedure Act; FAPA; SR 172.021).
- The Federal Supreme Court Act of 17 June 2005 (SR 173.110).

- The Federal Administrative Court Act of 17 June 2005 (SR 173.32).
- The Federal Act of 19 June 1992 on Data Protection (SR 235.1).

79. Occasionally, the Federal Parliament legislates by means of *federal decrees*, which, in the hierarchy of laws, is a lower form of legislation. In contrast to federal statutes, the possibilities to initiate a referendum against a federal decree are limited, as it is only permitted to the extent that the Constitution or statute foresees it (Article 141(1)(c) of the Constitution). For example, territorial modifications between cantons have to be approved by a federal decree (Article 53(3) of the Constitution). The lowest form of federal legislation is an *ordinance*, which is not submitted to a referendum.

§2. Law-Making Procedure

Selected Bibliography: *See*, *inter alia*, Häfelin, Haller, Keller & Thurnherr, §61; Rhinow, Schefer & Uebersax, §27; Tschannen, §45.

80. In a consensus-oriented democracy, the process for the adoption of a new law is complex and can take a minimum of twelve months to complete. In complicated or contested cases, it may take as many as twelve years. In essence, the law-making procedure usually consists of these following steps (as shown in Figure 3):

(1) Law-making procedures can be initiated by individual voters, interest groups, members of Parliament, the cantons, the Federal Council and the Federal Administration. In practice, it is mainly the Federal Council which retains the function to initiate the legislative process.
(2) If an important legislative project is at risk, the Federal Councillor managing the department in charge appoints an expert committee. Their function is to assist the administration with their professional knowledge and to establish a first draft (in less important cases, the bill will be drafted by the administration only).
(3) The expert draft is then submitted to a *consultation procedure* (Article 147 of the Constitution). During the preliminary procedure, the cantons, parties, associations and other groups with a particular interest in the subject are invited to state their position and propose modifications if any are necessary. Although the predominant aim is to make the expert draft public, the consultation procedure also acts as the first litmus test in order to assess the willingness of the relevant actors to compromise and evaluate the chances of the legislative project passing a popular referendum.
(4) The Federal Administration reviews the draft and submits it to the Federal Council, who can refer back to the text for further consideration. Finally, the Federal Council publishes the governmental proposal in the Federal Gazette, which consists of the proposed text of the bill often accompanied by a very detailed commentary (the latter is an important source for the courts in order to establish legislative intent in cases in which they have to interpret statutory provisions).
(5) Finally, the Federal Council transfers the draft on to the Parliament to be debated.
(6) The Presidents of the two Chambers of Parliament decide which Chamber will debate the proposal first. A *preparatory committee* of the chosen Chamber (the first Chamber) discusses the text and presents conclusions to the Chamber.

(7) The *first Chamber* may then decide the law is not necessary, in which case the matter is closed. Alternatively, it can refer the text back to the Federal Council or the committee for further revisions, prepare a new draft, or further debate the law in detail to reach a decision.
(8) Steps 6 and 7 are repeated in the *second Chamber*.
(9) If the decisions of both Chambers differ, a *conciliation procedure* is launched. The committee of the first Chamber assesses the differences and makes a proposal to their Chamber. This proposal may be to adopt all or some of the modifications suggested by the second Chamber, and/or choose to retain its own version.
(10) Following discussions in the first Chamber, the committee of the second Chamber considers the remaining differences and makes proposals to the second Chamber.
(11) If after three debates the differences are still not reconciled, a *conference of conciliation* constituting of members of the committees from both Chambers is convened in order to seek a compromise … .
(12) … which is then submitted to both Chambers for a *final vote*.
(13) The new statute, adopted by the two Chambers of Parliament, can then enter into force unless a *referendum* is demanded within 100 days (*see infra* Part II Chapter 2, §4).
(14) If a referendum is successfully demanded, a *popular* vote is scheduled.
(15) If a majority of the voters agree with the new piece of legislation, it is published in the Official Compilation of Federal Legislation and will enter into force.

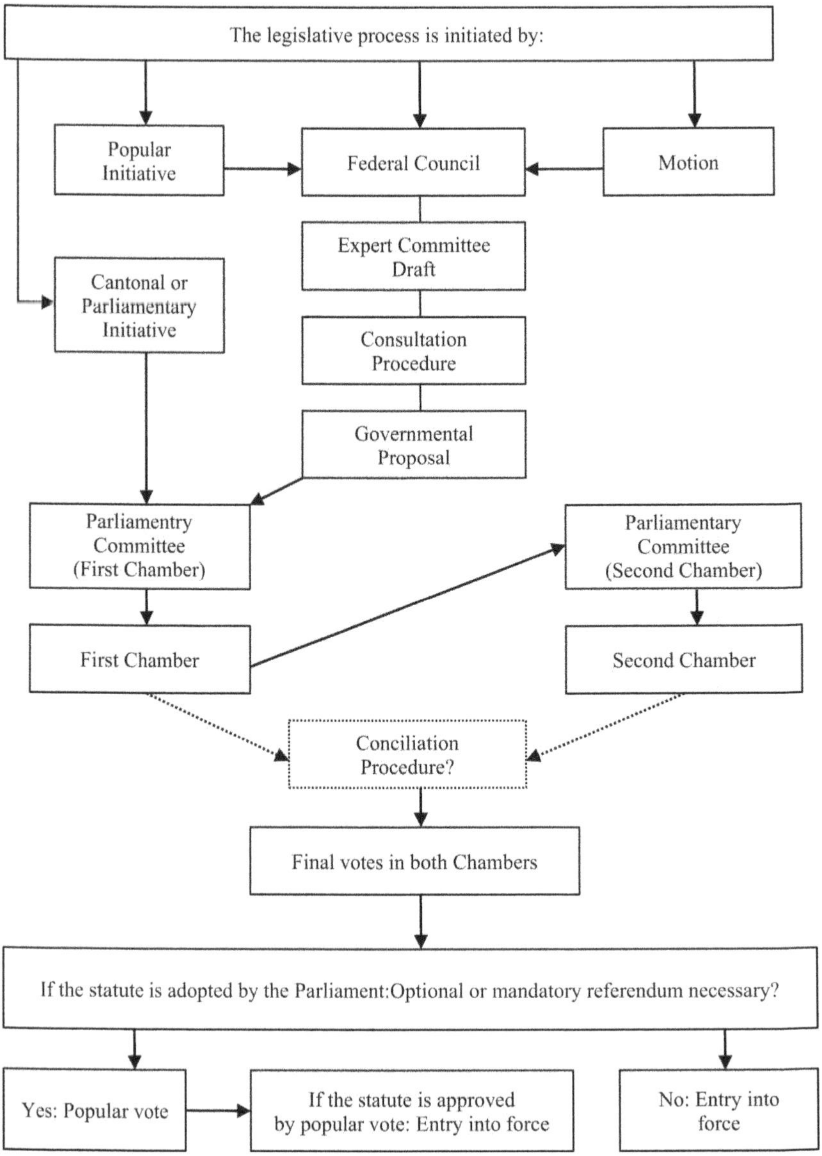
The legislative process is initiated by:
Popular Initiative
Federal Council
Motion
Expert Committee Draft
Cantonal or Parliamentary Initiative
Consultation Procedure
Governmental Proposal
Parliamentry Committee (First Chamber)
Parliamentary Committee (Second Chamber)
First Chamber
Second Chamber
Conciliation Procedure?
Final votes in both Chambers
If the statute is adopted by the Parliament:Optional or mandatory referendum necessary?
Yes: Popular vote
If the statute is approved by popular vote: Entry into force
No: Entry into force

Chapter 4. Case Law

Selected Bibliography: *See inter alia* Giovanni Biaggini. *Verfassung und Richterrecht, Verfassungs rechtliche Grenzen der Rechtsfortbildung im Wege der bundesgerichtlichen Rechtsprechung.* Basel: Helbing & Lichtenhahn, 1991; Egli, 17–18; Haller Walter. 'Verfassungsfortbildung durch Richterrecht'. In *Zeitschrift für Schweizerisches Recht [ZSR].* 2005 I, 5 et seq.

81. Due to their open texture most constitutional provisions need to be interpreted. As a consequence, the case law of the Federal Supreme Court is of utmost importance in Swiss constitutional law and practice. As shall be shown *infra*, Part IV, Chapter 2, §1 and §3, the Court performed an essential function in solidifying the development of the Constitution of 1874, especially with respect to the general equal protection clause (Article 4 of the Constitution of 1874) as well as to the development of fundamental rights, namely through the recognition of implied fundamental rights. For a detailed presentation of the Federal Supreme Court *see infra*, Part II, Chapter 5, §3. The most important questions regarding the judiciary and its eminent role in the protection of fundamental rights will be studied in detail *infra*, in Part IV, Chapter 2, §1 and §2.

82. As a result of the case law of the Federal Supreme Court playing an important role in Swiss constitutional law and practice, it seems useful to explain how the cases of federal courts are published and cited. All cases of the Federal Supreme Court (since the year 2000) and the lower federal Courts are published on the internet (*see* www.bger.ch [Federal Supreme Court]; www.bvger.ch [Federal Administrative Court]; www.bstger.ch [Federal Criminal Court]; www.bundespatentgericht.ch [Federal Patent Court]). A selection of the leading cases or other relevant decisions of the federal courts are published in an official compilation (*Amtliche Sammlung*) in the national language in which the parties addressed the court. Thus, no official translation of the decisions is provided. It is upon the discretion of the Federal Court to publish its leading cases. In order to avoid malpractice claims of their clients, these leading cases must be known to lawyers. The official compilations have the following abbreviations, which shall be also used in this monograph:

– 'BGE' (in German), 'ATF' (in French), 'DTF' (in Italian) for the Official Compilation of the Decisions of the Federal Supreme Court.
– 'BVGE' (in German), 'ATAF' (in French), 'DTAF' (in Italian), 'DTAF' (in Romansh) for the Official Compilation of the Decisions of the Federal Administrative Court.
– 'TPF' for the Official Compilation of the Decisions of the Federal Criminal Court.

83. In the Official Compilation, the case law of the Federal Supreme Court is published in five volumes:

(1) Volume I: Constitutional Law.
(2) Volume II: Administrative Law.
(3) Volume III: Civil Law.

(4) Volume IV: Criminal Law.
(5) Volume V: Social Security Law.

The case of the Federal Supreme Court is cited with the volume number (volume 1 compiles the cases between 1874 and 1875, volume 2 between 1875 and 1876, etc.) followed by the indication in Roman letters of the area of law concerned, the page number of the beginning of the case and the page numbers or the paragraph of the cited part of the case. Therefore, as an example, the abbreviation BGE 126 I 1, 5 means: Decision of the Federal Supreme Court, published in the Official Compilation in the year 2000, in the field of constitutional law, the case starts on page one, the relevant text is on page five. Another common citation of Federal Supreme Court cases (which is also used in this monograph) is the following: BGE 131 IV 1 E. 1. It means: Decision of the Federal Supreme Court, published in the Official Compilation in the year 2005, in the field of criminal law, the case starts on page one, the relevant portion is in paragraph 1 (*E.=Erwägung [German]; consid.=considérant [French] or considerazione [Italian]*). However, a paragraph can sometimes go over several pages. Hence, for the sake of precision, the Federal Supreme Court prefers to cite its cases by adding the page where the relevant passage of the paragraph can be found: BGE 143 V 50 E. 3.6 S. 58 (Decision of the Federal Supreme Court, published in the Official Compilation in the year 2017, in the field of social security law, the case starts on page fifty, the relevant portion is in paragraph 3.6 on page 58.

Chapter 5. Customary Law

84. Customary law plays a rather insignificant role in Swiss public law (for more details *see* Häfelin, Haller, Keller & Thurnherr, pp. 5–6). In theory, customary law may be recognized if three conditions are present. There must be:

(1) evidence of a continuous, uninterrupted and coherent practice;
(2) an *opinio iuris* of the law-applying agency and the concerned individual (or legal entity); and
(3) a lacuna in the written law.

Chapter 6. Administrative Ordinances and Administrative Orders

85. Federal acts often delegate considerable discretionary powers to the Federal Council or the Federal Administration, which usually act through administrative ordinances (synonymous to regulations). Administrative ordinances are the lowest rules of law in the hierarchy of norms. However in spite of this, they do play an important role in constitutional practice (*see infra* Part II, Chapter 4).

86. Article 5 of the FAPA (SR 172.021) provides a legal definition for the administrative order, according to which it is the final and unilateral decision of an agency, in a concrete and individual case, imposing upon the individual a set of obligations or granting a set of rights, based on federal public law (for a detailed analysis this definition *see infra* Part II, Chapter 5).

Chapter 7. Interpretation and Publication

§1. Interpretation of Constitutional Provisions

Selected Bibliography: Giovanni Biaggini, 'Über die Auslegung der Bundesverfassung und ihr Verhältnis zur EMRK'. In *Schweizerisches Zentralblatt für Staats- und Verwaltungsrecht [ZBl]*. 2013, 316 et seq.; Biaggini Giovanni. 'Verfassungsinterpretation in der Schweiz'. In *Festschrift Heinz Schäffer*. Vienna, 2006, 109 et seq.; Egli, 19 et seq.; Häfelin, Haller, Keller & Thurnherr, § 3; Haller. *Swiss Constitution*, 20 et seq.; Haller Walter. 'Verfassungsfortbildung durch Richterrecht'. In *Zeitschrift für Schweizerisches Recht [ZSR]*. 2005 I, 5 et seq.; Huber Hans. 'Der Formenreichtum der Verfassung und seine Bedeutung für ihre Auslegung'. In *Zeitschrift des Bernischen Juristenvereins [ZBJV]*. 1971, 172 et seq.; Kramer Ernst. *Juristische Methodenlehre*. 4th ed. Berne: Stämpfli 2013; Müller Jörg Paul. 'Verfassung und Gesetz: zur Aktualität von Art. 1 Abs. 2 ZGB'. In *recht 2000 (Sondernummer)*, 119 et seq.; Rhinow, Schefer & Uebersax, §4 III (with further references); Tschannen, §4; Tschannen. 'Verfassungsauslegung'. In Thürer et al., §9.

87. The famous Article 1 of the Swiss Civil Code emphasizes that legal rules can never regulate all facts of life, and that legal texts must be interpreted in order to establish their true meaning. Regarding the interpretation of constitutional provisions, the Federal Supreme Court follows 'the same methodological rules [...], as those developed for the interpretation of laws at the sub-constitutional level' (Decision of the Federal Supreme Court, BGE 116 Ia 359, 367, *Theresa Rohner*). Originating from the wording of a constitutional provision, the Federal Supreme Court establishes its meaning applying all known interpretation methods:

(1) The starting point of every interpretation is the *grammatical interpretation* of legal norms in which the ordinary use of language, including the meaning of terms, wording, grammar and syntax is relevant. Switzerland publishes its legal texts in the three official languages (German, French and Italian), of which all versions carry the same normative weight. If their meaning in the translations differs, the text, which – according to other interpretation techniques – reflects the true meaning, receives precedence.

(2) The *systematic interpretation* analyses the norm in light of the systematic context with other legal provisions within the concerned act. Compared to the Constitution of 1874, the Constitution of 1999 is characterized by a high degree of systematization. Thus the systematic interpretation may gain new relevance under the new Constitution and the Federal Supreme Court case law.

(3) The *historical interpretation* establishes the meaning of the norm at the time of its creation. In general, a norm should either be interpreted according to the historical will of the framers of the Constitution (*subjective* interpretation) or according to the general understanding of the norm by the People at the time of the adoption (*objective* interpretation).

(4) In contrast to the historical interpretation – with its inherent potential for ossification of the legal order – the *topical or contemporary interpretation* relies on the public understanding of the norm under modern circumstances.
(5) The *teleological interpretation* establishes the meaning of the norm by considering the aims (*telos*) that the legislator wanted to achieve. The norm must imply the goal. It is not permissible to subsume a non-implied goal from the norm.
(6) As a subsidiary method of interpretation, comparative law is increasingly gaining importance in constitutional law.

88. The Federal Supreme Court usually adopts a balancing approach, combining the different elements of interpretation. With regard to the interpretation of legal texts, the Court is led by a so-called pragmatic pluralism of methods (*pragmatischer Methodenpluralismus*). The Court refuses to 'subordinate the different elements of interpretation under a hierarchy of importance' (Decision of the Federal Supreme Court BGE 128 Ia 34, 41). The balancing of the different elements of interpretation may vary considerably, depending on whether an organizational provision or a constitutional right is at risk or not. When interpreting the new federal constitution, the rich history of its creation often plays an introductory role. In addition, according to the 'update idea' (*supra* Chapter 1, §3 III of the General Introduction), the practice and materials on the previous provisions of the Federal Constitution of 1874 are further valuable sources.

§2. Interpretation in Conformity with the Constitution

89. As a consequence of the hierarchy of norms and the unity of the legal order, statutes and ordinances are interpreted in light of the values expressed in the Constitution. Through this interpretation in conformity with the Constitution (*verfassungskonforme Auslegung*), the legal system can be harmonized. Furthermore, in the proceeding of abstract or concrete judicial review (*infra*, Part IV, Chapter 2, §7) the Court will only declare a cantonal decision or act unconstitutionally when an interpretation in conformity with the Constitution is not possible.

90. Probably the most famous example of such an interpretation in conformity with the federal constitution was the introduction of female suffrage in the Canton of Appenzell Innerrhoden (Decision of the Federal Supreme Court BGE 116 Ia 359, *Theresa Rohner*). The provisions of the cantonal constitution that attributed the right to vote to all 'Swiss [male] citizens' (*Schweizer*) was interpreted by the Federal Supreme Court to include men and women (*Schweizer und Schweizerinnen*), contrary to a historical, grammatical, systematic or teleological interpretation of the constitutional text.

91. Correspondingly, legal texts including constitutional provisions are interpreted in conformity with international law, particularly with the European Courts of Human Rights in Strasbourg. In such cases, Swiss courts will rely on the interpretation given by the highest authorities responsible for the application of the Convention. Regrettably, as shall be discussed in Part V, Chapter 1, §3 III, of this monograph, the widespread idea of international judges interpreting the ECHR extensively and deciding on that basis controversial matters that affect national legal systems has led to a rather uncomfortable climate of disagreement (not to say: hostility) in certain segments of the Swiss population.

§3. Publication

92. All Swiss federal legislation, including each cantonal constitution, is published in two official compilations. First, the legal text is published in a Chronological Compilation of Federal Legislation (called *'Amtliche Sammlung des Bundesrechts'* [abbreviation: *'AS'*]; *'Recueil officiel du droit fédéral'* [*'RO'*]; *'Raccolta ufficiale delle leggi federali'* [*'RU'*]), which is updated weekly. According to Article 8 of the Federal Publication Act, the publication in the AS is a prerequisite for the validity of the legal text. Second, several months later, the legal text is published in the Systematic Compilation of Federal Legislation (called *'Systematische Sammlung des Bundesrechts'* [abbreviation: *'SR'*]; *'Recueil systématique du droit fédéral'* [*'RS'*]; *'Raccolta sistematica del diritto federale'* [*'RS'*]). These texts are published in the three official languages – German, French and Italian – each version being equivalent to the other. The most important legal texts are also translated into Romansh, and even in English. For details *see* the English translation of the Federal Publication Act (www.admin.ch/ch/e/rs/170_512/index.html).

93. Cantonal laws are also published in official cantonal compilations, most of which are available on the internet. The internet platform 'Findlex' provides access to cantonal laws based on a standardized index (*see* www.findlex.ch).

Part II. State Organization

Chapter 1. General

Selected Bibliography: Abromeit Heidrun. *Interessenvermittlung zwischen Konkurrenz und Konkordanz.* Opladen, 1993; Abromeit Heidrun & Stoiber Michael. *Demokratien im Vergleich, Einführung in die vergleichende Analyse politischer Systeme.* Wiesbaden, 2006; Auer, Malinverni & Hottelier. Vol. I, 19 et seq.; Biaggini. Kommentar, Articles 136 et seq.; Egli, 85 et seq.; Fleiner & Basta Fleiner, 353 et seq.; Häfelin, Haller, Keller & Thurnherr, 425 et seq.; Haller. Swiss Constitution, 107 et seq.; Jaag, Bucher & Häggi Furrer, 111 et seq.; Mahon, 151 et seq.; Le Roy Katy & Saunders Cheryl (eds). *Legislative, Executive, and Judicial Governance in Federal Countries.* Montréal/Kingston: McGill-Queen's University Press, 2006; Linder, 128 et seq.; Linder Wolf. 'Grundzüge des politischen Systems'. In Thürer et al., 995 et seq.; Rhinow, Schefer & Uebersax, 383 et seq.; Tschannen, 377 et seq.

§1. A Form Sui Generis

94. The Swiss political system can neither be easily qualified as a parliamentary nor as a presidential or a semi-presidential system. It mainly derived from the directorial system of France (*see* General Introduction, Chapter 1, §3 I).

95. The following aspects resemble a parliamentary system or are contradictory to a presidential system:

(1) The Constitution establishes Parliament as highest authority (limited by the rights of the People and the Cantons).
(2) Parliament elects the government, which also functions as collective head of state; there is no directly elected head of state.
(3) The government/head of state cannot veto decisions of Parliament.

96. The following aspects resemble a presidential system or are unusual for a parliamentary system:

(1) Once elected, the members of government are not dependent on Parliament; there is no vote of no-confidence, no possibility of impeachment.
(2) The Swiss government is a multi-party government, however not based on a coalition agreement of parliamentary parties/governmental programme. Though

Parliament takes party membership (as well as other criteria) into account when electing the individual members of government, they do not necessarily elect the candidate that was proposed by the party.

(3) Members of government do not have to follow party line or programme. They decide as part of a collegium and are supposed to defend the decisions even if they disagree.

(4) There is no strong party discipline. Representatives in Parliament can vote against proposals of 'their' member of government minister.

(5) There has never been a complete change of government. In most cases, ministers who wanted to be re-elected by the Parliament were re-elected.

(6) Both Chambers of Parliament have equal powers; the National Council does not have a special role in the election of the government. Both Chambers of Parliament are involved in oversight activities towards the government.

§2. Consensus-Oriented Democracy

97. The Swiss political system is characterized by *consensus-oriented democracy*. It tries to generate, as much as possible, consensus and compromise by balancing the various interests of Switzerland's diverse population (*see* General Introduction, Chapter 2, §2). Swiss governmental institutions aim to institutionalize diversity by representing the entire spectrum of citizens; they aim at avoiding polarization and foster constantly changing majorities. Amongst others, the mechanisms of direct democracy create continuous pressure to seek for compromise. If politicians do not integrate and balance various interests in advance there is a high risk that their decisions will be challenged and fail in a popular vote. The 'Damocles sword' of the will of the people led to the development of a political culture that values consultations of all concerned and pre-negotiations among stakeholders. Consensus-oriented democracy developed out of respect for the pre-existing diversity – or at least out of the pragmatic realization that if any group feel like a perpetual loser it will be harmful for the stability and prosperity of Switzerland. The Swiss political system provides even small communities with the possibility to pursue their legitimate interests within the political system and thus can prevent the adoption of extra-political means and the alienation of a part of the population. Consensus-oriented democracy was and still is a crucial element of peaceful coexistence in multicultural Switzerland.

Chapter 2. The People

Selected Bibliography: Auer, Malinverni & Hottelier. Vol. I, 197 et seq.; Fleiner & Basta Fleiner, 283 et seq.; Häfelin, Haller, Keller & Thurnherr, 383 et seq.; Hangartner Yvo & Kley Andreas. *Die demokratischen Rechte in Bund und Kantonen der Schweizerischen Eidgenossenschaft.* Zurich: Schulthess, 2000; Linder, 109 et seq.; Mahon, 39 et seq., 155 et seq.; Rhinow, Schefer & Uebersax, 40 et seq., 381 et seq.; Tschannen, 201 et seq., 377 et seq.

§1. People as Sovereign and Opposition

98. The People, together with the Peoples of the cantons, are the supreme and sovereign power in Switzerland. Together they establish and revise the constitutional order and thus form the constituent power. The Swiss state is based on a double legitimacy as clarified in Article 142 of the Constitution: proposals submitted to the vote of the People and the Cantons (e.g., all constitutional amendments) require a majority of the People (Swiss citizens) and the majority of the cantonal electorates (cantonal voters).

99. In addition, the Swiss People fulfil the function of opposition. Swiss institutions are designed so as to represent the largest part of the Swiss population: In the executive, legislature and the judiciary, all the stronger political parties are represented, thus disabling them to act as an effective opposition force. Consequently, this function was taken over by the Swiss People, whereby direct democratic instruments empower them to control the political agenda (initiative) and to supervise the legislating activity (referendum).

100. In §2 political rights as fundamental rights will be addressed, in §3 the elections as a means of representative democracy will be regarded, followed by the initiative (§4) and the referendum (§5) as means of direct democracy.

§2. Political Rights as Fundamental Rights

101. Political rights are fundamental and enforceable rights (*see supra* Part IV, Chapter 2, §1). The Swiss Constitution confirms this in Article 34(1): 'The political rights are guaranteed.' This guarantee includes the right to participate in the act, e.g., of elections or referenda. In addition, it adds a qualitative element and aims at ensuring that citizens can form and express their political will.

102. The 'guarantee of political rights protects the free formation of opinion and the unaltered expression of the voter's will' (Article 34(2) of the Constitution). There is a rich case law by the Federal Supreme Court on the free formation and expression of political will. The court mainly interfered when authorities provided unbalanced information or propaganda in the wake of referenda, when authorities were deemed to have provided excessive funding for or against a pending decision or when referenda questions were formulated in confusing terms or combined separate matters in one question (*see*, e.g., Decisions of the Federal Supreme Court BGE 129 I 366, BGE 130 I 290).

103. In the view of the Federal Supreme Court, the guarantee in Article 34 of the Constitution does not include the right to vote by secret ballot. While the secrecy of vote is realized at the federal level, it is not fully applied in all cantons or municipalities. Most of all at the municipal level, many decisions are taken at municipal assemblies in open votes though citizens can request that a vote by secret ballot is conducted instead. Cantons and municipalities can and to some extent do establish the duty to take part in elections. For instance, the Canton of Schaffhausen (Article 23 of the Constitution of Schaffhausen), the Canton of Uri (Article 20 of the Constitution of Uri) and the Canton of Aargau (Article 59 of the Constitution of the Canton of Aargau) establish a duty to vote and the Canton of Schaffhausen even foresees a small fine in the case of non-participation. Some cantons and municipalities establish a duty to stand for elections and to accept an office if elected.

§3. Elections

Selected Bibliography: Auer, Malinverni & Hottelier. Vol. I, 215 et seq.; Biaggini. Kommentar, Article 136, Articles 143 et seq.; Buser Denise. *Kantonales Staatsrecht,* 119 et seq., 131 et seq.; Haller. *Swiss Constitution*, 104 et seq.; Lutz Georg & Selb Peter. Wahlen. In Knoepfel et al. (eds), 465 et seq.; Rhinow, Schefer & Uebersax, 392 et seq., 437 et seq.; Mahon Pascal. Die Aktivbürgerschaft im Schweizer *Staatsrecht*. In Thürer et al., 335 et seq.; Poledna Tomas. Wahlrecht im *Bund*. In Thürer et al., 363 et seq.; Poledna Tomas. Grundzüge des Wahlrecht in den *Kantonen*. In Thürer et al., 373 et seq.; Tschannen, 425 et seq., 625 et seq.

I. Types of Elections

104. Citizens may participate in federal, cantonal and local elections. On the *federal level*, Swiss citizens elect the members of the National Council, which is the Chamber of Swiss Parliament representing the Swiss People. For this election, the cantons serve as constituency. In the *cantons*, the citizens of the cantons elect the members of the Council of States, which is the Chamber of Federal Parliament that represents the cantons. Depending on the various cantonal systems, the citizens of the canton elect a cantonal parliament, the cantonal executive and in some cantons the judges. In municipalities with parliaments, the citizens of the municipality elect the municipal parliament as well as in most cases- the municipal executive. In some municipalities, the municipal people may even elect higher civil servants and teachers. The right to participate in elections normally encompasses the right to vote and to stand for election. The *members of the Federal Parliament* elect the Federal Council, which is the Swiss executive, and the judges of the Federal Court.

II. Constitutional Provisions

A. Distribution of Powers and Guarantee of Political Rights

105. Article 39(1) of the Swiss Constitution of 1999 regulates the *distribution of powers* between the federal level and the cantons in respect to the political rights in general, including the right to participate in elections. The Confederation shall regulate the execution of political rights in federal matters, while the cantons are empowered to regulate the execution of political rights in cantonal and municipal matters, within certain limits (*see* Article 39(2) of the Constitution).

106. Political rights are guaranteed by the Constitution. This guarantee protects the free formation and the genuine and unaltered expression of the opinion of the citizens in the political decision-making process (Article 34 of the Constitution). This guarantee can be enforced before the Federal Supreme Court by the citizens.

B. Political Rights for Federal Matters

107. Article 136 of the Constitution defines the bearer of political rights: All Swiss citizens who are 18 years or older, and who are not under guardianship because of mental illness or weakness, have equal political rights and obligations in federal matters (Article 136(1) of the Constitution). Furthermore, Article 136 mentions the areas of political participation at the federal level. The citizens may participate in elections to the National Council, in federal voting, and may launch, as well as sign popular initiatives and referenda in federal matters (Article 136(2) of the Constitution).

108. While Article 136(2) of the Constitution establishes who has the right to elect the National Council, Article 143 of the Constitution regulates the right to stand for election to the National Council as well as the Federal Government and the Federal Court. The latter two are elected by the Federal Assembly, i.e., in a joined session of both Chambers of Parliament. Every Swiss citizen who is entitled to vote for federal matters is also eligible to these three institutions.

109. The elections to the Council of States, the second chamber of the Federal Parliament, are regulated by cantonal law. Since the Council of States represents the cantons, it is left to the cantons to decide on the mode of election (Article 150(3) of the Constitution), which must, of course, be in accordance with the minimum requirements of the Constitution, for instance with the equality and non-discrimination clause (Article 8 of the Constitution).

C. Principles for the Exercise of Political Rights

110. In addition to the distribution of powers on election and the definition of the bearer of political rights for federal matters, the Constitution establishes some *principles for the exercise of political rights*:

- According to Article 39(2) of the Constitution, Swiss citizens cast their vote and can be elected at their *place of domicile*, the place where they reside and which is their centre of vital interests. The domicile requirement shall ensure that citizens exercise their political rights in the polity to which they are most connected and by whose decisions they are directly affected. For those who want to run for office, it shall avoid cherry-picking of constituencies. The Confederation and the cantons can create exceptions of the domicile requirement but these are very limited.

- Cantons can introduce a waiting period until Swiss citizens who move to their canton can exercise their political rights at the cantonal and municipal level. Such a waiting period must not be longer than three months (Article 39(4) of the Constitution). Such waiting periods shall ensure that citizens do not move with the purpose of influencing elections and that they have time to familiarize themselves with cantonal and municipal matters. Most cantons abolished such waiting periods.
- Furthermore, persons must not exercise political rights in more than one canton (Article 39(3) of the Constitution). Consequently, the cantons cannot give political rights to their cantonal citizens who have their domicile in a different canton.

In Switzerland, it is not necessary to specifically register to participate in the elections or popular votes as there are permanent registries of all domiciled persons in a locality which also serve as electoral rolls.

D. *Non-discrimination Principle*

111. Article 37(2) of the Constitution states a *non-discrimination clause*, according to which, a canton may not discriminate against any Swiss citizens because of his/her cantonal or municipal citizenship (on cantonal and municipal citizenship *see infra,* Part IV, Chapter 1, §1). In different words, cantons must not disfavour Swiss citizens who reside in their canton but who originally are from another canton. Equally, in respect to political rights, they cannot privilege to persons who are originally from their canton but now live in another canton. No Swiss citizen shall be entitled to any privilege or suffer prejudice because of his/her origin – except for the short waiting period for new residents mentioned above (*see supra* C.).

The non-discrimination principle applies to Swiss citizens domiciled within one canton. They must not be discriminated against compared to other citizens within the canton. However, there can be differences in political rights between cantons. While in general those who have political rights for federal matters also have so for cantonal and municipal matters, there can be variations from canton to canton, e.g.; for cantonal and communal elections, cantons can provide political rights to additional groups of people, for instance they can accord political rights to foreigners, e.g. several cantons (currently Fribourg, Basel-Stadt, Vaud, Neuchâtel, Jura, Grisons and Appenzell Ausserrhoden) foresee political rights for foreigners for municipal matters, the cantons of Neuchâtel and of Jura also provide the right to vote on cantonal matters. Therefore, a foreigner might have the right to vote in one canton and 'loses' the right to vote again when moving to another canton. Furthermore, cantons have the possibility to establish a higher age requirement than 18 for candidates to certain cantonal or communal offices; they can set maximum age limits for office holders, e.g. judges and cantonal ministers; or they can set a lower age requirement for participation in elections. For instance, the Canton of Glarus provides political rights from the age of sixteen onwards (in comparison to eighteen for federal matters, Article 56 of the Constitution of Glarus). However, because of the equality provision in Article 8 of the Constitution and the obligation to be governed democratically, cantons must not exclude groups of citizens, such as those who are indebted, do not pay taxes, or are convicted criminals. Prisoners can theoretically be elected however they cannot assume office while they are in prison.

E. Swiss Citizens Living Abroad

112. Finally, the Constitution mandates the Confederation to legislate concerning the political rights of *Swiss citizens living abroad.* According to Article 40(2) of the Constitution, the Confederation shall legislate the rights and obligations of Swiss citizens who have their domicile abroad. This mandate mainly concerns the exercise of political rights at the federal level, the duty to render military or alternative service, social assistance and social security (Article 40(2) of the Constitution). Swiss citizens who are registered at a Swiss embassy or consulate abroad can vote in federal elections by postal mail or in some cases via the internet.

F. Political Parties

113. The Swiss Constitution contains only two provisions that concern political parties. In Article 137 of the Constitution, it is stated that the political parties contribute to the formation of public opinion. Article 147 regulates the consultation procedure and mentions that political parties shall be consulted on important legal drafts including international agreements. Not only because of direct democracy but also because of the electoral systems, political parties have less power than in many other countries. Political parties are very easy to establish because the same rules apply as for any other form of association. The political parties at the federal level are mainly umbrella parties that unite cantonal party chapters. The major parties have members from all linguistic groups and aim at an inclusive composition of their main organs. Traditionally however, political parties catered to different religious groups. These distinctions based on religion have decreased decisively, and membership is relatively mixed today.

§4. Popular Initiative

Selected Bibliography: Auer Andreas (ed.). *Sans délais et sans limites? L'initiative populaire à la croisée des chemins.* Basel, Geneva & Munich 2001; Auer, Malinverni & Hottelier, Vol. I, 239 et seq.; Biaggini. Kommentar, Article 136, Articles 138 et seq.; Buser Denise. *Kantonales Staatsrecht,* 131 et seq.; Egli, 67 et seq.; Epiney Astrid & Stefan Diezig. Basler Kommentar, Articles 138–139b; Grisel Etienne. *Initiative et référendum populaire.* Bern: Stämpfli, 2004, passim; Grisel Etienne. 'Volksrechte im Bund'. In Thürer et al., 383 et seq.; Grisel Etienne. 'Volksrechte in den Kantonen'. In Thürer et al., 397 et seq.; Haller. *Swiss Constitution,* 108 et seq.; Linder, 92 et seq.; Mahon Pascal, 179 et seq.; Rhinow, Schefer & Uebersax. 414 et seq.; Sciarini Pascal & Tresch Anke, 'Votations populaires'. In Knoepfel et al. (eds), 463 et seq.

114. The popular initiative gives the people the possibility to influence and control the political agenda. For launching an initiative, a certain number of signatures must be collected within a given period of time. When the requested number of valid signatures has been attained and there is no procedural or substantial reason for the invalidity of the initiative, a popular vote (referendum) on the content will take place. The instrument 'initiative' exists at the federal, and at the cantonal level, as well as in many municipalities.

I. At the Federal Level

A. Forms of the Federal Initiative: Constitutional Initiative

115. The constitutional initiative provides the right to the People to amend the Constitution. By attaining the required 100,000 citizen signatures, a partial (Article 139 of the Constitution) or a complete (Article 138 of the Constitution) amendment of the Constitution can be demanded.

116. Initiatives for the partial amendment of the Constitution can be handed in as a general proposition or as a formulated draft (Article 139(2) of the Constitution). Initiatives for the total amendment of the Constitution can only be handed in as general proposition (Article 138 of the Constitution; *see* further explanations below).

1. General Proposition

117. Procedures differ in the case of general propositions for the partial and the total amendment of the Constitution.

118. In the event of general propositions for the *partial amendment* of the Constitution, the Parliament will concretize the proposition (by drafting or re-drafting a constitutional provision) when it approves of it. If Parliament is opposed to the general proposition, a popular vote on the proposition will take place. If approved through the vote, the Federal Parliament must then formulate a corresponding draft (Article 139(4) of the Constitution). It is a matter of debate how much discretion Parliament has in formulating a corresponding draft. There are only very few cases of initiatives for partial amendment of the Constitution as general proposition. The clear majority of initiatives are presented as formulated drafts.

119. When the proposition involves a *total revision* of the Constitution, the proposition must be presented to the people in a popular vote (Article 138(2) of the Constitution).

2. Formulated Draft

120. Formulated drafts will be put to a popular vote in their original form as they have been submitted by the citizens, in different words, Parliament must not reformulate the proposal. Parliament can introduce a counterproposal (Article 139(5) of the Constitution). In the popular vote, the project must receive a majority of the overall votes cast, and a majority in more than half of the Cantons (Article 139(6) of the Constitution).

B. Procedure

1. List Preparation for Signature Collection

121. When a citizen wishes to start an initiative, he/she must first prepare a list for the collection of signatures.

122. The list of signatures must include the following:

(1) the text of the initiative;
(2) the name and addresses of at least seven drafters of the initiative;
(3) an unconditional escape clause (the right of the drafters to withdraw the initiative);
(4) the warning that any fraud in the collection of signatures and/or the falsification of the collection of results is a crime under the Swiss Federal Criminal Code; and
(5) the name of the canton and municipality in which the signatories have the right to vote.

123. The list is sent to the Federal Chancery, which undertakes a preliminary control whether formal requirements are fulfilled according to Article 194 of the Constitution and publishes the initiative title and text in an official publication.

2. Collection of Signatures

124. The collection of signatures starts on the day of publication. The proponents have eighteen months to collect the requested 100,000 signatures. In international comparison, the number of required signatures is relatively low (about 2% of persons with the right to vote on federal matters). Any citizen who signs the initiative must give all necessary information to verify his/her identity, i.e., name, address and date of birth. Everyone can collect signatures. In about one out of three cases, the initiators fail to collect the necessary signatures within the given time frame.

3. Verification of Signatures

125. Before the end of the eighteen-month period, the lists must be sent to the respective cantonal authorities who verify that the signatories have the right to vote on federal matters in the indicated municipality. The lists are returned to the initiators, who submit the compiled signature lists at the Federal Chancery. The Federal Chancery then determines whether the necessary 100,000 signatures have been collected within the given time frame.

4. Validity of the Initiative

126. Within a year, the Federal Council must present a report on the validity of the initiative and a motion to the Parliament with the proposal to either accept, to reject or to formulate a counter proposal. When the Federal Council wants to propose to Parliament to introduce a counterproposal, the delay is extended to eighteen months during which the Federal Council can prepare and submit a counterproposal to parliament.

127. The Federal Parliament verifies the legal validity of the initiative. So far (until Autumn 2017) it happened only four times that the Parliament declared an initiative as invalid. There have been instances in which initiatives have been declared invalid in parts. Pursuant to the procedural requirements, the initiative must fulfil certain criteria which directly concern the form and substance of the initiative:

(1) The initiative must be consistent in its form. It must be either formulated as a concrete project or as a general proposition.
(2) The initiative must be consistent in its subject matter. Only matters that are interconnected can be regulated in one initiative so as to guarantee that the citizens can clearly express their opinion in the vote.
(3) The initiative must be in accordance with international *ius cogens* (Article 53 of the Vienna Convention on the Laws of Treaties, SR 0.111). If this is not the case, the Federal Parliament can declare the initiative invalid (which Parliament is reluctant to do based on the argument '*in dubio pro populo*'). Initiatives that are opposed to international agreements, which are not part of the ius cogens, must be presented to the People and to the Cantons. If possible the text of the initiative is interpreted in a way to render it consistent with international law. In most cases, initiatives that were inconsistent with international law were rejected by the People. However, lately, the People have accepted initiatives for which the consistency with international law is highly questionable. Doubts about the consistency arose for instance for an initiative of 8 February 2004 that provided that extremely dangerous sex-offenders must be kept in custody for life, or of 29 November 2009 to prohibit the building of minarets. Initiatives dealing with the expulsion of foreigners who committed certain crimes can showcase the stance of the parliament. Related constitutional provisions were introduced with an initiative of 28 November 2010. Because of dissatisfaction with the implementation of the provisions, a second initiative was launched ('Implementation-Initiative' of 28 December 2012) that aimed at providing interpretation and making the constitutional provision directly applicable. The parliament declared part of this second initiative as invalid because it included a narrow interpretation of ius cogens. However, the rest of the initiative was presented to the People despite of its critical nature considering international human rights obligations. The initiative failed in the popular vote.
(4) Finally, it must be possible to execute the initiative. The impossibility of its execution must be manifest and clear.

5. Decision on Support by the Parliament

128. After the validity of the initiative is declared, the Members of Parliament will decide whether to support it, and in the case of concrete proposals, whether they want to make a counter proposal. This decision must be taken within two years for general proposals, and within thirty months for concrete proposals.

6. Popular Vote on the Popular Initiative (Referendum)

129. Thereafter, the Federal Council will set a date for the popular vote. Up to this point, the initiator can withdraw the initiative. Under normal circumstances, it takes about five years from the launch of the initiative until the popular referendum takes place. The Federal Parliament can give a recommendation to the citizens how to vote in the referendum.

130. The initiative is presented in its exact wording to the People (*see* Article 99 of the Parliamentary Act). When a counterproposal is introduced, the citizens can cast a 'double yes' for the initiative and counterproposal, and can state their preference should it occur that both versions are approved. Before the possibility of a 'double yes' was introduced, Parliament used the counterproposal to split the votes of those who wanted a change of the *status quo*.

131. When the initiative is accepted by the sovereign (by a majority of those voting within Switzerland and within a majority of the cantons) the text of the initiative – as proposed – becomes part of the Constitution.

C. Excursus: Introduction of a General Initiative

132. Parliament had proposed a constitutional amendment to introduce a general initiative. This initiative was supposed to be similar to the constitutional initiative with the major difference that Parliament could decide whether an initiative should be considered as statutory or as a constitutional initiative depending on the nature and importance of the subject matter concerned in the initiative. In addition, the general initiative was supposed to always take the form of a general proposition. The People and the Cantons accepted the reform in a constitutional referendum on 9 February 2003.

133. A general initiative should prevent subject matters that could be regulated on a statutory level to be introduced in the Constitution, as is sometimes the case when the people can only initiate constitutional amendments but not amendments of ordinary legislation. In the Constitution of 1874, there was, for example, a provision on the prohibition of a certain type of alcohol (absinth) that could have been regulated by statute or even by decree.

134. However, provisions on the general initiative were never completely set into force and a little bit more than five years after its adoption, Parliament proposed the abolishment of the respective constitutional provision. On 27 September 2009, the People and the Cantons approved the renewed constitutional amendment for the abolishment of the general initiative. Parliament mainly argued for the abolishment based on considerations of practicability. Of course it can be asked why Parliament did not consider the practicability before proposing the introduction in the first place. Some cantons provide for and use general initiatives.

II. At the Cantonal Level

A. Forms of Cantonal Initiatives

135. All cantons provide for constitutional and legislative initiatives. With a constitutional initiative, the cantonal constitution can be amended in total or in part. With a legislative initiative, changes to cantonal ordinary law can be initiated. In addition, the cantons allow for administrative initiatives, which are directed at a specific project like the building of a school, the construction of an electricity plant or planned expenses. In a limited number of cantons, it is also possible to demand early elections for the executive or the Parliament.

B. Requirements and Procedure

136. The cantons regulate the number of signatures necessary and the procedure for pursuing an initiative. The Federal Constitution provides that each cantonal constitution must be subject to revision if the majority of the citizens in the canton so wishes (Article 51 of the Constitution). All cantons, however, set lower signature requirements. Otherwise, aside from this minimum requirement established by the Federal Constitution, the cantons are free to determine how, in what cases, and under what conditions an initiative may be sought. The regulations differ decisively from canton to canton.

C. Legal Validity

137. When the necessary numbers of signatures have been collected in accordance with the necessary procedure, the *legal validity* of an initiative depends on five criteria which apply to all cantons (and that are similar to the four criteria needed for federal initiatives, *supra* Part II, Chapter 2, §3 I). The Federal Court had an important influence for harmonizing these criteria, which are the following:

(1) The initiative must be limited to one subject matter, and the suggested provisions must be general in their application. Should the initiative have several parts, the different parts must be intrinsically connected.
(2) The initiative must either be formulated as a concrete project or as a general proposition. Initiatives that are formulated as a general proposition must then be concretized by the cantonal parliament. For initiatives that are formulated as concrete proposals, parliament can make a counterproposal.
(3) The initiative must either be conceived as a constitutional initiative or as a legislative initiative, taking caution not to mix either form. When an initiative is formulated as a legislative initiative but deals with constitutional matters, the cantonal authorities must treat it as a constitutional initiative.
(4) The constitutional initiative must not be in contradiction or violation of higher (federal and international) law or infringe upon the rights of other cantons. Legislative initiatives must additionally respect the cantonal constitution and

inter-cantonal treaties. Administrative initiatives must additionally respect cantonal ordinary law.

(5) The initiative must be possible to execute. Impossible initiatives are not valid. However, an initiative may not be defeated merely because it is irrational.

138. If an initiative is introduced successfully, a cantonal vote will take place in which the citizens of the canton can approve or reject the proposal.

III. Importance of the Initiative

139. Between the introduction of the constitutional initiative at the federal level in 1891 and Spring 2017, 320 initiatives have been successful insofar as the necessary number of signatures was collected and the initiative was declared valid. About one-third of them (97) were withdrawn before the date of the popular vote was set. Only 7% (22 initiatives) of valid initiatives that were supported by 100,000 signatures, were later approved by popular vote. In 2016, the people and cantons were called to vote on eight initiatives. None of them succeeded in the popular vote.

140. Regardless the statistics, which may suggest that the initiative is only of minor importance, the initiative is quite important in practice. Initiatives that are withdrawn (even though successfully introduced) are normally withdrawn after negotiations with the Swiss Parliament and government. The initiative can be a means to bring politicians to the negotiation table. In many instances, the politicians prefer the introduction of some of the demands through the Parliament to avoid having a popular vote on the topic.

141. Even initiatives that fail in the popular vote normally have repercussions on the political agenda. When an initiative manages to win the support of a major part of the population, the executive and Parliament tend to take up the demands in a more moderate way.

142. While low numbers of participation in elections and popular votes can be noticed, there is no decrease in the number of launched initiatives. Initiatives remain a useful mechanism to influence the political agenda.

§5. Referendum

Selected Bibliography: Auer, Malinverni & Hottelier. Vol. I, 239 et seq.; Biaggini. Kommentar, Articles 140 et seq.; Buser Denise. *Kantonales Staatsrecht,* 132 et seq.; Egli, 73 et seq.; Epiney Astrid & Stefan Diezig. Basler Kommentar, Articles 140–142; Grisel Etienne. 'Volksrechte im Bund'. In Thürer et al., 383 et seq.; Grisel Etienne. 'Volksrechte in den Kantonen'. In Thürer et al., 397 et seq.; Haller. *Swiss Constitution,* 108 et seq.; Linder, 92 et seq.; Mahon, 172 et seq.; Rhinow, Schefer & Uebersax, 420 et seq.; Sciarini Pascal & Anke Tresch. 'Votations populaires'. In Knoepfel et al. (eds), 463 et seq.

I. In General

143. The referendum accords the People the possibility to react. In a popular vote, the People can approve or reject constitutional amendment proposals introduced through a popular initiative or by the Parliament as well as legislative proposals introduced by the Parliament.

II. At the Federal Level

144. There are two types of referenda: mandatory and optional referenda. For certain issues the Constitution prescribes that a referendum must take place – e.g., for constitutional amendments (mandatory referendum). On other issues, the People can demand the referendum (optional referendum). Referenda at the federal level are always binding. There are no consultative referenda.

A. Mandatory Referendum

145. As is regulated in Article 140 of the Constitution, the mandatory referendum assures the legitimacy of certain types of decisions and Federal statutes that are deemed most important from a constitutional law perspective. There are two categories of mandatory referenda as follows.

146. (1) The first category of mandatory referenda requires a *double majority*. These referenda must be approved by the majority of the Swiss people and a majority of the cantons (Articles 140(1) and 142(2, 3, 4) of the Constitution). In practice: citizens fill in one ballot paper. For establishing the necessary overall majority (the majority of the Swiss people), all ballot papers are counted. For the cantonal majority, the ballot papers cast in each canton are counted per canton, and it is established in how many cantons a majority voted in favour.

147. The most important case of this type of mandatory referendum is the constitutional referendum. All revisions of the Constitution must be submitted to the vote by the People and the cantons. Furthermore, this category of mandatory referenda requiring a double majority encompasses as well:

(1) The entry into organizations for collective security.
(2) The entrance into supranational organizations.
(3) Federal Statutes declared urgent and adopted without constitutional basis by the Parliament, and whose validity exceeds one year.

148. (2) The second category of mandatory referenda requires a *simple majority* of the people. This category includes:

(1) the popular initiative for the total revision of the Constitution;
(2) the popular initiative for the partial revision of the Constitution in the form of a general suggestion which has been rejected by the Federal Parliament; and

(3) the question whether a total revision of the Constitution should be carried out if the two Chambers of Parliament disagree.

149. Normally, a positive result in the popular vote is a prerequisite for the subject matter of the referendum to enter into force. Only in the case of urgent legislation, the referendum has a dissolving effect. Once the urgent legislation has been rejected in the popular vote, it loses its binding force.

B. *Optional Referendum*

150. The optional referendum confers to the people a veto power, insofar as the people can veto decisions taken by the Federal Parliament. This was introduced in the Constitution of 1874 as a compensation for the stronger federal centralization. Within forty years (1970–2010), about eighty statutes or statutory revisions had to be submitted to the vote of the people, who rejected less than one-third of them. The optional referendum has a strong influence on Swiss law-making procedure. It creates pressure upon Parliament to find a compromise in order to prevent the people from demanding a referendum. Although a referendum may run the risk of discrediting the policy of Parliament, a negative referendum result has no direct personal consequences for the parliamentarians or for the Federal Councillor who suggested or promoted a legislative draft.

151. In the case of the optional referendum, (1) 50,000 Swiss citizens with their signature or (2) 8 cantons may demand a popular vote (Article 141 of the Constitution). In 2003, for the first time in Swiss constitutional history, eleven cantons decided to make use of the optional referendum against a federal taxation scheme decided by the Federal Parliament. The opposing cantons (Basel-City, Bern, Glarus, Jura, Obwalden, St. Gallen, Schaffhausen, Solothurn, Vaud and Valais) won and the federal taxation scheme was successfully rejected by the People. The optional referendum can be used for:

(1) federal statutes;
(2) federal statutes with a constitutional basis that have been declared urgent with a validity exceeding one year;
(3) federal decrees, insofar as the possibility of referendum is especially foreseen in the Constitution or in the statute; and
(4) international treaties which are:

 (a) of unlimited duration and;
 (b) may not be terminated, which;
 (c) provide for the entry into an international organization.

152. In most cases, a negative result following a popular vote prevents the parliamentary act from entering into force. If a piece of urgent legislation with a constitutional basis is rejected in a popular vote, then it becomes invalid no later than one year after its adoption, and it cannot be renewed.

C. Organization

153. Every year, several weekends are reserved for federal popular votes in which the citizens may vote on various issues at the time. In most cases, cantonal votes are also held on these dates. The federal popular votes are organized by the cantons on the specified weekends. The federal level prepares information including a short summary on the subject matter to be voted on, a statement of the referendum respectively the initiative committee, and the recommendations of the Federal Council. These are then distributed to the citizens some weeks in advance before the vote takes place. The citizens can either vote directly on the weekend in which the voting is taking place, or they can vote by postal mail beforehand. Some cantons plan to introduce the option of voting via the internet.

154. The cantons organize the counting of the votes, and in some cantons electronic counting machines have been introduced. However, electronic counting is only allowed with permission from federal authorities. In cases of violation of the voting rules, the votes must be recounted in the concerned cantons or municipalities.

III. At the Cantonal Level

A. Mandatory Referendum

155. As prescribed by federal law, the amendment of a cantonal constitution necessitates a referendum (Article 51 of the Constitution). Thirteen cantons also provide mandatory referenda for the adoption and revision of statutes, and one canton for directives issued by cantonal parliament. In seventeen cantons, public expenses exceeding a certain amount must be approved in a referendum (financial referendum). Six cantons conduct a mandatory referendum for inter-cantonal treaties.

B. Optional Referendum

156. The thirteen cantons that do not have a mandatory referendum for the adoption of statutes foresee an optional referendum. Twenty cantons provide for an optional financial referendum, and nine cantons provide an optional referendum for inter-cantonal treaties.

IV. Importance of the Referendum

157. The referendum accords the majority of the people the right to veto legislation (or at the cantonal level also certain other decisions). In cases of constitutional amendments both the majority of the people and of the cantons can veto constitutional changes. Although this seems contrary to the consensus-oriented approach of Swiss democracy, in the Swiss context, the right to referendum does not introduce elements of competitive democracy. On the contrary, it further enhances consensus-oriented democracy and promotes the legitimacy of decisions. Proposals are normally rejected in a popular vote when a basic consensus of the political elite is lacking.

158. There are several probable reasons for this phenomenon. When the major political parties and politicians are divided, the population tends to prefer to remain with the status quo. A party with a majority within parliament cannot be sure that its proposals will also carry a popular majority. Experience shows changing majorities, crossing party lines. Citizens cast their vote depending on the issue and not necessarily based on party allegiance.

159. Voting outcomes are regularly analysed for emerging more constant voting patterns. There were several referenda in which, for example, the German-speaking part of Switzerland was strongly opposed while the French-speaking part was in favour (e.g., on 26 September 2004, a new proposal to facilitate the naturalization of foreigners living in Switzerland for the second and third generation was clearly rejected by the German-speaking population and clearly accepted by the French-speaking population). Because of the larger German-speaking population, as well as the larger number of cantons dominated by German speakers, they were in the position to dominate the voting in these referenda. In several instances, a division between urban and rural areas can be noted, for instance in the vote 'against mass immigration' of 9 February 2014.

160. A relatively small number of popular vote proposals have been rejected even though a majority of the Swiss People have been in favour of it due to the negative vote of a majority of the cantons (e.g., a proposal on the facilitated naturalization of foreigners in 1994). Up to now only three constitutional amendments failed in the popular vote even though a majority of the cantons were in favour. For instance, in November 2002, an initiative that was aimed at the restriction of the rights of asylum seekers was rejected by the people but adopted by the majority of the cantons.

161. An *indirect* reason that safeguards the interests of minorities is the low turnout at ballots. Mainly those who feel strongly concerned participate in the vote. However, low turnout is problematic from a democratic point of view. Since referendum voting often attracts only 30% of the overall population, this means a strongly concerned minority of 16% can win the vote.

Chapter 3. The Legislature

Selected Bibliography: Aubert Jean-François. *Die Schweizerische Bundesversammlung von 1848 bis 1998.* Basel/Frankfurt: Helbing & Lichtenhahn, 1998; Auer, Malinverni & Hottelier. Vol. I, 31 et seq.; Biaggini. Kommentar, Article 153; Buser Denise. *Kantonales Staatsrecht,* 164 et seq.; Egli, 88 et seq.; Häfelin, Haller, Keller & Thurnherr, 443 et seq.; Haller. *Swiss Constitution,* 117 et seq.; Kiener Regina. *Die Informationsrechte der parlamentarischen Kommissionen.* Bern, 1994; Le Roy Katy & Saunders Cheryl (eds). *Legislative, Executive, and Judicial Governance in Federal Countries.* Montréal/Kingston: McGill-Queen's University Press, 2006; Linder, 182 et seq.; Lüthi Ruth. 'Das Parlament'. In Knoepfel et al. (eds), 169 et seq.; Mahon, 203 et seq.; Rhinow, Schefer & Uebersax, 437 et seq.; Sägesser Thomas (ed.). *Die Bundesbehörden: Bundesversammlung, Bundesrat, Bundesgericht: Kommentar, Beiträge und Materialien zum 5. Titel der schweizerischen Bundesverfassung.* Bern: Stämpfli, 2000; Sciarini Pascal. 'Le processus législatif'. In Knoepfel et al. (eds), 527 et seq.; Tschannen, 417 et seq.; Zimmerli Ulrich, 'Bundesversammlung'. In Thürer et al., 1027 et seq.

§1. Organization

I. The Status of Federal Parliament as Highest Authority

162. According to Article 148(1) of the Constitution, the Federal Parliament is the highest authority of the Swiss Confederation. The authority of Parliament is limited by the rights of the People and the Cantons that form together the constituent power (*pouvoir constitutant*).

163. A special feature of Swiss democracy is the militia system (*Milizsystem*). In congruence with the militia system, Members of Parliament are usually only part-time politicians who continue to work in their professions. This shall prevent the emergence of a political caste who depends on politics and a political career. Furthermore, it shall ensure that politicians remain integrated in the work force and therefore keep in touch with the citizens and their concerns. However, the number of full-time politicians is increasing.

II. Bicameral Parliament

164. Similar to the American system and based upon its direct influence, the Swiss Parliament is bicameral:

- In the National Council, the Swiss citizens are represented proportionally in accordance with the democratic principle.
- In the Council of States, similar to the Senate in the United States of America, the cantons are equally represented in accordance with the federal principle.

165. The National Council and the Council of States have equal powers, e.g. all legislation must pass both Chambers of Parliament to be adopted.

III. Composition

A. National Council

1. Distribution of Seats

166. Since 1963, the National Council has been composed of 200 members (Article 149(1) of the Constitution). Every four years, the representatives are elected by the people (Article 149(2) of the Constitution). Even for this chamber, tribute is paid to federalism. Each canton forms a constituency (Article 149(3) of the Constitution). The number of representatives elected within the constituency depends on the population size of the constituency. However, if proportionality were applied in its purest form, some of the smaller cantons would not be able to elect any National Councillor. Therefore, based on the principle of federalized democracy, the population of each canton can elect at least one representative (Article 149(4) of the Constitution).

2. Procedure for the Distribution of Seats

167. According to Article 17 of the Political Rights Act, the procedure for the distribution of seats per canton is the following:

- In the first round, the total number of all inhabitants is divided by 200. Cantons that have a population of less than the determined number receive one seat. These cantons and their share in the Swiss population are excluded from the further procedure.
- In the second round, the remaining population is divided by the remaining seats. Again, the cantons whose population is less than the determined number receive one seat, and they and their populations are, from then on, excluded from the procedure. This procedure is repeated until all remaining cantons have populations higher than the determined number.
- In the third round, for the distribution of the remaining seats, the population of each remaining canton is divided by the last determined number.

3. Outcome

168. This procedure leads to the following distribution of seats (as established in 2015): Zurich (35), Berne (25), Lucerne (10), Uri (1), Schwyz (4), Obwalden (1), Nidwalden (1), Glarus (1), Zug (3), Fribourg (7), Solothurn (6), Basel-City (5), Basel-Land (7), Schaffhausen (2), Appenzell Outer Rhodes (1), Appenzell Inner Rhodes (1), St. Gallen (12), Grisons (5), Aargau (16), Thurgau (6), Ticino (8), Vaud (18), Valais (8), Neuchâtel (4), Geneva (11) and Jura (2).

169. The distribution of seats is adapted periodically based on census data.

B. The Council of States

170. The Council of States is composed of forty-six members (Article 150(1) of the Constitution). Each canton elects two representatives, except for the so-called half-cantons (Obwalden, Nidwalden, Basel-City, Basel-Land, Appenzell Ausserrhoden, Appenzell Innerrhoden), which each elect one representative (Article 150(2) of the Constitution).

IV. Elections

A. The National Council

171. The Constitution prescribes that the members of the National Council shall be elected directly by the People according to the system of proportionate representation. Each canton forms a constituency (Article 149(2) and (3) of the Constitution). Owing to the disproportionate demographic size of the cantons, the actual effect of the electoral system differs decisively. In cantons that are entitled to elect one representative, the proportional system is de facto replaced by the majority principle (first past the post), which favours bipolarization among voters. As a consequence, the smaller cantons are rather dominated by the biggest political parties. In contrast, e.g., in the Canton of Zurich, a political party can gain a seat in the Federal Parliament with less than 3% of the cantonal votes. Therefore, a much more diversified political landscape can be observed.

172. For the election to the National Council, citizens can propose candidate lists. In most cases, these lists are proposed by political parties (party lists). The lists must not include more candidates than the number of representatives the concerned canton is attributed. The lists must be signed by 100–400 citizens of the concerned constituency, depending on the size of the constituency.

173. The election is limited to the candidates included on the lists and voters can (but need not) give as many votes as the number of representatives attributed to the canton. Voting citizens are provided with the proposed lists and with a blank list. Citizens can either use a list as proposed, they can modify the proposed lists or they can fill in the blank list. There are three permissible modifications to the proposed lists:

(1) Voters can add names to lists that contain less than the maximum number of candidates.
(2) They can strike out one or more names on the list.
(3) They can modify the lists to include candidates of different parties (or independent candidates) on one list (*panachage*). If a voter wants to increase a candidate's probability of being elected, he/she can *cumulate* – in other words, he/she can put the name of a candidate down twice.

174. In tallying the results, each candidate receives as many votes as he/she received on the voted for lists. In addition to these individual votes, the party vote is established. A vote for a candidate counts as a vote for that candidate's political party. In addition, the party receives votes for the blank spaces on the voted for party lists.

175. The distribution of seats is based on a formula that considers the individual votes and the party votes.

B. The Council of States

176. Whereas federal law regulates the election to the National Council, the election to the Council of States mainly is a cantonal matter (Article 150(3) of the Constitution). The cantons must respect the one man, one vote principle, the right to free formation of opinion by the citizens and the citizens' right to the unaltered expression of their will (Article 34(2) of the Constitution).

177. All cantons, except for the Canton of Jura, rely on the majority principle. As a general rule, in the first round, the candidate must receive an absolute majority of votes; in the second round, a relative majority is sufficient.

178. In most of the cantons, the representatives are elected by secret ballot. The half-canton of Appenzell Innerrhoden, still follows the practice of voting for its representatives in its *Landsgemeinde* (a publicly held assembly of all citizens).

V. Session Period

179. The provisions of the Constitution concerning session periods of Parliament are rather rudimentary. Article 151(1) of the Constitution prescribes that the two Chambers of Parliament shall meet regularly for ordinary sessions. It shall not depend on the will of political parties or the government whether sessions take place. Any further regulation is left to statutory law. Sessions take place in spring, summer, autumn and winter for a period of three weeks. The chambers can call additional sessions independent from each other, for instance to catch up on workload (Article 2(2) of the Law on Parliament). Furthermore, according to Article 151(2) of the Constitution, extraordinary sessions of both chambers must be called when one-quarter of the Members of a Chamber or Federal Parliament of the Federal Council (the executive) so request.

VI. Presidency

180. Both Chambers of Parliament elect their own Presidents, as well as first and second Vice-Presidents. The mandate of the President and the Vice-Presidents is limited to one year, and an immediate re-election is not possible (Article 152 of the Constitution).

181. According to protocol, the President of the National Council is the highest-ranking politician in Switzerland. The Presidents chair the sessions of their respective Chambers of Parliament. In the case of joint sessions, the President of the National Council acts as chairperson. Apart from purely representative functions, this is the only additional power accorded to the President.

VII. Parliamentary Committees and Groups

182. The impact of parliamentary committees on the decision-making process in Parliament cannot be underestimated. According to Article 153 of the Constitution, each Chamber shall appoint committees. Most of the committees have been designed as standing committees. For fulfilling their tasks, committees have the right to obtain information, to consult documents and to conduct inquiries as established by law. In addition to committees in each Chamber, there are also joint committees of both Chambers (Article 153(2) of the Constitution). The most important case of a joint committee is the Parliamentary Investigation Committee. This committee is not a standing committee but is instituted by the Parliament when there are signs of major state irregularities.

183. According to Article 154 of the Constitution, the Members of Parliament may form parliamentary groups, which include the party members of both Chambers and can include members of several parties of similar ideology. The parliamentary group must have at least five members in one of the Chambers. Members of one political party cannot form more than one parliamentary group. For the composition of parliamentary committees, the size of the parliamentary groups is taken into account. Membership in a parliamentary group is important for influencing parliamentary committees.

VIII. Parliamentary Services

184. Parliament relies on professional parliamentary services (Article 155 of the Constitution) which plan and coordinate the sessions of Parliament and the meetings of committees, and which equally act as a secretariat, take the protocol, and undertake translations. They also advise the presidents of the committees on substantive and procedural questions. The parliamentary services can request support from the services of the federal administration.

§2. Procedures

I. Separate and Joint Deliberations

185. In most cases, the National Council and the Council of States deliberate separately, in their individual chambers in Parliament with their own agenda. The National Council and the Council of States deliberate jointly only for elections, to decide on jurisdictional disputes between the highest federal authorities, and to rule on petitions for pardon. In addition, both chambers will assemble for special occasions and to hear declarations of the Federal Council (Article 157 of the Constitution). All meetings are open to the public unless the law provides otherwise (Article 158 of the Constitution).

II. Quorum and Majority

186. Deliberations in the chambers are valid if the majority of their members are present (Article 159(1) of the Constitution). The President of each chamber presides over the quorum. In the case of joint deliberations, the majority of the members of each chamber is required. Despite of the clear wording of the Constitution, which suggests that the quorum is required for deliberations it is normally only enforced for formal decision-making. Members of Parliament are obliged to be present in parliamentary sessions unless officially excused. In both chambers and in joint sessions, the decisions are taken by the majority of those voting (Article 159(2) of the Constitution). An absolute majority of the members of each chamber is required for the declaration of urgency of federal statutes, for provisions granting subsidies, authorizing credit lines, and establishing spending ceilings, which cause new one-time expenditures exceeding CHF 20 million, or new recurrent expenditures exceeding CHF 2 million as well as for an increase of the overall spending for extraordinary disbursement needs (Article 159(3) of the Constitution).

187. Decisions of the Federal Parliament require the approval of the exact same wording by both chambers (Article 156 of the Constitution). The Presidents of the two chambers or the lot decide which chamber deliberates first. The relevant parliamentary committee pre-discusses and formulates proposals, then the business is discussed in the plenary. In a first step, the chamber decides whether it wants to enter detailed deliberations. It can revert the business back to the committee. Once the detailed deliberation is finalized, the chamber votes on the business and upon successful vote transfers it to the second deliberating chamber. If one chamber rejects the business after detailed deliberations it is written off. If both chambers – after three detailed deliberations – approve the business but still adopt different wordings, a conference of the members of the respective parliamentary committees of both chambers is called for reaching an agreement. Once an agreement is achieved within the conference the business is once more submitted to the two chambers. If the agreed-on version is defeated in one of the chambers the business is written off. There are some cases for which the legislator is called upon to establish a procedure that guarantees that a decision is taken even in case of disagreement between the chambers. These cases are enumerated in the Article 156(3) of the Constitution:

- the validity or partial non-validity of initiatives (if the chambers disagree, the chamber in favour of the validity succeeds);
- the implementation of a successful initiative that was presented in the form of a general proposition (if the two chambers cannot agree on one version for the implementation of the general proposition, both are presented to the people as alternatives);
- the implementation of a federal decree, accepted by the people in a referendum, for the commencement of the process of a total revision of the Constitution (until now (Autumn 2017) the statute does not establish such procedure);
- the budget and supplementary budgets (in case the two chambers disagree, the lower amount is considered as adopted).

III. Rights to Initiatives and Motions

188. According to Article 160(1) of the Constitution, every Member of Parliament, every parliamentary committee or group, and every canton is entitled to submit parliamentary initiatives to the Federal Parliament. (For the initiative of the Federal Council *see infra* Part II, Chapter 4, §2 II A.) With the parliamentary initiative – not to be confused with the popular initiative – the initiator or the initiators can submit a draft for a new Act of Parliament, or the initiator can make a general proposition.

189. In a preliminary phase, after deliberations in the parliamentary committee, the concerned chamber of parliament decides whether to follow the initiative. In cases of rejection – contrary to the procedure of the popular initiative – the matter is put *ad acta*.

190. In those rare cases in which a canton introduces a parliamentary initiative, the concerned committee in *each* Chamber deliberates. Otherwise, the procedure and the effects are the same.

IV. Prohibitions of Instructed Mandates

191. The members of both chambers must not be instructed on how to vote by individuals, the cantons, nor by any interest groups (Article 161(1) of the Constitution). However, the militia system implies that the politicians are deeply rooted in different professions and civil society. Therefore, the Constitution mandates that Members of Parliament reveal their links with interest groups (Article 161(2) of the Constitution).

V. Immunity

192. Article 162(1) of the Constitution provides for absolute immunity for the Members of Parliament, as well as for the members of the Federal Council and for the Federal Chancellor. The absolute immunity applies for statements in parliament and before parliamentary organs – e.g., the parliamentary committees and groups. For these statements, immunity cannot be lifted. Statutory law may provide for further forms of immunity and can extend immunity to other persons (Article 162(2) of the Constitution).

193. In contrast to the American model, Members of Parliament and of the Government cannot be prosecuted for criminal offences *during sessions*, even if not connected with their office.

194. Outside of sessions, relative immunity applies for criminal acts that are connected to the political office. In these cases, prosecution is allowed only upon authorization of both chambers. The consent of the accused does not suffice because the relative immunity is supposed to safeguard the functioning of political institutions and is therefore within the exclusive power of Parliament. When in doubt, the Parliament assumes a connection between the criminal act and the political office and rejects the lifting of immunity.

§3. Powers

I. Legislation

195. A distinction must be drawn between federal statutes and decrees (Article 163(1) of the Constitution). The distinction is mainly relevant with respect to the rights of direct democracy, to judicial remedies and to the rules of delegation. Provisions of importance, which establish rules of law, must be enacted in the form of statutes. The Constitution provides examples of matters that have to be regulated in the form of statutes: the fundamental provisions on the exercise of political rights, the restrictions of constitutional rights, the rights and obligations of persons, the circle of taxpayers, and the object and the calculation of taxes, the tasks and services of the Confederation, the obligations of cantons when implementing and executing federal law, and the organization and the procedure of federal authorities (Article 164 of the Constitution). Court decisions provide for further criteria. Matters of lesser importance can use the form of a federal decree (Article 163(2) of the Constitution). A federal decree not subjected to referendum is called a simple federal decree.

196. According to Article 164(2) of the Constitution, Parliament can delegate, within a federal statute, the power to legislate unless the Federal Constitution prohibits the delegation. Legislative powers on matters that must be regulated in form of a federal statute cannot be delegated.

197. When the coming into force of a statute does not tolerate delay, the statute may be *declared urgent* by the absolute majority of the members of each chamber of Parliament and can be put into force immediately. A federal statute that shall be declared urgent must be limited in time (Article 165(1) of the Constitution). Urgent statutes lapse one year after their adoption unless they are approved in a popular vote before that date. Depending whether the statute has a constitutional basis, the statute must be approved by the People or by the People and the Cantons. Urgent Federal Statutes that have not been approved may not be renewed by the Parliament (Article 165(2)–(4) of the Constitution).

II. Further Tasks of Parliament

198. Aside from its powers in the fields of legislation, the Federal Parliament shall deal with all subjects that are within the powers of the Confederation and that are not attributed to another federal authority (Article 173(2) of the Constitution).

199. In addition to this general power, the Constitution enumerates some further tasks of the Federal Parliament:

(1) Foreign relations are mainly a task of the Federal Council. However, the Federal Parliament shall participate in the shaping of foreign policy and shall supervise foreign relations. Additionally, it has the right to approve international treaties unless a statute or an international treaty declares the treaty within the power of the Federal Government (Article 166 of the Constitution).

(2) The Federal Parliament decides on the spending, adopts the budget and approves the federal accounts (Article 167 of the Constitution).
(3) The Federal Parliament elects the members of the Federal Council, the Federal Chancellor and the judges of the Federal Supreme Court. In case of war, Parliament elects a general for the Swiss army (Article 168 of the Constitution). In times of peace, the Swiss army has no general.
(4) The Federal Parliament supervises the Federal Government, the Federal Administration, the Federal Supreme Courts, and the other organs entrusted with tasks of the state (Article 169 of the Constitution), and evaluates the efficacy of measures taken by the Confederation (Article 170 of the Constitution).
(5) The Federal Parliament may confer mandates to the Federal Government (Article 171 of the Constitution).
(6) The Federal Parliament maintains the relations between the Confederation and the cantons, it approves the cantonal constitutions and decides whether to approve inter-cantonal treaties or treaties between cantons and foreign countries, if the Federal Government or a canton raise objections against the treaty (Article 172 of the Constitution).
(7) The Parliament fulfils certain security related tasks to safeguard the internal and external security, the independence and the neutrality of Switzerland. For these tasks, the Federal Parliament can issue ordinances or simple federal decrees (that are not submitted to popular referendum). The Federal Parliament can order active military service and, to this end, can mobilize the army (Article 173(1)(a)–(d) of the Constitution).
(8) The Federal Parliament takes measures to enforce federal law, it decides on the validity of popular initiatives that meet the formal requirements, decides on individual acts in cases especially foreseen in a Federal Statute, rules on conflicts of jurisdiction between the highest federal authorities; and it decides on petitions for pardon and can declare amnesties (Article 173(1)(e)–(k). For instance, the Federal Parliament granted general tax amnesties in which persons can declare tax frauds (and pay the due tax amount) without being punished.

Chapter 4. The Executive

Selected Bibliography: Adam Elisabeth. 'La chancellerie fédérale dans l'histoire: aperçu sur les origines d'une institution bientôt bicentenaire'. In *Mélanges François Couchepin, Schlieren*: 1995, 163 et seq.; Altermatt Urs. *Die Schweizer Bundesräte, Ein biographisches Lexikon.* Zurich: Artemis & Winkler, 1991; Auer, Malinverni & Hottelier. Vol. I, 47 et seq.; Biaggini. Kommentar, Articles 174 et seq.; Brühl-Moser Denise. *Die schweizerische Staatsleitung.* Bern: Stämpfli, 2007; Egli, 94 et seq.; Häfelin, Haller, Keller & Thurnherr, 491 et seq.; Haller. *Swiss Constitution*, 139 et seq.; Rieder Stefan, Balthasar Andreas & Kissling-Näf Ingrid. 'Vollzug und Wirkung öffentlicher Politiken'. In Knoepfel et al. (eds), 563 et seq.; Klöti Ulrich, Papadopoulos Yannis & Sager Fritz. 'Regierung'. In Knoepfel et al. (eds), 193 et seq.; Linder. 182 et seq.; Mader Luzius. 'Bundesrat und Bundesverwaltung'. In Thürer et al., 1047 et seq.; Mahon, 235 et seq.; Rhinow René. *Wie weiter mit dem Bundesrat?.* Zurich/St. Gallen: Dike Verlag, 2011; Rhinow, Schefer & Uebersax, 469 et seq.; Tschannen, 494 et seq.

200. In Switzerland, the Federal Council forms the head of the executive branch. It is the most distinctive of the Swiss Federal institutions. Its composition and functioning demonstrates the Swiss stance towards diversity and Switzerland's compromise driven way of decision-making.

§1. Organization and Procedure

I. Federal Government as Highest Governing and Executive Authority of the Confederation

201. According to Article 174 of the Constitution, the Federal Government is the highest governing and executive authority of the Confederation.

II. The Government as Federal Council

202. The Federal Government is organized as a Federal Council. The French directorate inspired this institution (*see* General Introduction, Chapter 1, §3 I).

III. Composition and Election

203. The Federal Council consists of seven members, called Federal Councillors, who concurrently serve as head of state and ministers. Federal Councillors are elected by the Federal Parliament in a joint session of the two chambers of Parliament. They are elected for a four-year term among the Swiss citizens eligible for membership in the National Council after each full renewal of the National Council (Article 175(1)–

(3) of the Constitution), or for the remaining term after a Federal Councillor vacated his/her seat. The candidate must receive an absolute majority of the votes. The political parties normally propose candidates. In the first two rounds of voting, however, elections are free and the parliamentarians can vote for any eligible person. From the third round onwards, only candidates receiving at least ten votes in the previous round are eligible; after every new round, the candidate with the lowest number of votes is excluded from the coming rounds.

204. In the past, with exceptions in 1854, 1872, 2003 and 2007, Federal Councillors have always been re-elected when they stood for re-election. There is no official maximum term for Federal Councillors and no vote of no-confidence. In average, Federal Councillors serve for about ten years, then step down voluntarily – sometimes based on pressure from their party or the parliament. Since 1848 there has never been a complete renewal of the Federal Council which has provided continuity to government policy.

205. According to the Constitution, in the selection of the Councillors, Parliament shall consider that the various geographical and language regions be adequately represented (Article 175(4) of the Constitution). In accordance with this provision, the Federal Council normally includes two or three French- or Italian-speaking Councillors. The rule that all Councillors had to originate from different cantons was abolished in a popular vote of 7 February 1999.

206. Article 175(4) of the Constitution has differing wordings in the different language versions of the Constitution. While the German version states that 'linguistic regions' shall be adequately represented the French and Italian versions use the expression of 'linguistic communities'. Officially, all three versions have equal legal validity. The practical consequences became apparent when elections for a seat vacated by a French-speaking Federal Councillor took place in 2009. One candidate originated from the French-speaking region but his mother tongue was German. The French-speaking community questioned his candidacy. He lost the election.

207. In addition to these constitutional requirements, in 1956 the main political parties agreed on the so-called magic formula for the composition of the Council. According to this unwritten formula, the four biggest parties are to be represented in the Government. The number of Councillors per party had remained the same for several decades. From 1956 to 2003, the Free Democratic Party, the Social Democratic Party and the Christian Democratic Party had each been represented by two Federal Councillors. The Swiss People's Party had been represented by one Councillor. In 2003, the magic formula was adapted in respect to the distribution of seats per party. In consideration of the sharp increase in popularity of the Swiss People's Party (SPP), on 10 December 2003, the Parliament did not re-elect Federal Councillor Ruth Metzler, the representative of the Christian Democratic Party, and instead elected Christoph Blocher, a representative of the Swiss People's Party. With the election of Christoph Blocher, parliament accorded a second seat to the Swiss People's Party.

208. For a short period (2007–2015), there has been a deviation from the magic formula in so far that five parties have been represented in the Federal Council. In 2007, in a surprise move, Parliament denied re-election to Federal Councillor Christoph Blocher and instead elected Evelyn Widmer Schlumpf, also a member of the SPP – against the will of the SPP party leadership. The SPP reacted by excluding the cantonal party chapter of Ms. Widmer Schlumpf from the party. The cantonal party chapter formed a new party, the Conservative Democratic Party (CDP). Ms. Widmer Schlumpf remained in the Federal Council for two terms and stepped down at the end of 2015. In her place, again a representative of the SPP was elected, returning to the distribution of seats as of 2003.

209. On 2 October 1984, the first woman, Elisabeth Kopp from the Free Democratic Party, was elected to the Federal Council. However, in 1990, Ms. Kopp decided to resign when it became known that she had informed her husband, who was Vice-President of the board of directors of the Shakarchi Inc., about a criminal money-laundering investigation against the company. The Federal Supreme Court did not classify the telephone call to her husband as a violation of an official secret in the sense of Article 320 of the Criminal Code and the sentence was one of acquittal (Decision of the Federal Court BGE 116 IV 56 et seq.). Since then, six women representatives were elected to the Federal Council: Ruth Dreifuss from the Social Democratic Party (1993–2002), Ruth Metzler from the Christian Democratic Party (1998–2003), Micheline Calmy-Rey from the Social Democratic Party (2002–2011), Doris Leuthard from the Christian Democratic party (elected in 2006), Evelyn Widmer Schlumpf now from the Conservative Democratic Party (2007–2015) and Simonetta Somaruga from the Social Democratic Party (elected in 2010). For a short period of time (2010–2011), the Federal Council had a majority of female Federal Councillors.

210. As shown above, the Federal Council is composed of different political parties. Nevertheless, the Swiss government is not a classic coalition government, i.e., the government is not based on a coalition agreement or pre-negotiated government programme. Government formation is by and large formula based (like in Northern Ireland) though the formula is an informal, unwritten one.

211. The constitutional and informal requirements for the composition of the Federal Council have the effect that there is almost no political opposition as all main political forces and groups are part of the government. It is particularly in light of this lack of opposition that the instruments of direct democracy are important. Through them, the people can act as opposition. The system of government formation also has the effect that Federal Councillors are relatively independent from their political parties. The mode of election by the Parliament requires that the candidate is acceptable to the majority of parliament. The Parliament considers amongst others whether the candidate is a team player and can constructively interact with his or her follow Federal Councillors. Political parties tend to propose candidates that do not polarize to increase the chance that their preferred candidate gets elected.

IV. Presidency

212. Parliament elects the President and the Vice-President of the Confederation from among the Federal Councillors. The term of the presidency and of the vice-presidency are limited to one year and are not renewable (Article 176 of the Constitution) and thus the presidency rotates among the Federal Councillors. As a general rule, Federal Councillors are elected president in the order of their election to the Federal Council. Thus, every Federal Councillor who serves two terms will be president at least once. The President is *primus inter pares*. The presidential office does not confer additional powers, but includes representative duties. He or she continues to preside over a department (ministry). The Swiss presidency is a very weak one, and decisions are taken by the Federal Council *in corpore*.

V. Principle of Collective Authority

213. In order to ensure continuity, consistency and stability within the executive branch of government, the Federal Council takes its decisions as a collective body (Article 177(1) of the Constitution) by majority vote. Thus, in practice, decisions must at least be based on the consensus of two political parties. According to Articles 4 and 12 of the Federal Act on the Organization of the Federal Council and the Federal Administration of 21 March 1997, all members of the Federal Council have the same legal status, and their decisions are taken as a collective body and represented as such uniformly towards the public regardless of the personal opinion of the Federal Councillor (duty of identification with collective decision). Consequently, to the extent possible, the voting behaviour of the individual Federal Councillors is kept secret.

VI. Federal Administration

214. According to Article 178 of the Constitution, the Federal Council directs the Federal Administration with the duty to insure its efficient administration and the effective fulfilment of its tasks.

215. The Federal Administration is divided into Departments (ministries) and each member of the Federal Council is head of a Department (Article 178(2) of the Constitution). Because the Constitution limits the number of Federal Councillors to seven there are also only seven Departments. The distribution of Departments is based on free choice and not necessarily on qualification. In practice, the Federal Councillors gather behind closed doors and – not bound by any rule of law – decide who will head which Department. The seven Departments are the following:

(1) Federal Department of Foreign Affairs;
(2) Federal Department of Home Affairs;
(3) Federal Department of Justice and Police;
(4) Federal Department of Defence, Civil Protection and Sports;
(5) Federal Department of Finance;
(6) Federal Department of Economic Affairs; and
(7) Federal Department of Environment, Transport, Energy and Communications.

216. Influenced by New Public Management, Article 178 of the Constitution provides the general basis for the delegation of administrative tasks to organizations and persons of public or private law outside of the Federal Administration.

VII. Federal Chancery

217. Central services are provided by the Federal Chancery. The Chancery is directed by a Chancellor who is elected in a joint session of both chambers of Parliament for a period of four years (Article 179 of the Constitution). Although the Constitution is silent on the tasks of the Federal Chancery, its importance should not be underestimated. It provides services to the Federal Council and the Parliament.

218. The Chancellor attends the weekly sessions of the Federal Council in an advisory capacity and may table motions. The Chancery organizes the sessions of Parliament including the setting up of the agenda for deliberation. It redacts Federal Council decisions and ensures the timely internal distribution of information. A legal division of the Chancery advises the Federal Council in its legislative process and supports the law-drafting committees of the two chambers of Parliament. Further, a language division ensures that legislation is drafted in such a way that it can be easily understood by the public. A political division advises initiative and referendum committees, verifies the submitted lists of signatures, organizes federal votes and elections and deals with complaints concerning votes and elections.

219. As part of the Federal Chancery, a Federal Data Protection Commissioner and a Federal Data Protection Commission work to safeguard the privacy of individuals whose data are processed by federal bodies or by private individuals and organizations. The Commissioner can conduct investigations, issue recommendation and counsel private individuals as well as government agencies on questions concerning data protection. The Federal Data Protection Commission presides over appeals against decisions of most federal bodies and of the Commissioner's office, and it acts as arbitration commission for recommendation of the Commissioner in the private sphere. Judgments of the Commission can be appealed before the Federal Supreme Court.

220. In addition, the Chancery is involved in public relations and communication, in the publication and distribution of laws, and in personnel matters concerning training, equal opportunities, logistics and budget, payments and auditing.

§2. Powers

I. Government Policy

221. The Federal Council is responsible for the strategic planning and coordination of all governmental activity. It determines the goals and the means of its government policy (Article 180 of the Constitution). Transparency of governmental activity shall be assured by timely information to Parliament (Article 187(1)(b) of the Constitution) and to the public, whenever not opposed by preponderant public interests. Federal Parliament exercises oversight over the Federal Council (Article 169 of the Constitution).

II. Powers in Respect to Legislation Issued by the Parliament

A. Initiative

222. The Federal Council can submit parliamentary initiatives to parliament. (For the discussion on parliamentary initiatives, *see supra* Part II, Chapter 3, §2, III.)

B. Draft Legislation

223. In nearly all cases, drafts for legislation are prepared by the Federal Council based on its own initiative or on the request of Parliament. The Federal Council submits these drafts to Parliament (Article 181 of the Constitution).

C. Preliminary Procedure (Consultation Procedure)

224. The Federal Council directs the preliminary procedure of the legislative process, including the consultation of the cantons, of political parties, of associations and of economic, social, environmental and other interest groups (Article 147 of the Constitution). The preliminary procedure is a specific feature of Swiss law-making which aims at creating consensus in a very early stage of the legislative process, even before the draft enters Parliament. The Federal Council selects experts and organizes hearings to accomplish this goal.

D. Entry into Force of Acts of Parliament

225. Many acts of Parliament foresee that the Federal Council determines the date for the entry into force.

III. Own Legislative Powers

226. The separation of powers is based more on an *institutional separation* than on a functional separation of powers. The Federal Council has important legislative powers and can issue ordinances. However, it cannot legislate on the level of the Constitution or of statutes. Two types of ordinances can be distinguished: the dependent and the independent ordinance.

A. Dependent Ordinances

227. Usually, the Federal Council issues dependent ordinances, which are based upon an express delegation in a Federal Statute (Articles 164(2) and 182(1) of the Constitution).

B. Independent Ordinances

228. Independent ordinances are based upon a Constitutional provision, such as ordinances for the implementation of statutes (Article 182(2) of the Constitution), ordinances for safeguarding the interests of the country (Article 184(3) of the Constitution) and police ordinances in case of imminent danger of public order (Article 185(3) of the Constitution).

IV. Judicial Powers of the Federal Council

229. See infra, Part IV, Chapter 4, §3.

V. Further Tasks

230. Additional tasks of the Federal Council include the preparation of the financial plan, the budget, the federal accounts and the supervision of the financial management (Article 183 of the Constitution). Other important tasks include foreign relations (Article 184 of the Constitution, *infra* Part V, Chapter 1, §3), external and national security (Article 185 of the Constitution, *infra* Part V, Chapter 1, §1) and the relation between the Confederation and the cantons (Article 186 of the Constitution, *infra* Part III, Chapter 1).

Chapter 5. The Judiciary

§1. Independence of the Judiciary: Institutional Principle and Fundamental Right

Selected Bibliography: Biaggini Giovanni. 'Rechtsprechung'. In Thürer et al., 1153 et seq.; Biaggini. Kommentar, Article 30 and Article 191c; Eichenberger Kurt. *Die richterliche Unabhängigkeit als staatsrechtliches Problem*. Berne: Stämpfli, 43 et seq.; Häfelin, Haller, Keller & Thurnherr, §26; Haller. *Swiss Constitution*, 220–221; Kiener Regina. *Richterliche Unabhängigkeit*. Berne: Stämpfli; Koller Heinrich, Basler Kommentar BGG, Article 2; Haller Walter. Kommentar BV 1874, Article 106, note 30 et seq.; Misic. *Verfassungsbeschwerde*, 234 et seq.; Müller, Schefer & Uebersax, 540 et seq.; Reich Johannes, Basler Kommentar BV, Articles 30 and 191c; Steinmann Gerold. St. Galler Kommentar, Article 30 (with further references).

I. Independence of the Judiciary as Institutional Principle

231. Deriving from the *Rechtsstaat* principle (*supra* General Introduction, Chapter 2, §4), the *independence* of the judiciary is one of the prerequisite of the modern constitutional state. According to the Constitution, it is guaranteed in two ways: Not only is independence of the judiciary a *fundamental right* that grants protection to the parties of a particular case (Article 30(1) of the Constitution), but it is also an *institutional principle*. The latter is emphasized in Article 191c of the Constitution: 'The judicial authorities shall be independent in the exercise of their judicial powers and shall be bound only by the law.' The institutional principle (in combination with the fundamental right) shall safeguard – as the Federal Supreme Court has pointed out with almost Solomonic words – the judge's main function as a 'righteous mediator' ('*ein rechter Mittler*' *see* Decision of the Federal Supreme Court BGE 33 I 146 [1907]). Thus, all non-judicial branches of government shall refrain from any form of impediment that may impair the independence of the judiciary. The judiciary shall not receive directives from other branches of government. But – aside from this distinct separation of aspects of powers – the principle goes further and obliges the judiciary itself, e.g., the Federal Supreme Court in the exercise of high supervision over the administration of business in the lower federal courts (*see* Article 1(2) of the Federal Supreme Court Act). Furthermore, courts shall not be influenced by the parties of the case, or by other interest groups, such as by political parties, political pressure groups, lobbyists or the media. Finally, the character of a judge must show high integrity and a resistance towards personal prejudices and bias (or at least a high degree of abstraction between her/his personal opinions and emotions and the issues at stake in a given case). Of course, the independence of the judiciary is not absolute and finds its limits within the law itself. Since all non-judicial branches of government have to respect the independence of the judiciary and – in the sense of

Article 35(2) of the Constitution – to contribute to its implementation, the legislative branch is also directed to take appropriate positive measures (*see* Article 40a of the Parliamentary Act regarding the so-called judicial commission assessing the professional and personal qualification of potential candidates and proposing candidates to the Federal Assembly).

232. Article 191c of the Constitution grants independence to *every* judicial authority of the Confederation (Article 191a of the Constitution) and of the cantons (Article 191b of the Constitution), including arbitration tribunals (Decision of the Federal Supreme Court BGE 135 I 14 paragraph 2). According to the Strasbourg and Lausanne case law, to be recognized as such, a judicial authority must fulfil the conditions of Article 6(1) of the ECHR, of Article 191c and of Article 30 of the Constitution. In a leading case, the Federal Supreme Court summarized it as follows (Decision of the Federal Supreme Court BGE 126 I 228 paragraph 2a/bb): A court is an authority taking binding decisions in a dispute in a fair procedure according to and in the forms of the law (*'nach Gesetz und Recht'*). The authority must not be incorporated into the ordinary judiciary of a state, but it must be independent and impartial vis-à-vis other authorities as well as the parties of the case from an organizational and personal point of view (such as the procedure of its appointment, the period of office, the protection from external inferences and manipulations and the outward appearance). The ECHR and the Federal Constitution are not violated if representatives of the authority belong to a certain profession as long as they are not officers bound by instructions (*weisungsgebundene Funktionäre*). The independence of the judiciary not only applies to the judges, but to every person involved in the decision-making process of a judgment (such as registrars; *see also* Decision of the Federal Supreme Court BGE 124 I 255 paragraph 5c/aa).

II. Independence of the Judiciary as Fundamental Right

233. Article 30(1) of the Constitution contains the *fundamental right to independence and impartiality* of the judge. In contrast to Article 29 of the Constitution, this provision does not grant access to justice and it is only limited to *judicial* proceedings (whereas Article 29 of the Constitution is broader in its scope and applicable to all proceedings before a judicial or administrative authority).

234. According to this provision, influenced by Article 6(1) of the ECHR, Article 14(1) UN-Pact II and the case law of the Strasbourg Court, every person, whose case must be decided in judicial proceedings, has the right to a competent, independent and impartial court established by law. In essence, Article 30(1) of the Constitution shall guarantee a correct and fair trial. The judge shall not be influenced by off-topic facts that may alter the final decision in favour or in disfavour of a party of the case. The primary function of this fundamental procedural right is to contribute to the openness (disinterestedness) of the procedure that is necessary to reach an equitable judgment in a particular case. According to the case law of Federal Supreme Court, a court is *presumed* to be dependent and partial, if certain circumstances are present that are (from an objective point of view) likely to cause distrust about the impartiality and disinterestedness of a judge. Such circumstances may arise from certain behaviours of the judge in question or from particular external circumstances of a functional or organizational nature. The distrust in the impartiality must be justified by objective criteria and not by the subjective sentiment of the parties involved. It is sufficient, and Article 30(1) of the Constitution is violated, if circumstances exist that are objectively indicating the *appearance* of the lack of impartiality and bias. Hence, the disqualification of a judge does not imply per se that she/he was really biased (cf. with further references Decision of the Federal Supreme Court BGE 136 I 207 paragraph 3.1). Article 30(1) of the Constitution equally applies to arbitration tribunals (Decision of the Federal Supreme Court BGE 135 I 14 paragraph 2).

235. Article 34 of the Federal Supreme Court Act defines situations in which a judge must withdraw from a particular case due to lack of impartiality (this provision also applies to the Federal Administrative Court, *see* Article 38 of the Federal Administrative Court Act, for civil and criminal courts, *see* Article 47(1) of the Federal Code of Civil Procedure and Article 56 of the Federal Code of Criminal Procedure). The list in Article 34 of the Federal Supreme Court Act is non-exhaustive and contains standard withdrawal situations, such as personal interest of the judge in a case, personal relationship of the judge with a party or its counsel (through marriage, cohabitation, kinship), special friendship with, or personal hostility towards, a party or its counsel. Note that according to the provisions of the codes of civil and criminal procedure, mere friendship between a judge and a party or its counsel may already constitute a reason to withdraw (*see* for a recent case the decision of the Federal Supreme Court 1B_55/2015 of 17 August 2015 [friendship between judge and counsel; regular sports activities and sailing holidays]). Of course, the disqualification of a judge should remain the exception; this provision shall not serve as a tool for the parties to choose judges at their own will. The participation of judges in a leading case or pilot decision does not disqualify them per se from judging in other cases that are dealing with the same questions (*see* the interim decision of the Federal Administrative Court A-6743/2010 [13.12.2010], where the party requested, *inter alia*, that the whole first division of the Federal Administrative Court must withdraw due to the participation of the judges at pilot decisions regarding mutual assistance in tax matters between the United States and Switzerland; request rejected and decision affirmed by the Federal Supreme Court in 1C_573/2011 [07.01.2011]).

§2. Judicial Organization

Selected Bibliography: Alvarez et al. (eds). Schweizerische Zivilprozessordnung. Berner Kommentar. 3 volumes. Stämpfli: Berne 2012–2014. Biaggini. Kommentar, Articles 122 and 123; Donatsch Andreas et al. (eds), *Kommentar zur Schweizerischen Strafprozessordnung.* 2nd ed. Schulthess: Zurich 2014; Geiser et al. (eds). Prozessieren vor Bundesgericht. 4th ed. Basel: Helbing & Lichtenhahn 2014; Häfelin, Haller, Keller & Thurnherr, §58; Haller. *Swiss Constitution*, 148 et seq.; Imboden Max. 'Erfahrungen auf dem Gebiet der Verwaltungsrechtsprechung in den Kantonen und im Bund'. In *Zeitschrift für Schweizerisches Recht [ZSR].* 1947 II, 1 et seq.; Kley Andreas. St. Galler Kommentar, Article 29a; Koller Heinrich. 'Die Verwaltungsrechtspflege des Bundesrates als Residuat'. In *Festschrift für Bundesrat Arnold Koller.* Berne/Stuttgart/Vienna,

1993, 359 et seq.; Kölz, Häner & Bertschi, 96 et seq. (with further references); Moser André, Beusch Michael & Kneubühler Lorenz. *Prozessieren vor dem Bundesverwaltungsgericht.* 2nd ed. Basel: Helbing & Lichtenhahn, 2013; Rhinow et al., §10 and §11; Sutter-Somm Thomas et al. (eds), *Kommentar zur Schweizerischen Zivilprozessordnung (ZPO).* 3rd ed. Zurich: Schulthess, 2016; Tophinke Esther. Basler Kommentar BGG, Article 86.

I. Overview

236. The following paragraph gives a short overview of the organization of the administrative, private and criminal law judiciary at both the cantonal and federal levels.

237. In Switzerland, as in most other federal states, the organizational structure of the judiciary shows a certain degree of complexity due to the horizontal and vertical levels of government that have to be distinguished from each other (while at the same time being intertwined as well). Generally, there are – on the cantonal level – several *district courts*, followed by a *Court of Appeal*, both applying federal and cantonal law. Based upon the public/private law distinction, typical of all the civil law countries of the European Continent, a different organizational structure of the judiciary exists for administrative law matters; in general, each canton has at least one separate administrative law court applying both federal and cantonal administrative law (*see infra* Part II, Chapter 5, §3).

238. In other words, Switzerland did not adopt the concept of dual judicial federalism as known in the United States. Most – but not all – lawsuits take their course in cantonal courts even when federal law is at stake. Thus, on the cantonal level, there are no federal district courts or federal courts of appeal. On the federal level, there are three *lower federal courts*: the Federal Administrative Court, the Federal Criminal Court and the Federal Patent Court.

239. Finally, on the top of the judicial pyramid, the Federal Supreme Court, which shall be discussed *infra* in §3 of this Chapter, operates as the court of last resort. In the wording of Article 188(1) of the Constitution, it is the highest judicial authority of the Confederation (*see also infra*, Part IV, Chapter 5, §4).

II. The Judiciary in Administrative Law Cases

A. *The Creation of Administrative Law Courts in Switzerland*

240. The introduction of independent administrative courts took more time to be achieved in the cantons than in the Confederation. One of the main reasons for this delayed evolution was due to the nineteenth century being dominated by the doctrine of the supremacy of the democratic principle over the *Rechtsstaat* principle (*see supra* General Introduction, Chapter 2, §1 and §4). This may explain why significant portions of the population were fairly hostile to the 'aristocratic and elitist idea' of creating administrative courts in order to control the administration. This aversion originated from the fact that cantonal and municipal administrations were (and often still are) integrated in relatively small communities conferring individuals democratic instruments to defend themselves against arbitrary and capricious actions. The various, democratically legitimized, local governments were somewhat unwilling to confer on administrative courts the authority to have the last word with regard to the way statutes are operated. In the Canton of Zurich, for example, the People rejected the creation of an administrative court in 1933, with the prevailing concern that it would obstruct the way of governmental endeavours. The first administrative tribunal, albeit with very limited jurisdiction, was established in the Canton of Valais in 1877. The cantonal Administrative Court Act of Basel-City created the first genuine administrative court with general jurisdiction in 1905, followed by the Canton of Berne in 1907. In later years, administrative courts would be created in the Canton of Zurich (1959), in the Canton of Basel-Land (1959), in the Canton of Solothurn (1960) and the Canton of St. Gallen (1965). Although Article 114*bis* of the Federal Constitution of 1874 (introduced in 1914) provided for the creation of a Federal Administrative Court, the opposition to such an institution greatly outweighed it. A federal act of 1 March 1929 created a federal administrative judiciary with very limited competences, which were gradually increased by further revisions in 1943, 1968 and 1991. Instead of a federal administrative court with general jurisdiction, the model of specialized administrative courts was preferred. This led to the creation to over thirty independent federal appeals and arbitration commissions (*Rekurs- und Schiedskommissionen*).

241. Despite their eventual development, even where cantonal administrative courts were established, not all administrative cases and controversies could be brought before these judicial authorities. Rather, some could be heard only by a political body. After the termination of the administrative procedure issuing an administrative order, the order could be appealed before an internal administrative authority. This administrative authority did not constitute a court (in the sense of Article 6(1) ECHR, and of Article 191c and of Article 30 of the Constitution), but was normally a superior administrative instance. After its verdict, one could only appeal – in cases of cantonal law – before the council of the canton (*Regierungsrat*), a political body of the executive branch of government. In cases of federal law applied by cantonal administrations, appeal was open to the Federal Council or the Federal Supreme Court. With time, the Federal Supreme Court got broader and extended jurisdiction over most federal administrative law cases. However, some cases remained that could only be brought before a political authority.

242. In 1991, due to the reluctance of some cantons to establish independent administrative courts with general jurisdiction, the Confederation decided to amend the former Federal Judicial Act of 1943 (which was replaced by the Federal Supreme Court Act of 2005, in force since 1 January 2007). Article 98(a) of the Federal Judicial Act declared that cantons were compelled to create 'judicial authorities', which functioned as cantonal judicial instances of last resort regarding cases that could be brought before the Federal Supreme Court concerning:

(1) cantonal administrative orders *that should have been based upon federal administrative law*;
(2) cantonal administrative orders based upon dependent cantonal executory laws *purely in implementation of exhaustive federal laws*; or

(3) administrative orders based upon cantonal law which have a *narrow substantive nexus* with federal administrative law.

This provision positively impacted the cantons, in that those that had yet to do so, finally introduced administrative courts. However, they differed substantially from each other mainly because their jurisdiction was not general and broad, but sometimes tailored in a way to neatly satisfy the requirements of Article 98(a) of the Federal Judicial Act. Parallel to the evolution in the cantons, the Confederation instituted so-called *independent federal commissions of appeals*, for instance, in the fields of asylum and refugee law, competition or broadcasting law. These tribunals decided either as last instance with no appeal to the Federal Supreme Court (i.e., in the field of asylum and refugee law) or as first judicial instance with the possibility to appeal before the Federal Supreme Court.

B. The Impact of the Reform of the Judiciary on the Access to Administrative Justice

243. The reform of the judiciary, which entered into force on 1 January 2007 (*see also supra* General Introduction, Chapter 2, §3), did not only change the federal administrative judicial system and its organizational structure considerably, but it also had (and still has) effects upon the cantonal judiciary in administrative matters. From a constitutional perspective, one of the most remarkable features of the reform of the judiciary was the introduction of *the fundamental right to access to justice* in the catalogue of fundamental rights. According to Article 29a of the Constitution, everyone has the right to have legal disputes judged by a judicial authority. Article 191b(1) of the Constitution guarantees this fundamental right on an institutional level. Note that the fundamental right grants access to a court (be it cantonal or federal) but not access to the Federal Supreme Court. Since the ECHR requires its Member States to only create courts in private and criminal law matters (an obligation Switzerland had fulfilled already long before the reform of the judiciary), Article 29a of the Constitution was mainly introduced to battle the salient problem that in some cantonal (but also federal) administrative matters, one could often only appeal before a political authority (and not a court). Thus, regarding its scope of application *ratione materiae*, this provision goes a step further than the ECHR.

244. Although Article 29a of the Constitution can be rightly regarded as a milestone in a long history of attempts to create independent administrative courts in Switzerland, the constitutional provision still leaves the door open for exceptions. According to the second sentence of Article 29a of the Constitution, the Confederation and the cantons may exceptionally preclude access to the courts by statute (of course, such a parliamentary act may be subject to a referendum if demanded by the concerned population). It is too early to fully assess the consequences of that exception. However, constitutional scholars agree so far, that the exclusion of the fundamental right to access to justice now requires cogent reasons and the case law of the Federal Supreme Court indicates the exceptional character of that provision (Decision of the Federal Supreme Court BGE 136 I 42 paragraph 1.5.3: '*ne doit être exclu que de manière exceptionnelle*').

C. *Organizational Structure of the Administrative Judiciary*

1. The Federal System

245. With the reform of the judiciary, the organizational structure of the administrative judiciary of the Confederation has undergone considerable modifications. Generally, after the conclusion of the federal administrative procedure issuing an administrative order (*see* for the administrative process and the control of its regularity, *infra*, Part IV, Chapter 5 §3 and §4), an appeal is possible before the Federal Administrative Court and subsequently (but not always; *infra* Part IV, Chapter 5, §3) before the Federal Supreme Court as court of last resort. In some rare cases an appeal can be brought before the Federal Council. The control of federal orders by internal administrative bodies has been almost completely abolished (one of these rare exceptions in Article 32(2) of the Federal Film Act of 14 December 2001 [SR 443.1] was abolished in 2012). According to Article 85 of the Federal Act of 24 March 2006 on Radio and Television, the Independent Complaints Authority for Radio and Television is the only remaining special administrative court dealing with complaints about the content of editorial programmes and the selection and supervision of the ombudsman services.

246. From a historical perspective, the Federal Council used to have considerable judicial competencies in administrative matters. However, considering that the Federal Council is the supreme governing and executive authority of the Confederation (Article 174 of the Constitution) and in view of Article 6(1) of the ECHR, the reform of the judiciary has reduced the judicial functions of the Federal Council to a minimum, basically to cases with a predominantly political and non-justiciable impact. Nowadays, according to Article 72 of the FAPA, an administrative appeal is only admissible against administrative orders relating to the internal and external security of the country, neutrality, diplomatic protection and other matters *relating* to external relations, *unless international law confers the right to have the matter judged by a court* (subsidiarity of the administrative appeal before the Federal Council). Furthermore, an administrative appeal is possible as well against administrative orders on the performance-related element of the salaries of federal personnel.

2. The Federal Administrative Court

247. The Federal Administrative Court, which started to operate from 1 January 2007, is the general administrative court of the Confederation (Article 1 of the Federal Administrative Court Act). It is the Court of First Instance in federal administrative matters that can be subsequently brought to the Federal Supreme Court. However, since Article 83 of the Federal Supreme Court Act excludes a wide range of administrative matters in order to alleviate the Federal Supreme Court, the Federal Administrative Court acts as Court of Last Instance in some areas of the law involving mass procedures (e.g., asylum and refugee law). Note that Article 83 of the Federal Supreme Court Act may be revised in the future. According to a proposal, an appeal in public law matters before the Federal Supreme Court shall be exceptionally admitted only if the case raises a legal question of fundamental importance.

248. From a historical perspective, the Federal Administrative Court was the result of a 'merger' of over thirty preceding independent federal appeals commissions (*Rekurs- und Schiedskommissionen*) that were competent in administrative appeals of first and sometimes last instance, especially on the subject of asylum and refugee law (where a subsequent appeal to the Federal Supreme Court was and still is excluded). The Federal Administrative Court has its permanent seat in St. Gallen. Before June 2012, since the court building in St. Gallen was in the process of construction, the provisional seats of the Court were in Berne and Zollikhofen. The Federal Administrative Court is the largest federal court with seventy-two judges (2015). In order to handle a caseload of 8000–9000 cases per year, approximately 200 registrars and administrative personnel are at the disposal of the judges. The judges are elected by the Federal Assembly for a term of office of six years (*see also* Articles 5 et seq. of the Federal Administrative Court Act regarding incompatibilities, impeachment and immunities of the judges).

249. The President of the Federal Administrative Court represents the Court in all external matters. He/she chairs the United Court and the Administrative Commission (Article 15 of the Federal Administrative Court Act). The United Court, the highest organ of the Federal Administrative Court, is competent, *inter alia*, for issuing regulations (e.g., for the organization and administration of the Court, the assignment of the areas of laws falling within the jurisdiction of each division of the Court, information, legal fees, etc.; *see* Article 16 of the Federal Administrative Court Act). The Conference of the Presidents of the six divisions of the Federal Administrative Court is another organ, which coordinates, *inter alia,* the uniformity and coherence of the case law of the divisions of the Court (*see* Article 18 Federal Administrative Court Act). The Administrative Commission of the Federal Administrative Court, formed by the President and the Vice-President of the Court and at most three judges, deal with the organization and administration of the Court (Article 18 of the Federal Administrative Court Act). Finally, the administrative staff and the scientific services are governed by the Secretary General.

250. The Federal Administrative Court consists of six divisions which are subdivided into chambers. According to the annex of the Rules of the Court of 17 April 2008 (SR 173.320.1), the divisions of the Federal Administrative Court have substantive jurisdiction over various matters:

- The First Division: Public torts law, taxes and customs, infrastructure, national roads, zoning, expropriation, energy, environmental law, radio and television, protection of data, employment law of the personnel of the Confederation, mutual administrative assistance and mutual legal assistance in criminal matters (if the matter concerns an area of law within the jurisdiction of the division) and much more.
- The Second Division: Public procurement, intellectual property, competition law, agriculture, money-laundering, supervision over stock exchanges, mutual administrative assistance and mutual legal assistance in criminal matters (if the matter concerns an area of law within the jurisdiction of the Second Division) and much more.

- The Third Division: Monument conservation, pharmaceutical products and drugs, various social security insurances, mutual administrative assistance and mutual legal assistance in criminal matters (if the matter concerns an area of law within the jurisdiction of the Third Division) and much more.
- The Fourth and the Fifth Divisions: Asylum law, mutual administrative assistance and mutual legal assistance in criminal matters (if the matter concerns an area of law within their jurisdiction).
- The Sixth Division: Citizenship and immigration law (if the fourth and fifth division are not competent), recognition of statelessness, restriction of illicit assets of politically exposed persons, entry bans for national security reasons, mutual administrative assistance and mutual legal assistance in criminal matters (if the matter concerns an area of law within the jurisdiction of the Sixth Division) and much more.

3. The Cantonal Administrative Courts

251. According to Article 86(2) of the Federal Supreme Court Act, the cantons are obliged to create superior courts for all cases that can be brought before the Federal Supreme Court. This provision predominantly concerns the access to cantonal *administrative* justice (since in all private and criminal law matters the cantons have already created superior courts in order to fulfil the requirements of Article 6(1) of the ECHR). Nowadays, all cantons finally have administrative courts. Of course, Article 86(3) of the Federal Supreme Court Act gives the cantons the option to exclude courts in cases with a 'preponderant political character', which means that the case will be judged by a non-judicial, political authority. Here, again, the Federal Supreme Court has emphasized the exceptional and narrowly tailored scope of application of that provision; the Court may allow exceptions from the fundamental right to access to justice (Article 29a of the Constitution) in situations where the political aspect of the case prevails without discussion (Decision of the Federal Supreme Court BGE 136 I 42 paragraph 1.5.3: 'l'aspect politique prévaut sans discussion'). Since the Federal Supreme Court can only review severe errors in fact (and sometimes not all questions of law), the central idea behind the obligation to create cantonal administrative courts was that at least one cantonal court must possess the power to fully review all factual and legal questions of a case. Thus, if a canton chooses the option of Article 86(3) of the Federal Supreme Court Act, factual questions of a case can never be reviewed by a court (which stands in contradiction to the whole reform of the judiciary).

252. From an organizational perspective, the cantons have created administrative courts with general jurisdiction, sometimes in combination with specialized and autonomous administrative courts (especially in the field of tax law, expropriation or social security). As an example, the Canton of Berne has created an administrative court with general jurisdiction, whereas the superior administrative courts in the Canton of Zurich are the Administrative Court in Zurich and the Social Insurance Court in Winterthur.

III. The Judiciary in Private Law Cases

A. Diversity of Organizational Arrangements in the Cantons

253. According to Article 122(2) of the Constitution, the organization of the courts and the administration of justice in private law matters are within the competence of each canton, unless the law provides otherwise. Since its entry into force on 1 January 2011, the Federal Code of Civil Procedure confirms this constitutional arrangement in favour of the cantons (Article 3) and contains only a few provisions (in Articles 5 and 6) concerning the obligation of the cantons to designate a cantonal court which will have exclusive jurisdiction over certain cases (mainly in the field of intellectual property) and the creation of cantonal commercial courts. Due to the self-rule principle of Swiss federalism, the organization of private law courts varies from one canton to another. For example, some very small cantons like the Cantons of Basel-City or Schaffhausen are not subdivided into court districts. Here, the trial court has general jurisdiction for the whole cantonal territory, while in most other cantons, it usually corresponds to the territory of each district (district court, *Bezirksgericht, tribunal d'arrondissement*). Since the Constitution is silent on the personal and professional qualifications of judges, there is no constitutional right to a legally trained judge (Decision of the Federal Supreme Court BGE 134 I 16 paragraph 4). However, in cantons with large populations, they are almost always legally trained and experienced professionals working on a full-time basis, while in cantons with smaller populations, justices of peace and usually district court judges may be laymen working part-time. The institution of laymen judges is very old in Switzerland and deeply rooted in the idea to bring 'common sense' to the courtroom (which – in the view of the 'ordinary citizen' – legally trained professionals may sometimes lack). This is not mere folklore. Although the institution was abolished in several cantons between 2010 and 2016, such as in Lucerne, Neuchâtel and Zurich, laymen judges still play an important role, especially in rural cantons and where particular expertise is required (medical doctors, nurses, architects, etc.). In the Canton of Vaud, one out of five judges is such a 'specialized' layman ('*juge assesseur*'); of course, this model requires strict scrutiny with regard to bias.

B. Justices of the Peace and District Courts in Private Law Cases

254. For the following the Canton of Zurich shall serve as an example for the cantonal organization of the judiciary in private law matters. As a general rule, before the parties can file a suit before a district court, they must try to settle their dispute before a mediation body (*Schlichtungsbehörde; see* for further details and exceptions Articles 197 et seq. of the Federal Code of Civil Procedure). According to §55 of the Act regarding the Organisation of the Judiciary in Civil and Criminal Cases of the Canton of Zurich of 10 May 2010 (hereinafter: Zurich Judiciary Act) this (pre-trial) mediation procedure is chaired by Justices of the Peace (*Friedensrichter*), who are generally laymen. They fulfil an important function in the administration of justice (approximately 40% of all cases are settled by the Justices of the Peace). Every political municipality usually has one Justice of the Peace, but bigger municipalities, like the

City of Zurich, may decide to have several Justices of the Peace (*see* §53 of the Zurich Judiciary Act). Furthermore, the Federal Code of Civil Procedure prescribes a mediation procedure for controversies in the field of landlord and tenant law and for disputes under the Federal Equality Act of 24 March 1995 (SR 151.1). In these cases the mediation board consists of three persons: a legally trained person (who chairs the board and who is a member of the district court) and one general representative each for the employers' and the employees' interests who are chosen out of a pool of sixteen members; both sexes must be represented (*see* §59 and §61 of the Zurich Judiciary Act).

255. The twelve district courts of the Canton of Zurich are the courts of first instance competent in the field of private and criminal law matters (provided that the Zurich Superior Court and the Commercial Court do not have exclusive jurisdiction over a legal matter, *see* for further details §§8 et seq. of the Zurich Judiciary Act). The district court judges are elected by the people of the district. In major private law cases (including disputes in the field of employment law and landlord and tenant law) the district courts are generally composed as a collegiate tribunal of three judges (*see* §§19 et seq. of the Zurich Judiciary Act). Of greater practical importance, however, is the single district court judge who hears most cases (usually of a lower litigation value). According to §22 of the Zurich Judiciary Act, summary and simplified procedures are usually confined to a single trial judge (for more details *see, inter alia*, Articles 243 [cases with litigation value lower than CHF 30,000], 198(e) [certain bankruptcy actions], 248 et seq. [summary procedure in a multitude of private law cases], 274 et seq. [divorce cases], 295 et seq. [family law cases regarding children's interests], 335 et seq. [execution of judgments] of the Federal Code of Civil Procedure). In landlord and tenant law as well as employment law cases, the President of the district court presides as a single judge in disputes with a litigation value lower than CHF 30,000. However, if the litigation value is CHF 15,000 the President may, ex officio or upon request of the parties, delegate the case to the district court composed as a collegiate (*see* §§25 and 26 of the Zurich Judiciary Act).

C. *The Courts of Appeal in Private Law Cases*

256. All cantons have instituted a second instance of appeal – the cantonal superior courts (*Obergericht*) – which fulfils the requirements of Article 6(1) of the ECHR. In some exceptional cases, they act as the court of first instance (e.g., in the field of intellectual property law). In the Canton of Zurich, the Superior Court has general jurisdiction in private and criminal law cases. Its seat is in the City of Zurich. The judges are elected by the cantonal parliament (*Kantonsrat*). Furthermore, the Superior Court also fulfils the function of the Commercial Court and has certain competencies in arbitration law cases (for more details *see* §§43 et seq. of the Zurich Judiciary Act). As a rule, cantonal superior courts have general jurisdiction over all factual and legal questions that arise before the district court. As a Court of Appeal, the Zurich Superior Court is subdivided into three chambers dealing with private law cases. Each chamber decides generally in a composition of three superior court judges. Apart from its function as a court, the superior courts have a supervisory role over their chambers, the Commercial Court and the lower cantonal courts. They also supervise the notary public and the various public institutions dealing with the administration of bankruptcy cases (§80 of the Zurich Judiciary Act).

D. Courts with Limited Jurisdiction

257. As shown above, the aim of courts with limited jurisdiction in private law cases is to combine expertise and speedy procedure, especially in the field of employment law, commercial law, and landlord and tenant law. Special statutes regulate their organization. The basic idea is that the expertise of the judges, who are often experienced professionals in the area involved, shall increase the parties' confidence in the judicial process. However, not all cantons have courts with limited jurisdiction in private law cases (e.g., commercial courts have been created only in the Cantons of Zurich, Berne, St. Gallen and Aargau so far).

IV. The Judiciary in Criminal Law Cases

A. Overview

258. According to Article 123(1) of the Constitution, the Confederation is responsible for legislation in criminal law matters as well as in criminal procedure. Since 1 January 2011, the latter is regulated by the Federal Code of Criminal Procedure (SR 312.0), the Federal Juvenile Criminal Procedure Act (SR 312.1) and the Federal Act of 19 March 2010 concerning the Organisation of the Criminal Authorities of the Confederation (SR 173.71). According to Article 123(2) of the Constitution, the cantons shall be responsible for the organization of the cantonal criminal courts, the administration of justice in criminal cases as well as for the execution of penalties and measures, unless the law provides otherwise.

B. The Federal Criminal Court

259. In 2004, based upon Article 191a(1) of the Constitution, Parliament established a Federal Criminal Court in Bellinzona, the capital of the Canton of Ticino, consisting of 15–35 Federal Judges (Article 41(1) of the Federal Act of 19 March 2010 concerning the Organisation of the Criminal Authorities of the Confederation). The Court consists of a single Criminal Chamber and two Chambers of Appeals. Provided that the Office of the Attorney General has not delegated the case to the cantonal authorities, the Criminal Chamber of the Federal Criminal Court as the Court of First Instance has substantive jurisdiction over federal criminal matters as listed in Articles 23 and 24 of the Federal Code of Criminal Procedure, such as crimes committed against persons protected by international public law, crimes against federal officers or members of the Federal Assembly, crimes with explosives and toxic gases, felonies and misdemeanours against public order, financing terrorism, white collar crimes, money-laundering, felonies and misdemeanours against the state and national security. Additional substantive jurisdiction may derive from other federal legislation, such as from the Federal Act of 22 June 2007 on the Swiss Financial Market Supervisory

Authority (SR 956.1), or the Nuclear Energy Act of 21 March 2007 (SR 732.1). The decisions of the Criminal Chamber can be subject to an appeal in criminal matters before the Federal Supreme Court (Article 78(1) of the Federal Supreme Court Act).

260. The first Chamber of Appeals of the Federal Criminal Court has jurisdiction, *inter alia*, over constraint measures. Ordered by the criminal authorities (e.g., a detention order), these measures secure pieces of evidence, the presence of persons during the procedure, or the execution of a final decision (*see* Article 393 together with Article 196 of the Federal Code of Criminal Procedure). Since these measures may affect or even violate the fundamental rights of the person concerned, they can be reviewed by the Court and by the Federal Supreme Court (*see* Article 79 of the Federal Supreme Court Act). The second Chamber of Appeals of the Federal Criminal Court has jurisdiction over cases regarding international mutual legal assistance in criminal matters (such as extradition requests by foreign states) governed by the Federal Act on International Mutual Assistance in Criminal Matters (SR 351.1). Decisions of the Federal Criminal Court can only be reviewed by the Federal Supreme Court if the latter holds that a 'case of special importance' is at stake, meaning that there are reasons to believe that elemental procedural principles have been violated or that the procedure abroad is manifestly deficient (Article 84 of the Federal Supreme Court Act).

C. *Cantonal Criminal Courts*

261. According to Article 123(2) of the Constitution, the organization of the courts in criminal law matters is within the competence of each canton, unless the law provides otherwise. Although there is a great organizational variety among the cantons, the criminal judiciary corresponds largely to the following organizational structure: the districts courts are the criminal courts of first instance followed by a cantonal superior court as a Court of Appeal. The organization of these courts has been already shown above in the context of private law cases (for more details *see, inter alia,* §§3, 22, 27, 49 of the Zurich Judiciary Act). With the new Federal Code of Criminal Procedure, jury courts were abolished in all cantons with the exception of the Canton of Ticino ('*assessori-giurati*').

262. According to the second phrase of Article 30(1) of the Constitution, *exceptional tribunals* acting outside the constitutional order and instituted just for a single case are prohibited. *Ordinary criminal courts* dispose of a general jurisdiction and hear all cases that are not delegated by statute to a court with special jurisdiction. *Criminal courts with special jurisdiction,* for example military courts, juvenile courts, or economic crime courts, are only permitted if their competencies and organizational structures have been established by statute and if there is an objective reason for their creation.

§3. The Federal Supreme Court

Selected Bibliography: Auer, Malinverni & Hottelier. Vol. I, 679 et seq.; Biaggini. Kommentar, Vorbemerkungen *ad* Articles 188–191c; Corboz Bernard et al., *Commentaire de la LTF.* 2nd ed. Berne: Stämpfli, 2013; Donzallaz Yves. *Loi sur le Tribunal federal,*

Commentaire. Berne: Stämpfli, 2008; Egli, 99 et seq.; Errass Christoph. Basler Kommentar BGG, Zur Geschichte des Bundesgerichts; Fleiner & Giacometti, §§81–94; Häfelin, Haller, Keller & Thurnherr, §58; Haller. *Swiss Constitution*, 148 et seq.; Kiss Christina & Koller Heinrich. St. Galler Kommentar, Article 188 and Article 191–191b; Niggli Marcel, A., Uebersax Peter & Wiprächtiger Hans (eds). *Bundesgerichtsgesetz*. Basler Kommentar, Basel: Helbing & Lichtenhahn, 2008; Rhinow et al., §§25–28; Schubarth Martin. 'Bundesgericht'. In Thürer et al., §68; Seferovic Goran. *Das Schweizerische Bundesgericht 1848–1874*. Zurich: Schulthess, 2010; Seiler Hansjörg, Von Werdt Nicolas, Güngerich Andreas & Niklaus Oberholzer. *Bundesgerichtsgesetz* (BGG). 2nd ed. Berne: Stämpfli, 2016; Tschannen, §§ 40–43.

I. The Federal Supreme Court as Highest Judicial Authority of the Confederation

263. In the early stage of the Swiss Confederation, between 1848 and 1874, the Federal Supreme Court was only a non-permanent organ with very limited jurisdiction over private and criminal cases. Its role was negligible in cases regarding the protection of fundamental rights, owing to the fact that it only had jurisdiction if the Federal Assembly delegated the case to the Federal Supreme Court (which only happened once in a period of twenty-six years). As a permanent court with substantive jurisdiction the Federal Supreme Court was founded in 1874, with nine full-time and nine part-time judges, when the second Federal Constitution entered into force. Its seat is in Lausanne, the capital of the Canton of Vaud; since 1914, the social security department of the Court is traditionally located in Lucerne, the capital of the Canton of Lucerne.

264. The official name of the Court is *Bundesgericht* (in German), *Tribunal fédéral* (in French), *Tribunale federale* (in Italian) and *Tribunal federal* (in Rumantsch). This denomination – the correct English translation being 'Federal Court' – has historical reasons. Until recently – before the creation of lower federal courts – there existed only two federal courts in the Swiss Confederation: The Federal Court in Lausanne and the Federal Insurance Court in Lucerne (with the reform of the judiciary the latter was integrated into the Federal Court in 2006). Since then, more federal courts have been established: the Federal Criminal Court started to operate in 2004, the Federal Administrative Court in 2007, and the Federal Patent Court in 2011. Thus, the use of the term 'Federal Court' may become increasingly misleading for foreign readers attempting to understand the Swiss system of the federal judiciary. For reasons of clarity, the term 'Federal Supreme Court' is used throughout this monograph in order to denominate the highest judicial authority of the Swiss Confederation.

265. As the highest judicial authority of the Swiss Confederation, the Federal Supreme Court has to fulfil various functions which are not explicitly mentioned in the Constitution, such as:

(1) the protection of the constitutional order, especially the fundamental and constitutional rights (the Federal Supreme Court as guardian of the Constitution);
(2) assuring the unity of the law in the Confederation (federal function);

(3) interpreting statutes and the Constitution, developing a consistent case law, and, if necessary, creating new implied fundamental or constitutional rights;
(4) granting judicial protection as a court of last resort on the national level against decisions of the cantonal courts and the lower federal courts. But note that exceptions may apply where the Federal Supreme Court is not the court of last resort (*see* Articles 73, 74, 79 and 83–85 of the Federal Supreme Court Act).

266. The Federal Supreme Court is independent in its judicial function and free of interference from other branches of government (*see supra* Part II, Chapter 5, §1). Only the law binds the Federal Supreme Court (Article 191c of the Constitution and Article 2(1) of the Federal Supreme Court Act). The high supervision of the Federal Assembly over the Federal Supreme Court, as stipulated in Article 169(1) of the Constitution and Article 3 of the Federal Supreme Court Act, is not intended to constitute an instrument to influence or to control the decision-making process of the Court. Generally, the high supervision is limited to the formal control of the regularity of judicial affairs and the organizational and financial management of the Court.

II. Election of the Federal Supreme Court Judges

A. Eligibility and Incompatibilities

267. All Swiss citizens who are 18 years or older and are not under custody because of mental illness or weakness are eligible for membership in the Federal Supreme Court (Articles 143 in conjunction with Article 136 of the Constitution). Of course, even though not constitutionally required, the Court is composed of experienced and distinguished judges, lawyers, practitioners or (rarely) law professors from all parts of the country.

268. Judges of the Federal Supreme Court may not at the same time be members of the National Council, of the Council of States or of the Federal Government (Article 144(1) of the Constitution). They are not entitled to undertake another function of the Confederation or a canton, nor may they exercise another remunerative private activity (Article 144(2) of the Constitution and Articles 6 of the Federal Supreme Court). Articles 7 and 8 of the Federal Supreme Court Act contain further incompatibilities regarding the secondary exercise of non-remunerative activities and incompatibilities due to a personal relationship between judges (e.g., marriage, cohabitation or kinship).

B. Election and 'Impeachment'

269. Since Article 190 of the Constitution requires the Federal Supreme Court to apply federal statutes even when they are in conflict with the Constitution (*see infra* Part IV, Chapter 2, §7) Federal Supreme Court judges 'are less exposed to the political limelight than their colleagues in Washington and Karlsruhe' (Haller, note 328). Aside from that fact, their election is of course still a political issue and one of great importance. As a rule of thumb, the distribution of the seats in the Court mirrors the strength of all political parties (and not only of the parties represented in the Federal Council). The exact election and re-election procedure is laid down in Articles 40a and 135 et seq. of the Federal Act on the Federal Assembly of 13 December 2002 (SR 171.10). After a screening process of potential candidates before the Judiciary Commission, the Commission submits a recommendation to the parliamentary groups and requests their opinion; it then reaches a final decision on the proposals to make to the Federal Assembly, taking that opinion into account. To date, the candidates proposed by the Judiciary Committee have always been elected by the Federal Assembly. The members of the Federal Supreme Court are elected by the Federal Assembly (Article 168(1) of the Constitution and Article 5(1) of the Federal Supreme Court Act) for a term of six years (Article 145 of the Constitution). With regard to the independence of the judiciary, this short term of office is delicate but somehow compensated by the customary rule that the probability of being re-elected is very high (although on recent occasions some segments of the political system tend to overstretch their liberty of opinion by ‘thinking out loud’ about not re-electing certain Federal Supreme Court judges who have participated in judgments certain politicians are in strong disagreement with). According to Article 9 of the Federal Supreme Court Act, the judges retire at the end of the year in which they reach their 68th birthday (in particular cases an extension for two more years is possible [*see* Article 20 of the Personnel Ordinance of the Federal Supreme Court, in force since 1 January 2011; AS 2011 639]). – In its evaluation report of 15 March 2017, the Council of Europe anti-corruption body (GRECO) underlined that the recruitment and re-election system in Switzerland allows subtle pressure to be exerted on the judiciary and recommended several measures (e.g., ensuring that no non-reelection of judges of the federal courts by the Federal Assembly is motivated by these judges’ decisions, etc.).

270. Neither the Constitution nor the Federal Supreme Court Act contain an impeachment procedure or a disciplinary procedure against Federal Supreme Court judges (whereas impeachment is possible against the judges of the lower federal courts, *see* Article 10 of the Federal Administrative Court Act and Article 49 of the Federal Act of 19 March 2010 concerning the Organization of the Criminal Authorities of the Confederation). The absence of an impeachment or disciplinary procedure got new impetus in Parliament when in 2003, in the foyer of the Federal Supreme Court, a judge tried to spit in the face of a journalist, but missed and hit a registrar who was standing next to the journalist. Later on, the judge claimed that he had a coughing fit. He was immediately suspended from his judicial duties (which was of course an understandable, but from a constitutional point of view questionable reaction). Although the President of the Federal Supreme Court advised him to resign, the judge refused to do so, averring that the whole story was part of an intrigue conducted against him. However, perhaps due to an inspection report of the Parliamentary Control Committees and enormous pressure from the media, he left office in the beginning of 2004, four years before the expiration of his ordinary term of office. Despite that very strange and extraordinary event, unprecedented in the whole history of the Federal Supreme Court, the Parliament did not seize the opportunity to introduce an impeachment procedure in the Federal Supreme Court Act.

III. Organization of the Federal Supreme Court

A. *Personal Composition of the Federal Supreme Court*

271. According to Article 1(3) of the Federal Supreme Court Act, the number of full-time positions may vary between thirty-five and forty-five. Article 1(4) of the Federal Supreme Court Act further states that the number of part-time judges may not be higher than two-thirds of the appointed full-time positions. The exact number of judges is determined by an ordinance of the Federal Assembly (SR 173.110.1), according to which the Federal Supreme Court is composed of thirty-eight full-time judges and nineteen part-time judges. This ordinance also obliges the Federal Supreme Court to set up a control system serving Parliament as a basis for the determination of the numbers of position needed in the future. In view of the new ordinance which will enter into force in 2012, the Committees for Legal Affairs of the National Council and the Council of States are proposing to connect the future position planning of the Court to further indicators. The search for qualitative and quantitative criteria is unproblematic as long as these indicators are not serving as a back door in order to affect the independence of the Court, but rather are aiming at enhancing the efficiency and the management of judicial business operations. Since Article 188(3) of the Constitution grants administrative autonomy to the Federal Supreme Court, the above-mentioned ordinance points out that the decision on how the control system will be implemented and operated *in concreto* is up to the Court.

272. Upon proposition of the Federal Supreme Court, the President and the Vice-President of the Court, who must be full-time judges, are elected for a term of office of two years by the United Federal Parliament; a re-election is possible but only for one additional term (Article 14(2) of the Federal Supreme Court Act). The President represents the Court in all external matters and chairs the United Court and the Administrative Commission (Articles 14(3), 15 and 17 of the Federal Supreme Court Act, for more details *see also* the Rules of the Federal Supreme Court of 20 November 2006 [SR 173.110.131]).

273. Currently, the Supreme Court judges are provided with approximately 140 registrars and 155 administrators. The position of the registrar (*Gerichtsschreiber/ greffier*) does not exist in most countries and needs a short explanation. It dates back to ancient times when most judges were laymen (and sometimes illiterate) and the registrar often the only legally trained person in the courtroom responsible to deliver a written and legally reasoned decision in accordance with the orally pronounced sentence. According to Article 24 of the Federal Supreme Court Act, the registrar participates in the instruction and the decision-making process of a case. Under the supervision of a judge, they write the draft of the judgment (*Referat*) that will circulate among the panel of judges. Given that some of the registrars of the Federal Supreme Court are highly qualified experts in a certain area of law, it is not unusual that their drafts are transformed into the final judgment as such or with just slight editorial alterations. The registrars not only have the right to express their opinion *vis-à-vis* that of the judges before the decision is taken, but they also have the duty to point out contradictions or inadequacies in the legal reasoning or other legal mistakes in the judgment. A judgment can only be pronounced after this participatory right of the registrar has been respected. Thus, due to their key position, which some scholars have described maybe too emphatically as ‘de facto judges’, the registrars of the Federal Supreme Court are not comparable to law clerks who are usually graduates fresh from law school working one or two years at a court.

B. The Divisions of the Federal Supreme Court

274. Pursuant to Articles 26 et seq. of the Rules of the Federal Supreme Court of 20 November 2006 (SR 173.110.131), the Court has seven divisions – two each in the area of public, private and social security law and one in the area of criminal law – with jurisdiction over the subject matters set out in Articles 29 et seq. of the Rules of the Federal Supreme Court, such as:

- The First Public Law Division: political rights, naturalization, international mutual legal assistance in criminal matters, construction and land use planning law, expropriation, environmental law, traffic law, etc.
- The Second Public Law Division: alien and immigration law, tax law, public economic law (e.g., public torts law, the laws regarding education, the acquisition of real estate by persons from abroad, film, the protection of animals, subsidies, concessions and monopolies, public procurement, energy, transport, radio and television, public employment, agriculture, supervision over banks, insurances and stock exchanges, cartels and price surveillance, etc.).
- The First Private Law Division: contracts (including insurance contracts), torts, liability for medical malpractice, private competition law, intellectual property law, international arbitration law, etc.
- The Second Private Law Division: family law, inheritance law, property law, bankruptcy law, etc.
- The Criminal Law Division: substantive criminal law and criminal procedure.
- The First Social Security Law Division: disability insurance, accident insurance, unemployment insurance, military insurance, social welfare benefits, family income supplements, etc.
- The Second Social Security Law Division: old-age and survivors’ insurance, disability insurance, income replacement schemes (including maternity), health insurance.

Part III. The State and Its Subdivisions

General Bibliography for Part III (selection): Aubert & Mahon. commentaire, Articles 42–135; Auer, Malinverni & Hottelier. Vol. I., 315 et seq.; Biaggini. Kommentar, Articles 42–135; Biaggini, Giovanni. 'Föderalismus im Wandel'. In *Zeitschrift für öffentliches Recht [ZÖR]*. 2002, 359 et seq.; Biaggini, Giovanni. *Theorie und Praxis des Verwaltungsrechts im Bundesstaat.* Basel/Frankfurt a.M.: Helbing & Lichtenhahn, 1996; Egli, 35 et seq.; Fleiner & Basta Fleiner, 529 et seq., 593 et seq.; Fleiner Thomas & Misic Alexander. 'Föderalismus als Ordnungsprinzip der Verfassung'. In Thürer et al., §27; Frenkel Max. *Föderalismus und Bundesstaat.* 2 vol. Bern: Lang Publ., 1984/1986; Häfelin, Haller, Keller & Thurnherr, 289 et seq.; Haller. *Swiss Constitution*, 45 et seq.; Hänni Peter (ed.). *Schweizerischer Föderalismus und europäische Integration.* Zurich: Schulthess, 2000; Jaag, Bucher & Häggi Furrer, 85 et seq.; Kincaid John. 'From Cooperative to Coercive Federalism'. *Annals of the American Academy of Political and Social Science 509* (1990): 139–152; Knapp Blaise. 'La répartition des compétences et la coopération de la Confédération et des cantons'. In Thürer et al., §29; Koller Heinrich. 'Subsidairität als Verfassungsprinzip'. In *Festschrift Yvo Hangartner.* St. Gallen, 1998, 675 et seq.; Linder. 43 et seq.; Mahon. 101 et seq.; Rhinow René. 'Bundesstaatsreform und Demokratie'. In René L. Frey (ed.). *Föderalismus zukunftstauglich?!.* Zurich: NZZ Libro, 2005, 63 et seq.; Rhinow, Schefer & Uebersax, 111 et seq.; St. Galler Kommentar *ad* Articles 42–135; Saladin Peter. 'Bund und Kantone'. In *Zeitschrift für Schweizerisches Recht [ZSR].* 1984 II, 431 et seq.; Schindler Dietrich. 'Schweizerischer und europäischer Föderalismus'. *In Schweizerisches Zentralblatt für Staats- und Verwaltungsrecht [ZBl].* 1992, 193 et seq.; Tschannen, 239 et seq.; Waldmann Bernhard (ed.). *1. Nationale Föderalismuskonferenz: Der kooperative Föderalismus vor neuen Herausforderungen.* Basel: Helbing & Lichtenhahn, 2005; Watts Ronald, L. *Comparing Federal Systems.* 3rd ed. Montreal/Kingston: McGill-Queen's University Press, 2008.

Chapter 1. Switzerland as a Federal State

§1. Federalism as Legitimizing Element of State Organization

Selected Bibliography: Agranoff Robert (ed.). *Accommodating Diversity: Asymmetry in Federal States.* Baden-Baden: Nomos, 1999; Basta Fleiner Lidija, R. 'Minority and Legitimacy of a Federal State: An Outsider Perception of the Swiss Model'. In Basta Fleiner & Fleiner, 99–102; Egli, 35 et seq.; Fleiner Thomas. 'Legal Instruments and Procedures to Prevent and Solve Ethnic Conflicts: Experiences from the Swiss Constitution'. In Basta Fleiner & Fleiner. 145–164; Fleiner Thomas. 'Die schweizerische Verfassung im Kontext eines gemeinsamen europäischen Verfassungsrechts'. In Sitter-Liver, 431 et seq.; Fleiner & Basta Fleiner, 593 et seq.; Haller. *Swiss Constitution,* 45 et seq.; Schoder Charlotte. *Vom Minderheitenschutz zum Schutz verwundbarer Gruppen.* Zurich: Schulthess, 1999 (with further references); Töpperwien Nicole. *Nation-state and Normative Diversity.* Basel: Helbing & Lichtenhahn, 2001, 241–283.

I. Introduction

275. Swiss federalism can only be understood from a historical perspective, as it is the pragmatic answer to internal and external developments in the nineteenth century (*see supra* General Introduction, Chapter 1). Swiss history is characterized by a slow centralization of power without cultural homogenization. Switzerland has a population that is characterized by its cultural, religious and linguistic diversity. There was no pre-constitutional homogeneity that could be taken for creating national unity. Nevertheless, there is a Swiss nation based on a feeling of 'Swissness' that transcends and holds together the different cantonal, language and religious identities. The Swiss nation is composed of the peoples of the cantons, as well as of the various cultures that cut across cantonal borderlines. The basis of the common Swiss national identity is the broad recognition of *political* Switzerland, that is, primarily of federalism and semi-direct democracy (*see supra* General Introduction, Chapter 2). The homogeneity of the state and the nation is to be found within an internalized common understanding of the 'political' which translates into the political will to form a nation. The political identity is the reason why, for example, a French-speaking Swiss citizen does not see herself/himself as a member of the French nation. Federalism and semi-direct democracy provide reasons to belong because they enable groups to influence their own destiny and the destiny of the common state. Swiss identity and unity cannot be taken for granted. They can ultimately only be preserved through the provision of far-reaching cantonal autonomy and by the participation of all cultures in the federal consensus – to ensure that all composing groups continue to feel part and see reasons to belong to the Swiss nation.

276. The decision for federalism was a pragmatic one. It acknowledged the need to maintain empowered cantons as well as the necessity for common decision-making. Switzerland adopted its first federal constitution in 1848. This constitution, as well as the constitutions of 1874 and 1999, enabled a balance between self-rule and shared rule and provided a compromise between non-centralization and centralization. While the constitutions included elements of centralization, they also maintained the sovereignty of the cantons. With the 1999 Constitution – as well as amendments to the different constitutions, the balance between shared rule and self-rule has shifted. Self-rule of the cantons has diminished while their capacity to effectively participate on federal issues has risen. For better cooperation and coordination, cantons introduced new mechanisms, namely the Conferences of the cantons and in particular the Conference of Cantonal Governments. In 2004, the majority of the citizens and of the cantons adopted several amendments of the constitution which reinforced federalism with some basic federal principles such as the principle of subsidiarity (Article 5a) and a more pronounced concept of financial solidarity and fiscal equalization among rich and poor cantons. At several moments throughout Switzerland's history there have been debates on constitutional reforms that have been essential for reconfirming Swiss identity and for fine-tuning the overall power balance.

II. Diversity Promotion in the Constitution

277. One of the main features of Swiss federalism is considerable autonomy of the cantons. Cantons on their turn accord autonomy to local governments. Through cantonal and local autonomy, cantonal and local diversity is accommodated. In addition, there are further mechanisms to manage diversity, e.g. the provisions for national and official languages to accommodate linguistic diversity.

278. Diversity is not seen as a burden or as an impediment to national unity, but rather as the engine that ensures constant dialogue and debate and therefore fosters vitality, innovation and creativity within the federation. The Constitution recognizes diversity as an asset and a value – though of course diversity can also cause challenges. The Preamble of the Constitution of 1999 relies on a concept of diversity in unity: 'We, the Swiss People and the Cantons … are determined to live our diversity in unity respecting one another.' Article 2 of the Federal Constitution, which states the goals of the Swiss Confederation goes further by declaring that the 'Swiss Confederation … shall promote … the cultural diversity of the country.'

279. Switzerland's stance towards diversity, the achievement of unity that incorporates and transcends diversity, and the instruments Switzerland developed to balance diverse interests regularly spark the interest of other countries that seek to deal with their own diversity. However, there are limits to the Swiss success story. For instance, structurally only traditional diversity is regarded as a value (for the migrant population and minority issues *see infra* Part IV, Chapter 3.)

III. Federalized Democracy

280. Federalism and participatory democracy are the primary means to promote diversity (*see* already General Introduction, Chapter 2, §3). Federalism was not introduced as a corrective to a majoritarian democracy, but unites the participatory democracies of the cantons under a common federal government. Federalism enables a multilevel democracy through which decisions can receive multilevel legitimacy. Decisions can be left to the democratic decision-making unit of the level that is most concerned by the decision. Local and group interests can be channelled into the democratic decision-making process so as to enable appropriate political solutions. Understood in this way, federalism can facilitate the democratic self-determination of different groups. For instance, harmonization of education was mainly achieved through democratic decision-making at cantonal level and inter-cantonal cooperation. Centralized decision-making would probably have been faster, however, would have been counter to cantonal sensitivities.

§2. Elements of Federalism

Selected Bibliography: *See* General Bibliography for Part III and, *inter alia*, Aubert & Mahon. commentaire, Remarques liminaires, 381–384; Biaggini. Kommentar, Vorbemerkungen, Articles 42–135 (with further references); Biaggini, Giovanni. 'Vertragszwang im kooperativen Föderalismus: Verfassungsrechtliche Richtpunkte für den Einsatz der in Article 48a BV vorgesehenen Zwangsmittel'. In *Schweizerisches Zentralblatt für Staats- und Verwaltungsrecht [ZBl]*. 2008, 345–377; Biaggini Giovanni. 'Föderalismus quo vadis?'. In *Herausforderung Harmos: Bildungspolitik, Föderalismus und Demokratie auf dem Prüfstein*, edited by Andreas Auer. Zürich: Schulthess, 2010, 107–119; Fleiner Thomas & Basta Fleiner Lidija, R. 'Federalism, Federal States and Decentralization'. In Basta Fleiner & Fleiner, 1–40; Fleiner Thomas & Misic Alexander. 'Der Föderalismus in der Schweiz'. In *Krise und Reform des Föderalismus*, edited by Meier-Walser Reinhard & Hirscher Gerhard. Munich: Hans-Seidel-Stiftung/Olzog, 1999, 246–264; Stauffer Thomas & Töpperwien Nicole. 'Balancing Self-Rule and Shared Rule'. In Basta Fleiner & Fleiner, 41–74; Rhinow, Schefer & Uebersax, 113 et seq. (with further references). *See* for further references (especially regarding the distribution of powers between the Confederation and the cantons) the Basler Kommentar *ad* Articles 3 and 42–135 (various authors) as well as the St. Galler Kommentar *ad* Articles 3 and 42–135 (various authors).

I. Definition

281. Federalism can be defined as 'constitutionally guaranteed self-rule and shared rule'. A federal state can be understood as a state with sub-entities (in the case of Switzerland: the cantons), each of which has a constitutionally guaranteed right to these forms of rule. Self-rule is understood here as a substantive decision-making and self-governing power. Shared rule can but does not necessarily mean shared competencies, but rather presupposes an institutionalized and guaranteed special input from the subunits in the decision-making process of the federal level. In Switzerland, this special input is guaranteed, for example, through the representation of the cantons in the second chamber of Parliament (*see supra* Part II, Chapter 3). In addition, any federation needs coordination and dispute resolution mechanisms.

The Constitution establishes some general principles related to the tasks of the confederation and the cantons (Title 3 section 1 of the Constitution). It regulates the cooperation between the confederation and the cantons (Title 3 section 2 of the Constitution). It guarantees the autonomy of municipalities as far as the cantonal constitutions provide local autonomy (Title 3 section 3 of the Constitution). And finally, it provides some specific guarantees regarding the cantonal autonomy and their territories (Title 3 section 4 of the Constitution).

II. Relations Between the Confederation and the Cantons

282. The Confederation has to respect the autonomy of the cantons (Article 47(1) of the Constitution). In particular, it has to leave the cantons sufficient tasks and must respect the organizational autonomy of the cantons. Cantons have their own constitution and decide on their concept of direct democracy, governmental organization, their court organization and their territorial organization with regard to districts and municipalities.

283. The powers of the federal level are expressly defined by the Constitution (Article 42 of the Constitution). In different words, the federal level can only assume powers that are attributed to it by the Constitution. The residual power is with the cantons. The cantons determine their tasks within the scope of their powers (Article 43 of the Constitution). In Article 43a, the Constitution develops the basic principles for the distribution of tasks between the Confederation and the cantons. This provision does not only bind the legislature in concretizing the distribution of powers but also gives guideline to the constitution-maker for future amendments to the distribution of powers. It establishes that:

- the federal level shall only fulfil such tasks that exceed the capacity of the cantons or require uniform regulation;
- the unit of government that profits from a service covers the costs thereof;
- The unit that covers the costs of the service decides on the service.

From this provision also follows that decision-making power must go hand in hand with the attribution of financial resources and financial autonomy. Article 47(2) of the Constitution obliges the Confederation to leave to the cantons sufficient sources of revenue and even to contribute financially to enable cantons to fulfil their tasks. The guidelines on the attribution of tasks also contribute to accountability: Those who take decisions also bear the consequences (financial and others). At the same time the Constitution puts some limits: basic services shall be available to all persons in a comparable manner and they shall be provided in a need-oriented and cost effective way.

284. Contrary to federations embedded within the common law system, in particular the United States, in Switzerland federal law is usually not implemented by federal agencies and Federal Supreme Courts but by the cantonal administration and cantonal courts. The principle of implementation of federal law by the cantons is stated in Article 46 of the Constitution. This implies that all provisions concerning the distribution of powers providing for federal powers are mainly limited to legislative power. However, the Confederation and the cantons can agree on targets for the cantons, and the Confederation can financially support cantonal programmes for achieving these targets. Only in exceptional cases, there are constitutional provisions that transmit a responsibility and power to the Confederation not only to legislate but also to administer the federal task with proper administrative agencies. This is, e.g., the case in the field of communication with the postal services.

285. Federal systems can only function if there is cooperation among federal units (horizontal cooperation) as well as between federal units and the federal level (vertical cooperation). The principle of cooperation is stated in Article 44 of the Constitution, which requires the Confederation and the cantons to cooperate in the fulfilment of their tasks and to support each other within their responsibility.

286. Over time, because of complexity and interconnectedness of different policy decisions, high expectations towards service-delivery, as well as higher mobility of populations, the pressure to harmonize policies has increased. Harmonization has been achieved by centralizing certain powers as well as through cooperation among cantons. For instance, since 2008, the Confederation oversees land surveys – here centralization was the means of choice. In many other fields, preference has been given to cooperation. For enhanced cooperation, cantons developed a rich body of treaties. Almost all areas of cantonal autonomy are subject to inter-cantonal cooperation and treaties. The federal level can be part of inter-cantonal treaties – if also federal powers are concerned. In line with this trend towards formalized cooperation, the 1999 Constitution includes more detailed provisions on inter-cantonal treaties than previous ones. Article 48 of the Constitution empowers cantons to enter into inter-cantonal agreement and even to establish joined organizations and common institutions. For instance, cantons can jointly establish infrastructure, or decide that a water purification plant of one canton can also be used by one or several other cantons. Cantons can jointly deliver services, can agree on harmonized policies, e.g. in the area of school curricula, and can even delegate legislative powers to regional organizations and institutions, provided the legislative powers are clearly determined by the treaty, and the legislative procedures correspond to the respective cantonal constitutions and inter-cantonal law (Article 48(4) of the Constitution). Inter-cantonal treaties must not be in contradiction of federal law or impede on the interests of the Confederation or other cantons. In addition, there are constitutional provisions that aim at creating incentives for harmonization and cooperation, for instance Article 62(4) of the Constitution provides for a negative incentive: if cantons do not manage to harmonize the school entry age and compulsory school attendance, the duration and objectives of levels of education, and the transition from one level to another, as well as the recognition of qualifications, the Confederation can issue coordinating and harmonizing regulations. As an example of a positive incentive, the Confederation can for instance provide financial support to cantonal universities (Article 63a of the Constitution).

287. As a matter of principle, cantons are free to decide whether they want to conclude or join an inter-cantonal treaty. However, based on Article 48a of the Constitution – on request of eighteen cantons – the Federal Parliament can declare certain inter-cantonal agreements as generally applicable. Furthermore, on request of half of the cantons who are part of the agreement, Federal Parliament can force other cantons to join and participate in agreements. The Constitution provides an enumeration of policy areas for which such a declaration of general applicability or an obligation to participate can be established, including for instance certain aspects of education, highly specialized medical care or certain aspects of traffic regulations. The people and the cantons can demand a referendum against a declaration of general applicability whereas decisions on an obligation of individual cantons to join a treaty are not submitted to referendum. The provisions of Article 48a of the Constitution were introduced considering good experiences with the declaration of general applicability of Collective Labour Agreements, however, the provisions are in tension with the autonomy of the cantons to decide within their sphere of powers.

288. The Constitution envisages that the cantons participate in the federal decision-making process, in particular in the process of developing legislation. It obliges the Confederation to inform cantons in a comprehensive and timely manner and to seek their opinion on all matters that affect their interests (Article 45 of the Constitution). The Confederation has the obligation and responsibility to intervene as mediator in case of disputes between the cantons. As far as possible, disputes shall be settled by negotiation.

III. 'Bottom-Up' Federalism

289. Switzerland is a bottom-up federation with the municipalities as the lowest level of government. Municipalities have political, administrative and fiscal autonomy. When Napoleon conquered Switzerland (General Introduction, Chapter 1), he established a general system of local authorities. He equalized the powers of villages, towns and cities throughout Switzerland. The system of local authorities (municipalities/communes) with autonomous powers has survived the defeat of Napoleon, however, Swiss cantons have regained the power to decide on their territorial organization and the extent of local powers. Despite of the importance of the local level within the Swiss system of governance, the Constitution dedicates only one article to local government: Article 50 of the Constitution. This article acknowledges the power of the cantons by providing municipalities with an indirect guarantee of local autonomy. Because the cantons are in charge of legislating on the local level, the organization and powers of municipalities vary among cantons and with that also the extent of local autonomy. The Constitution guarantees local autonomy to the extent that the different cantons grant autonomy to their municipalities. Thus, the constitutional guarantee of local autonomy established in Article 50 of the Constitution is dependent on the cantonal legislation (*see infra,* Part III, Chapter 3, §1).

290. In addition, the Constitution, in Article 50(2) and (3) of the Constitution, obliges the Confederation to consider the potential impact of its acts on the local level and to be considerate of the special needs of cities, agglomerations and mountainous regions.

IV. Overview on Federal Guarantees

291. The Constitution provides for three special federal guarantees: It guarantees (1) the cantonal constitutions, (2) the cantonal order, and (3) the territory and existence of the cantons. The following provides a short overview. For more details, *see infra*, Chapter 2, §1. Each canton has constitution-making power and substantial decision-making space how to organize itself. However, the Constitution sets some requirements for cantonal constitutions.

(1) It establishes minimum rules to guarantee the legitimacy of cantonal constitutions. The cantonal constitution must be adopted by the cantonal People and must be amended if a majority of the citizens so demands (Article 51 of the Constitution). All cantons set lower thresholds for the amendment of their cantonal constitution than required in Article 51 of the Constitution.
(2) Furthermore, the Constitution aims at ensuring that the cantonal constitutions are in line with the overall legal order. The cantons must submit their constitution to the Federal Parliament for approval. The Federal Parliament must approve the cantonal constitution if its provisions are in line with federal law (Articles 51 and 172(2) of the Constitution).

292. The Confederation guarantees the constitutional order of the cantons (Article 52 of the Constitution). This instrument was last used in 1932. It is noteworthy that the Confederation (Federal Council or Parliament) can only become active as ultima ratio if neither the canton on its own nor the canton with the help of other cantons can restore the cantonal constitutional order (Article 52 of the Constitution). Upon request of the canton, in cases of serious unrest, the army can be deployed when the canton cannot resolve the situation with its own police force as well as with the assistance from police forces of other cantons. The Federal Parliament decides who will cover the costs for any intervention.

293. Article 53 of the Constitution guarantees the existence and the territories of the cantons. The guarantee protects the legal existence and the legal status of the cantons and protects them from changes to their territory. While already former constitutions provided a guarantee of the existence and territories of cantons, the 1999 constitution additionally includes a procedure for changing cantonal boundaries. Article 53 of the Constitution regulates the procedures for three different types of territorial changes:

(1) Any change of the number of the cantons (because of internal secession or the merger of cantons) needs the approval of the concerned populations, the concerned cantons as well as of the majority of the People and the Cantons. This leads to a cascade of referenda at local, cantonal and federal level.
(2) Changes of territory between cantons require the approval of the concerned populations and of the cantons as well as the approval of Federal Parliament. This leads to local and cantonal referenda while a federal referendum is not needed.
(3) The cantons can agree on minor boundary adjustments in the form of a cantonal treaty.

Including a procedure for boundary change recognizes that there can be demands for reconfiguring the federal map. The provision provides a procedure that allows to pursue such demands with political means and ensures that potential new cantons and resulting boundary lines have democratic legitimacy.

V. Constitutionally Guaranteed Self-Rule

A. Principle

294. According to Article 3 of the Constitution, the cantons have original or residual powers: They exercise all powers that are not constitutionally transferred to the Confederation. *E contrario*, the Confederation has only powers that are explicitly attributed to it by the Constitution (Article 42(1) of the Constitution). Title III, Chapter 2 of the Constitution contains the enumeration of federal powers (*see infra* 2.).

295. Article 43a of the Constitution provides for general principles for the allocation of tasks between cantons and the Confederation (*see also supra* Part III, Chapter 1, §2). According to paragraph 1, the Confederation shall only assume tasks when the cantons either are not able to perform this task or when a uniform regulation is required. Paragraph 2 provides for a cost-benefit principle as it requires that always the collective body which has the benefit of public service should pay for it. Furthermore, the one who pays shall also have the power to decide (paragraph 3). In addition, the article gives also guidelines to the cantons concerning the basic services for the People. Basic services must be available to everyone in a comparable manner. The cantons have to find the ways and means to provide those services. Only if the cantons are unable to perform then the Confederation might intervene. Finally, the provision stipulates that Confederation, cantons and municipalities are to fulfil state tasks economically and in accordance with demand. Thus, Article 43a of the Constitution has to a certain extent substantiated the principle of subsidiarity provided in Article 5a of the Constitution. These principles cannot be enforced by court decisions. They are guidelines for the legislature without any judicial remedy.

296. Articles 46 and 47 of the Constitution explicitly assign the Confederation to respect the autonomy, including the financial autonomy of the cantons.

297. In the following section, the constitutionally guaranteed distribution of powers between the Confederation, and the cantons shall be depicted.

B. Distribution of Powers

298. In general, the federal level is attributed powers that are of importance for sovereignty, e.g. the coinage of money, that concern matters of high complexity, or that would require a high level of coordination, e.g. atomic power, and that are based on shared values, e.g. criminal law. Cantons maintain many powers that have more regional implications, e.g. regional road infrastructure, that concern basic services, e.g. health care, and that are linked to identity, e.g. culture or the relationship between state and religion. Cantons entrust the local level with powers that primarily are of local relevance, e.g. local road infrastructure, kindergartens, zoning.

As the residual power is with the cantons it would suffice to list the powers of the federal level (in contrast to many of the newer federations that enumerate exclusive and concurrent powers of the federal level, of federal units and sometimes even of local governments). However, also the Swiss Constitution includes more than a list of federal powers.

(1) Tasks are more and more interconnected. Many provisions spell out the interplay between federal and cantonal powers, e.g. provisions on education (Article 61a of the Constitution) and therefore do not only enumerate federal powers but also mention related cantonal powers.
Provisions go further than mentioning the power as such, e.g. security or foreign relations, and additionally provide goals and policy directives to the federal level for fulfilling the power. For instance, based on Article 54(1) the federal level is in charge of foreign affairs. According to Article 54(2) of the Constitution, the Confederation shall shape its foreign relations with the goal that it contributes to the reduction of poverty in the world, promotes the protection of human rights and democracy, as well as facilitates the peaceful cohabitation of peoples and the preservation of natural resources. This extent of detail can be explained as follows: For each constitutional amendment – and with that for any new attribution of power to the federal level – it needs a mandatory referendum and the approval by the majority of the People and of the cantons. In such votes, majorities can only be achieved if citizens are convinced that the provision does not provide the federal level with too broad powers and that they will benefit from implementation of the outcome. The constitution-maker can only arrive at the needed majorities if constitutional provisions balance different interests. Furthermore, there is no constitutional review of federal legislation. Therefore, there is a more acute need to have constitutional provisions that give precise direction.

299. Since 1999, there have been several successful popular initiatives for constitutional amendments that are problematic from a human rights perspective. Although they are not in direct connection to the distribution of powers, they have been introduced into the chapter dealing with the distribution of powers. Those texts are the prohibition of the construction of minarets (Article 72 paragraph 3 of the Constitution), the incarceration for life of extremely dangerous and violent sex-offenders (Article 123a of the Constitution), no time limit for the right to prosecute or for penalties for sexual or pornographic offences involving prepubescent children (Article 123b of the Constitution), the life-long prohibition for certain sex-offenders to work with children and dependent persons (Article 123c of the Constitution) and the obligation to expel foreign criminals (Article 121(2) and (3) of the Constitution).

1. Relations with Foreign Countries

300. Foreign relations are one of the prerogatives of the sovereign state and are a federal matter (Article 54(1) of the Constitution). Even when the Confederation lacks explicit power in a certain policy field (cp. taxation) it still has the right to conclude treaties with foreign states (e.g., double taxation treaties). However, the cantons shall participate in the preparation of decisions of foreign policy that concern their powers or their essential interests. Furthermore, cantons have to be informed in a timely matter and shall be consulted. The position of the cantons shall have particular weight when their powers are concerned. In these cases, the interested canton can also directly participate in international negotiations, delegated by the Confederation (Article 55 of the Constitution).

301. As a rule, the relations of the cantons with foreign countries are conducted by the Confederation on behalf of the cantons. However, within the scope of their powers, the cantons have a limited treaty-making power with foreign countries, and they may deal directly with lower ranking foreign authorities. The Conference of the Cantonal Governments has a permanent observer at the EU in Brussels. The treaties of the cantons, e.g., with neighbouring states may neither be contrary to the law and the interests of the Confederation nor infringe on the rights of other cantons. To guarantee this, the cantons must inform the Confederation before concluding a treaty. This is an improvement of the position of the cantons in comparison to the situation under the Constitution of 1874, which required that the cantons must not only inform the Federal level, but ask for federal approval.

2. Security, National and Civil Defence

302. *See infra* Part V, Chapter 1.

3. Education, Research, Culture, Languages and Religion

303. Education, research and culture are sensitive areas because, on the one hand, cantons want to maintain their autonomy as fields are connected to cultural identity and different cantonal traditions, and, on the other hand, the Confederation is interested in ensuring mobility and high quality education throughout Switzerland and promoting Switzerland's capacity to compete internationally. The constitutional provisions aim at balancing the different interests and needs and provide for unification without complete centralization. Article 61a of the Constitution stipulates that Switzerland forms one educational area and that to ensure high quality and general accessibility of education, the Confederation and the cantons shall coordinate and cooperate.

304. Primary and secondary education are part of cantonal autonomy and responsibility (Article 62 of the Constitution). However, there are several constitutional provisions that limit cantonal autonomy:

(1) The federal level determines the start of the school term (Article 62(5) of the Constitution).
(2) Cantons must ensure adequate primary school education which is free of charge, mandatory and supervised by the state (read: the canton).
(3) The Constitution obligates the cantons to ensure that all children with disabilities receive adequate education up to the age of 20 (Article 62(2), (3) of the Constitution).

Based on Article 62(4) the Confederation can further intervene to harmonize cantonal school education if the cantons cannot achieve coordination on their own. For the elaboration of any federal legislation in the field of primary and secondary education, the federal level must invite the cantons to participate.

305. Vocational and professional education are a federal power, with the aim to foster equal opportunities in the employment market. Article 63 of the Constitution obliges the Confederation not only to regulate professional and vocational education; the Confederation must also ensure a diverse and accessible system of vocational education. Furthermore, the Confederation and the cantons shall promote that general education and vocational education have a comparable social status (Article 61a(3) of the Constitution).

306. With regard to university education, the Constitution balances and interlinks cantonal and federal powers:

(1) General university education remains a cantonal power. Cantons can decide whether they want to establish a cantonal university. Currently, there are ten cantonal universities and several institutions of higher applied education. The Confederation runs technical universities. Currently, there are two technical universities, one in Zurich, one in Lausanne. The Constitution allows the Confederation to establish, to take over or to run additional universities (Article 63a(1) of the Constitution).
(2) Confederation and cantons are jointly in charge of coordination and quality assurance within the Swiss university system. In pursuing this task they have to respect the autonomy of universities and treat institutions with equal tasks equally (Article 63a(3) of the Constitution). The already long-term cooperation among cantons in the field of higher education has been extended to include the Confederation. For this purpose, they have established the Swiss University Council, a council of all rectors as well as a council for accreditation. Mainly three legal texts govern the cooperation in the field of education: a federal law on the promotion and coordination of higher education, an inter-cantonal treaty on higher education as well as a cooperation agreement between the Confederation and the cantons.
(3) An important part of university funding is provided by the cantons. The main funder of cantonal universities is the canton where the university is located. As not all cantons can afford their own university and as there is student mobility between universities, the cantons pay for their students who visit a university in another canton. In addition, since 1968, the Confederation has supported cantonal universities with important subsidies. The federal right to fund is established in Article 63a(2) of the Constitution. Based on Article 63a(5) of the Constitution, the Confederation can use funding as an incentive for harmonization and cooperation, i.e., to promote harmonized financing principles as well as cooperation among universities in cost-intensive areas. Furthermore, Article 66 of the Constitution explicitly provides the Confederation with the power to support cantons in providing scholarships for universities and other institutions of higher learning.
(4) Similar as regarding primary and secondary education, the federal level has subsidiary power in case coordination is not effective. If the Confederation and cantons do not achieve the set aims by cooperation the Confederation can enact

rules on an enumerated number of issues, including on the accreditation of universities and recognition degrees (Article 63a(5) of the Constitution).

307. In addition to the federal competences concerning regulation of harmonization in the field of educational statistics (Article 65 of the Constitution), the Constitution entrusts the Confederation with the power to regulate continuing education (Article 64a of the Constitution). Furthermore, the Confederation can promote scientific research and innovation and run its own research institutes. Finally, the Confederation has the power to operate a sports school and to encourage education in sports (Article 68 of the Constitution) as well as, in cooperation with the cantons, to promote musical education (Article 67a of the Constitution). In all its activities, the Confederation must ensure that the special needs of children and young people are taken into account and that they receive encouragement and protection (Article 67 of the Constitution).

308. Article 69(1) of the Constitution establishes the general rule that the cantons are responsible for cultural matters. However, the confederation can support cultural initiatives that are of Swiss interest and can promote art and music. When the confederation supports cultural activities, it is obliged to consider the cultural and linguistic diversity of the country (Article 69(2)–(3) of the Constitution). Article 71 of the Constitution gives the Confederation an additional power to promote diversified and qualitative Swiss cinema and film production.

309. Language is crucial for identity. While during the nineteenth century, religion was the most important dividing line in Switzerland, in the twentieth century, linguistic diversity has gained in importance. This has also reflected on the number of provisions related to language. For instance, the Constitution of 1999 added provisions on language, including on the linguistic composition of the Federal Council. In 2007 Switzerland enacted its first federal language law (SR 441.1). The Swiss Constitution distinguishes between national and official languages. Article 4 of the Constitution stipulates that German, French, Italian and Romansh are national languages. This recognition is mainly of symbolic relevance. Article 70 of the Constitution defines the official languages at federal level. The four national languages are also recognized as official languages at federal level. While German, French and Italian have an equal status, i.e., all authorities of the Confederation need to address the People in these languages, all legislation is prepared and published in those three languages, and no language has legal priority, Romansh has a slightly lower status. Romansh is an official language at federal level in respect to native Romansh-speakers (0.5% of the population). Consequently, Romansh-speakers can address the Confederation in their language and have the right to receive an answer in that language, however, not all laws and not all communication of the Confederation are translated into Romansh. While a Romansh-speaking member of parliament can address parliament in Romansh, Parliament is not obliged to have legislative drafts and other documents translated into Romansh.

310. The cantons determine their own official languages (Article 70(2) of the Constitution). While in principle cantons are free in determining their official languages, the Constitution stipulates that for communal harmony the cantons shall consider the language communities that are traditionally present in their areas and shall show respect to linguistic minorities (Article 70(2) of the Constitution). Most cantons – as they are by and large monolingual – have only one official language (German, French or Italian).

Three cantons in which two traditional language communities are present have two official languages (Berne, Fribourg and Valais). The canton of Grisons has three official languages namely German, Italian and Romansh. The Constitution mandates the confederation, in cooperation with the cantons, to promote the understanding and exchange among the different linguistic communities, to support cantons with more than one official language and to help the cantons of Grisons and Ticino in protecting and promoting Romansh and Italian (Article 70(3–5) of the Constitution).

311. While in respect to linguistic diversity, the approach is largely one of recognition and accommodation, in respect to religion, the Confederation aims at taking the role of a neutral arbiter. In order to avoid dispute at the federal level and among the cantons, the Constitution leaves it up to the cantons to define the relations between state and religion within their territory (Article 72(1) of the Constitution). In line with its role as neutral arbiter, the Confederation can take measures to safeguard public peace among the members of different religious denominations (Article 72(2) of the Constitution). Introduced by a popular initiative, Article 72(3) of the Constitution includes a prohibition of the construction of minarets. The initiators argued that the provision established just a construction regulation, did not interfere with possibilities to practice the religion and therefore was not in contradiction with fundamental rights, however the constitutional provision is problematic in light of the principle of non-discrimination and of religious freedom enshrined in the Swiss Constitution and in the ECHR (Articles 9 and 14).

4. Environment and Zoning

312. The Preamble of the Constitution expresses the respect for the environment by stressing the People's responsibility towards the Creation and for future generations. Sustainable development is considered as one of the core responsibilities of the Confederation and the cantons (Article 2 of the Constitution). This commitment to sustainable development is confirmed in Article 73 which requires that the Confederation and the cantons strive to establish a durable equilibrium, balancing the interests that nature can renew itself and that people can make use of nature's resources.

313. Environmental protection (Article 74 of the Constitution), zoning and spatial planning (Article 75 of the Constitution), national land survey (Article 75a of the Constitution), water (Article 76 of the Constitution), forestry (Article 77 of the Constitution), nature and cultural heritage (Article 78 of the Constitution), fishery and hunting (Article 79 of the Constitution), as well as the protection of animals (Article 80 of the Constitution) have traditionally been powers of the cantons. Still today the cantons are actively legislating in these fields. However, step-by-step, the Confederation has been given legislative powers. For instance, already in 1897, the Confederation has adopted a constitutional amendment to protect and to sustain the existing forests in Switzerland. Industrialization had let to the destruction of many forests and the cantons asked the Confederation to assume powers for protection and reforestation. In respect to the above-mentioned policy areas, powers of the federal level and of the cantons are intertwined and therefore they all merited their special provisions in the Constitution within a chapter entitled Environment and Zoning. In most instances, the Federal Parliament has only the authority to enact framework legislation or to define basic principles and standards for specific matters. Remaining matters, more detailed policies and implementation measures are decided by the cantons. For example, regarding environment protection, the federal legislature's powers are limited to enacting provisions that focus on the protection of human beings and their natural environment so as to protect people from damages to their health and other nuisances. The regulation of other matters and implementation are left to the cantons (Article 74 of the Constitution). Similarly, in respect to water, the federal level is attributed with the power to define principles and standards, e.g. in respect to the protection of bodies of water, the preservation of water and the security of dams. The cantons decide on the use of water. In regard to zoning regulations (Article 75 of the Constitution), the federal level is only allowed to enact framework legislation, however, the density of federal norms differs from very vague principles, which leave important discretion for implementation and further legislation to the cantons to detailed provisions that must be applied directly by the cantons (Article 24 of the Federal Zoning Act, SR 700). Also in the policy area of fishery and hunting the federal level has only the power to enact framework legislation. For animal protection, on the other hand, the federal level has far-reaching authority. The cantons mainly maintain the task to implement the federal policies. In 2012, a new provision (Article 75b of the Constitution) was added to the chapter on Environment and Zoning. It was introduced by popular initiative. It limits the number of secondary (holiday) residencies within municipalities to 20%.

5. Public Works and Transportation

314. The Confederation has the authority to establish public works that are in the interest of the whole of the country or important parts thereof (Article 81 of the Constitution). Switzerland has an extensive road and rail network. Even the smallest villages are connected to the road system and public transportation. By popular initiative, in 2016, a constitutional provision was introduced that mandates the federal level and the cantons to provide for sufficient transportation infrastructure for traffic by rail, road, water and ropeways in all parts of the country. An adequate part of the costs shall be covered by the users (Article 81a of the Constitution). With this provision, as one of the objectives, the initiators wanted to prevent that public transportation in more remote areas is being reduced.

315. The Confederation legislates on road and rail traffic, cable cars, navigation, aviation and space travel (Articles 82 and 87 of the Constitution). Additionally, it can define principles and standards for footpaths and hiking trails (Article 88 of the Constitution). The federal level is mandated to enact legislation on road traffic and to supervise roads of national importance (Article 82 of the Constitution). Furthermore, the federal level is in charge of constructing, maintaining and financing national highways (Article 83 of the Constitution). All cantonal and municipal roads are cantonal matters. Due to Switzerland's important geostrategic position in Middle Europe, with the Alps forming a natural barrier between the North and South, most of Europe's heavy north-south traffic runs through Switzerland. The Gotthard tunnel is one of the few throughways as well as the shortest connection from north to south of Europe. Improved mobility created a nuisance mainly for the alpine region. As a result, a popular initiative that aimed at limiting trans-alpine border-to-border transit on the roads by mandating rail transportation was introduced and finally approved by popular referendum in the 1990s (Article 84 of the Constitution). For this reason, Switzerland has decided to construct a new tunnel under the Gotthard in order to transport also the big trucks by train from Basel to Chiasso. The federal level can levy several taxes and fees, including a consumption tax and motorway tax (Article 86 of the Constitution). The Constitution provides detailed provisions how such revenues are to be used. For instance, the consumption tax and motorway tax shall be used for road infrastructure, the promotion of combined (rail-road) traffic – as envisaged for the trans-alpine transit – as well as for improving transportation infrastructure in agglomerations, for financing main roads, for constructing protective structures against the forces of nature, and for providing subsidies to the cantons for their tasks as well as to cantons without national highways.

6. Energy and Communication

316. Switzerland has own energy resources, mainly from water. The water sources located in Switzerland are nourishing four different Seas: the Atlantic (River Rhine), the Mediterranean (River Rhone) the Adriatic Sea (River Tessin) and the Black Sea (River Inn). According to the Constitution, the Confederation and the cantons shall strive to ensure sufficient, diversified, renewable and reliable energy supply compatible with the protection of the environment as well as an economical and efficient use of energy. Furthermore, the Confederation is entitled to establish principles for the use of domestic and renewable energy, while measures concerning the use of energy in buildings are primarily a cantonal matter (Article 85(1–4) of the Constitution). In its energy policy, the Confederation is called upon to balance the interests and efforts of the cantons, municipalities and business actors as well as to consider the conditions in the different parts of the country and the economic sustainability (Article 85(5) of the Constitution).

317. In respect to nuclear energy, the Confederation has general legislative power and responsibility (Article 90 of the Constitution). Based on Article 196(4) of transitional provisions of the Constitution, the Confederation was barred to give any licence for a new nuclear power-plant up to the year 2000. In 2003, the People rejected an initiative to prolong the prohibition. In 2011, in a consultative vote, the People of the canton Berne gave a positive opinion on the renewal of the licence of their (already existing) atomic power-plant.

318. Furthermore, the Confederation has wide ranging powers with regard to transportation and supply of electrical energy. In the field of liquid and gaseous fuel, it can even regulate the systems for transmission and distribution (Article 91 of the Constitution).

319. In 2017, in a popular vote, the people approved a law that aims at reforming the energy sector. It envisages reducing the consumption of energy, increase energy efficiency and the use of renewable energy sources. In addition, the law prohibits the construction of new atomic power plants. Existing atomic power plants can continue their operation as long as they are deemed safe. Thus, the law provides for a stepwise exit from nuclear energy.

320. Postal services have been part of the powers of the Confederation since 1848. The constitution not only assigns the power to legislate to the Confederation but the responsibility to ensure adequate, universal and reasonably priced postal services. The Swiss Post is a special stock corporation that is entirely owned by the Confederation. However, there is pressure to open the market and allow competing private companies. At the time of writing (Spring 2017), the Swiss Post still has a monopoly for the transportation of letters up to 50g that are posted and addressed to places within Switzerland. Despite of detailed legal regulations, there are continuous discussions about the interpretation of the constitutionally required level and accessibility of postal services throughout Switzerland.

321. Telecommunication is also purview of the Confederation. Telecommunication services have been privatized in the nineties. The original agency in charge of telecommunication has been changed into a stock corporation in which the Confederation has the majority of capital (51%). This company is in competition with other, private companies.

322. Radio and television are sensitive areas in multicultural and multilingual Switzerland. Article 93 gives responsibility to legislate to the Confederation. It assigns the federal legislature to guarantee that public broadcasting companies are independent and autonomous regarding their programming. However, they must consider the particularities of the country and allow the diversity of opinions to be adequately expressed. Currently, Switzerland has one broadcasting association which covers the entire country. The association is composed of four regional corporations covering the German, French, Italian and Romansh languages. Those four regional corporations take care of the programming and broadcasting. The association is financed by the special taxes paid by the users of radio, television and internet. To support smaller language communities, the association ensures some financial equalization between the different cultures and language communities. Besides this Swiss broadcasting association, there are many private institutions which have licences to broadcast by radio or television.

7. Economy

323. The Confederation and the cantons must respect the principle of economic freedom, as stipulated in Article 94 of the Constitution. With this, Switzerland is one of the few countries that does not only guarantee property rights, free access to any profession and the freedom right to conclude contracts but that also guarantees the system of the free market. The Confederation and the cantons are called upon to create framework conditions that are conducive to strengthening the private economy. Measures that restrict economic freedom are only admissible based on an explicit constitutional provision or in connection with cantonal monopolies (mainly salt). The Constitution allows a deviation from economic freedom, for instance for the purpose of economic stabilization (Article 100(3) of the Constitution), for safeguarding the interests of the Swiss economy internationally (Article 101(2) of the Constitution), for ensuring the availability of essential goods (Article 102(2) of the Constitution), for supporting regions of the country that are under economic threat as well as endangered specific economic sectors and professions (Article 103 of the Constitution). Furthermore, the Confederation can restrict economic freedom in protection of farms that cultivate land (Article 104(2) of the Constitution).

324. The regulation of alcohol, in particular for the protection of the consumers, gambling and lotteries as well as weapons and military equipment are federal matters (Articles 105–107 of the Constitution). Up to 80% of revenues from gambling can be used for the pension fund.

325. According to Article 95(2) of the Constitution, the Confederation shall strive to create a unified Swiss economic area. It shall guarantee that university degrees as well as federal and cantonal educational certificates, or certificates recognized by one canton permit the holder to exercise his/her profession throughout Switzerland.

326. Furthermore, money and currency, including monetary policy for the protection of the Swiss franc, are federal matters. The Confederation has the exclusive right to coin money and to issue bank notes. As an independent central bank, the Swiss National Bank shall follow a monetary policy that serves the general interest of the country. The Bank is also charged with creating sufficient money reserves from its profits; a part of these reserves shall be held in gold. At least two-thirds of the net profits of the Swiss National Bank shall be distributed to the cantons (Article 99 of the Constitution).

327. According to Article 100 of the Constitution, the Confederation shall take measures to ensure a balanced economic development and, in particular, to prevent and fight unemployment and inflation. Additionally, the Confederation shall safeguard the interests of the Swiss economy abroad (Article 101 of the Constitution).

328. Introduced as part of neutrality and in reaction to food shortage during World War II, the supply of essential goods and services is still an issue in Swiss politics. The Confederation shall ensure the country's supply of essential goods and services in the event of threats of military or economic war, or in cases of severe shortage to which the economy cannot respond by itself (Article 102 of the Constitution). A popular initiative showed that the topic is still of relevance. In September 2017, the People and the Cantons approved a counter proposal to popular initiative and with it introduced a new provision to the Constitution on food security (Article 104a of the Constitution). The provision mandates the Confederation to ensure that there are conditions that allow the availability of sufficient food. Measures include safeguarding land for agriculture, resource-efficient production of food, market-oriented land and food policies, the use of international relations for a sustainable land and food economy, as well as a resource-conscious use of with food items. This constitutional provision overlaps with the provision on essential goods (Article 100 of the Constitution) and the provision on agriculture (Article 104 of the Constitution). It shows the intent of the citizens to influence land and food policy through a popular initiative but brings only small additions to federal powers (mainly land related).

329. The Confederation has relatively broad powers in the field of agriculture. The Constitution foresees six measures designed to ensure food security, to conserve natural resources and the rural scenery and to provide decentralized forms of settlement. The measures are (Article 104(3)(a–f) of the Constitution):

– direct payments to secure a fair and adequate remuneration for the services rendered, provided that compliance with ecological requirements is proven;

- economic incentives, to promote forms of production which are close to nature and friendly to environment and livestock;
- legislation on the declaration of origin, quality, production and food processing methods;
- protection of the environment against pollution due to excessive use of fertilizers, chemicals and other auxiliary substances;
- encouragement of agricultural research, counselling, and education, and subsidies for investments;
- legislation on the consolidation of rural property.

8. Housing, Work, Social Security and Health

330. The overwhelming majority of the Swiss People hold property by lease or rent (nearly 70%). The Constitution promotes the construction and ownership of housing and aims to prevent abuses in the field of landlord and tenant relationships, particularly with respect to abusive rent practices (Articles 108 and 109 of the Constitution). The Confederation can declare frame lease contracts generally binding.

331. The Confederation has limited powers concerning labour regulations. It may legislate on the protection of employees, the relationship between employees and employers and placement services. According to Article 110(2) of the Constitution, the Confederation can confer a binding effect on collective labour contracts if justified minority interests and regional differences are taken into account and the principle of equality before the law (Article 8(1) of the Constitution) as well as the freedom to unionize (Article 28 of the Constitution) are respected.

332. The basis of the Swiss system of social security is laid down in Article 12 of the Constitution and guarantees to everybody a fundamental right to assistance, when in need. This right has already been enforced by the Federal Supreme Court when asylum seekers had been refused the necessary minimum means. The system of social security is based on individual responsibility and solidarity. The principles of individual responsibility and solidarity are already incorporated in the Preamble of the Constitution, stating: and in the knowledge, that '… only those who use their freedom remain free, and that the strength of a people is measured by the well-being of its weakest members'. In addition, Article 6 of the Constitution underlines the responsibility of everyone for his or her proper development, as well as solidarity towards the state and society.

333. About 20% of the population in Switzerland receive contributions from the system of social security at least once during their professional life. Although the system as such is undisputed, there are many who fear that the system cannot be financially sustained in its current form. Discussions about the reform of the system and the financing modalities are ongoing. The main challenge is to balance the various interests, including of companies interested in an internationally competitive economy, of individuals who contribute, as well as of the receivers of assistance.

334. Regarding social security, the Confederation and the cantons cooperate. According to the Constitution, the cantons of residence are the main providers of assistance (Article 115 of the Constitution). However, the Constitution sets up a rather detailed system of social security. On most issues, the Confederation is attributed with legislating powers and defines goals, principles and standards while the cantons are mainly implementing. Social security is primarily provided through an insurance-based system which involves cantonal and private institutions.

335. The Swiss social security covers the following areas:

(1) Old-age, survivors' and disability insurance (Article 112 of the Constitution). Already in 1926, the People and the cantons adopted a constitutional amendment that attributed the Confederation with the power and responsibility to guarantee a general pension for elderly people and later also for disabled persons. The first legislative draft for a pension scheme was rejected by the People in a referendum. Only in 1946, after World War II, the People accepted a law that introduced compulsory contributions for old-age pensions. This law is still in force, but it was amended several times. It provides a pension that shall ensure a minimum living standard. The current working generation pays for the pension of the retired population. The active generation transfers some of its earnings to the elderly people hoping, claiming and trusting that they will later also profit from such transfers by the next generation.
The contributions for the old-age-pensions are paid at the place of residence of the contributing person. All persons with residence in Switzerland must contribute, regardless of their nationality. The obligation to contribute starts at 18 for all with gainful activities and at 20 for persons who are not employed or self-employed. It normally ends at 64 for women and 65 for men, the current official retirement age. If persons continue a gainful activity beyond this age they still must contribute, however, they benefit from an exempt amount. Persons pay proportionally to their income. Half of the contributions of employees are covered by the employer. The work of not employed spouses is also considered as a contribution so that they receive a pension when reaching the retirement age. The amount any contributor paid during his active life only determines to some extent the amount of the actual pension. Persons with high incomes get at most twice as much as persons with no or low income. The system leads to a rigorous redistribution.

- In 1959, the federal legislature introduced a general, mandatory insurance for disabled persons. Like the old-age pension scheme, also the insurance for disabled persons is paid by the active working generation. Accordingly, for employed contributors, again employee and employer contribute, proportionally to the employee's income. The insurance covers costs for living, reintegration, as well as costs for therapies. The Constitution puts an important emphasis on the reintegration into the workforce of disabled persons.
- Additional pension plans. The general old-age pension, as described above, only covers very basic needs but does not necessarily ensure that people can maintain their standard of living after retirement. In 1972, the general old-age pension has been supplemented by two more pillars, leading to a three-pillar pension system, the first pillar being the general old-age pension system described above, the second pillar establishing a mandatory employee pension scheme. For the second pillar, the employer and the employee are obliged to contribute in equal parts to a pension fund of the employer's choice. In contrast

to the first pillar which leads to a redistribution of money, funds from the second pillar are not redistributed. The employee is supposed to receive the total of the savings with interest (Article 113 of the Constitution). The third pillar is voluntary and encourages employees and self-employed persons by providing tax cuts to further economise and set aside money for the old age.

- Unemployment insurance (Article 114 of the Constitution). In 1951, the Confederation had established some basic principles for different public or private insurances covering unemployment. In 1976, the Constitution was amended to introduce a general insurance against unemployment. The contribution to this insurance is paid half by the employer and half by the employed. The respective law was adopted in 1982 and was revised since. Based on this law, as a rule, unemployed persons get a percentage of their salary for two years. The insurance can also pay additional costs for education and professional training.
- Assistance to needy persons (Article 115 of the Constitution). According to Article 12 of the Constitution persons in need have a constitutional enforceable right for assistance. Cantons are in change of assistance to the needy. Such need can for instance arise, once unemployment benefits run out.

(2) In addition, the Constitution provides for supplementary benefits in cases the system of social insurances cannot cover the basic living costs, i.e., supplementary benefits to the old-age and disability pension, for instance for persons who do not receive a full pension (Article 112a of the Constitution), rehabilitation of disabled peoples (Article 112b of the Constitution) and aid for elderly people and people with disabilities who are tended to at home (Article 112c of the Constitution):

- Family allocation and maternity insurance (Article 116 of the Constitution). Since 2009, general legislation has been enforced which principally guarantees family allowances for every child in Switzerland until the age of 16 and for their later education until they have reached the age of 25. The system is implemented by the existing cantonal agencies for the old-age scheme. The minimal rate is CHF 200 per month per child for children up to the age of 16 and CHF 250 per month up to the age of 25 for those children and young adults who continue their education. The cantons can increase this Swiss-wide guaranteed minimal rate. Although foreseen in the Constitution, there is still no general insurance covering the costs of maternity leave. Legislation obliges employers to pay 80% of the salary or a maximum of CHF 196 – per day to young mothers for a fourteen-week maternity leave. This system might lead to factual discrimination. Employers might be reluctant to employ women in order to avoid additional costs in case of maternity absence.
- Health and accident insurance (Article 117 of the Constitution). All persons with residence in Switzerland are obliged to be insured for health and accident. Insurances are provided by private insurance companies. Notwithstanding that the insurances are private they have the obligation to accept everyone. Contrary to the pension system, the health insurance is based on a flat rate contribution not dependent on the person's income or personal risk factors.

The insurance must cover necessary and economically reasonable therapies of illnesses as well as palliation. The insured pays a small part of the costs amongst others to raise the awareness about health costs. There is a special public foundation to provide for an equalization of the risks between the different insurance companies.

336. Traditionally, the cantons are in charge of health. They ensure hospital services, give medical licences and organize the system of health care within the canton. However, the Confederation has been assigned some powers in the field of health, mainly in response to developments of science and research. The Constitution sets clear goals and limits which the Confederation must achieve and respect. The Confederation's main obligation is the protection of health. For that, it regulates the handling of food and medical products, narcotics, organisms, chemicals and other substances that could harm health, it establishes provisions for the control of transmissible and particularly harmful diseases and for the protection of ionizing radiation (Article 118 of the Constitution). Though protection of health is the major goal, the Confederation is e.g. also called upon to protect the dignity of persons and of all living beings as well as to protect the biosphere. The Confederation and the cantons shall provide room for complementary medicine (Article 118a of the Constitution). Furthermore, the Confederation regulates research on human beings as far as necessary for the protection of human dignity and the personality of persons (Article 118b of the Constitution), and ensures the protection of human beings from the misuse of fertility medicine and gene technology (Article 119 of the Constitution). This provision is also a good example of detailed limitations, as it establishes principles that the legislator must abide to, including the prohibition of cloning or surrogate motherhood. In addition, the Confederation has the power to regulate organ transplant medicine (Article 119a of the Constitution) as well as gene technology focusing on animals and plants (Article 120 of the Constitution).

9. Residence and Domicile of Foreigners

337. The Confederation is in charge of regulating the residence and domicile of foreigners as well as of granting asylum. Within the last ten years there have been several amendments to this section of the Constitution, triggered by popular initiatives. For instance, in 2010 a popular initiative introduced a revocation of the right of residence when a person commits certain crimes or misuses the social security system. Also based on a popular initiative, the Confederation is called upon to independently regulate immigration (which potentially is in tension with agreements with the EU) and to determine a maximum number of residence permits for immigrating foreigners per year (*See also infra* Part IV, Chapter 4, §3).

10. Civil and Criminal Laws, Weights and Measures

338. Legislations in the areas of civil and criminal law are federal matters (Articles 122 and 123 of the Constitution). As set out *supra* in Part II, Chapter 5, §2 III and IV, the organization of the judiciary in civil and criminal matters (as well as penitentiaries) are within the competencies of the cantons. However, criminal and civil procedures are determined at the federal level. The laws on Civil and Criminal Procedure are in force since January 2011. In addition, the Confederation can legislate on the penal system and provide subsidies to the cantons for the establishment of penal institutions, to improve the execution of sentences, as well as to support institutions that implement educational measures for children and young adults. The Confederation and the cantons ensure support to victims of crimes (Article 124 of the Constitution).

339. In addition, as already mentioned above, the section on criminal law in the Constitution includes several articles that do not directly concern the distribution of powers between the Confederation and the cantons. Such provisions include the unlimited incarceration of highly dangerous sex offenders and violent felons (Article 123a of the Constitution), the non-applicability of the statute of limitation for sex-related and pornographic crimes with children (Article 123b of the Constitution) as well as the prohibition to work with minors or dependents for certain sex-offenders (Article 123c of the Constitution).

340. Legislation on weights and measures is also a federal matter.

VI. Constitutionally Guaranteed Shared Rule

341. The cantons are accorded a special input in the decision-making of the federal level. Because most aspects of shared rule have already been mentioned above, the following shall serve as a short summary.

342. The cantons are included in the constitution-making process. For the adoption of a new constitution or a constitutional amendment (for joining organizations for collective security or supranational organizations as well as in the case of certain federal statutes declared urgent), it requires a popular vote with a majority of the Swiss citizens and a majority of cantons voting yes (Articles 140(1) and 142 of the Constitution). *See supra* Part I, Chapter 2, §1 II and Part II, Chapter 2, §3 I and §4 II.

343. The cantons are represented in the second chamber of Parliament (Council of States), which has powers equal to those of the first chamber of Parliament. Although cantons regulate the election of their representatives in the second chamber (Article 150(3) of the Constitution), the direct influence of the cantons on the Council of States is limited. For instance, the cantonal governments may not instruct their Councillors (Article 161 of the Constitution). *See supra* Part II, Chapter 3.

344. The cantons are involved in the law-making process and are included in the preliminary phase of legal drafting (Article 147 of the Constitution). In most cases, it is the cantonal governments that participate in the preliminary procedure, whereas in other cases of cantonal involvement, the cantonal Parliament acts, as is the case in most cantons for the parliamentary initiative and the referendum. Each canton can launch parliamentary initiatives (not to be confounded with the popular initiative, *see supra* Part II, Chapter 2, §3). Eight cantons are needed to initiate a referendum against federal statutes, federal statutes declared urgent with a validity exceeding one year, federal decrees when foreseen by the Constitution or the statutes and international treaties which are (a) of unlimited duration, and (b) may not be terminated, which (c) provide for the entry into an international organization, or (d) contain important provisions that require a nomotechnical transformation into federal statutes (Article 141(1) of the Constitution).

345. Article 55 of the Constitution introduces the participation of the cantons in the preparation of foreign policy decisions, which concern cantonal powers or their essential interests. The Confederation shall inform the cantons and consult them. The opinion of the cantons shall particularly be taken into account when cantonal powers are concerned. In such cases, the cantons can directly participate in international negotiations – on behalf of the Confederation.

§3. Selected Aspects

Selected Bibliography: *See* General Bibliography for Part III and, *inter alia*, Abderhalden Ursula, 'Der kooperative Föderalismus'. In Fleiner et al., 213–221 (with further references); Biaggini Giovanni. 'Allgemeine Pflichten und Rechte bei der Umsetzung von Bundesrecht durch die Kantone'. In *Mensch und Staat*. Festgabe für Thomas Fleiner zum 65. Geburtstag, Schulthess 2003, 3 et seq.; Egli Patricia. *Die Bundestreue*. Zurich: Schulthess, 2010 (with further references); Forster Peter. 'Eigenständigkeit der Kantone, Vorrang und Einhaltung des Bundesrechts und Bundesgarantien'. In Fleiner et al., 133–134; Häfelin Ulrich. 'Der kooperative Föderalismus in der Schweiz'. *In Zeitschrift für Schweizerisches Recht [ZSR]*. 1969 II, 549 et seq.; Kälin Walter. 'Überprüfung kantonaler Verfassungsbestimmungen durch das Bundesgericht'. In *recht* 1986, 161 et seq.; Kölz Alfred. 'Bundestreue als Verfassungsprinzip?'. In *Schweizerisches Zentralblatt für Staats- und Verwaltungsrecht [ZBl]*. 1980, 145 et seq.; Roberts Julian. 'Solidarität und Gerechtigkeit als Verfassungsinhalte'. In Sitter-Liver, 27–42.

I. Supremacy Clause

346. According to European continental law systems, the legal order forms a unity in which the Constitution, different treaties, statutes, and ordinances of federal, cantonal and municipal governments are hierarchically classified. This is apparent both in the German Basic Law and in the system of the EU.

347. In Article 49, the Swiss Constitution determines that all levels of federal law take precedence over contrary cantonal law. According to this principle, even ordinances of the Federal Council (*supra* Part II, Chapter 4, §2 III) take precedence over cantonal constitutional law. The Confederation has the duty to ensure that the cantons respect federal law. The federal assembly is given the constitutional power to enforce federal law within the cantons (Article 173(e) of the Constitution).

348. Federal statutory law prevails irrespective of whether it is constitutional. The supremacy of federal law that is in accordance with the Constitution follows from the general rule of Articles 3 and 42 of the Constitution. Furthermore, unconstitutional federal statutory law prevails over cantonal law because of Article 190 of the Constitution, which orders the Federal Supreme Court to apply federal law regardless of its constitutionality.

349. The supremacy clause is a recognized constitutional right of the citizen (*verfassungsmässiges Recht*; *see infra* Part IV, Chapter 2, §1 I C). Contrary cantonal law is null and void – there is no need to engage further judicial proceedings. In case of doubt, an appeal in public law matters (*infra* Part IV, Chapter 5, §3 III) is available as a remedy to establish whether cantonal law contradicts federal law.

II. Partnership Between Confederation and Cantons

350. A federation can only exist based on the solidarity of its partners. In addition to the constitutionally instituted cooperation, Swiss federalism finds a complementary balance in a network of informal cooperation at all levels of government, as well as between labour unions and economic entities (the so-called social partners) although, due to its informal character, this network may often not be apparent. It is this *comity* of different partners that contributes to the unity of Switzerland.

351. Moreover, the complexity of state tasks and state obligations requires not only cooperation among magistrates and elected authorities, but also among civil servants of federal and cantonal administrations. This is the underlying philosophy of Article 44 of the Constitution. According to the constitutional provision, the Confederation and the cantons shall cooperate and support each other in the fulfilment of their tasks. Rather a political maxim than a normative principle (Decision of the Federal Supreme Court BGE 125 II 152, 163), the cantons and the Confederation owe each other *mutual consideration and support*, and shall grant each other administrative and judicial assistance.

352. The duty of solidarity is further illustrated in Article 44(3) of the Constitution, which states that disputes between cantons, or between cantons and the Confederation, shall whenever possible be resolved through mediation and negotiation.

III. Cantonal Autonomy Versus Cooperative Federalism

353. Although the Constitutions of 1848 and 1874 placed clear priority on competitive federalism and the autonomy of the cantons, since 1874, as a result of approximately 150 constitutional amendments and a total revision of the Constitution, the originally extensive powers of the cantons have slowly shifted to the federal level. This process of centralization gradually diminished cantonal autonomy. As a counterbalance, the Constitution of 1999 places more emphasis on the principle of cooperation than previous constitutions. Three major changes have been introduced in the Constitution of 1999:

(1) the right of cantons to participate in foreign policy decisions of the federal government;
(2) the general right to participate in the preparation of federal legislation; and
(3) the general possibility for cantons to regulate matters of general concern through international or inter-cantonal treaties.

354. The strengthening of the shared rule principle has not led, as one might expect, to a strengthening and widening of the powers of the second Chamber, as this chamber is already attributed with equal powers as the first chamber. The shared rule principle has been implemented instead by strengthening the possibilities for cantonal executive bodies to participate in the decision-making processes of the federal government. Cantonal executives created a new body, which represents all the cantonal governments. Thus, the widening of the shared rule principle at federal level has caused the establishment of a presidential council of cantonal governments. This, in turn, has led to better cooperation between cantonal governments and enabled the cantons to use new ways and means for cantonal and inter-cantonal partnership as well as cooperation. These new aspects of cooperative federalism lead Switzerland to a greater flexibility: For example, in the field of university education, the legislature has established a body – composed of representatives of cantonal governments and the Federal Council – who must plan and establish strategies for developing federal and cantonal universities. With this new 'superstructure', combining shared rule and self-rule in the field of higher education, Switzerland tries to meet the challenge of a 'European Area of Higher Education', proclaimed in the Bologna Declaration of 1999. There also are new tendencies that may lead to supra-cantonal cooperation on a regional basis, which are already partially realized in the field of professional education.

355. In addition, there are also forms of cooperation that include the municipalities. As a rule, the federal level has no direct contact with the municipalities. All its relations with the municipalities go through cantonal authorities. For instance, if the Confederation wants to provide subsidies to mountainous areas it gives them to the canton and the canton redistributes the money to the concerned municipalities. However, some exceptions to this rule exist. For instance, a tripartite conference on agglomerations was created in 2001 that includes representatives of all three levels of state and has the purpose to develop common policy for the fast-growing agglomerations in Switzerland. Thus, Swiss federalism is open for new administrative bodies, and new executive branches, as well as distinct regional organizations, potentially even regional parliaments, to fulfil specific tasks in an efficient and effective manner.

IV. Administrative Federalism

356. Contrary to the American system of dual federalism, the cantons implement federal law (administrative federalism). Consequently, the federal administration is rather small, with 34,915 full-time positions in 2016, and would be incapable of executing the federal law by itself. In comparison, the Canton of Zurich has an administration with approximately 33,800 full-time positions. While federal law binds the cantons in how they implement federal law, the Confederation must leave them as much leeway of action as possible as well as take the financial burden for and the particularities of the cantons into account (Article 46 of the Constitution). Depending on federal regulation, the cantons have varying degrees of discretion in the execution of federal norms. Due to the diversity among cantons with respect to size, topography, demography and other structural elements, it is nearly impossible for the Confederation to consider the particularities of the cantons unless it grants the cantons broad discretion.

V. Non-promotion of Equal Living Conditions

357. Article 72(2) of the German Basic Law provides general federal legislative power in case that a standardization of law should be necessary for the establishment of equal living conditions throughout the country. A similar provision is found in Article 130 of the Spanish Constitution, which provides that the 'public authorities shall attend to the modernization and development of all economic sectors, particularly of agriculture, livestock raising, fishing and handicrafts, in order to equalize the standard of living of all Spaniards'. Thus, these constitutions aim at equal opportunities and equal results.

358. The Swiss Constitution, however, guarantees neither equal opportunities nor equal results. Swiss federalism does *not* promote equality of living conditions among the cantons. Cantons and municipalities offer different standards of services, there are differences in respect to social assistance, and the tax burden differs. Diversity and autonomy can only be upheld if a certain degree of economic discrepancies among the different cantons – and even among the different municipalities – is permitted. Swiss federalism has always accepted this inequality for the sake of the autonomy of the cantons. Equalization would mean centralization. However, Article 43a(4) of the Constitution, now guarantees a comparable standard at least with regard to basic services. (For financial equalization, *see infra* Part V, Chapter 2, §2.)

359. The EU promotes an open market based on equal opportunities. Switzerland took some steps to put into force a law guaranteeing equal opportunities with regard to the internal market in Switzerland (Federal Internal Market Act, SR 943.02). According to this Act, several cantonal legislative modifications would be required in order to eradicate inter-cantonal discrimination. However, according to assessments not all cantons have followed these federal obligations.

360. In a state with a fragmented society, the issue of equality pertains not only to individuals, but also to the status of different cultural communities and religions. In Switzerland, equality of communities has often been given priority over equality of individuals. The term 'equal rights' can be understood in two ways:

(1) the *right to be equal*; and
(2) the *right to equal rights*.

If persons belonging to the small indigenous Romansh community had only equal rights, they would always be considered or would consider themselves second-class citizens. In a society relying solely on the concept of individual equality, the Romansh community would remain a tiny minority that could easily be outvoted and therefore might feel de facto discrimination. Also, a quality radio programme in Romansh is likely to cost more per Romansh-speaking listener than one catering to the much bigger German-speaking community. If the Romansh community shall have the right to be equal, they must be accepted on equal terms as a cultural community. Switzerland is seeking a balance between equal individual rights and the right to be respected as equal even when belonging to a different cultural group.

Chapter 2. The Cantons

§1. The Position of the Cantons in the Confederation

Selected Bibliography: *See* General Bibliography for Part III and, *inter alia,* Abderhalden Ursula. *Möglichkeiten und Grenzen der interkantonalen Zusammenarbeit.* Fribourg, 1999; Jaag Tobias. 'Die Rechtsstellung der Kantone in der Bundesverfassung'. In Thürer et al., §30; on sovereignty *see* especially Fleiner & Basta Fleiner, 306 et seq.; Ruch Alexander. 'Äussere und innere Sicherheit'. In Thürer et al., §56; Forster Peter. 'Eigenständigkeit der Kantone, Vorrang und Einhaltung des Bundesrechts und Bundesgarantien'. In Fleiner et al., 136–140; Basta Fleiner & Lidija, R. 'Minority and Legitimacy of a Federal State: An Outsider Perception of the Swiss Model'. In Basta Fleiner & Fleiner, 90–94; Frey Bruno, S. *Ein neuer Föderalismus für Europa: Die Idee der FOCJ (Functional, Overlapping, Competing Jurisdictions).* Tübingen, 1997; Mahon, 101 et seq.; Saladin Peter. 'Bund und Kantone, Autonomie und Zusammenwirken im schweizerischen Bundesstaat'. In *Zeitschrift für Schweizerisches Recht [ZSR].* 1984, 431 et seq. For further references *see also* St. Galler Kommentar and Rhinow, Schefer & Uebersax, 152 et seq.

361. The cantons formed the Confederation based on a system of treaties among cantons and transformed into a federation with the adoption of the Constitution of 1848. The Swiss Confederation is a bottom-up federation which has been developed out of the sovereignty of the cantons. The nation-building process of the nineteenth century focused mainly on the democratization of the cantons. The diversity of the cantons regarding language, culture and religion is obvious. However even within the same language community or religion there are important diversities. Zurich is a canton which developed out of guilds and which since the thirteenth century has always been the pace-maker regarding the development of democracy. Basel-Land has separated from the city (Basel Stadt) based on a revolution of the Bourgeois who were strongly influenced by ideas from Rousseau against the Aristocrats of the city. As a consequence, for instance, the organization of courts is much less aristocratic in Basel-Land than in the canton of Berne with the strong aristocratic tradition of the City of Berne. Cantons with two or more languages differ in organization from monolingual cantons. Cantons which traditionally faced divisions between the catholic and the protestant denomination have different concepts about communal schools. Each canton developed its governance system according to its very specific context. Thus, each canton has not only its cultural, religious and language identity, but it has also its special constitutional and political identity. Although today mobility of the population is rising, many Swiss citizens still feel closely attached to their canton of origin.

362. The cantons are territorially based legal entities with a special public law status, whose rights and duties are equal, even though the status of the half-cantons is slightly inferior to the status of the other cantons. Half-cantons have only one representative in the Council of States, in contrast to the two seats of the other cantons (Article 150(2) of the Constitution, *supra* Part II, Chapter 3, III and IV). Additionally, in cases of mandatory referendum for which the approval of the People and the cantons is needed, the half-cantons are attributed only half a vote (Article 142(3) of the Constitution). In all other aspects – for instance in respect to their autonomy – the half-cantons are equal to the other cantons.

363. Cantons have a relatively high degree of autonomy, particularly with respect to their own organization, legislation and finances, but their autonomy is also restricted by federal law. As a counterbalance to these restrictions, the federal level guarantees the cantonal constitutional order and assures the existence and territorial integrity of the cantons.

364. The discussion below focuses on the constitutionally established notion of cantonal sovereignty, cantonal autonomy and its restrictions, the federal guarantees and the political organization of the cantons.

I. Cantonal Sovereignty

A. Principle

365. As a bottom-up federation, in 1848, the sovereign cantons gave only very few powers to the federation. It seems that the cantons were only prepared to accept federal powers for subject matters that were considered necessary for this new polity to survive. The constitutional settlement between the formerly conflicting cantons required a clear compromise between the liberal cantons which preferred a strong democratic and liberal new nation-state and the conservative mostly catholic cantons which resisted any development which could affect their traditional identity and sovereignty. Thus, according to Article 3 of the Constitution, the cantons are sovereign insofar as their sovereignty is not limited by the Constitution. The content of this provision as well as its wording and its place as Article 3 remained unchanged through the revision of 1874 and of 1999, although the content of the sovereignty of the cantons has de facto diminished considerably since 1848.

B. Concept of Sovereignty

366. Since the development of the theory of sovereignty by its founder Jean Bodin in the sixteenth century, sovereignty remains a disputed concept in relation to federations and in the theory of federalism. While some argue that in federal systems, either the federal state or the subunits have undivided sovereignty (Laband, Jellinek), others argue for a sovereignty of the *Gesamtstaat*, encompassing the federal level and the subunits (Nawiasky), or for divided sovereignty between the federal state and the sub-entities (Tocqueville, Madison, Fleiner). Based on the difficulties of finding a concept of sovereignty which corresponds with the reality of the federal state, some do not rely on the sovereignty argument at all. Three different issues should be kept in mind:

(1) In accordance with Article 3 of the Constitution which mentions cantonal sovereignty, the cantons kept their residual power. Unless the federal constitution

transmits powers to the Confederation, the cantons are the sole decision-makers. This can be considered as an argument in favour of cantonal sovereignty.

(2) However, based on a procedure established in the Constitution, the federal constitution can always confer new powers to the Confederation. The Confederation thus has the so-called competence-competence. Many authors argue that the cantons have lost their sovereignty because the federal constitution can, based on a double majority, always diminish their powers.

(3) This reduction of sovereignty to a mere legal and formal formula does not fit to the actual reality. The emergence of new semi-sovereign international organizations such as the EU requires a more realistic and therefore relative concept of sovereignty.

C. Relative Sovereignty

367. In the era of globalization, sovereignty as the idea of the 'Big Bang' to which the state owes its existence and from which all state authority flows is not congruent with reality. Because of internationally established formal and informal limitations, the state can only claim to hold a part of sovereignty. Thus, if sovereignty is divisible, then it can be divided internally (among the federal level and federal units) and can even be transferred externally, e.g. in the case of adhesion to supranational organizations. This presupposes a new concept of sovereignty. Sovereignty is not simply power or authority, but rather the foundation of the *legitimacy* of the state. The division of powers and tasks according to the principle of subsidiarity, but also legitimacy and democratic decision-making, are the foundations of genuine federalism. International or regional integration – if the people opt for it – is a natural and organic progression for a polity that has developed bottom up from the municipality to the federal unit up to the federation (*see also infra* Part III, Chapter 2, II).

368. According to this view, the formulation in Article 3 of the Constitution has not only its historical reasons but it is also based on the idea that the cantons as well as the Confederation have some kind of state quality because they have the legitimacy of their population to exert public authority and public power.

D. Missing State-Hood Quality According to International Law

369. Cantons have a cantonal territory and a cantonal People as well as relative sovereignty. Many cantons call themselves a *State* or a *Republic* (e.g., the cantons of Ticino, Neuchâtel, Geneva and Jura). However, international law considers the state as the direct addressee of international law. From an international law perspective, the cantons are not considered an active (treaty-making power) or passive (respondent in an international court) subject to international law – despite of their limited treaty-making power based on Article 56 of the Constitution. A treaty-based relationship between cantons and foreign states can only be established by the Confederation on behalf of the cantons. The parties of such treaties remain the sovereign states (Article 6 of the Vienna Convention on the Law of Treaties).

E. Federation or Confederation?

370. The official name of Switzerland is *Confoederatio Helvetica*. The Latin name, from which the official abbreviation of Switzerland *CH* derives, was maintained because, in 1848, it was not possible to reach consensus on a new name. In German, the name is traditionally Schweizerische Eidgenossenschaft which for lack of terminology cannot be translated in either of the other Swiss languages.

371. Although by name Switzerland calls itself a Confederation it is nevertheless, a federation, not a Confederation. Even in the title of the French, Italian and Romansh version of the Constitution, there is a clear contradiction as it is called 'Federal Constitution of the Swiss Confederation'. A Confederation is an international comprehensive organization of sovereign powers coordinated by an international treaty which can only be changed by a unanimous consent of the Member States. Since 1848, Switzerland is however based on a Constitution which can be amended, changed and even totally revised by a double majority of the People and the cantons. Individual cantons have no veto power. Federalism can be defined as 'constitutionally guaranteed self-rule and shared rule'. The cantonal autonomy (self-rule) and their participation in the decision-making at the federal level are guaranteed by the constitution of the Confederation. The existence of the cantons, their autonomy and the scope of their powers can only be changed by Constitutional amendment in a procedure in which the cantons participate from the initial stage and which requires the consent of at least half of the cantons.

372. In addition, the cantons now have a constitutional guarantee that the Confederation must respect the principle of subsidiarity in the allocation and performance of all tasks (Article 5a of the Constitution). With this provision, the federal constitution has followed the example of Article 3a of the treaty of Lisbon establishing the EU.

373. In this monograph, the terms 'federation' and 'Confederation' are used inter-changeably with respect to Switzerland. While the term' federation' is technically speaking correct, the term 'Confederation' is commonly used due to historical reasons.

II. Cantonal Autonomy and Its Restrictions

A. Cantonal Autonomy

374. In comparison to other federations, the cantons have maintained a relatively large amount of autonomy despite the strong trend towards centralization. They have the residual power – all powers that the federal constitution does not attribute to the federal level remain with the cantons (Articles 3, 42 and 43 of the Constitution). In addition, they are also granted autonomy by the principle of subsidiarity now enshrined in Article 5a of the Constitution. Autonomy is further ensured by the relatively high level of financial autonomy.

375. Cantonal autonomy includes the autonomous right of self-organization, under which the cantons have adopted their own constitution, their own coat of arms and in some cases even their own cantonal anthem. The cantons decide on their concept of direct democracy, their form of government and the structure of cantonal institutions, although with some limitations. The limitations mainly concern minimum requirements in respect to the democratic organization of the polity and the political rights of the peoples including the people's right to initiate constitutional amendments and the non-discrimination of citizens from other cantons. In addition, the cantons decide within the principle of the rule of law on the organization of their judiciary. The territorial organization of the cantons including the cantonal system of districts and municipalities also forms part of the organizational autonomy of the cantons. It is also up to the cantons to decide how much autonomy they accord to their municipalities. Further, the cantons maintain financial autonomy through their power to tax citizens; within their autonomy they decide on their taxes and expenditures (*see infra* Part V, Chapter 2, §1). The cantons are responsible to maintain order and security within their territory. To fulfil this task, cantons have their own police (Article 57 of the Constitution).

376. Should the federation violate its mandate to respect the cantonal autonomy (Articles 5a and 47 of the Constitution), the cantons can take recourse to the Federal Supreme Court. The possibility of recourse is however limited by the fact that the federal tribunal has no power to review federal statutes even though they might violate constitutionally guaranteed cantonal autonomy (Article 190 of the Constitution). The protection of cantonal autonomy is not only in the abstract interest of cantonal authorities it also is in the political interest of the citizens because their possibility to influence legislation through their democratic rights are even more robust at the cantonal than at the federal level.

377. By conferring powers and tasks to the Confederation, the Constitution restricts cantonal autonomy. First, we shall look into the restrictions and then into the support and promotion of cantonal autonomy by the Confederation.

B. Federal Restrictions on Cantonal Autonomy

1. Approval of the Cantonal Constitution

378. Cantons have the right and the duty to adopt their own subnational constitution. According to the federal Constitution, the adoption and revision of cantonal constitutions must be approved by the Confederation. On behalf of the Confederation, the Federal Parliament (Article 172 of the Constitution) shall grant the approval if the cantonal constitution is not contrary to federal law (Article 51(2) of the Constitution). The question of approval or denial of approval is a legal question. The Federal Parliament has no political discretion in its decision. The federal approval is a prerequisite for the validity of the cantonal constitutional provisions. The non-validity of single provisions does not impede the validity of the overall constitution. However, the Confederation does not have the means to prevent the cantons from including not approved provisions in the cantonal publication of the Constitution. The official cantonal publication of the Constitution of the Canton of Jura for example, includes a provision that declares the aim to reunite a part of the geographical region, which is currently part of the Canton of Berne, with the Canton of Jura. This provision was not approved by the Confederation because of its opposition to the federal guarantee of the territory of the cantons (*see infra* Part III, Chapter 2, §1 III) and the solidarity principle. While the *official federal publication* of the Constitution of the Canton of Jura omits this disputed provision, within the cantonal publication it had remained although with a footnote saying that the federal assembly has not approved this provision (*see* Article 138 of the Constitution of the Canton of Jura https://rsju.jura.ch/fr/viewdocument.html?idn=20002&id=36641 (last visited June 2017)).

379. Federal Parliament is very reluctant to deny the approval of constitutional provisions. There are only a limited number of additional cases in which approval was denied, for instance the Federal Parliament denied approval of a provision on the electoral system in the Constitution of the Canton of Schwyz that was not in line with long-standing rulings of the Federal Supreme Court; furthermore, Federal Parliament denied approval for a provision in the Constitution of the Canton of Geneva that excluded clergy from the right to be elected as member of the auditing institution. On the other hand, for instance, Federal Parliament approved a constitutional provision that mandated a canton to take all possible measures to prevent the establishment of a nuclear power-plant on the cantonal territory, even though this provision can be regarded as opposed to the principle of comity (*see supra* Part III, Chapter 1, §3 II) as well as a constitutional provision in the Canton of Ticino that mandates the canton to set minimum wages. In the latter case, the Federal Council in its message to the Federal Parliament argued that it is possible to interpret this provision in conformity with the federal Constitution and thus should be approved (*see*, BBl 2017, 1505). The Canton of Ticino is seeking the approval of a further constitutional amendment that wants to give employment preference to persons domiciled within the Canton of Ticino. It is not clear yet whether the Parliament will grant approval.

2. Federal Restrictions Concerning the Cantonal Organization

380. The federal constitution, the federal statutory law and the Federal Supreme Court established a series of restrictions concerning cantonal organization, based on their interpretation of federal and international law. The list given below is not all-inclusive:

(1) *Written constitution.* According to Article 51(1) of the Constitution, the cantons must adopt a cantonal constitution. In accordance with this provision, all the cantons have adopted *written constitutions.*
(2) *Democratic constitution.* The federal constitution sets minimum standards for the content of cantonal constitutions. According to Article 51(1) of the Constitution, the cantonal constitution must be *democratic.* It is from this provision that the requirement of cantonal *separation of powers* is deducted.
(3) *Constitutional Referendum.* The canton must hold a popular vote in order to *adopt or amend* its cantonal constitution.
(4) *Constitutional Initiative.* The federal constitution mandates the cantons to foresee a *constitutional initiative.* A majority of the People of the cantons can demand that a proposal for the amendment of the constitution is submitted to the People in a cantonal vote. However, all cantons have established a lower requisite number of signatures for the constitutional initiative than the one established in the Federal constitution (*see supra* Part II, Chapter 2, §3 II).

(5) *Cantonal Elections and Voting*. Under Article 39(2) of the Constitution, the cantons are restricted in defining their *electorate*. The Federal constitution proscribes that all Swiss domiciled in the canton have the same political rights. Therefore, the cantons cannot give special political rights to their citizens who live outside of the canton, and they cannot exclude Swiss citizens who do not have cantonal citizenship (for citizenship *see infra* Part IV, Chapter 1). Based on the non-discrimination principle established in Article 8 of the Constitution (or Article 4 of the Constitution of 1874), the Federal Supreme Court deduced several restrictions for the cantonal organization. Several cases concerned cantonal elections and voting. In *Theresa Rohner* (Decision of the Federal Court BGE 116 Ia 359) the Court held that the cantons must allow women the right to vote and hold public office. Further, in the *Quota* case (Decision of the Federal Court BGE 123 I 152), the Court decided that allowing women a quota in relation to their share in the cantonal population in the cantonal parliament, government and the courts is in violation of the non-discrimination principle.

(6) *Cantonal Authorities*. In several cases based on the ECHR, the Federal Supreme Court established criteria for the establishment of the right to an independent judge, to independent courts (Decisions of the Federal Supreme Court BGE 123 I 87, 121 II 53) and access to justice (Article 29a of the Constitution). The cantons must also establish independent judicial authorities for all administrative law matters that can be brought to the Federal Supreme Court (*see* Part II, Chapter 5, §2).

381. The federal level can define which or what kind of cantonal authorities shall implement federal law; in some cases, federal law proscribes the creation of new institutions. For instance, the cantons have the duty to establish cantonal laboratories for food control purposes. In other instances, federal law mandates that the cantons establish judicial authorities, e.g., the authority for the surveillance of tutelage.

3. Federal Restrictions Concerning the Cantonal Activities

382. Cantonal activities, including legislative activities, must not be opposed to federal law and shall be based on the principle of comity (*see supra* Part II, Chapter 1, §3 II).

To assure that federal law is not violated, the Confederation must take the necessary measures to ensure the implementation of federal law, cantonal constitutions and inter-cantonal treaties (Articles 186(4) and 173(1)(e) of the Constitution. Two different types of federal control can be distinguished: preventive control and repressive control.

383. The duty to submit the cantonal constitutions for approval is one case of a *preventive control*. Formerly, under the Constitution of 1874, cantonal treaties also required approval of the Confederation. Today, cantonal treaties need only the approval of Federal Parliament when the Federal Council or another canton protests the treaty (*see infra* Part V, Chapter 1, §3). Cantonal statutes and regulations will only be submitted to preventive control when a federal act explicitly foresees such approval procedure.

For instance, the Federal Civil Code requires that the cantons must submit their introductory legislation for approval.

384. Repressive control can consist of:

(1) the revocation of a cantonal act – this is mainly problematic when the cantonal act has already entered into force, normally such control is limited to a legality control unless federal statutes foresee a more far-reaching control;
(2) the curbing of subsidies – there must however be a nexus between the violation of a cantonal duty and the subsidy in question;
(3) the execution by substitution – in this case federal authorities act instead of the canton to fulfil the cantonal duty, and as *ultima ratio*;
(4) the military federal executive measure – under which the Confederation can use military means to force the cantons to fulfil their duties.

In contrast to the federal intervention (*see infra* C 1) which aims to support cantonal authorities, the military federal executive measure is directed against cantonal authorities who do not fulfil their duties. So far, this has never been applied.

III. Federal Guarantees

385. However, the Confederation does not only restrict the cantonal authority but also supports the cantons to uphold their autonomy. The Confederation guarantees the cantonal constitutional order, as well as the existence and territory of the cantons.

A. Guarantee of the Cantonal Constitutional Order

386. According to Article 52(1) of the Constitution, the Confederation shall protect the constitutional order of the cantons. In this provision, constitutional order is understood in a narrow sense. It encompasses security within the territory of the canton as well as the proper functioning and integrity of constitutionally established cantonal institutions. The constitutional provision establishes a duty to protect in the case of unrest and constitutional crises. While primary responsibility for ensuring constitutional order lies with the cantons (Article 57 of the Constitution), the Confederation and the other cantons are called to support the concerned canton if the canton cannot ensure its own constitutional order (*principle of comity*). This duty of support is based on Article 44(1) and (2) of the Constitution, which states that the Confederation and the cantons shall support each other in the fulfilment of their tasks.

387. A *federal intervention* is foreseen when the inner order of a canton is disturbed or threatened and cannot be protected by the canton alone or with the help of other cantons (Article 52(2) of the Constitution). The Confederation will only intervene when the general support to the canton is not sufficient to re-establish the constitutional order and when the disturbance of the constitutional order does not emanate from a cantonal institution or agency. The measures to be taken for reestablishment of the constitutional order are decided by the respective federal agency – in most cases, the Federal Council. In several instances, the Confederation has delegated a commissioner to the concerned canton to act as representative of the Federal Council and to issue orders towards the cantonal executive and legislature. As *ultima ratio*, the Confederation can intervene with military force. There have been ten such military interventions since 1848, with the last one taking place in Geneva in 1932. In that case, leftists had tried to disturb a meeting of right-wing extremists. When the situation got out of hand, the Canton of Geneva requested the support of the Federal Council, who sent military troops. Federal Parliament can decide who covers the costs for the intervention.

388. As an alternative to federal intervention, the Federal Military Act of 3 February 1995 (SR 510.10) foresees the possibility that the Confederation can provide the concerned canton with troops that act under the direction of the canton. Troops may only be sent when there is a serious threat to the cantonal order, and the decision to send troops must be taken by Federal Parliament. If there is an absolute immediate threat and Federal Parliament is not in session, the Federal Council has authority to put troops of a limited number and for a limited time at the disposal of the canton. For any extension of the mandate, Federal Parliament must be convened. Through this measure, the canton can continue to act independently while relying on military forces.

B. Guarantee of the Existence and Territory of the Cantons

389. At the time of the formation of the federation in 1848, the cantonal territory was not disputed, and only some areas that had been subject to disagreements had later been defined in treaties or in court opinions.

390. The Confederation has the duty to protect the existence and territory of the cantons (Article 53(1) of the Constitution). Changes in the number of cantons or the redistribution of territory are only permissible in accordance with the constitutional procedure of Article 53(2) and (3) of the Constitution.

391. The former Constitutions of 1848 and 1874 did not foresee a procedure for territorial modifications. The rules introduced in Article 53 of the Constitution are the result of experiences with territorial modifications. The most important example of a territorial modification was the creation of the Canton of Jura in 1978.

392. The now established procedure for territorial changes includes as its main element the consent of the concerned populations. Article 53 of the Constitution distinguishes three different cases of modification that concern the existence and territory of the cantons.

393. (1) The modification can concern the total number of cantons, or it can change their status (Article 53(2) of the Constitution). The number of cantons can be increased – e.g., through the creation of a new canton as in the case of the creation of the Canton of Jura – or the number can be decreased – e.g., through the merger of two cantons. The status of the cantons can be changed – e.g., by elevating a half-canton to the status of ordinary canton. In these cases, the modification must be based of the consent of the populations concerned, of the cantons concerned, and of the People and the cantons. The procedure requires a cascade of popular votes on the district and/or communal level, on the cantonal level, and on the federal level to create the highest possible legitimacy for the new boundaries. The creation of a new canton needs the consent of:

(1) the population inhabiting it;
(2) the population inhabiting the canton that the territory formerly belonged to;
(3) the Swiss population; and
(4) a majority of cantonal populations.

Changes in the number and the status of the cantons must fulfil the requirements of a constitutional amendment because the constitutional text must be changed (Article 1 with the enumeration of the cantons, in the case of a change of status additionally Articles 142 and 150(2) of the Constitution). Switzerland is one of the very few countries that has an established procedure for such internal secession. The creation of the Canton of Jura is the main case of a change in the number of cantons in recent history. The attempt to create a 'new' bigger Canton of Jura failed. In addition, the Canton of Basel Stadt and the Canton of Basel Land considered merging. However, this attempt failed in 2014 when the People of Basel Land voted against it.

394. (2) The modification can concern the cantonal territory without changing the number of cantons or their status – e.g., through the change of the municipality of one canton to another canton, as was the case with the municipality of Vellerat, which left the Canton of Berne to join the Canton of Jura (Article 53(3) of the Constitution). Similarly, in June 2017 the municipality of Moutier decided to leave the Canton of Berne and become part of the Canton of Jura. According to the established procedure, such modifications must be based on the consent of the population concerned and of the cantons concerned. At the federal level, the assent of Federal Parliament in the form of a federal decree (not submitted to a popular referendum) suffices.

395. Before the introduction of Article 53(3) of the Constitution, territorial changes were also submitted to the approval of the People and the Cantons based on the argument that even though no explicit change of the federal Constitution was necessary, the procedure for the amendment of the Constitution should be applied because of the federal guarantee of cantonal territory and the possible effect on the internal power balance in Switzerland. The framers of Article 53 of the Constitution decided on a lower standard in order to avoid popular votes on the federal level that in most cases directly affect only a small number of inhabitants.

396. (3) Finally, the modification can concern small boundary settlements. Such border settlements can be made by treaties between the cantons concerned.

IV. Inter-cantonal Treaties and Cooperation

397. The tasks the cantons are supposed to fulfil have become more and more complex and interconnected. The complexity and interconnectedness of tasks creates on the one hand a pressure towards the unification of cantonal law and, on the other hand, pressure towards an enhancement of cooperation between cantons. In order to prevent the transferal of powers to the federal level, the cantons try to reach the necessary unification of law and cooperation through *inter-cantonal treaties*.

398. According to Article 48(1) of the Constitution, the cantons may conclude inter-cantonal treaties (called *concordats*). Such concordats may not be opposed to the law, including the distribution of powers between the Confederation and the cantons, the interests of the Confederation, and the rights of other cantons. The Confederation must be notified of such treaties (Article 48(3) of the Constitution).

399. Inter-cantonal treaties can regulate subject matters, such as administrative agreements or a unification of legislation, and can create common institutions. Political inter-cantonal treaties are prohibited if they violate the principle of comity laid down in Article 44(2) of the Constitution. Concordats can be concluded between two or more cantons, and the Confederation can be party to the treaty and/or can participate in the common institutions (Article 48(2) of the Constitution). This provision is of relevance in areas where the federal level and the cantons have parallel powers. For instance, the Confederation is party to the concordat on the equivalence of scientific degrees. Based on this concordat, the criteria for the equivalence of high school diplomas were unified. The concordat may not transfer cantonal powers to the federal level, and the Confederation may only get involved in areas where the Constitution foresees a federal power.

400. Inter-cantonal institutions are mainly introduced for implementation purposes. In some cases, the concordat delegates to these institutions the power to issue regulations. Due to the legality principle, these regulations may only concern issues of minor importance.

401. Inter-cantonal treaties allow for flexible cooperation between cantons and the Confederation. The cooperation for schooling can be different from one for environmental protection or land planning. Frey suggests a system of functional overlapping of competing jurisdictions (FOCJ). According the FOCJ system, more competition shall be introduced. The possibility of free choice is enhanced because different overlapping subunits offer services to the People. This can create a system that is difficult for citizens to understand. For politicians and the civil servants, the multiple forms of cooperation create the necessity of a high level of coordination. The main challenge for these kinds of cooperation is to assure democratic control of inter-cantonal bodies.

402. The cantons regulate the procedure for joining inter-cantonal treaties. The Canton of Grisons demands a mandatory referendum for all inter-cantonal treaties, while in many other cantons the cantonal parliament can decide on the adhesion without the possibility of a referendum (e.g., Obwalden, Zug, Schaffhausen, Appenzell Innerrhoden, St. Gallen, Fribourg, Ticino and Geneva). All other cantons require a mandatory referendum for the more important inter-cantonal treaties, particularly those that include the unification of law.

403. The number of concordats is rising steadily. They can be found on a full-text search by Lex-Find (www.lexfind.ch). With Article 48a of the Constitution, the Confederation has even got the power to declare concordats that are open to all cantons and concern a number of issues enumerated in the Constitution as generally applicable.

404. The cantons rely today on very close inter-cantonal cooperation affecting almost all areas of cantonal powers. Although small cantons and cantons depending economically on each other would rationally have an interest to merge emotionally the people are connected to their cantonal identity and are not willing to abandon their symbol of independence. For this reason, proposals planning the merger of cantons have up to now been rejected for political reasons. Even proposals to completely review the federal system and to decentralize the Confederation on economical and functional bases have never had any real political support.

§2. Organization of the Cantons

Selected Bibliography: *See* General Bibliography for Part III and, *inter alia,* Germann Raimund, E. 'Die Kantone: Gleichheit und Disparität'. In Klöti et al., 398–401; Nuspliger Kurt. 'Grundzüge der Behördenstruktur im Verfassungsrecht der Kantone'. In Thürer et al., §69.

I. Right to Self-Organization

405. Within the limitations established by federal law, the cantons have the right to self-organization (for the federal limitations, *see supra* §1, II, B). This allows the cantons to develop their institutions in accordance with their traditions and to preserve their specificities. The organization of the cantons is established in the cantonal constitutions. The cantonal constitutions differ decisively from each other mainly depending on the date of their adoption. The older constitutions often include only rudimentary provisions and seem relatively unsystematic. The newer constitutions – those adopted in the last twenty years – are normally very systematic and include a Bill of Rights, along with provisions concerning the organization of the cantons and providing for the political rights of the citizens of initiative and referendum.

406. The cantons can decide on the organization of their territory (*see supra* General Introduction, Chapter 3; *infra* Part III, Chapter 3), on the setup of institutions, and how those institutions operate. They can limit their own cantonal powers or they can delegate part of their powers to districts or municipalities. While the actual organization of the cantons shows some similarities between cantons, and between the cantons and the Confederation, there are nevertheless important nuances in cantonal organization. Besides their concept of decentralization, they differ mainly regarding their concept of direct democracy.

II. Forms of Cantonal Organization

A. Cantonal People

407. The possibilities of the cantons to determine to whom they want to confer political rights are limited (*see supra* Part III, Chapter 2, §1 II B). The cantons have the option to give non-Swiss persons the right to vote, elect and be elected. Presently, the cantons of Jura and Neuchâtel are the only cantons that accord the right to vote and elect to foreigners. All persons who are domiciled in the canton for a certain period of time can participate in elections and voting at the cantonal level. So far, for cantonal elections, no canton provides the right to foreigners to stand for election. (For political rights at the municipal level, *see infra* Chapter 3, II B.)

408. The citizens are more powerful at the cantonal level than at the federal level. For instance, in the cantons, the citizens elect the members of the cantonal parliament, the cantonal government and in some cases, they can also elect some of the judges, civil servants and the teachers. Further, the cantons provide more direct democratic rights to influence cantonal policies than the Confederation for federal policies (*see supra* Part II, Chapter 2, §3 and §4).

409. In most cantons, elections are decided by secret ballot. However, two cantons, the Canton of Appenzell Innerrhoden and the Canton of Glarus, are still governed by an assembly of the People (*Landsgemeinde*), which is derived from the thirteenth century. This institution includes all citizens that inhabit the canton, and it normally convenes once a year. The *Landsgemeinde* elects the cantonal government (Appenzell Innerrhoden), the members of the higher courts and higher civil servants. In addition, the *Landsgemeinde* has constitution-making, legislative as well as certain executive powers. The voting takes place by raising the hand, the votes are estimated and only exceptionally they are counted. Switzerland does not consider that such open voting in small assemblies violates the principle of secrecy of voting. (Note: Switzerland has signed but not ratified the first protocol of the European Human Rights Convention which in Article 3 guarantees freedom of election.)

410. The cantons of Nidwalden, Appenzell Ausserrhoden and Obwalden respectively abolished their *Landsgemeinde* in 1996, 1997 and 1998.

B. Cantonal Parliament

411. All cantons have a parliament. These parliaments are composed of one chamber and they meet in regular sessions. Similar to Federal Parliament, the cantonal parliaments are based on the militia system. Members of parliament are not full-time parliamentarians – they are expected to continue working in their professions.

412. The number of members of parliament differs in each canton. The Canton of Obwalden has the smallest parliament with fifty-five representatives. The Canton of Berne has the largest parliament with 200 members. All cantons, except for the cantons of Ticino and Grisons, elect their representatives based on the proportional system. Finally, the cantons of Lucerne, Uri, Obwalden, Nidwalden and Appenzell Innerrhoden require elected citizens to accept their election to the parliament (*Amtszwang*).

413. The cantonal parliaments' principal tasks are legislation, budgeting and control of cantonal administration. However, due to the more important role of direct democracy at the cantonal level, the powers of the cantonal parliaments are more limited than those of Federal Parliament. According to Article 43 of the Constitution, the cantons can decide within their powers what tasks they want to fulfil. In other words, the cantons are not obliged to assume the powers they have. Some cantons self-restrict their right to assume tasks. For example, the constitutions of the cantons of Aargau and Basel-Land foresee that the assumption of new tasks needs a basis in the cantonal constitution. If the canton wishes to assume new tasks, it must first amend the cantonal constitution so as to introduce the necessary constitutional basis. These provisions are designed to prevent an over-regulation by the state.

414. In addition to being involved in the legislative process, the cantonal parliaments determine cantonal taxes, vote on the budget, approve accounts and decide on spending. Here again the powers are limited by the means of direct democracy, especially by the financial referendum (*see supra* Part II, Chapter 2, §4 III).

415. In a majority of the cantons, the parliament elects the members of the higher courts. In all cantons, the members of the executive are elected by the People.

416. The sessions of the parliamentary meetings differ decisively depending on the tradition, size and demography.

C. Cantonal Executive

417. The cantonal executive has a position similar to the Federal Council *see supra* Part II, Chapter 4). Historically, the members of the cantonal executive are independent from the parliament. They decide as council normally by consensus or by majority. The executive functions as a collegial organ in which all members are peers to each other. The President has no exceptional powers; he/she determines, prepares and facilitates the meetings. Most cantons have seven members in the executive. Some cantons have only five. In contrast to the Federal Council, the cantonal governments are not elected by the Parliament but directly by the People. In most cantons, the election of the government is based on the majority principle, although the cantons of Zug and Ticino elect their government members according to the proportional system. Three cantons require a minimum age for the members of cantonal government (twenty-five in the cantons of Fribourg and Schwyz, twenty-seven in the Canton of Geneva). Some smaller cantons have a government based on the militia system, but the more populous cantons have governments composed of remunerated full-time members.

418. The cantons of Lucerne, Uri, Schwyz, Obwalden and Appenzell Innerrhoden require citizens to serve in the cantonal government if elected (*Amtszwang*).

419. The function of cantonal governments is to rule and represent the canton and to manage the cantonal administration. Cantonal governments have collective decision-making structures, and every member of government is also head of a department (ministry) of the cantonal administration. Finally, the President of the government is elected either by the People (Canton of Uri), the *Landsgemeinde* (Appenzell Innerrhoden and Glarus), by the cantonal parliament (German-speaking cantons), or by the government itself (French-, Italian- and Romansh-speaking cantons). As a rule, three to five political parties are represented in the cantonal government. Only the government of the Canton of Appenzell Innerrhoden is a one-party council (however, including two independent members).

D. Cantonal Courts

420. The cantons have important autonomy with respect to the court system, which differs significantly not only among cantons, but also between the different administrative, civil, criminal and specialized courts within the canton; *see supra* Part II, Chapter 5.

Chapter 3. The Municipalities

Selected Bibliography: *See* General Bibliography for Part III and, *inter alia,* Braaker Christa. 'Die Gemeindeautonomie'. In Fleiner et al., 225–246; Dafflon Bernard. 'Structure communales: qu'est-ce qui distingue la collaboration intercommunale, l'agglomération et la fusion?'. *Journée d'étude: Réformes et Politiques communales*. Berne, 5 November 2002; Horber-Papazian Katia & Jacot-Descombes Caroline. 'Communes'. In Knoepfel et al., 275 et seq.; Kölz Alfred & Kuster Susanne. 'Der Städteartikel der neuen Bundesverfassung'. In *Zeitschrift für Schweizerisches Recht [ZSR]*. 2002 I, 137 et seq.; Ladner Andreas & Steiner Reto. 'Die Schweizer Gemeinden im Wandel'. *Swiss Political Science Review* 9, no. 1 (2003): 233–259; Steiner, Reto. *Interkommunale Zusammenarbeit und Gemeindezusammenschlüsse in der Schweiz.* Berne: Haupt etc. 2002; Steiner, Reto. *New Public Management in the Swiss Municipalities.* Berne: Haupt, 2000; Seiler Hansjörg. 'Gemeinden im schweizerischen Staatsrecht'. In Thürer et al., §31; Thürer Daniel. *Bund und Gemeinden.* New York/Berlin/Heidelberg: Springer, 1986; Zimmerli Ulrich. 'Bund-Kantone-Gemeinden'. In *Berner Tage für die juristische Praxis [BTJP].* Berne: Stämpfli, 1999, 35 et seq.

§1. The Position of the Municipalities in the Confederation

421. The municipalities form the grassroots level of the Swiss federal system and are territorially defined legal entities with a special public law status. They are often depicted as the cradle of Swiss democracy. For a long time, municipalities have been considered as within the exclusive realm of the cantons. The extent of municipal autonomy differs among cantons. In early history, municipalities developed according to the customs of the different tribes who settled in Switzerland. The Alemans built the farm houses around the church; the Celts built their houses in the middle of their field. As a consequence, municipalities in the German-speaking cantons, derived from Aleman settlements, have been more populous and have been granted more autonomy. The French-speaking municipalities are mainly influenced by dispersed settlements of Celtic tradition and were accorded less autonomy.

422. From a historical point of view, most municipalities are older than the cantons or the Confederation. Many Swiss citizens have strong emotional links to their municipality of origin. Constitutionally speaking, however, the cantons are the constituting entities of the state (Article 3 of the Constitution). As part of cantonal autonomy, cantons can determine their territorial organization, create and dissolve municipalities and can confer or revoke municipal autonomy. However, any cantonal decision limiting communal autonomy must be based on formal cantonal legislation. Most cantons accord their municipalities a high degree of autonomy that corresponds to the municipalities' historical and emotional importance. The municipalities thus continue to play a decisive role in politics.

I. Types of Municipalities

A. *Political Municipality*

423. The Swiss system recognizes different types of municipalities. The most important one being the *political municipality*, which is formed by all the Swiss inhabitants of the municipality. A decisive element for membership is the domicile (*see infra* Part IV, Chapter IV, §3 on domicile and residence). Within the political municipality, Swiss citizens have equal political rights irrespective of his/her municipal or cantonal citizenship.

B. *Bourgeois Municipality*

424. The political municipality can be distinguished from the ancient *burghers or bourgeois municipality*, which only includes persons who are citizens of the municipality (*see infra* Part IV, Chapter 1, §1), or descendants of one of the old families (burghers). Historically, municipalities were cooperatively organized by their burghers. The Constitution of 1874 required that all Swiss citizens living in a municipality enjoy the same political rights, irrespective whether they are burghers. For this reason, municipalities were forced to reorganize themselves. Several of them created a *bourgeois municipality* for their *citizens or* burghers, and a political municipality for all Swiss inhabitants of *the* municipality (including the burghers) based on equal political rights. The creation of the *bourgeois municipality* was one way to maintain some privileges for the burghers or the municipal citizens, while ensuring political equality through the political municipality. The *bourgeois municipality* does not exist in all cantons. The French-speaking cantons of Geneva, Vaud and Neuchâtel as well as the Canton of Glarus have only political municipalities.

425. The *bourgeois municipalities* are remnants of aristocratic or oligarchic institutions. Democracy in Switzerland before 1798 (the year of the French invasion) was not all-encompassing, but rather limited to certain families. The preservation of the *bourgeois municipality* was a concession to convince the former ruling families to accept inclusive suffrage. Today, the role of the *bourgeois municipality* is decreasing. In some cases, they can decide on municipal citizenship or burgher membership, administer their own patrimony and cultural heritage (e.g., forests, buildings, vineyards) and can provide social services.

426. In the dualistic system, the *bourgeois municipalities* have their own institutions (e.g., Fribourg, Schwyz, Zurich), whereas in the so-called mixed system, they are represented by the institutions of the political municipality. In cases that concern matters of *the bourgeois municipality*, only those members of the political municipality who are also members of the *bourgeois municipality* have the right to vote.

C. *Specialized Municipalities, Agglomeration*

427. The specialized municipalities have powers in a limited number of clearly defined subject matters while the *political municipalities* have general powers. Not all cantons have specialized municipalities. It is mainly the German-speaking cantons that rely on specialized municipalities in addition to the *political* and *bourgeois municipality*.

428. An important case of the specialized municipality is the *school municipality*, which does not necessarily have to correspond geographically with the political municipality, but can include a smaller or a larger territory. As indicated by its name, the school municipality fulfils functions in the area of schooling.

429. Some cantons foresee specialized *municipalities for the poor* that have the task to support the needy members of the municipality.

430. Some cantons confer the status of *ecclesiastic municipality* to the parishes of the main religious denominations (*see infra* Part V, Chapter 3 on State and religion). Their territory and members do not necessarily coincide with the ones of the political municipalities. Only adherents of the religion are included. The cantons request certain standards of democratic organization of the ecclesiastic municipalities. Therefore, as a side effect, the main religious groups (Catholic and Protestant) rely on a relatively democratic form of organization.

431. To take the special situation of cities and the surrounding municipalities into account, several cantons created legislation on *agglomerations*, which are designed as legal entities and are conferred certain powers. Bernard Dafflon calls the agglomeration a 'fusion sélective', a selective merger. In other words, they can be described as a new form of specialized municipality. They are territorially based legal entities with a special public law status and with selective powers, including for instance traffic and planning.

II. Municipal Autonomy

A. Provisions in the Federal Constitution

432. The Constitution dedicates one provision to the municipalities, mainly dealing with municipal or local autonomy. The Constitution, however, does not establish municipal autonomy (*see supra* Part III, Chapter 1, §2 II), it guarantees municipal autonomy to the extent that the cantons confer autonomy to the municipalities (Article 50(1) of the Constitution). In different words, the Confederation respects the cantonal right to self-organization and leaves it to cantons to define the municipal autonomy. Only in cases where the cantons illegally violate the municipal autonomy the Confederation will protect municipal autonomy.

433. Federal law, however, sets the maximum scope of municipal autonomy. The cantons cannot attribute more autonomy than they have themselves under the Constitution.

434. In addition to the guarantee of municipal autonomy, the Confederation is called to take the possible consequences of its activities for the municipalities into account. In particular, it shall pay attention to the special situations of the cities, agglomerations and mountainous regions (Article 50(1) and (2) of the Constitution).

B. Cantonal Provisions

435. Due to the cantonal powers, there are twenty-six different regimes of municipal autonomy. While all cantons and half-cantons accord autonomy to a local level of government, the form of the cantonal attribution of local autonomy and the scope of accorded autonomy differ decisively. The following is a general outline of the cantonal provisions.

1. Form of the Attribution of Local Autonomy

436. Local autonomy is either based on the cantonal constitution, on cantonal statute(s), or – as in most cases – on a combination of both. If the status of their municipalities is defined by statutory law, the municipality's autonomy is far less protected than when status is determined by the cantonal constitution. When status is determined by statute, the cantons can change the status of the municipalities with the normal legislating procedure. In cases of constitutional guarantees, however, a constitutional revision is necessary. According to the Federal Supreme Court, even the abolition of a municipality or the forced merger of municipalities in accordance with cantonal law is not opposed to the guarantee of municipal autonomy in the Constitution (Decision of the Federal Supreme Court BGE 104 Ia 387, *Comune et patriziato di Fusio*). An increasing number of cantons foresee the possibility to force municipalities to merge.

2. Scope of Attributed Autonomy

437. By relying on simplification, it can be said that the more important the municipalities have been in the history of the canton the more powers they are attributed. For instance, in the French-speaking cantons, the municipalities are less embedded in the cantonal history than in most German-speaking cantons. Therefore, for example, the Canton of Geneva is much more centralized than the cantons of Berne, Valais or Grisons. Culturally diverse cantons like the Canton of Grisons tend to accord more autonomy than homogeneous ones. In some cantons – e.g., the cantons of Aargau and Glarus – the municipalities have even residual powers. In the Canton of Glarus, the Landsgemeinde of the canton has decided to reduce all its municipalities to only three municipalities which are now the bearer of many public tasks.

438. In most cases, the municipalities have a limited right to self-administration and legislative and administrative powers in areas that directly concern the local level or that are culturally sensitive, such as municipal citizenship, primary education, municipal police and municipal infrastructure. In addition, all municipalities have the right to raise their own taxes (*see infra* Part V, Chapter 2, §1 III). However, judicial powers are in most cases very limited. In some cases, federal law delegates powers not globally to the cantons but directly to the municipalities. An example is the area of zoning, in which the cantons are mandated to make general plans which then serve as a basis for the municipal zoning plans.

C. Cantonal Support and Control

439. The cantons have extensive control and support powers over the municipalities. Measures aim to guarantee that the municipal order functions well. Furthermore, in cases when municipalities execute cantonal law, the cantonal control can include a control of appropriateness. When municipal powers are concerned, the canton is limited to a control of legality. Here three different kinds of measures shall be regarded: supportive, preventive and repressive measures. The controlling instruments and measures that cantons apply to the municipalities are more extensive and more frequently used than those applied from the federal level towards the cantonal level. Generally, control mechanisms are stricter when the municipalities execute federal or cantonal law than when they act within their own powers.

1. Supportive Measures

440. Supportive measures aim at strengthening the municipal order. There are multiple examples for supportive measures, which can be financial, e.g., through the mechanisms of financial subsidies and grants as well as financial equalization; they can be operational by providing the preconditions, framework and infrastructure so that the municipal institutions functions well, e.g., through information and counselling, e.g. on how to do the municipal accounts, or the creation of a legal framework for voluntary inter-municipal cooperation; or they can be educational, e.g., through the provision of training programmes. Because many municipalities are faced with a lack of well-trained personnel, the cantons normally provide voluntary or mandatory training programmes for the empowerment of the municipal civil servants. Judicial measures can be included in the category of supportive measures as well. The cantons can accord remedies against the infringement of municipal autonomy; the system of remedies differs from canton to canton.

2. Preventive Measures

441. Preventive measures shall ensure that the municipality does not neglect the fulfilment of its tasks. The least intrusive case of preventive measures is the oversight of municipal activities. These oversight programmes can include control in the form of reporting, information and inspection, and they can be combined with the (mandatory) self-control and self-evaluation done directly by the municipality. For instance, municipalities do their own audit of accounts. In addition, the canton might check whether the account plan follows the rules set by the canton. Preventive measures – like the requirement of approbation of legislation and decrees, requirements concerning planning and budgets, or the setting of minimal standards for the management of the municipality and for its services – curb municipal autonomy.

3. Repressive Measures

442. Repressive measures are applied when the municipality does not satisfactorily fulfil its tasks. These repressive measures can include legal actions, revocation of municipal acts, of financial subsidies and contributions, execution by substitution, disciplinary measures, forced cooperation between municipalities to assure better services, or tutelage. Tutelage is the *ultima ratio* of repressive measures because it results in cantonal authorities acting in place of municipal authorities. This tutelage will be restricted in time and will only be applied when the municipality is temporarily not able to fulfil its tasks. For instance, at one-time, the municipality of Leukerbad was bankrupt and no longer able to establish a balanced budget on its own. Therefore, the Canton of Valais put it under tutelage. In most such cases, the canton will not put the municipality under tutelage for all subject matters, but rather act for the municipality to fulfil one task, as was in 1995, when the municipality of the City of Berne was not able to pass a budget in accordance with the financial powers of the city, the canton forced the city to adopt higher taxes. That same year, the Canton of Zurich forced a new zoning law on the municipality of the City of Zurich because the one passed by the City of Zurich had triggered hundreds of complaints.

D. Judicial Protection of Municipal Autonomy by the Federal Supreme Court

443. Based on Article 50 of the Constitution, which guarantees the autonomy of municipalities within the limits fixed by cantonal law, the Federal Supreme Court provides a remedy against the violation of municipal autonomy. This remedy can be invoked by all forms of municipalities (i.e., political municipalities, special municipalities, etc., *see supra* A).

444. According to the Federal Supreme Court, municipalities are autonomous in areas where they have a *relatively important discretion and decision-making power*. In other words, the municipalities must have the right to make a choice between different self-defined options based on their own responsibilities (Decision of the Federal Supreme Court, BGE 101 Ia 259, *Municipality of Ritzingen*). Municipalities can therefore even be deemed autonomous when they implement cantonal or federal law as long as they have a relatively important decision-making power.

445. Additionally, the municipalities are competent to interpret their own regulations. The canton cannot arbitrarily impose a specific reading to a municipal legal act (Decision of the Federal Supreme Court, *Municipality of Lausanne,* 108 Ia 74); rather, the cantons are bound by the legality principle. All cantonal involvement in municipal affairs that is not based on cantonal powers is in violation of municipal autonomy. For example, the cantonal authorities may not review the appropriateness of municipal action when the cantonal law only requires a legality control (Decision of the Federal Supreme Court BGE 114 Ia 364, *Political Municipality of Obfelden*).

446. In case of violation of the municipal autonomy, federal law allows remedies against the violation of municipal autonomy (*see infra* Part IV, Chapter 5 and Article 189(1)(e) of the Constitution).

447. The guarantee of municipal autonomy is a constitutional right of the municipalities (*see infra* Part IV, Chapter 2, §1), so standing is normally limited to municipalities. Individuals can claim the violation of municipal autonomy only in combination with other grievances, not as an independent cause of action. The scrutiny of the Federal Supreme Court is normally limited to the arbitrary and capricious test, unless the violation of federal or cantonal constitutional law is invoked. In such cases, the Court has free scrutiny.

III. Inter-municipal Cooperation and Mergers of Municipalities

448. Considering the size of the country, Switzerland has a high number of (political) municipalities. In March 2017, there have been 2,240 municipalities with an average population of 3,764 inhabitants. Municipalities are facing increasing difficulty fulfilling the tasks they are accorded. Generally, small, financially weak municipalities have insufficient capacities to respond to the challenges of a globalized world. In order to prevent a centralization of the tasks, that they are no longer able to fulfil, the municipalities can either rely on cooperation or on mergers with other municipalities.

449. Cooperation provides the flexible interplay between different governments without changing the distribution of powers or the territorial organization. However, it usually reduces the scope of the political rights of the peoples. Inter-communal cooperation agreements normally give the executives of the municipalities more decision-making powers than they would otherwise have – with repercussions on the role of communal parliaments and possibilities of direct democracy.

A. Inter-municipal Cooperation

450. In most cases, cooperation is limited to municipalities of one canton. There are however also cases of trans-border cooperation. The clear majority of Swiss municipalities has intensified inter-municipal cooperation in recent years, primarily with the goal to improve the quality of services.

451. Cooperation requires that the municipalities are legally and factually able to cooperate. The cantons provide the legal framework for cooperation, either by allowing and promoting voluntary cooperation or even by mandating cooperation. For instance, the *Cantonal Act on Municipalities* of the Canton of Berne establishes a three-step procedure to 'convince' the municipalities to optimize their services through cooperation:

(1) first, the Canton created a legal framework favouring voluntary cooperation;
(2) second, when the municipalities do not cooperate even though a cooperation would be economical, the Canton can revoke subsidies and grants as incentives for cooperation; and
(3) finally, when the municipalities are still not willing to cooperate on a voluntary basis, the Cantonal Act allows the possibility to force cooperation.

452. Most municipalities have concluded multiple cooperations with neighbouring municipalities. Cooperation can be either constitutionally or legally institutionalized cooperation, or contractual cooperation. For example, contractual cooperation can include the establishment of stock corporations (for tasks that need important financial means) or leasing contracts, such as those implemented in the Canton of Ticino, where some municipalities concluded police leasing contracts with the City of Chiasso to avoid having to establish its own police force. Most of the larger cities that provide infrastructure which is also used by inhabitants of surrounding municipalities, attempt to conclude cost-sharing agreements with benefitting municipalities. These cases are being more and more regulated in special legislation on agglomerations (*see supra* Part III, Chapter 3, §1 I).

B. Merger of Municipalities

453. Mergers of municipalities are promoted and conducted in light of discussions on the optimal size of local government. The merger of two or more municipalities shall guarantee a more efficient and effective government by cutting costs and establishing joint administrations. As a result, decisions can be made in a more organized, centralized and supposedly more efficient way, thus allowing development and infrastructure policies to be introduced with less externalities. Additionally, it can be argued that mergers promote democracy because, even though the influence of each individual citizen will be reduced nominally, the actual influence could increase due to the higher importance and the better financial position of the larger municipality. The creation of larger units may lead to less input from each individual, but perhaps – at least for some time – it could assure more effective influence of the municipality. Larger units may, however, seem less accessible to the citizens and the incentive to be politically active might decrease.

454. However, the merger of municipalities does not necessarily guarantee the needed flexibility and can provoke a legitimacy crisis, particularly where identity arguments are involved.

455. The number of municipalities decreased quite significantly. Since 2000, in average, Switzerland has seen a reduction of the number of municipalities by thirty-nine per year. The Canton of Fribourg and the Canton of Ticino lead the statistic of mergers. The most decisive reform was conducted in the Canton of Glarus when it merged its twenty-five political municipalities, eighteen school municipalities, sixteen municipalities for the poor and nine bourgeois municipalities into three municipalities. Many cantons foresee the possibility to force the merger of municipalities (e.g., Ticino, Bern) while other cantons try to give (financial) incentives for mergers. In the case of the municipality Ausserbinn in the Canton of Valais, the Federal Supreme Court decided that the forced merger of the municipality was legal because cantonal law did not guarantee the territory and existence of the municipality (Federal Supreme Court Decision 131 I 91 E. 2, p. 94). However, in a recent case regarding an initiative in the Canton of Ticino to merge seventeen municipalities with the city of Locarno and sixteen municipalities with the city of Bellinzona without prior consultation of the concerned municipalities the Court held that the cantonal initiative violated international law, in this case the European Charter of Local Self-Government of 15 October 1985, and declared the initiative null and void (*see* the Decision of the Federal Supreme Court BGE 142 I 216).

§2. Organization of the Municipalities

I. Right to Self-Organization

456. To a large extent, the form of municipal organization is regulated by cantonal law. The municipal right to self-organization is therefore very limited. Municipalities cannot decide on their form of government to the extent that the cantons can define their own form of cantonal organization. Some cantons accord municipalities a limited autonomy to define their body politic, e.g., with respect to the participation of foreigners. Other cantons give municipalities the option to choose between a people's assembly or a municipal parliament, while yet other cantons allow municipalities to adopt an electoral system of their choice for the municipal parliament.

II. Form of Municipal Organization

A. In General: Bipartite and Tripartite Organization

457. Municipal organization is to a large extent regulated by cantonal law. All municipalities have at least two institutions: the electorate (the People) and the municipal government (*bipartite or ordinary municipal organization*), and some cantons even have a municipal parliament (*tripartite or extraordinary municipal organization*). The highest authority lies with the municipal People.

458. Approximately five out of six Swiss municipalities are organized based on the bipartite organization, with only the People and the government as municipal institutions. All cantons, except for the cantons of Geneva and Neuchâtel, have the ordinary municipal organization. In some cantons (Uri, Schwyz, Obwalden, Nidwalden, Glarus and Appenzell Innerrhoden), the bipartite organization is mandatory for all municipalities. All other cantons designate bipartite organization for the smaller municipalities.

459. About one out of six municipalities is organized based on the tripartite organization. Although only a relative small number of municipalities rely on this form of organization, about half of the Swiss population lives in these municipalities. In the cantons of Neuchâtel and Geneva, all municipalities are organized in the form of the tripartite form of organization, while in most other cantons the tripartite form of organization is reserved for the more populous ones. Some cantons give larger municipalities the choice between the bipartite and the tripartite form of organization.

460. The municipalities have hardly any judicial functions. Courts are normally situated at the district level, and some cantons accord the municipalities the right to introduce Justices of Peace (*see supra* Part I, Chapter 5, §2 III).

461. Finally, many municipalities have introduced the so-called *Amtszwang*, mandating that persons who are elected to office must accept the office.

B. Municipal People

462. The municipal People are the highest authority of a municipality.

463. The canton is not completely free to define the body politic of the canton or municipality, because restrictions based on federal law that apply to the canton also apply to the municipalities (for these restrictions, *see supra* Part III, Chapter 2, II). Normally, the definition of the body politic at the municipality level corresponds with the one at the cantonal level. However, there are some variations. Four cantons provide foreigners the right to vote and to be elected at municipal level (Jura (with the exception of the position of mayor), Neuchatel, Vaud and Fribourg). In the Canton of Geneva, foreigners have the right to vote at the municipal level but not to stand for elections. Cantons can also leave some autonomy in this respect to the municipalities. For instance, the Canton of Appenzell Ausserrhoden accords the municipalities the right to give foreigners political rights at a municipal level upon demand and after ten years of residency in Switzerland, with a minimum of five years in the canton. Three of the twenty municipalities made use of this right. Similar rights also have the municipalities in the cantons of Grisons and Basel-Stadt. In the Canton of Thurgau, foreigners have a consultative vote at the municipal level, whereas in other cantons (e.g., the Canton of Solothurn), foreigners can participate in the decision-making of ecclesiastic municipalities.

464. In cases of bipartite organization, the People vote on all municipal legislation, on the municipal budget and accounts, as well as on certain administrative acts. In cases of tripartite organization, where mandatory or facultative referenda are foreseen, the People can sign and vote on initiatives and referenda as well as elect the members of municipal government. Only in the Canton of Neuchâtel, members of municipal government are elected by the municipal Parliament. Further, in municipalities with parliaments, the People additionally elect their parliamentary representatives.

465. In municipalities with a tripartite organization, the People mainly vote by secret ballot whereas those municipalities with a bipartite organization normally take decisions in the municipal or people's assembly – which is comparable to the *Landsgemeinde* (*see supra* Part III, Chapter 2, §2 II). The municipal assembly is made up of all the inhabitants of the municipality with political rights, and votes are taken by a showing of hand. Some municipalities use vote by secret ballot for more important decisions or when demanded. In municipalities with a bipartite organization, the influence of political parties is much smaller than in those with a tripartite organization.

C. Municipal Parliament

466. About one-sixth of Swiss municipalities – including all those in the cantons of Geneva and Neuchâtel – have a parliament. In the Canton of Vaud, municipalities with more than eight hundred inhabitants rely on a parliament. In the German-speaking cantons, the urban centres are generally accorded parliaments. Bigger municipalities sometimes have the choice between the tripartite or the bipartite form of organization. For instance, in the Canton of Solothurn, the City of Olten with close to 17,000 inhabitants opted for a parliament while the City of Solothurn with about 16,000 inhabitants decided against.

467. The parliament is always elected by the municipal People, and in most cantons the municipality can decide on the mode of election. Most municipal parliaments are elected based on proportional representation.

468. Municipal parliaments have the ordinary functions of a parliament. They legislate, supervise the municipal administration and executive and adopt the budget, the accounts as well as the zoning plans, and in some cases the parliamentarians elect or nominate civil servants. Ultimately, the powers of municipal parliaments are, however, limited by direct democracy.

D. Municipal Executive Government

469. Similar to the government at cantonal and federal levels, municipal government is normally composed of a five- to fifteen-member council. In all cantons, except in the Canton of Neuchâtel, the government is directly elected by the people. The municipal government prepares legislative drafts and can issue regulations. The council is normally headed by a President who exercises his/her function on a full-time basis, while the other members of government are normally on a part-time basis. In contrast to the situation at federal and cantonal levels, in most municipalities the President is not *primus inter pares*, but has additional powers and responsibilities.

Part IV. Citizenship and the Administration of Justice

Chapter 1. Rules Concerning Citizenship and Relevance of Citizenship

Selected Bibliography: Biaggini. Kommentar, Articles 37–40 (with further references); Brubaker Rogers. *Citizenship and Nationhood in France and Germany.* Cambridge: Harvard University Press, 1998; Ehrenzeller Bernhard. 'Schweizer werden – Aktuelle Rechtsfragen des Einbürgerungsverfahrens in der Schweiz'. In *Festschrift für Wolfgang Mantl.* Vienna/Cologne/Graz: Böhlau Publ., 2004, 239 et seq.; Fleiner Thomas & Misic Alexander. 'Der Föderalismus in der Schweiz'. In *Krise und Reform des Föderalismus*, edited by C. Meier-Walser Reinhard & Hirscher Gerhard. Munich: Olzog, 1999, 246 et seq.; Häfelin, Haller, Keller & Thurnherr, 383 et seq. (with further references); Haller. *Swiss Constitution*, 93 et seq.; Hartmann Karl & Laurent Merz. 'Einbürgerung: Erwerb und Verlust des Schweizer Bürgerrechts'. In *Ausländerrecht*, edited by Uebersax Peter et al., 2nd ed. Basel: Helbing & Lichtenhahn, 2009, §12; Misic, 142 et seq. (with further references); Schaffhauser René. 'Bürgerrechte'. In Thürer et al., §19; Rhinow & Schefer, §3 II (with further references); Spescha Marc et al., *Migrationsrecht.* 4th ed. Zurich: Orell Füssli, 2015; Tschannen, 206 et seq.; Uebersax Peter. 'Das Bundesgericht und das Bürgerrechtsgesetz, mit Blick auf das neue Recht'. In *Basler Juristische Mitteilungen 2016*, 169 et seq.

§1. Rules Concerning Swiss Citizenship

I. In General

A. Citizenship and Nationality

470. Citizenship and nationality are often used as synonyms. Citizenship, however, is a status, the legal link between a person and the state. It is often understood as including political rights. Nationality, however, denominates belonging to a nation. Whenever the nation incorporates all citizens, citizenship and nationality are identical. However, when the definition of nationhood does not rely on citizenship but rather on other criteria, such as ethnicity, then nationality and citizenship diverge. The United States and France are examples of nation-states where citizenship coincides with nationality, while for instance Germany is an example of a nation-state where a person can be a citizen but not a national, a national but not a citizen, both, or neither. While citizenship can be defined by relying on legal criteria, nationality normally evades objective definition.

471. In Switzerland, it is debated whether there is a Swiss nation, and therefore whether the Swiss nationality exists. Those who argue in favour of a Swiss nation, define it based on shared political values such as federalism, direct democracy and neutrality, and/or on belonging to one of the cantons. Often the Swiss nation is depicted as a *Willensnation* – a nation based on the will of the People to belong to the state and the nation. This Willensnation can also be described as a composed nation based on the argument that the nation is composed of different groups who in addition to loyalty to their group also share a feeling of belonging to the Swiss nation. Those who argue that a Swiss nation does not exist claim that the cultural diversity of the Swiss population – and moreover, the Swiss respect for that given diversity – eliminates the possibility of nationhood, and Switzerland therefore can at best be regarded as a multinational state.

472. Both concepts of Swissness, based on a voluntary nation or as a multinational state, suggest a society open to newcomers. This is however not entirely so. In particular, political parties belonging to the right spectrum of the political landscape are constructing a Swiss identity that relies on political values but draws a sharp distinction between persons of Swiss origin and naturalized citizens. They question the willingness and ability of immigrants to fully share Swiss (political) values and thus to become truly Swiss. Those who negate a Swiss nation might still argue in favour of 'Swissness' that is based in the different cultures existing in Switzerland. Also based on this understanding, foreigners or naturalized Swiss citizens do not necessarily share the attributes of 'Swissness'.

473. The individual definition of 'a nation' normally influences the criteria required to establish citizenship. Nation-states that rely on an ethnic understanding of the nation tend to apply foremost the *ius sanguinis* principle, according to which citizenship is accorded based on descent. Nation-states that define their nation as the totality of its citizens are more likely to apply at least some forms of the *ius soli* principle, under which one's residency or birth in the territory is decisive for the attribution of citizenship.

474. Nation-states relying on ethnic concepts are normally very restrictive in their naturalization policies. The request will be granted only when the citizenship candidate can prove that he/she is completely assimilated and loyal foremost to the country from which he/she is requesting citizenship. Nation-states relying on civil concepts are normally more willing to naturalize and either pre-suppose integration and/or demand only the acceptance of some (mainly political) values.

475. Switzerland predominately applies the *ius sanguinis* principle and is rather restrictive in its naturalization policy. Integration is one of the main criteria for naturalization. The citizenship policy is derived from the above-mentioned notions that in order to belong to the Swiss state, the person must share and identify with the political values and institutions to such an extent that only descent or integration and assimilation into one of the Swiss communities can guarantee. Essentially, Switzerland has *turned its politics into a quasi-ethnicity*.

476. To some extent, Swiss direct democracy contributed to the rather strict Swiss citizenship law. Proposals to facilitate naturalization of second-generation foreigners or other attempts to make Swiss citizenship more accessible accumulated significant numbers of 'no' votes in popular votes. To avoid referenda or further popular initiatives, the legislature established a rather restrictive citizenship law.

B. Three-Level Citizenship

477. The three-level federal system in Switzerland has an important influence on citizenship law in Switzerland. This influence is not only visible in the distribution of powers, which still leaves considerable power to the cantons, but even more in the phenomenon of a *three-level citizenship*. Every Swiss citizen has at least three citizenships. He/she is citizen of Switzerland, of a canton, and of a municipality. Although these three citizenships are distinguishable, they also form a unity, and federal and cantonal citizenship cannot be obtained without municipal citizenship. Cantonal citizenship derives from municipal citizenship, and cantonal and municipal citizenship are a necessity for federal citizenship. Thus, according to Article 37(1) of the Constitution, every person in possession of citizenship of a municipality and of the canton to which the municipality belongs has Swiss citizenship. This three-level citizenship – constructed from the bottom up – stresses the importance of bottom-up democratization and the idea of federalized democracy. Cantonal and municipal citizenship do not depend on a person's place of residence – as in the United States for state citizenship – but are ascribed through descent, adoption or marriage, or are attributed through naturalization. Double or multiple citizenship on all three levels is permitted.

II. Obtaining Swiss Citizenship

A. Constitutional Provision

478. The Constitution contents itself with the determination of the *distribution of powers* and does not set special principles or substantive requirements for obtaining Swiss citizenship except that the Confederation is mandated to facilitate naturalization for stateless children and third-generation immigrants (whose grandparents and parents have already lived in Switzerland).

479. According to the Constitution, it is the federal level, which establishes the rules concerning the obtaining and reinstating of *Swiss citizenship through status* like birth, marriage and adoption. Furthermore, it shall facilitate the naturalization of stateless children and third-generation immigrants (Article 38 of the Constitution). The cantons are in charge of ordinary naturalizations; however, the federal level sets minimum requirements for naturalizations by the cantons, grants naturalization permits and regulates the loss of Swiss citizenship.

B. *Other Legal Sources*

480. Until the end of 2017, the most important federal source next to the Constitution was the Federal Act on the Obtaining and Loss of Swiss Citizenship of 29 September 1952 (SR 141.0), however, in June 2014, Parliament adopted a new Federal Citizenship Act which will enter into force on 1 January 2018. On the same date, also a Federal Decree on citizenship will enter into force. The following is based on the 2014 Federal Citizenship Act. In addition, the case law of the Federal Supreme Court has gained high importance, and the *cantons* have their own legislation concerning naturalization that also must be consulted.

C. *Swiss Citizenship Based on Status*

481. As a rule, citizenship is acquired by birth. In principle, Switzerland accords citizenship based on the *ius sanguinis* principle. Citizenship is accorded based on descent, rather than the place of birth.

482. As a rule, children of a married couple, of which at least one of the spouses is Swiss, automatically receives Swiss citizenship. Any child born to a Swiss woman will receive Swiss citizenship, irrespective of the citizenship of the father or the marital status of the parents. A child who is born to a woman who is not Swiss but whose father is, will automatically receive Swiss citizenship when the father officially recognizes fatherhood while the child is still a minor. In case the minor child already has own children, they also receive Swiss citizenship (Article 1 of the Federal Citizenship Act).

483. In addition to Swiss citizenship, the child automatically also receives *cantonal and municipal citizenship*. If its parents are both Swiss it will get the cantonal and municipal citizenship of the parent whose name it carries (parents must select one name as family name), if only one parent is Swiss, the child receives the cantonal and municipal citizenship of this parent (Article 2 of the Federal Citizenship Act).

484. The *adoption* of a minor child will lead to the ascription of Swiss citizenship as if the child had been born to the person or persons who adopted it.

485. Formerly, a woman obtained citizenship automatically when she married a Swiss citizen, and a Swiss woman would automatically lose citizenship when she married a foreigner, if she had gained Swiss citizenship because of her marriage to a Swiss man. Divorce did not influence citizenship.

486. Today, *marriage* has no direct influence on citizenship, but it gives access to a facilitated naturalization for spouses of Swiss citizens, male and female. The spouse can obtain Swiss citizenship after three years of marriage when he/she has lived a total of five years in Switzerland and resided there at least the year prior to naturalization (Article 21 of the Federal Citizenship Act). When the couple does not live in Switzerland, the spouse can receive Swiss citizenship after six years of marriage when he/she has links to Switzerland (Article 21 of the Federal Citizenship Act). Marriage and divorce do not lead to the loss of citizenship.

487. Living in a registered partnership does not provide access to facilitated naturalization but registered partners of a Swiss national benefit from shorter delays within the procedure of the ordinary naturalization.

D. Ordinary Naturalization

488. The federal level has limited competencies concerning ordinary naturalization. The Confederation can set minimum requirements for naturalization. The cantons have the right to complement the requirements and, within the principles established by the Confederation, can regulate the details of naturalization.

489. For the ordinary naturalization, it needs a federal naturalization authorization as well as a cantonal naturalization decision. The procedure for naturalization is divided into three stages. The first stage of the procedure is cantonal, once the canton can assure that the canton (and the municipality) are positive on the naturalization, the naturalization request is forwarded to the Federal Office of Migration. The second stage of the procedure is federal. At its end, in the positive case, the Federal Office of Migration issues a federal naturalization authorization. The federal naturalization authorization is valid for one year, during which the canton (stage 3) has to take its official naturalization decision. During the third stage, naturalization can only be refused if since the issuance of the federal naturalization permit new facts came to light that prevented the issuance of the federal naturalization permit (Article 13 of the Federal Citizenship Act). Minor children are normally included in the naturalization procedure of the parent. In addition, in the case that the naturalization procedure was initially started without including the children, the federal naturalization authorization can be extended to include the minor children (Article 13(4) and Article 30 of the Federal Citizenship Act).

490. In accordance with the Constitution, federal legislation establishes minimum requirements for the naturalization of foreigners which apply to adults and in a modified form to children above the age of 12.

491. Some of the requirements are formal: when applying for Swiss citizenship, the candidate must be in the possession of a Swiss settlement permit or he/she must have lived in Switzerland for at least ten years of which three years must have been within the last five years. Years lived in Switzerland during the age of 8 and 18 count double, however the candidate must have lived a minimum of six years within Switzerland (Article 9 of the Federal Citizenship Act). Shorter delays exist for persons who live in a registered partnership with a Swiss partner (Article 10 of the Federal Citizenship Act).

492. Other requirements aim at ensuring that the candidate is successfully integrated, is familiar with life in Switzerland and does not pose a threat for the internal or external security of Switzerland (Article 11 of the Federal Citizenship Act). The Act also establishes criteria to assess the requirements, these are even further concretized in the Federal Decree on Citizenship. Legally established criteria include: the respect for law and order, respect for the values of the Swiss constitution (the decree establishes that this includes amongst others the respect for the equality between men and women), the ability to communicate in one of the official languages, the participation in the economic life or in education, as well as the promotion of the integration of the spouse or partner as well as of minor children (Article 12 of the Federal Citizenship Act).

493. The canton can determine additional requirements for naturalization. Previously, the cantons had important discretion in determining how many years a candidate had to live within the canton and a specific municipality before being eligible for receiving citizenship. Now, the Federal Citizenship Act establishes that cantons determine a time between two and five years (Article 18 of the Federal Citizenship Act). Also in respect to integration-related requirements, the cantonal discretion is somewhat more limited because the Federal Citizenship Act provides far more detailed guidelines than the Act of 1952. It was one of the objectives of the federal legislator to contributor to comparable standards for naturalization across cantons. However, the cantons still have the right to add integration-related criteria.

494. The cantons determine the authority to which naturalization requests are to be directed (Article 13 of the Federal Citizenship Act), and they regulate the cantonal and municipal procedure for naturalization (Article 15 of the Federal Citizenship Act). Cantonal and municipal authorities are involved in the naturalization process, and in most cantons, both must give assent to naturalization. Cantons do not only check the cantonal requirements but also the above-mentioned federal requirements and criteria (Article 34(1) of the Federal Citizenship Act). While many cantons give a major role to a naturalization commission, the Act explicitly provides for the option that cantons foresee a direct democratic decision-making procedure, i.e., that the citizens at a municipal assembly decide on naturalization (Article 15(2) of the Federal Citizenship Act).

495. Naturalization through direct democratic decision-making was focus of several court decisions. In a landmark decision in 2003, the Federal Supreme Court ruled that a denial of citizenship without proper reasoning violated the Swiss Constitution, in particular the right not to be discriminated (Article 8(2) of the Constitution) and the right to be heard (Article 29(2) of the Constitution; Decision of the Federal Supreme Court BGE 129 I 217). The Federal Supreme Court clarified in another decision, that this does not exclude that municipalities make use of direct democratic instruments in the naturalization procedures. For instance, the citizens' assembly can still decide on naturalization demands if the decision is based on a proper discussion and voting (Decision of the Federal Supreme Court 130 I 140). The Federal Citizenship Act follows these decisions, mandating the cantons to ensure that any rejection of a naturalization demand must be accompanied by a reasoned explanation in the sense of Article 29(2) of the Constitution (*see infra* Part IV, Chapter 2, §6), and that citizens can only reject a naturalization demand if a reasoned petition for rejection was raised (Article 16 of the Federal Citizenship Act). In addition, the cantons must protect the privacy of the candidates. Citizens shall receive information on the current citizenship, the duration of residency in Switzerland as well as other necessary information, in particular on the integration of the candidate and family members included in the naturalization demand (Article 17 of the Federal Citizenship Act). Thus, citizens still receive far-reaching information on the candidate and his/her family.

496. Against all cantonal decisions of last instance regarding ordinary naturalizations an appeal can be lodged with a cantonal court (Article 46 of the Federal Citizenship Act). In addition, the person requesting citizenship, the concerned canton and municipalities can lodge an appeal to the Federal Supreme Court (Article 47 of the Federal Citizenship Act). A constitutional appeal is restricted to the control of the violation of constitutional rights (*see infra* Part IV, Chapter 2, §1), especially the non-discrimination clause of Article 8(2) of the Constitution (*infra* Part IV, Chapter 2, §3 III).

E. Facilitated Naturalization and Reattribution of Swiss Citizenship

497. The *facilitated naturalization* is regulated exclusively by federal law. Therefore, the cantons must not introduce additional criteria. The procedure is established by federal authorities. According to Article 25 of the Federal Citizenship Act, the federal authorities decide on naturalization after consultation with the canton. In addition, the federal authorities mandate the cantonal authority to assess naturalization requirements. Also, candidates for facilitated naturalization are assessed whether they are integrated or pose threat to the internal or external security of Switzerland (Article 20 of the Federal Citizenship Act). The familiarity with Switzerland is not necessarily regarded. A negative decision can be appealed before the Federal Supreme Court with an appeal in public law matters (*see infra* Part IV, Chapter 5, §3 III).

498. The Federal Citizenship Act allows five groups of persons to benefit from facilitated naturalization:

(1) the spouse of a Swiss citizen living in Switzerland or living abroad (Article 21 of the Federal Citizenship Act);
(2) persons who based on good faith believed that they were Swiss citizens (Article 22 of the Federal Citizenship Act);
(3) a stateless child (Article 23 of the Federal Citizenship Act);
(4) a child of less than 22 years who has not been included in the naturalization of its parent (Article 24 of the Federal Citizenship Act);
(5) third-generation immigrants (Article 38(3) of the Constitution).

499. While spouses of Swiss citizens benefit from facilitated naturalization, the partner of a Swiss citizen who lives in a registered (same-sex) partnership does not. However, he/she benefits from a shorter waiting period until he/she can demand naturalization (Article 10 of the Federal Citizenship Act).

500. There have been proposals to facilitate naturalization of second-generation immigrants and to attribute Swiss citizenship automatically to third-generation immigrants. However, on September 2004, the People and the cantons clearly rejected both proposals. The facilitated naturalization of third-generation immigrants was adopted in a popular vote in 2017.

501. Persons can be *reattributed* citizenship upon their demand if they are successfully integrated or have close links with Switzerland, respect law and order as well as the constitutional values of Switzerland and do not pose a threat to the internal and external security of Switzerland.

III. Losing Swiss Citizenship

502. Swiss citizenship can be lost based on the intervention of Swiss authorities and based on the request of the citizen to give up Swiss citizenship.

503. There are three cases in Swiss law in which Swiss citizenship is lost ex officio:

(1) when the link of parentage to the person who transferred Swiss citizenship is annulled unless the child would become stateless (Article 5 of the Federal Citizenship Act);
(2) when a Swiss child is adopted by foreigners and receives the foreign citizenship (Article 6 of the Federal Citizenship Act); and
(3) at the age of 25 in case the person was born outside of Switzerland, has another citizenship and was never registered with a Swiss authority outside or within Switzerland nor declared that he/she wants to maintain Swiss citizenship (Article 7 of the Citizenship Act).

504. The *Swiss authorities can intervene to annul citizenship* when citizenship was attained through false declarations or the misrepresentation of essential facts (Article 36 of the Federal Citizenship Act). With the consent of the concerned canton, Swiss authorities can also annul citizenship, when the person has double citizenship, if the person's conduct seriously jeopardizes the interests and the reputation of Switzerland (Article 42 of the Federal Citizenship Act).

505. Additionally, all Swiss citizens living abroad who have a dual citizenship or who are guaranteed another citizenship can request to be dismissed from their Swiss citizenship (Article 37 of the Federal Citizenship Act). Minors of less than 16 years who do not reside in Switzerland, who have dual citizenship or are guaranteed another citizenship are included in their parents' dismissal from Swiss citizenship. From the age of 16 onwards, the minor's written consent is needed for the dismissal.

§2. Relevance of Swiss Citizenship

506. *See also* discussion *infra* Part IV, Chapter 4 on foreigners.

507. Swiss citizenship status establishes special rights and duties. The main differences in rights concern political rights. Fundamental rights are guaranteed to Swiss citizens and foreigners alike, with the exception of the right to choose their place of residence. Political rights on the federal level, which are only accorded to citizens, include the right to participate actively and passively in elections, to organize and take part in initiatives, and to demand and vote in referenda. On the cantonal and municipal levels, foreigners can receive political rights.

508. Swiss citizens have the right to a Swiss passport, an identification card and to an act of origin. They further have the right to live in Switzerland, to choose freely their place of domicile in Switzerland and to leave Switzerland (Article 24 of the Constitution, *see infra* Part IV, Chapter 2, §4 VI). Swiss citizens benefit from diplomatic protection outside of Switzerland. Also, Swiss citizens must not be expelled from Swiss territory and can only be extradited to foreign authorities when he/she gives his/her consent (Article 25 of the Constitution, *see infra* Part IV, Chapter 2, §4 VI).

509. Citizenship also establishes duties and restrictions for the citizen. Swiss citizens have a general duty to be loyal to Switzerland. Men must do military service or alternative service (*see infra* Part V, Chapter 1, §2). When they cannot do either, they must pay a tax (Article 59 of the Constitution). Swiss citizens are prohibited to serve in the army of a foreign country. This is mainly problematic for persons with double citizenship. Some international treaties allow exceptions so as to dispense persons from Swiss military and allow foreign military service and vice versa. For instance, it is permitted to serve in the army of the Vatican. Additionally, Swiss citizens have a duty to assist at elections for collecting and for counting votes and, in some cantons they must serve jury duty when so requested. Also, in some cantons and municipalities Swiss citizens must accept political office if elected (*supra* Part III, Chapter 2).

Chapter 2. Fundamental Rights

Selected Bibliography: Aubert & Mahon. commentaire, Articles 7–36; Auer, Malinverni & Hottelier. Vol. II; Biaggini. Kommentar, Vorbemerkungen *ad* Articles 7–36, and Kommentar, Articles 7–36; Egli, 161 et seq.; Fleiner Thomas. *What Are Human Rights?*. Sydney: Federation Press, 1999; Fleiner Thomas & Basta Lidija. *Constitutional Democracy.* 163 et seq.; Frowein Jochen & Peukert Wolfgang. *EMRK-Kommentar.* 3rd ed. Kehl/Strassburg/Arlington: N.P. Engel Verlag, 2009; Grabenwarter Christoph & Katharina Pabel. Europäische Menschenrechtskonvention 6th ed. Munich/Basel/Vienna: Beck/Helbing/Manz, 2016. Grisel Etienne. *Droits fondamentaux.* Berne: Stämpfli, 2008; Häfelin, Haller, Keller & Thurnherr, §§6 et seq. (with further references); Haefliger Arthur & Schürmann Frank. *Die Europäische Menschenrechtskonvention und die Schweiz.* 2nd ed. Berne: Stämpfli Verlag, 1999; Haller. *Swiss Constitution.* Part V; Kälin Walter & Künzli Jörg. *The Law of International Human Rights Protection.* Oxford U.P., 2009; Kälin Walter, Malinverni Giorgio & Nowak Manfred. *Die Schweiz und die UNO-Menschenrechtspakte.* 2nd ed. Basel/Frankfurt a.M.: Helbing & Lichtenhahn, 1997; Kiener & Kälin. Grundrechte, passim; Kley Andreas. 'Der Grundrechtskatalog, der nachgeführten Bundesverfassung'. In *Zeitschrift des Bernischen Juristenvereins [ZBJV].* 1999, 301 et seq.; Merten Detlef & Papier Hans Jürgen (eds). *Handbuch der Grundrechte in Deutschland und Europa.* Vol. VII/2: Grundrechte in der Schweiz und in Liechtenstein. Heidelberg/Zurich/St. Gallen: C.F. Müller/Dike, 2007; Meyer-Ladewig, Nettesheim & von Raumer (eds). *EMRK- Europäische Menschenrechtskonvention.* Handkommentar. 4th ed. Baden-Baden etc.: Nomos etc., 2017; Misic Alexander. *Verfassungsbeschwerde*, 284 et seq.; Misic Alexander. 'Der Grundrechtskatalog'. In Fleiner et al., BV–CF 2000, 71 et seq.; Müller Jörg Paul. *Elemente einer schweizerischen Grundrechtstheorie.* Berne: Stämpfli, 1982; Müller Jörg Paul. 'Allgemeine Bemerkungen zu den Grundrechten'. In Thürer et al., §39; Müller Jörg Paul & Schefer Markus. *Grundrechte in der Schweiz.* 4th ed. Berne: Stämpfli, 2008; Peters Anne & Altwicker Tilmann. *Einführung in die Europäische Menschenrechtskonvention.* 2nd ed. Munich: Beck, 2012; Rhinow, Schefer & Uebersax, §§11 et seq.; Rossinelli Michel. *Les libertés non écrites.* Lausanne, 1987; Rütsche Bernhard. *Rechtsfolgen von Grundrechtsverletzungen.* Basel/Frankfurt a.M.: Helbing & Lichtenhahn, 2002; Schindler Benjamin. 'Zu Begriff und Verständnis der Grundrechte' in der neuen Bundesverfassung'. In *Neue Akzente in der nachgeführten' Bundesverfassung*, edited by Gächter Thomas & Bertschi Martin. Zurich: Schulthess, 2000, 51 et seq.; Thurnherr Daniela. 'The Reception Process in Austria and Switzerland'. In *A Europe of Rights: The Impact of the ECHR on National Legal Systems*, edited by Keller Helen & Stone Sweet Alex. Oxford U.P., 2008, 311 et seq.; Tschannen, §7; Villiger Mark, E. 'EMRK und UNO-Menschenrechtspakte'. In Thürer et al., §40; Villiger Mark, E. *Handbuch der Europäischen Menschenrechtskonvention* (EMRK). 2nd ed. Zurich: Schulthess, 1999.

§1. General Introduction

I. The Catalogue of Fundamental Rights of the Federal Constitution

A. Fundamental Rights, Human Rights and Constitutional Rights

510. Fundamental rights (*Grundrechte, droits fondamentaux, diritti fondamentali*), as set out in Chapter 1 of Title 2 of the Constitution, are commonly defined as enforceable rights (or entitlements), which – due to the substance and values enshrined therein – are classified as essential for every individual. Consequently, restrictions of fundamental rights can only be tolerated if they fulfil the conditions set forth in the Constitution (*infra* §1 IV. of this Chapter). Usually, a distinction is drawn between fundamental rights and human rights (*Menschenrechte, droits de l'homme, diritti dell'uomo*). Based upon the theory of natural law, the latter are pre-constitutional, inalienable, indivisible, belong to every individual and are, as such, independent of the existence of a state; in contrast, fundamental rights are legal rules binding the state (thus pre-supposing its existence). In this chapter, the term 'human rights' shall encompass all justiciable provisions as contained in the international human rights treaties ratified by the Swiss Confederation. According to the concept of monism, the ECHR and the self-executing provisions of other international human rights conventions ratified by the Swiss Confederation have the same procedural status as domestic fundamental rights. They are directly enforceable by the courts and agencies of both the cantons and the Confederation.

511. Furthermore, constitutional rights (*verfassungsmässige Rechte, droits constitutionnels, diritti costituzionali*) play a considerable role in constitutional litigation. The content of these rights is defined and determined by the case law of the Federal Supreme Court. According to the Court's formula, constitutional rights are constitutional provisions, which confer to the individual spheres protected from undue interference by the state, or provisions, which, though predominantly serving the public interest, aim at the protection of individual interests as well; specifically the justiciability of the provision in question and the need for judicial protection must be taken into account (*see* Decision of the Federal Supreme Court BGE 131 I 366 paragraph 2.2). In a nutshell, constitutional rights include (1) all fundamental rights of Chapter 1 of Title 2 of the Federal Constitution as well as (2) all self-executing provisions of the international human rights conventions ratified by the Swiss Confederation, (3) all fundamental rights of the relevant cantonal constitution of the plaintiff, if they confer, in substance, more protection than the Federal Constitution, and (4) some rights outside Chapter 1, Title 2 of the Federal Constitution. The last category, which can be invoked by plaintiff in constitutional litigation as well, includes:

- the principle of legality in criminal matters (Article 5(1) of the Constitution) and in taxation matters (Article 5(1) and/or Article 127 of the Constitution);
- the prohibition of discrimination based on municipal citizenship (Article 37(2) of the Constitution);
- the supremacy of federal law (Article 49(1) of the Constitution);

- municipal autonomy as guaranteed within the limits fixed by the respective cantonal laws (Article 50 of the Constitution);
- the prohibition of inter-cantonal double taxation (Article 127(3) of the Constitution).

B. *Structure of Chapter 1, Title 2 of the Federal Constitution*

512. Following the example of the German Basic Law, Chapter 1 of Title 2 of the Federal Constitution opens with the human dignity clause (Article 7 of the Constitution; *infra* §2 I. of this Chapter) as the philosophical and normative foundation of, and guiding principle for, all fundamental rights. The subsequent provisions guarantee equality before the law, protection against arbitrariness and good faith (Articles 8–9 of the Constitution; *infra* §2 II., 2. III, and §3 of the Chapter). Then, in Articles 10–34, the Constitution enumerates several civil liberties (*Freiheitsrechte, libertés, libertà*; *infra* §4 of the Chapter), social fundamental rights (*Sozialgrundrechte, droits sociaux fondamentaux, diritti sociali fondamentali*; *infra* §5 of the Chapter), fundamental procedural guarantees (*Verfahrensgrundrechte, garanties générales de procédure, garanzie procedurali generali; infra* §6 of the Chapter) and the right to petition and political rights (*see supra* Part II, Chapter 2, §2). Chapter 1 of Title 2 of the Federal Constitution closes with two important provisions regarding the implementation and limitation of fundamental rights (Articles 35–36 of the Constitution; *infra* §1 III. and IV. of this Chapter). Note that the Constitution does not establish a hierarchy between the different provisions and that some fundamental rights cannot be enforced by a court (such as the content of the third sentence of Article 8(3) and Article 8(4) of the Constitution).

C. *Open Codification of Fundamental Rights*

1. The Catalogue of Fundamental Rights

513. Following the example of most modern constitutions, Chapter 1 of Title 2 of the Federal Constitution contains an extensive catalogue of fundamental rights (*Grundrechtskatalog, catalogue des droits fondamentaux, catalogo dei diritti fondametali*), which condenses four layers of Swiss fundamental rights history: (1) the written fundamental rights of the Federal Constitutions of 1848 and 1874; (2) the implied (unwritten) fundamental rights recognized by the Federal Supreme Court between 1959–1995; (3) the substantive principles and procedural guarantees derived from Article 4 of the Constitution 1874; and (4) the rights covered by the European Convention of Human Rights and Fundamental Liberties ('constitutionalization' of the ECHR) and other human rights treaties. The catalogue of fundamental rights of the Federal Constitution is *not exhaustive*. According to the concept of open codification, the Federal Supreme Court may recognize further implied fundamental rights that might emerge in the evolution of fundamental rights; but, owing to the generality of the catalogue, the expansion of the scope of protection of a written fundamental right through judicial interpretation is more likely than the recognition of further implied fundamental rights. Open codification means that further fundamental rights might be anchored in the catalogue through constitutional amendments as well. The inclusive character of the catalogue of fundamental rights is uncontested. However, a very disputed question is whether fundamental rights, once introduced into the catalogue, can be abolished again through constitutional amendment (*infra* §5 of this Chapter).

2. Codification of the Written Fundamental Rights of the Federal Constitution of 1874

514. The Federal Constitution of 1874 contained only a very limited set of written fundamental rights, such as the equal protection clause (Article 4 of the Constitution of 1874), the right to economic freedom, freedom of domicile, freedom of religion and conscience, freedom of marriage, freedom of the press, freedom of association and the right to petition. In the early Federal Supreme Court case law, only these written fundamental rights could be invoked by a plaintiff. Moreover, judicial protection was only granted by the Federal Supreme Court if the plaintiff's cantonal constitution contained an explicit textual basis for *further protection* beyond that provided by the Federal Constitution of 1874. Thus the protection of fundamental rights in Switzerland was to a certain extent lacunary. This narrow concept of enumerated fundamental rights was criticized, mainly on the grounds that the explicitly mentioned fundamental rights in the Constitution of 1874 should be merely construed as articulations of an underlying general system of fundamental rights (e.g., the freedom of the press *presupposes* the freedom of speech, the right to economic freedom *presupposes* the rights to property, etc.).

3. Codification of the Implied Fundamental Rights Recognized by the Federal Supreme Court

515. Gradually, the concept of enumerated fundamental rights was revealed to be too rigid. It did not allow the Federal Supreme Court to take into account various social, political and economic factors and actual threats to the individual, the democratic order and the *Rechtsstaat*. Since 1959 the Federal Supreme Court recognizes implied (unwritten) fundamental rights of the Confederation under certain conditions (*see, inter alia*, Decision of the Federal Supreme Court BGE 121 I 367 paragraph 2a). In order to be recognized as 'fundamental', the right in question must:

- constitute a *precondition* for the exercise of other written fundamental rights of the Federal Constitution;
- be *essential to the democratic order of the Confederation and to the Rechtsstaat principle*;
- reflect an already *widely shared constitutional practice in the cantons*; and
- be *generally accepted.*

516. Based on this formula, the Federal Supreme Court gradually recognized between 1959 and 1995 the following unwritten fundamental rights:

- the right to property (recognized in 1959/1960 in an *unpublished* decision of the Federal Supreme Court [*see* the decision of the Federal Supreme Court of 11 May

1969, re-printed in Schweizerisches Zentralblatt für Staats- und Verwaltungsrecht [ZBl] 1961, 69, which refers to two unpublished decisions in 1959 recognizing the right to property as an unwritten fundamental right of the Confederation]). Note: by popular vote in 1969, the right to property and the expropriation clause were incorporated into the Constitution of 1874 and thus became written fundamental rights;
- freedom of expression (recognized in 1961; *see* Decision of the Federal Supreme Court BGE 87 I 114 paragraph 2);
- personal freedom (recognized in 1963; *see* Decision of the Federal Supreme Court BGE 89 I 92 paragraph 3);
- freedom of language (recognized in 1965; *see* Decision of the Federal Supreme Court BGE 91 I 480 paragraph II/1);
- freedom of assembly (recognized in 1970; *see* Decision of the Federal Supreme Court BGE 96 I 219 paragraph 4 [leaving the question open whether the freedom to demonstrate constitutes an implied fundamental right as well]);
- the right to aid in distress (recognized in 1995; *see* Decision of the Federal Supreme Court BGE 121 I 367 paragraph 2a–c).

4. Codification of Substantive Principles and Procedural Guarantees (Article 4 of the Constitution 1874)

517. Apart from the acknowledgement of unwritten fundamental rights, the Federal Supreme Court has also derived substantive principles and procedural rules from the general equal protection clause of Article 4 of the Constitution of 1874 (*All Swiss are equal before the law*). This judge-made law is now incorporated in the catalogue of fundamental rights as well, *inter alia*:

- the protection against arbitrariness and the principle of good faith (Article 9 of the Constitution);
- fundamental procedural fairness before courts and agencies (Article 29(1) of the Constitution);
- the right to be heard (Article 29(2) of the Constitution);
- the right to free legal assistance and the right to a free legal counsel (Article 29(3) of the Constitution);
- general guarantees in judicial proceedings (Article 30 of the Constitution);
- (outside the catalogue of fundamental rights) the principle of legality in criminal matters (Article 5(1) of the Constitution);
- (outside the catalogue of fundamental rights) the principle of legality in taxation matters (Article 5(1) and/or Article 127(1) of the Constitution).

5. Constitutionalization of the European Convention of Human Rights

518. In November 1974, later than in other Western European countries, the Swiss Confederation finally ratified the ECHR. Following ratification, based on the concept of monism, the Federal Supreme Court held that the provisions of the Convention had the same *procedural* status as the domestic fundamental rights. The provisions of the Convention are therefore *directly applicable* by the courts and agencies of the cantons and the Confederation. However, being a revocable international treaty, the provisions of the ECHR were incorporated into the new Constitution ('constitutionalization' of the ECHR), in order to formalize their equivalence to the other fundamental rights of the Constitution. Hence, the catalogue of fundamental rights reflects the impact of the ECHR upon Swiss constitutional law and practice (*see* Table 1 below). Most additional protocols to the ECHR were ratified by Switzerland as well (with the exception of the additional protocols No. 1, No. 4 and No. 12).

519. Other international human rights conventions ratified by Switzerland are *inter alia*: the UN Covenant on Economic, Social, and Cultural Rights (UN-Pact I; SR 0.103.1), the UN Covenant on Civil and Political Rights (UN-Pact II; SR 0.103.2), the Second Optional Protocol to the UN-Pact II aiming at the abolition of the death penalty (SR 103.22), the UN Convention Against Torture and Other Cruel, Inhuman or Degrading Treatment or Punishment (SR 0.105) and its Optional Protocol (SR 0.105.1), the UN Convention on the Rights of the Child (SR 0.107) and its Optional Protocols on the involvement of children in armed conflicts (SR 0.107.1) and on the sale of children, child prostitution and child pornography (SR 0.107.2). The self-executing provisions of these conventions must be judiciously examined from case to case. In the case law of the Federal Supreme Court, the self-executing provisions of the UN-Pact II and the UN Convention on the Rights of the Child have played a substantial role so far and are regularly invoked before the Court (for recent decisions of the Federal Supreme Court *see* BGE 133 I 286 [*ad* Article 10(2)(b) UN-Pact II]; BGE 137 I 16 [*ad* Article 14(1) UN-Pact II]; BGE 136 I 332 [*ad* Article 19 UN-Pact II], BGE 124 III 90 [*ad* Article 12 UN Children Convention]). Regarding UN-Pact I, the Federal Supreme Court has held that these provisions are generally not self-executing (Decision of the Federal Supreme Court BGE 120 Ia 1 paragraph 5, *see also* recently BGE 135 I 161 paragraph 2.2 [*ad* Article 2(2) UN-Pact I]).

Table 1 Constitutionalization of the European Convention on Human Rights

	ECHR	Swiss Constitution of 1999
Right to Live	Article 2 and Additional Protocol 6	Article 10(1)
Prohibition of Torture	Article 3	Articles 10(3) and 25(3)
Prohibition of Slavery and Forced Labour	Article 4	Article 10(2)
Right to Liberty and Security	Article 5	Articles 10(2) and 31
Right to a Fair Trial	Article 6	Articles 29, 30 and 32
No Punishment without Law	Article 7	Constitutional right in all areas not covered by Article 1 of the Swiss Criminal Code
Right to Respect for Private and Family Life	Article 8	Article 13
Freedom of Thought,		
Conscience and Religion	Article 9	Article 15
Freedom of Expression	Article 10	Articles 16, 17, 20 and 21
Freedom of Assembly and Association	Article 11	Articles 22, 23 and 28
Right to Marry Right to an Effective Remedy	Article 12 Article 13	Article 14 Article 29a
Prohibition of Discrimination	Article 14	Article 8(2)

II. Addressees and Beneficiaries of Fundamental Rights

Selected Bibliography: *See* General Bibliography of this chapter and: Auer, Malinverni & Hottelier, 51 et seq.; Biaggini. Kommentar, Article 35; Biaggini Giovanni. 'Sind öffentliche Unternehmen grundrechtsberechtigt?'. In *Festschrift Peter Forstmoser*. Zurich: Schulthess, 2003, 623 et seq.; Patricia Egli. Drittwirkung von Grundrechten. Zürich: Schulthess 2002; Egli, 113 et seq.; Häfelin, Haller, Keller & Thurnherr, §7 and §8; Haller. *Swiss Constitution*, 166 et seq.; Haller. 'Menschenwürde, Recht auf Leben und persönliche Freiheit'. In *Handbuch der Grundrechte*, edited by Merten & Papier, §209; Hangartner Yvo. 'Grundrechtsbindung öffentlicher Unternehmen'. In *Aktuelle Juristische Praxis [AJP].* 2000, 515 et seq.; Häsler Philipp. *Geltung der Grundrechte für öffentliche Unternehmen.* Berne: Stämpfli, 2005; Mahon. commentaire, Articles 35; Misic. *Verfassungsbeschwerde*, 211 et seq.; Schweizer Rainer, J. St. Galler Kommentar, Article 35 (with further references); Thürer Daniel. 'Der Status der Ausländer'. In *Handbuch der Grundrechte*, edited by Mertens & Papier, §206; Waldmann

Bernhard. Basler Kommentar BV, Article 35; Weber-Dürler Beatrice. 'Träger der Grundrechte'. In *Handbuch der Grundrechte*, edited by Merten & Papier, §205.

A. Addressees: The State

520. Fundamental rights are primarily conceived as enforceable rights of the individual against the state (regarding the other 'dimensions' or 'facets' of fundamental rights *see infra* §1 III of this Chapter), which is obliged to tolerate the constitutionally protected spheres of human existence, to refrain from undue intrusion therein and to safeguard legal institutions, such as marriage and property. Thus, the addressee of fundamental rights is 'the State' and anyone exercising a 'public function' (*see* Article 35(2) of the Constitution). Of course, this broad-brush distinction can be tricky in practice and calls for some differentiation, which shall be discussed below in the context of Article 35 of the Constitution (*infra* §1 III. of this Chapter).

B. Natural Persons as Beneficiaries of Fundamental Rights

521. As a rule, most fundamental rights and constitutional rights apply to and can be invoked by every natural person. However, there are constitutional or judge-made exceptions that restrict the circle of beneficiaries (right-holders) of fundamental rights. Such restrictions may be based on citizenship, age or the immigration status of a person. The capacity to invoke, as a party, a subjective right derived from a fundamental right is conferred to *living* natural persons. Of course, the question regarding the beginning of life is controversial and has been left open by the European Court of Human Rights and the Federal Supreme Court (for the right to legal termination of pregnancy *see infra* §4 II,C of this Chapter and Article 119 of the Federal Criminal Code [SR 311]). The unborn child (*nasciturus*) is a right-holder of fundamental rights and may invoke them under the condition that it is born alive. Article 9(1) of the Federal Transplantation Act (SR 810.21) defines death as the irreversible cessation of all functions of the entire brain, including the brain stem (for further questions regarding the rights of a corpse *see* Decision of the Federal Supreme Court BGE 123 I 112 paragraph 4; regarding the post-mortal protection of the personality of a dead person *see* BGE 129 I 302 paragraph 1.2 and of next of kin *see* BGE 109 II 353 paragraph 4).

522. Restrictions based on citizenship and age of a natural person: According to Article 24(1) of the Constitution, only Swiss citizens have the right to establish their residence anywhere within the country. No Swiss citizen may be expelled from the country; they may only be extradited to a foreign authority with their consent (Article 25(1) of the Constitution). No one should enjoy privileges or be discriminated against because of their municipal and cantonal citizenship (Article 37(2) of the Constitution). Furthermore, only Swiss citizens who are 18 years or older and are not under guardianship because of mental illness or incapacity, shall have political rights in federal matters (Article 136(1) of the Constitution; but *see* Article 39(1) of the Constitution where the cantons may regulate the exercise of political rights at the cantonal and municipal level, which also includes the exercise of political rights for foreigners [e.g., in the Cantons of Fribourg, Vaud, Neuchâtel, Jura, Grisons and Appenzell Ausserrhoden]).

According to Article 11(1) of the Constitution, only children and young people have the right to special protection of their personal integrity and to the encouragement of their development. Furthermore, only children and young people have the right to a sufficient and free primary school education (Article 19 and Article 62(2) of the Constitution).

523. Restrictions based on the immigration status of a natural person: Another important restriction of the circle of beneficiaries is judge-made and concerns the guarantee of economic freedom (Article 27 of the Constitution). According to the Federal Supreme Court, foreign natural persons are only beneficiaries of economic freedom if they have a *permanent* residence permit (*see* Article 34 of the Federal Immigration Act [SR 142.20]: *Niederlassungsbewilligung; autorisation d'établissement; permesso di domicilio*) or if they possess a statutory or international treaty-based right to a residence permit (*see* Article 33 of the Federal Immigration Act: *Aufenthaltsbewilligung; autorisation de séjour; permesso di dimora*). Consequently, citizens from outside the EU and the European Free Trade Area who have a residence permit without a statutory or treaty-based right of extension may not invoke economic freedom (Decisions of the Federal Supreme Court BGE 129 II 401 paragraph 4.3; BGE 123 I 19 paragraph 2).

C. Legal Persons as Beneficiaries of Fundamental Rights

524. National legal persons (i.e., incorporated in Switzerland and established under private law, no matter if dominated by foreigners) are beneficiaries of all procedural fundamental rights, the equal protection clause, the protection against arbitrariness, the guarantee of property and, of course, economic freedom. However, they are generally not beneficiaries of the right to free legal assistance and to free legal counsel (Article 29(3) of the Constitution; for a very narrow exception *see* Decision of the Federal Supreme Court BGE 131 I 223, 226–227 paragraph 1.1). *E contrario*, fundamental rights, which by their nature exclusively protect natural persons (such as personal freedom, freedom of religion, or the right to marry), cannot be invoked by legal persons. Foreign legal persons established under private law are, as well, right-holders of the fundamental rights listed above; however, they may only invoke economic freedom if they are permitted the exercise of their business in Switzerland (*see*, e.g., Article 5 of the Agreement on the Free Movement of Persons between the Swiss Confederation and the EU [SR 0.142.112.681]).

525. Fundamental rights are directed against the state. Consequently, as a rule, *legal persons established under public law* may not invoke fundamental rights unless they are acting on the grounds of private law and are affected by a state activity in the same manner as an individual. So far, the Federal Supreme Court has left open whether mixed companies, such as Swisscom, which is a corporation established under the Federal Telecommunication Act (SR 784.11) with the Swiss Confederation as majority shareholder (*spezialgesetzliche Aktiengesellschaft*), may invoke economic freedom and the guarantee of property (Decision of the Federal Supreme Court BGE 131 II 13 paragraph 6.4.1). It is interesting to note that the Federal Data Protection Act, which essentially substantiates Article 13(2) of the Constitution, applies to the processing of data pertaining to 'legal persons' by federal bodies (Article 2(1) a of the Act). It is questionable whether the legislator had fully premeditated the consequences of this broad formulation of the scope of application *ratione personae* because it includes legal person established under public law as well. In such a constellation, the state is the addressee as well as the beneficiary of the fundamental right concerned. At least from a dogmatic perspective this is difficult to reconcile with the traditional concept of fundamental rights. In practice, there is a tendency to ignore the problem and just to apply the law (e.g., Decision of the Federal Administrative Court A-4571/2015 of 10 August 2016). Consequently, the Parliament plans to amend Article 2(1) of the Federal Data Protection Act and to narrow its scope of application down to natural persons only (hence striking out all legal persons established under private law as well). In a recent case, the Federal Supreme Court has held that public or mixed corporations may not directly invoke Article 13(2) of the Constitution in order to protect their privacy (Decision of the Federal Supreme Court 1C_428/2016).

526. Regarding municipalities, the Federal Supreme Court has held that they are only beneficiaries of fundamental rights if: (1) their autonomy, existence or territorial integrity is violated; (2) they appear as actors in the area of private law; or (3) when a decision or judgment affects them in the same way as private persons (Decision of the Federal Supreme Court BGE 132 I 140 paragraph 1.3.1).

III. Implementation of Fundamental Rights

Selected Bibliography: *See* General Bibliography for this chapter and: Auer Andreas. 'Freiheitsrechte im Dreiecksverhältnis zwischen Staat, Gesellschaft und Individuum'. In *Schweizerisches Zentralblatt für Staats- und Verwaltungsrecht [ZBl]*. 1992, 2 et seq.; Biaggini. Kommentar, Article 35; Haller. *Swiss Constitution*, 166 et seq.; Häner Isabelle. 'Grundrechtsgeltung bei der Wahrnehmung staatlicher Aufgaben durch Private'. In *Aktuelle Juristische Praxis [AJP]*. 2002, 1144 et seq.; Hangartner Yvo. 'Grundrechtsbindung öffentlicher Unternehmen'. In *Aktuelle Juristische Praxis [AJP]*. 2000, 515 et seq.; Kälin Walter et al., *Auslagerung von sicherheitspolizeilichen Aufgaben, Beiheft zur Zeitschrift für Schweizerisches Recht [ZSR]* no. 46. Basel, 2007; Mahon. commentaire, Article 35; Müller Jörg Paul. *Grundrechtstheorie*, 45 et seq.; Müller Jörg Paul. 'Geschichtliche Grundlagen, Zielsetzung und Funktionen der Grundrechte'. In *Handbuch der Grundrechte*, edited by Mertens & Papier, §202; Schweizer Rainer, J. St. Galler Kommentar, Article 35 (with further references); Rhinow, Schefer & Uebersax, §12; Rhinow et al., Chapter 6; Vogel Stefan. *Der Staat als Marktteilnehmer.* Zurich: Schulthess, 2000.

527. According to Article 35(1) of the Constitution, fundamental rights must be implemented throughout the entire legal system (all state authorities at every level). In the context of this provision, the Federal Supreme Court has pointed out on several occasions that fundamental rights are not only subjective rights of the individual, conferring enforceable protection from undue interference of the state (defensive function; *individuelles Abwehrrecht*), but also provisions with an objective content (*objektiv-rechtlicher Gehalt*), permeating the entire legal order (Decisions of the Federal Supreme Court BGE 130 III 353 paragraph 2.1.1; *see also* BGE 134 I 49 paragraph 2.4 and BGE 134 I 56 paragraph 4.4 [both concerning the refusal to naturalize persons wearing a headscarf]). In sum, the Federal Supreme Court case law includes the various facets of most fundamental rights under current Swiss constitutional doctrine: (1) a *directly justiciable facet*: fundamental rights are conceived as subjective and enforceable rights of the individual vis-à-vis the state; (2) an *indirectly justiciable facet*: law-applying authorities may interpret and concretize ordinary statutory provisions in the light of fundamental rights; and (3) a *programmatic facet*: the objective content and the inherent values of fundamental rights may serve as a mandate for legislative action at the federal and/or cantonal level. Note that the notion 'throughout the entire legal system' is to be interpreted in a general sense (e.g., in cases regarding international mutual legal assistance, *see* Decision of the Federal Supreme Court BGE 126 II 324 paragraph 4c [underlining 'la portée générale de l'obligation de respect des droits fondamentaux']; *see also* BGE 136 I 158 paragraph 3.2 [although the European Court of Human Rights had affirmed a violation of Article 10 of the Convention, a *subsidiary* of the Swiss Radio and Television Company, established under private law, still refused to broadcast a political advertisement of an animal rights' activist group; the Federal Supreme Court held that fundamental rights must be implemented, otherwise legal measures pertaining to the broadcasting concession must be examined].

528. Article 35(2) of the Constitution states that whoever exercises a state function must respect fundamental rights and contribute to their implementation. The term 'state function' must be understood in a broad sense. The Federal Supreme Court has always pointed out that fundamental rights bind all public authorities of all branches of the State and at every level thereof (federal, cantonal, municipal), even if acting on a purely private law basis (*see*, *inter alia*, Decision of the Federal Supreme Court BGE 127 I 90 paragraph 4c [regarding the right of the Canton of Lucerne, conceded to a private company, to exclusively advertise on public transport vehicles; the refusal of the company to place the advertisement of an animal rights group on a bus does not violate the freedom of opinion as set out in the Federal Constitution and the ECHR]). All entrepreneurial activities of public authorities must observe fundamental rights (for an interesting case regarding the refusal of the City of Geneva to lease a theatre, owned by the municipality as 'patrimoine financier', for security reasons *see* Decision of the Federal Supreme Court 1C_312/2010 of 8 December 2010 [Dieudonné]). The action of public authorities may be formal (e.g., administrative orders, public or private contracts, etc.) or informal (e.g., *actus realis*; *see* Decision of the Federal Supreme Court BGE 133 I 49). Note that in a semi-direct democracy like Switzerland, state functions are also fulfilled by the People, e.g., when municipal assemblies are voting on requests for naturalization (*see* Decision of the Federal Supreme Court BGE 135 I 275 paragraphs 4.2 and 4.3). Private individuals or corporations fulfilling *delegated* public functions or private holders of legal monopolies or concessions are bound by fundamental rights (Decision of the Federal Supreme Court BGE 127 I 84 paragraph 4c; BGE 133 I 49 paragraph 3.2). Public authorities may not evade the observance of fundamental rights by outsourcing state functions to private persons or corporations.

529. Finally, according to Article 35(3) of the Constitution, public authorities (i.e., all organs of the legislative, executive and judicial branch of the state) shall ensure that fundamental rights, wherever applicable, also take effect in relationships between individuals. This provision obviously stands in a certain antagonistic tension to the classical definition of fundamental rights according to which private parties can never or only under very exceptional cases be addressees of fundamental rights. By anchoring the so-called theory of third-party effect (*Drittwirkungstheorie*) in the Constitution, Article 35(3) takes into account that not only the state, but also natural or legal persons may threaten fundamental rights in an intolerable way (*see also* Decision of the Federal Supreme Court BGE 130 III 28 paragraph 4.2: '[L]es droits fondamentaux servent en premier lieu à défendre les individus contre les atteintes des pouvoirs publics, mais leur portée peut se révéler utile dans la détermination de ce qui est tolérable dans les relations entre particuliers.'). According to the theory of third-party effect, fundamental rights constitute an overarching value system permeating all sub-constitutional areas of law as well. Despite other positions among Swiss constitutional scholars, probably with the exception of the right of men and women to equal pay for work of equal value (Article 8(3) of the Constitution), the Federal Supreme Court case law indicates that fundamental rights have no *direct* third-party effect between private parties (e.g., in a civil action, John Doe cannot invoke Article 15 of the Constitution against Jane Doe for her critique of his religious beliefs, *see* Decision of the Federal Supreme Court BGE 118 Ia 46 paragraph 3c; in the decision *Tavel v. Switzerland* of 7 January 2014, 41170/07, the ECHR carefully avoided the issue with regard to a Swiss family foundation charter allegedly discriminating against the offspring of the female members of the family). However, in connection with the freedom to coalition (Article 28 of the Constitution), the Federal Supreme Court has admitted and applied the theory of *indirect* third-party effects in a labour law torts action (*see* Decision of the Federal Supreme Court BGE 132 III 122 paragraph 4.4.1: '[L]e juge, qui est appelé, dans le cadre d'une action aquilienne, à se prononcer sur la licéité d'un moyen de combat en droit collectif du travail, est tenu de prendre en compte les garanties constitutionnelles en cause.'). Thus, the theory of indirect third-party effect implies that law-applying authorities interpret and concretize private or criminal law provisions *in the light of the fundamental rights at stake*. An often cited example for legislative action are Articles 28 et seq. of the Civil Code (SR 210) balancing the interest to protect the personality of the individual vis-à-vis the interest of the media to inform the public (*see also* Decision of the Federal Supreme Court BGE 132 III 641 paragraph 5). – Of course, the Federal Constitution leaves the questions unresolved *how* fundamental rights should take effect between individuals and whether the fulfilment of this task primarily falls upon the legislative or judicial branch of the state.

IV. Limitations (or Restrictions) of Fundamental Rights

Selected Bibliography: Aubert & Mahon. Article 36; Auer, Malinverni & Hottelier, Vol. II, 77 et seq.; Biaggini. Kommentar, Article 36 (with further references); Egli, 114 et seq.; Epiney Astrid. Basler Kommentar BV, Article 36 (with further references); Häfelin, Haller, Keller & Thurnherr, §9; Haller. *Swiss Constitution*, 170 et seq.; Kiener & Kälin, 70 et seq.; Moor Pierre. 'Systématique et illustration du principe de la proportionnalité'. In *Mélanges Fromont*, Strasbourg, 2001, 319 et seq.; Müller Jörg Paul. *Grundrechtstheorie*, 103 et seq.; Müller Markus. *Das besondere Rechtsverhältnis.* Berne: Stämpfli, 2003; Rhinow, Schefer & Uebersax, §13 (with further references); Schefer Markus. *Die Kerngehalte von Grundrechten.* Berne: Stämpfli, 2001; Schefer

Markus. *Die Beeinträchtigung von Grundrechten* Berne: Stämpfli, 2006; Schefer Markus. 'Beeinträchtigung von Grundrechten'. In *Handbuch der Grundrechte*, edited by Mertens & Papier, §208; Schweizer Rainer, J. St. Galler Kommentar *ad* Article 36 (with further references); Tanquerel Thierry. 'Le juge comme arbitre de l'intérêt public'. In *Mélanges Perrin*, Geneva, 2002, 221 et seq.; Weber-Dürler Beatrice. 'Der Grundrechtseingriff'. In *Veröffentlichung der Vereinigung Deutscher Staatsrechtslehrer [VVDStRL]*. 1998 [57], 57 et seq.; Wiederkehr René. *Die Kerngehaltsgarantie am Beispiel kantonaler Grundrechte*. Berne: Stämpfli, 2000; Zimmerli Ulrich. 'Der Grundsatz der Verhältnismässigkeit im öffentlichen Recht'. In *Zeitschrift für Schweizerisches Recht [ZSR]*. 1978 II, et seq.; Zünd Andreas & Errass Christoph. 'Die polizeiliche Generalklausel'. In *Zeitschrift des Bernischen Juristenvereins [ZBJV]*. 2011 261 et seq.

A. The Conditions for the Limitation of Fundamental Rights in General

530. The exercise of fundamental rights is not absolute and may be subject to constitutional limitations. According to Article 36 of the Constitution, which codifies the case law of the Federal Supreme Court, four conditions – each of which must be satisfied individually – must be met in order to limit the scope of protection of a fundamental right:

(1) there must be a legal basis or a clear and present danger (Article 36(1) of the Constitution);
(2) the limitation must be justified by a public interest or by the need to protect the fundamental rights of others (Article 36(2) of the Constitution);
(3) the limitation must be proportionate to the goal pursued (Article 36(3) of the Constitution); and
(4) the essence (*Kerngehalt*) of the fundamental right(s) at stake may not be violated (Article 36(4) of the Constitution).

531. The heading of Article 36 (fundamental rights) is usually considered to be over-inclusive because the Federal Supreme Court case law under the Constitution of 1874 was only designed for limitations of *civil liberties* (*Freiheitsrechte, libertés, libertà*). Under the new Constitution, it is undisputed that Article 36 applies to all civil liberties. This leads to the question whether Article 36 of the Constitution is also applicable to other provisions of the catalogue of fundamental rights, such as human dignity, equality before the law, fundamental procedural guarantees, fundamental social rights or political rights (Articles 7–9, 10(3), 12, 19 or 29–32 of the Constitution), which – at least in theory – cannot tolerate any limitation (e.g., an administrative order violates or does not violate the protection against arbitrariness in Article 9 of the Constitution; it cannot be 'a little bit' arbitrary). In recent cases, the Federal Supreme Court has chosen a pragmatic approach and has held that the limitations of Article 36 of the Constitution are *partially applicable per analogiam* to certain fundamental social rights (Decisions of the Federal Supreme Court BGE 142 I 7 paragraph 7.2.4 [with regard to Article 12 of the Constitution; *see also* BGE 131 I 166]; BGE 129 I 12 [regarding the right to primary school education; Article 19 of the Constitution]).

The current case law is still in flux and not always coherent (*see* Decision of the Federal Supreme Court BGE 130 I 312 where the Court has held that the guarantee of access to justice of Article 29a of the Constitution unconditionally falls under Article 36).

532. Note that the four conditions enumerated in Article 36 of the Constitution are not always exhaustive. Depending on the fundamental right at stake, further conditions may apply (e.g., regarding the *special* restrictions of economic freedom, *see infra* §4 VIII of this Chapter, regarding Article 94(1) of the Constitution). As already discussed above, in certain cases the criteria of Article 36 apply only partly *per analogiam* or even not at all.

B. Any Limitation Requires a Legal Basis

533. According to Article 36(1) of the Constitution, any limitation of a fundamental right requires a legal basis. In substance, the limitation must be described in general and abstract terms in a statute or ordinance (*Vorbehalt des Rechtssatzes*), whereby 'general' refers to an indeterminable number of persons and 'abstract' to an indeterminable number of facts. Except for grave limitations of fundamental rights (second sentence of Article 36(1) of the Constitution), the requirement of a legal basis does not exclude the delegation of legislative competencies to the executive branch (notably to the administration). Furthermore, based on the principle of legality (Article 5(1) of the Constitution), the rule must be 'sufficiently and adequately' precise (Decisions of the Federal Supreme Court BGE 141 I 203 paragraph 4.1 and BGE 132 I 49, 58; *see also* BGE 133 I 110 paragraph 6.1; BGE 134 I 322 paragraphs 2.6.1–2.6.3; BGE 136 I 1 paragraph 5.3.1; BGE 136 I 87 paragraph 3.1) to permit the addressees of the rule to foresee the consequences of their actions to a degree of certainty and previsibility (Decision of the Federal Supreme Court BGE 117 Ia 472 paragraph 2e). However, vagueness and generality cannot always be circumvented (e.g., in the area of police laws). The degree of precision required depends on multiple criteria, such as the identity of the addressees of a rule, the gravity of the limitation of the constitutional rights concerned, the complexity and the previsibility of a (possible and adequate) decision in a given case (Decision of the Federal Supreme Court BGE 128 I 327 paragraph 4.2; *see also* BGE 132 I 49 paragraph 6.2; 135 I 169 paragraph 5.4.1; 136 I 87 paragraph 3.1).

534. The underlying idea of the requirement of the *adequate legal form* (*Vorbehalt des Gesetzes*) is that governmental interference into the constitutionally protected spheres of the individual must be democratically legitimized. Therefore, grave limitations of fundamental rights must be *expressly* foreseen by a *statute* (Article 36(1) of the Constitution), such as – on the federal level – by federal statutes subject to a referendum (Articles 141 and 164(1)(b) of the Constitution) or treaties based on international public law (*see* Decision of the Federal Supreme Court BGE 141 I 215 paragraph 3.2 assessing the gravity of the interference). Minor limitations can be regulated by *administrative ordinances*. The distinction between grave and minor limitations of fundamental rights is sometimes challenging to draw in practice and requires thorough consultation of the widely ramified Federal Supreme Court case law on the subject.

535. It is evident that not all threats and dangers to security and to public order can be foreseen by statute. Therefore, in case of a clear and present danger, the general police clause (*polizeiliche Generalklausel*) in the third sentence of Article 36(1) of the Constitution, may serve as the *constitutional basis* for police actions. It can temporarily replace the requirement of an express statutory basis (even in cases of grave limitations of fundamental rights, *see* Decision of the Federal Supreme Court BGE 125 II 417 paragraph 6b; *see also* BGE 141 I 210 paragraph 4.6; BGE 132 I 49 paragraph 6.2; BGE 134 I 322 paragraph 2.4; BGE 136 I 87 paragraph 3.1). The Federal Supreme Court has already affirmed the constitutionality of the general police clause under the Constitution of 1874. This was reaffirmed in the *World Economic Forum* case (Decision of the Federal Supreme Court BGE 130 I 369; *see also* BGE 126 I 112 paragraph 4), where the Court also held that the addressees of the police clause must respect the general principles of constitutional and administrative law, and – above all – the principle of proportionality.

C. *Any Limitation Must Be Justified by Public Interest*

536. Any limitation of a fundamental right must be justified by public interest (Article 36(2) of the Constitution). The public interest at stake must outweigh competing private or other public interests. There can be no abstract and clear-cut formula of what public interests are – they can vary from place to place and change over the course of time. According to the Federal Supreme Court, one important and traditional category constitute *police interests*, which may impose limitations of fundamental rights for the protection of 'public order, peace, security, health, morality, and good faith in business relations' (Decision of the Federal Supreme Court BGE 91 I 457 paragraph 2).

537. The notion of public interest also includes other areas, such as the protection of the environment (Article 74 of the Constitution), spatial planning (also known as 'zoning'; Article 75 of the Constitution), and social, cultural or economic interests. Also, conflicts between a fundamental right and the fulfilment of a public task often occur in the area of free speech (*see, inter alia,* Decision of the Federal Supreme Court BGE 132 I 256 paragraphs 4.4–4.6 [regarding the denial of a demonstration on National Day] or in property law cases (e.g., conflicts between the owner of land and the public interest to maintain or create affordable housing or a functional infrastructure; *see, inter alia,* Decision of the Federal Supreme Court BGE 113 Ia 126, *Armengol*).

538. Article 36(2) states *in fine* that the limitation of fundamental rights may also be justified by the protection of fundamental rights of others. However, a mere inconvenience for third persons may not justify the limitation of fundamental rights; the danger for other persons must be imminent and grave (Decision of the Federal Supreme Court BGE 130 I 16 paragraph 5.2 regarding forced medication of a paranoid schizophrenic person in a psychiatric clinic).

D. *Any Limitation Must Be Proportionate to the Goals Pursued*

539. According to Article 36(3) of the Constitution, any limitation of fundamental rights must be proportionate to the goals pursued. The underlying idea of the doctrine of proportionality is that a limitation of a fundamental right should not go further than is required by the public interest or – as set out in Article 36(2) of the Constitution – for the protection of fundamental rights of others.

540. The threefold proportionality test of the Federal Supreme Court cumulatively requires that:

(1) the measure is *adequate* to achieve a legitimate public purpose;
(2) the measure must be suppressed if *milder means to attain the goal pursued are available*; and
(3) the public interest is *necessary to prevail over the private interest (balancing of interests)*.

541. The proportionality test has led to a widely disseminated Federal Supreme Court case law, which cannot be recounted here (for recent Decisions of the Federal Supreme Court *see* BGE 131 I 223 paragraph 4.3 [abstract review of a cantonal statute prohibiting litigation financing agreements in the light of economic freedom; proportionality test is not met]; BGE 132 I 49 paragraph 7.2 [expel and removal orders of the police against groups of persons consuming alcohol in and around the Bernese railway station; proportionality affirmed]; BGE 132 I 229 paragraph 11.3 [blocking of certain of Mobutu Sese Seko's assets not proportional]; BGE 133 I 81 paragraph 4.1 [abstract review of a cantonal police regulation regarding the temporary storage of data from the surveillance of public places and streets; temporary storage for 100 days held proportional]; BGE 133 I 110 paragraph 7.1 [validity of a popular initiative in the Canton of Geneva aiming at the prohibition of smoking in public places; proportionality test is met]; BGE 134 I 140 paragraph 6.2 [measures against domestic violence, such as restraining orders, proportional]; BGE 134 I 214 paragraph 5.7 [statutory prohibition on begging in Geneva held proportional]; BGE 135 I 169 paragraph 5.6 [observation of an insured person by a private detective held proportional]; BGE 135 I 176 paragraph 8.1 [monument preservation measures for a small fishermen's cabin held proportional]; BGE 135 I 233 paragraph 3.1 [abstract review of a cantonal statute regulating the use of secondary residences; the generous quotas held proportional]; BGE 136 I 17 paragraph 4.4 [abstract review of a Bernese statute aiming at the protection from passive smoking; proportionality of the ban of water pipe smoking affirmed]; BGE 136 I 29 paragraph 4.2 [abstract review of a Bernese statute aiming at the protection from passive smoking; regulation regarding smoking rooms held proportional]; BGE 136 I 87 paragraph 3.2 [abstract review of the Zurich police law]; BGE 137 I 31 paragraph 7.5.2 [measures against hooliganism met proportionality test]).

E. The Essence of Fundamental Rights Is Inviolable

542. According to Article 36(4) of the Constitution, the essence or the core (*Kerngehalt*) of fundamental rights is inviolable. The concept of a *Kerngehalt* of fundamental rights, which is in substance rooted in human dignity (Article 7 of the Constitution), is relatively new to Swiss constitutional law and is mainly influenced by Article 19(2) of the German Basic Law. Depending on the fundamental right in question, the *Kerngehalt* describes a sphere of constitutional protection, which cannot be limited under any circumstances by the state. The normative substance of the

Kerngehalt cannot be described in general or abstract terms. The case law on the expropriation clause and on the right to personal freedom illustrate that the Federal Supreme Court has given preference to a pragmatic approach, which does not allow clear-cut conclusions.

543. In accordance with Article 15(2) of the ECHR, the catalogue of fundamental rights of the Swiss Constitution contains specific guarantees, which are per se inviolable. Hence, Article 36 does not apply to certain fundamental rights, such as the prohibition of the death penalty in the second sentence of Article 10(1) of the Constitution and the prohibition of torture in Article 10(3) of the Constitution.

F. Limitations based upon a Special Status of a Category of Persons

544. Basically, every natural person is a beneficiary of fundamental rights. However, in case of a special relationship (*Sonderstatusverhältnis*) between a certain category of persons and the state, these freedoms may be subject to restrictions. Mainly, the addressees of the limitations are public officers, soldiers and other members of the Army, students and prisoners. In order to be constitutional, the limitation must be expressly foreseen by statute, justified by the public interest and meet the proportionality standard (*see*, e.g., Decision of the Federal Supreme Court BGE 98 Ib 301 paragraph 2a). Thus, for example, the liberty of opinion of public officers may be restricted by their duty of loyalty (for a recent case *see* Decision of the Federal Supreme Court BGE 136 I 335); regarding restrictions to the right to freely chose one's domicile *see infra* §4 VI of this Chapter.

§2. Human Dignity, Protection Against Arbitrariness and Good Faith

Selected Bibliography: Aubert Jean-François. 'Willkürverbot und Vertrauensschutz als Grundrechte'. In *Handbuch der Grundrechte*, edited by Merten & Papier, §228; Auer, Malinverni & Hottelier. Vol. II, 531 et seq.; Biaggini. Kommentar, Articles 7 and 9 (with further references); Egli, 119–120 and 152–154; Engi Lorenz. 'Was heisst Menschenwürde?'. In *Schweizeisches Zentralblatt für Staats- und Verwaltungsrecht [ZBl]*. 2008, 659 et seq.; Grisel, *Egalité*, passim; Haefliger. *Alle Schweizer sind vor dem Gesetze gleich*, 183 et seq., 217 et seq.; Haller Walter. 'Menschenwürde, Recht auf Leben und persönliche Freiheit'. In *Handbuch der Grundrechte*, edited by Merten & Papier, 199 et seq.; Haller Walter. *Swiss Constitution*, 175–176, 215–216–202; Kiener & Kälin, §31; Kley Andreas. 'Sakralisierung von Staatsrecht und Politik'. *Mélanges Pierre Moor*. Berne, 2005, 95 et seq.; Mahon. commentaire, Article 9; Mastronardi Philippe. 'Menschenwürde als materielle "Grundnorm" des Rechtsstaates?'. In Thürer et al., §14; Mastronardi Philippe. St. Galler Kommentar, Article 7 (with further references); Misic. *Verfassungsbeschwerde*, 319 et seq. (with further references); Moor Pierre. 'De la place de la prohibition de l'arbitraire dans l'ordre juridique'. In *Festschrift Yvo Hangartner*, edited by Ehrenzeller et al., 605 et seq.; Müller Georg. Kommentar BV 1874, Article 4; Müller & Schefer, Chapter 1; Rhinow, Schefer & Uebersax, §20; Rohner Christoph. St. Galler Kommentar, Article 9 (with further references); Rouiller Claude. 'Protection de l'individu contre l'arbitraire et protection de la bonne foi'. In Thürer et al., 677 et seq.; Thürer Daniel. 'Das Willkürverbot nach Art. 4 BV'. In *Zeitschrift für Schweizerisches Recht [ZSR]*. 1987 II, 413 et seq.; Tschentscher Axel. Basler Kommentar BV, Article 9; Uhlmann Felix. *Das Willkürverbot (Art. 9 BV)*. Zurich: Schulthess, 2005; Weber-Dürler Beatrice. *Vertrauensschutz im öffentlichen Recht*. Basel/Frankfurt a.M.: Helbing & Lichtenhahn, 1983; Weber-Dürler Beatrice. 'Neuere Entwickungen des Vertrauensschutzes'. In *Schweizerisches Zentralblatt für Staats- und Verwaltungsrecht [ZBl]*. 2002, 281 et seq.

I. Human Dignity

545. Following the example of the German Basic Law and some recently amended cantonal constitutions (e.g., §9 of the Constitution of the Canton of Aargau [1980] or Article 9 of the Constitution of the Canton of Berne [1993]), the catalogue opens with the human dignity clause (Article 7 of the Constitution) as the philosophical and normative foundation of and guiding principle for all fundamental rights and their implementation. The fundamental idea of human dignity is that human beings shall not be degraded to mere replaceable objects (*see* Article 3 of the ECHR and Article 10 UNO-Pact II); human dignity shall not have a market price (*see* the famous Kantian formula: 'In the kingdom of ends everything has either a price or a dignity. What has a price can be replaced by something else as its equivalent; what on the other hand is above all price and therefore admits of no equivalent has a dignity.'). The essence of human dignity cannot be conclusively defined *in abstracto*, let alone in terms of positive law. Paraphrasing a leading case of the Federal Supreme Court, human dignity encompasses the idea of the ultimately incomprehensible being-as-such of an individual or of individuals and the recognition of every individual's unique- and otherness; as the innermost value and basis of civil liberties, it serves for their interpretation and concretization (Decision of the Federal Supreme Court BGE 132 I 49 paragraph 5.1).

546. The position of the human dignity clause in Chapter 1, Title 2 equally indicates that human dignity is a legally enforceable subjective right as well. As a default fundamental right (*Auffanggrundrecht*), it has an independent and justiciable content, which is in practice – owing to the generality of the wording of the other fundamental rights in the Constitution – rather limited. Unless a 'hard case' is at stake, the invocation of the human dignity clause constitutes an *ultima ratio* and has relatively small chances of success in ordinary constitutional litigation. Already under the Constitution of 1874, the Court held that the right to a decent burial (Decision of the Federal Supreme Court BGE 129 I 311 paragraph 1.2.5) and the prohibition of incarceration in order to enforce the settlement of debts (*Schuldverhaft*) are subjective rights falling within the penumbra of human dignity (now under Article 7 of the Constitution; *see* Decision of the Federal Supreme Court BGE 134 I 293 paragraph 3.2; *see also* BGE 22 24 et seq. [unpaid military taxes may not be 'paid' by obliging the person to physical labour in military barracks]). Furthermore, the Court has pointed out that the human dignity clause stands as a guiding principle in a special relationship to the constitutional protection of personality (Decision of the Federal Supreme Court BGE 127 I 6 paragraph 5b), to the non-discrimination clause in Article 8(2) of the

Constitution (Decisions of the Federal Supreme Court BGE 134 I 49 paragraph 3.1; BGE 134 I 56 paragraph 5.1; BGE 135 I 49 paragraph 4.1), to the right to receive assistance when in need (Decisions of the Federal Supreme Court BGE 131 I 166 paragraphs 3.1 and 7.1; BGE 135 I 119 paragraph 7.3; BGE 136 I 254 paragraph 6.2), and to the guarantees of fair procedure (Decision of the Federal Supreme Court BGE 135 I 265 paragraph 4.5). The human dignity clause is violated when – despite the unwillingness of an asylum seeker to cooperate with the authorities – the denial of the right to receive assistance when in need (Article 12 of the Constitution) puts the survival of the person in question (Decision of the Federal Supreme Court BGE 131 I 166 paragraph 7.1; *see* also BGE 142 I 5 regarding the question whether the assistance payment according to Article 12 of the Constitution could be terminated if the person in need continues to refuse to participate in an employment scheme, which is not remunerated). Systematic strip-searches and full body searches of prisoners do not violate the human dignity clause (Decision of the Federal Supreme Court BGE 141 I 144 paragraph 6.3). The requirement to continue to work in prison after the detainee has reached retirement age was held compatible by the Court (Decision of the Federal Supreme Court BGE 139 I 182 paragraphs 1.3 and 2.4; reaffirmed by the ECHR with regard to Article 4 of the Convention in *Meier v. Switzerland* of 9 February 2016, 10109/14, §79 ('The compulsory work performed by the applicant while in detention, including the work carried out since he reached retirement age, can therefore be regarded as "work required to be done in the ordinary course of detention" within the meaning of Article 4 §3(a) of the Convention.')).

II. Protection Against Arbitrariness

547. In Switzerland, in contrast to most other constitutional systems and international human rights treaties, the protection against arbitrariness is a subjective and fully enforceable fundamental right binding all State organs and public authorities and therefore encompassing all their actions (*all-embracing character* of the protection against arbitrariness clause). Its function is to safeguard a minimum standard of justice in the *Rechtsstaat* and to correct grave manifestations of injustice (*absolute character* of the protection against arbitrariness clause). As a subsidiary fundamental right (*Auffanggrundrecht*), it is usually invoked as an *ultima ratio* in constitutional and administrative litigation when no other fundamental right is available. The protection against arbitrariness and the equal protection clause in Article 8(1) of the Constitution are closely intertwined (*see* Decision of the Federal Supreme Court BGE 131 I 394 paragraph 4.2 (with further references): 'L'inégalité de traitement apparaît [...] comme une forme particulière d'arbitraire, consistant à traiter de manière inégale ce qui devrait l'être de manière semblable ou inversement.').

548. It is not sufficient that the grounds of a decision issued by a public authority prove to be *untenable*: the *result* must be arbitrary – even if another, maybe more adequate or reasonable solution seems possible – regardless of the motives that led to the given decision (Decision of the Federal Supreme Court BGE 141 I 53 paragraph 3.4 [family reunification]).

549. According to the case law of the Federal Supreme Court, arbitrariness can be identified in the process of *law-making* when a statutory provision is not based on serious and objective grounds or if it is senseless or useless (Decisions of the Federal Supreme Court BGE 131 I 1 paragraph 4.2 [Municipality of Grindelwald; duty of real estate owners to maintain and clean the communal road network *in persona* ten to twenty hours per year or to pay a tax instead; *see also* BGE 138 II 129 paragraphs 5.4.3 and 5.4.4 regarding a municipal statute holding real estate owners per se responsible for the littering situation on public places in the City of Berne]; BGE 132 I 157 paragraph 4.1 [Glarus; cantonal statutes regarding the taxation and valuation of real estate]; BGE 133 I 249 paragraph 3.3 [Valais; cantonal statute prohibiting twelve dangerous breeds of dogs]; BGE 133 I 259 paragraph 4.3 [Basel-City; new cantonal notary public statute]; BGE 134 I 23 paragraph 8 [Valais; public retirement funds statute]; BGE 136 I 241 paragraph 3.1 [Geneva; cantonal statute prohibiting smoking in public places]).

550. The protection against arbitrariness in the process of *law-application* plays a considerable role in constitutional litigation before the Federal Supreme Court (although with relatively low chances of success). A violation may be affirmed by the Court when a decision (a) is manifestly unfounded, (b) stands in obvious contradiction with the factual situation, (c) violates a provision or an undisputed principle of law, *or* (d) violates the idea of justice in an shocking manner ('de manière choquante'; *see* for recent cases Decisions of the Federal Supreme Court BGE 141 I 53 paragraph 3.4 [family reunification]; BGE 141 I 110 paragraphs 3.5.2–3.6 [doubling the court fee on the grounds that the trial in court lasted less than a day and because plaintiff asked for the deliverance of a written judgment]; BGE 131 I 467 paragraph 3.1 [arbitrary grading of a bar exam thesis]; BGE 132 I 175 paragraph 1.2 [denial of an amortization of a piece of real estate without further examination of the factual circumstances by the cantonal tax authorities]; BGE 133 I 149 paragraph 3.1 [arbitrary delimitation between public waters and adjacent private real estate]; BGE 133 II 257 paragraph 5.1 [arbitrary application of cantonal procedural provisions regarding an anti-discrimination torts action]; BGE 134 II 124 paragraph 4.1 [calculation of the period of possession for the tax on profit from real estate not arbitrary]; BGE 135 II 356 paragraph 4.2.1 [judicial appreciation of evidence and arbitrariness]; BGE 136 I 316 paragraph 2.2.2 [Municipality of Zermatt; 'dynamic' reference as applied by the cantonal superior court held arbitrary]; BGE 137 I 1 paragraph 2.4 [application of the Zurich information and data protection act held not arbitrary]). In a recent case, the Federal Supreme Court decided that the Lucerne police statute cannot hold violent participants of a demonstration per se liable for the maximal amount of CHF 30,000 irrespective of the concrete damage caused by each individual (the case will be published in volume I of BGE 142).

551. Article 115(b) of the Federal Supreme Court Act requires a 'legally protected interest' (*rechtlich geschütztes Interesse*) in order to have standing in constitutional appeals (*Verfassungsbeschwerde, recours constitutionnel, ricorso costituzionale*; *see infra* Part IV, Chapter 5, §3 III). The Federal Supreme Court has repeatedly held that so-called *special fundamental rights* with a specific scope of protection, which is tied to a specific area of human existence (such as personal integrity, communication or economic freedom) or to a specific legal institution (such as marriage or property), confer *as such* and *immediately* a legally protected interest (*see*, *inter alia*, Decisions of the Federal Supreme Court BGE 133 I 185 paragraph 4 and BGE 135 I 265 paragraph 1.3). In contrast, the protection against arbitrariness in Article 9 of the Constitution and the equal protection clause in Article 8(1) of the Constitution are *general* fundamental rights because they are not linked to a specific scope of protection. Consequently, the Court denies standing in constitutional appeals solely grounded on these fundamental rights unless plaintiff can demonstrate an entitlement deriving from international public law (especially and above all the ECHR) or from sub-constitutional provisions. In public law, however, such provisions are rare. Therefore, this case law, which was established to avoid a congestion of the Federal Supreme Court in the mid-1960s, is highly controversial. Nevertheless, after the entry in force of the Federal Supreme Court Act in 2007, the Court reaffirmed its case law in a very tight 20/19-decision (Decision of the Federal Supreme Court BGE 133 I 185). Since 2009, the newly introduced Article 15b of the Swiss Citizenship Act (SCA; SR 141.0) demands that reasons must be given in order to reject an application for naturalization. This provision led the Federal Supreme Court to revise its case law regarding standing in constitutional appeals in the field of ordinary naturalizations (Decision of the Federal Supreme Court BGE 138 I 305). The Court held that standing shall be granted to plaintiffs to invoke the violation of Articles 9 and 8(1) of the Constitution if the naturalization eligibility requirements according to federal and cantonal law are evidently met and the rejection of their applications is clearly untenable ('unhaltbar') and violates the equal protection clause ('rechtsungleich').

III. Good Faith: The Protection of Confidence

552. Good faith is not only a constitutional principle (Article 5(3) of the Constitution) and one of the fundamental principles of private law (Article 2 of the Civil Code [SR 210]), but also a fundamental right (Article 9 of the Constitution) with a threefold content: it encompasses the right to the protection of confidence (which plays a considerable role in constitutional and administrative litigation), the prohibition of abuse of rights and the prohibition of *actus contrarius*.

553. According to the case law of the Federal Supreme Court, Article 9 of the Constitution confers on every person the right to rely in good faith on assurances issued by authorities (Decision of the Federal Supreme Court BGE 131 II 627 paragraph 6.1; *see also* BGE 141 V 538 paragraph 6.2), if four conditions are met: (1) a basis for good faith (*Vertrauensgrundlage*), i.e., a conduct of the administration (e.g., an unconditional assurance) raising a certain expectation in the individual; this can also be a misinformation (Decision of the Federal Supreme Court BGE 131 V 472 paragraph 5) or the constant practice of an agency; (2) a legitimate expectation (*berechtigtes Vertrauen*), i.e., that the person who claims a right from the protection of good faith was entitled to trust on that basis, whereby the assurance of the authority must not be abstract, but related to a given issue; (3) a disposition made in good faith (Vertrauensbetätigung), i.e., that the concerned person has made, based on the conduct of the administration, a disadvantageous disposition, which cannot be undone; and; (4) the absence of preponderant public interests(*see* especially Decision of the Federal Supreme Court

BGE 129 I 161 paragraph 4.1). Surprisingly, in *Steiner-Fässler v. Switzerland* of 7 October 2014 (application No. 18600/13), the European Court of Human Rights pointed out 'that Article 8 of the Convention does not contain – as such – an autonomous right to be treated by the authorities in good faith such as guaranteed under the Swiss Constitution'. In Switzerland, advance tax rulings are written and binding confirmations of the competent tax authorities with regard to particular tax consequences (or, more importantly, that there are no tax consequences). They do not confer preferential taxation but rather constitute an important tool especially for multinational undertakings to plan their business (e.g., obtain clearance in respect of any potential risk prior to the realization of an undertaking), future restructuring strategies (fiscal consequences of an M&A), or to allocate international or inter-cantonal profits, etc. In a recent case, the Federal Supreme Court held that a basis for good faith is no longer given if the cantonal tax administration revokes an advance tax ruling (BGE 141 I 169 paragraphs 4.1–5.4).

§3. Equality

Selected Bibliography: Auer, Malinverni & Hottelier, Vol. II, 473 et seq. (with further references); Biaggini. Kommentar, Article 8 (with further references); Biaggini. Giovanni. 'Die Einführung des Frauenstimmrechts im Kanton Appenzell I.Rh. kraft bundesgerichtlicher Verfassungsinterpretation'. In *recht* 1992, 65 et seq.; Bigler-Eggenberger Margrith. 'Art. 4 Abs. 2/8 Abs. 3 BV – eine Erfolgsgeschichte?'. In *Schweizerisches Zentralblatt für Staats- und Verwaltungsrecht [ZBl].* 2005, 57 et seq.; Dworkin, Ronald. *Sovereign Virtue. The Theory and Practice of Equality.* Cambridge: Harvard University Press, 2000; Egli, 148 et seq.; Grisel Etienne, *Egalité,* Berne: Stämpfli 2000; Haefliger Arthur. *Alle Schweizer sind vor dem Gesetze gleich.* Berne: Stämpfli, 1985; Müller Georg. 'Der Gleichheitssatz'. In *Veröffentlichung der Vereinigung Deutscher Staatsrechtslehrer [VVDStRL].* 1989 [47], 37 et seq.; Haller. *Swiss Constitution,* 208 et seq.; Hangartner Yvo. 'Diskriminierung – ein neuer verfassungsrechtlicher Begriff'. In *Zeitschrift für Schweizerisches Recht [ZSR].* 2003 I, 97 et seq.; Klein Caroline. *La discriminisation des personnes handicapées.* Berne: Stämpfli, 2002; Martenet Vincent. 'La protection contre les discriminations émanant des particuliers'. In *Zeitschrift für Schweizerisches Recht [ZSR].* 2006 I, 419 et seq.; Müller Jörg Paul. 'Die Diskriminierungsverbote nach Art. 8 Abs. 2 der neuen Bundesverfassung'. In Zimmerli (ed.), 103 et seq.; Müller & Schefer, 651–761; Peters Anne. 'Diskriminierungsverbote'. In *Handbuch der Grundrechte,* edited by Mertens & Papier, §211; Previtali Adriano. *Handicap e diritto.* Fribourg, 1998; Rhinow, Schefer & Uebersax, §§18–19; Waldmann Bernhard. *Das Diskriminierungsverbot von Art. 8 Abs. 2 BV als besonderer Gleichheitssatz.* Berne: Stämpfli, 2003; Waldmann Bernhard. Basler Kommentar BV, Article 8; Weber-Dürler Beatrice. 'Rechtsgleichheit'. In Thürer et al., §41; Weber-Dürler Beatrice. 'Zum Anspruch auf Gleichbehandlung in der Rechtsanwendung'. In *Schweizerisches Zentralblatt für Staats- und Verwaltungsrecht [ZBl].* 2004, 1 et seq.; Weber-Dürler Beatrice. 'Gleichheit'. In Handbuch der Grundrechte, edited by Mertens & Papier, §210.

I. Introduction

554. When Switzerland became a federal State (*see supra* General Introduction, Chapter 1), Article 4 of the Constitution of 1848 declared that '[a]ll Swiss are equal before the law'. This general equal protection clause gained its real importance with the creation of the Federal Supreme Court under the Constitution of 1874 (*see supra* Part II, Chapter 5, §3). Earlier in 1876, the Federal Supreme Court held that the equal protection clause did not grant *absolute* equality. As a result, the Federal Supreme Court introduced the concept of *relative* equality in 1880 stating that, under the Constitution of 1874, 'the equality before the law calls for equal treatment under the condition of the equality of all relevant factual conditions' (Decision of the Federal Supreme Court BGE 6, 174, *Jäggi:* 'Das Prinzip der Gleichheit vor dem Gesetze verlangt Gleichheit der Behandlung unter der Voraussetzung der Gleichheit aller erheblichen tatsächlichen Verhältnisse.'). This case was a milestone in Swiss constitutional law and Article 4 of the Constitution of 1874 became the focal point for the highly creative case law of the Federal Supreme Court.

555. As listed above in the introduction of this Chapter, the Federal Supreme Court also derived substantive principles and procedural rules from the equal protection clause of Article 4 of the Constitution of 1874. This judge-made law, which was also influenced by Articles 5 and 6 of the ECHR, is now incorporated in the catalogue of fundamental rights (*see, inter alia,* Articles 5, 9 and 29–32 of the Constitution). One of the innovations of the new Constitution (also in terms of comparative constitutional law) was the introduction of a non-discrimination clause in the catalogue of fundamental rights (Article 8(2) of the Constitution). Later in 1981, the guarantee of equal rights of men and women was added to Article 4 of the Constitution of 1874, which corresponds now with Article 8(3) of the Constitution. Finally, Article 8(4) of the Constitution obliges the lawmaker to provide for measures to eliminate discriminations against disabled people.

556. Article 8 of the Constitution is a fully justiciable legal norm (with the exception of the second sentence of Article 8(3) and 8(4) of the Constitution), which can be invoked by everyone (i.e., natural and legal persons; *supra* §1 II of this Chapter). It binds everybody exercising a state function (*supra* §1 III of this Chapter). Note that Switzerland has not ratified the Additional Protocol No. 12 to the ECHR of 4 November 2000 yet.

II. Equality Before the Law

557. 'Everyone is equal before the law.' – The formula that 'equals should be treated equally, unequals unequally' consists of and denotes a *relation* between at least two factual situations (persons, objects, circumstances, etc.) and at least one quality requiring a *classification* (*tertium comparationis*) defining the respect in which the equality or the inequality shall apply. Politically and socially rooted in the ideals of the French Revolution (of course with philosophical strings stretching further back to the Age of Enlightenment and as far as Ancient Greece), the general equal protection clause still poses a number of challenging problems not only in terms of its content and its interpretation, but also, for example, in regard to the notion of equality (what does the formula that 'equals should be treated equally, unequals unequally' really mean, if it is not to be devoid of any meaning?) and according to which criteria or parameters should the law distinguish equals from unequals. In a larger context, the importance of equality in a liberal society (the 'value' of equality) and the relationship between freedom, justice and equality are still controversial (as Ronald Dworkin pointed out: 'People who praise it or disparage it disagree about what they are praising or disparaging.').

558. The case law of the Federal Supreme Court, which shall be discussed below, draws a distinction between equality before the law *in the process of law-making* and equality before the law *in the process of law-application.*

559. In the process of law-making, a statute or a provision thereof violates the general equal protection clause if the challenged legislation (1) draws distinctions without a reasonable or objective cause and justification; or (2) ignores significant factual differences (Decision of the Federal Supreme Court 141 I 90 paragraph 9.1; *see* for recent decisions regarding this established formula of the Federal Supreme Court BGE 141 IV 263 paragraph 2 [victims of criminal acts who received free legal assistance based on Article 29(3) of the Constitution or pursuant to cantonal legislation must restitute the costs for proceedings while victims exempted from costs according to the Federal Victims Act [SR 312.5] are not obliged to do so]; BGE 131 I 1 paragraph 4.2 [Municipality of Grindelwald; duty of real estate owners to maintain and clean the communal road network in persona ten to twenty hours per year or to pay a tax instead]; BGE 133 I 249 paragraph 3.3 [in the regulation of identical matters – here: regarding the prohibition of dangerous dog breeds – the cantons may foresee different solutions]; BGE 135 I 130 paragraph 6.2 [cantonal levy for the prevention of hooliganism does not violate the general equal protection clause]; BGE 136 II 120 paragraph 3.3.2 [denial of a residence permit for the children of a naturalized Swiss citizen]).

560. The legal assessment of whether a statute is based upon a reasonable or objective cause may change in the course of time and require an adjustment or a change of the Court's case law (*see, inter alia,* Decision of the Federal Supreme Court BGE 131 I 1 paragraph 4.2; an often cited example is the admission of women to the bar [denied by the Court in the *Spyri* case in 1887, BGE 13, 1, but held unconstitutional in the *Roeder* case thirty-six years later, BGE 49 I 14]). Regarding the question whether a provision of a cantonal statute violates the general equal protection clause, the Federal Supreme Court allows the cantons considerable discretion (*see, inter alia,* Decisions of the Federal Supreme Court BGE 131 I 1 paragraph 4.2; BGE 136 I 1 paragraph 4.1; BGE 136 I 297 paragraph 6.1) – with the exception of the respect of the equality between men and women in Article 8(3) of the Constitution, where the Court generally applies a strict scrutiny test (Decision of the Federal Supreme Court BGE 131 I 105 paragraph 3.1).

561. Judicial restraint of the Federal Supreme Court: There are, among others, two main reasons for the Federal Supreme Court's reluctance to become too involved. The Swiss concept of federalism demands that federal authorities should not interfere with the competencies of the cantons as long as the cantons do not manifestly violate Article 8(1) of the Constitution; the general equal protection clause leaves the cantons wide discretion, and their decisions must be tolerated by the federal branches of government. Furthermore, the democratic principle and the principle of separation of powers demand that the realization (*Konkretisierung*) of the general equal protection clause in the process of law- and rule-making is primarily a task to be fulfilled by the democratically legitimized legislature, and not by the Federal Supreme Court.

562. In the process of *law-application and adjudication*, the general equal protection clause prescribes that the law must be applied equally in all similar cases. The general equal protection clause is violated in cases where a public authority treats two similar factual situations differently without objective grounds (Decision of the Federal Supreme Court BGE 125 I 161 paragraph 3a). However, the Federal Supreme Court held that cantonal laws and regulations, even with the same or similar wording of the norm, can be applied differently in different cantons (Decision of the Federal Supreme Court BGE 91 I 480, 491, *Association de l'Ecole Française*). For recent cases of the Federal Supreme Court *see* BGE 131 I 91 paragraph 3.4 (coercive merger of municipalities); BGE 131 I 105 paragraph 3.1 (equal pay for work; Article 8(1) confers only a right to correct the unequal payment in an adequate manner and within reasonable time, paragraphs 3.6–3.8); BGE 136 I 345 paragraph 5 (revocation of a driving licence on probation).

563. Furthermore, the unlawful application of a norm does not confer to other beneficiaries of the norm the right to be treated unequally as well (Decisions of the Federal Supreme Court BGE 132 II 485 paragraph 8.6; BGE 135 IV 191 paragraph 3.3; BGE 136 I 65 paragraph 5.6). In these cases, the principle of legality supersedes Article 8(1) of the Constitution. However, the Court has indicated that Article 8(1) of the Constitution may prevail in those rare and exceptional cases where: (1) a public authority constantly derogates from the applicable norm; and (2) a public authority indicates that, from now on and in the future, it will not adjudicate in conformity with the law. In this case, the Court has affirmed the right to be treated unequally as well (Decisions of the Federal Supreme Court BGE 122 II 446 et seq.; BGE 131 V 9 paragraph 3.7; BGE 134 II 272 paragraph 4.7; BGE 136 I 65 paragraph 5.6).

III. Non-discrimination

564. The non-discrimination clause in Article 8(2) of the Constitution prohibits discrimination grounded on origin, race, sex, age, language, social position, lifestyle, religious, philosophical and political convictions, or corporal or mental disabilities. It is the first explicit use of the term 'discrimination' in a federal constitution worldwide. The enumeration in Article 8(2) of the Constitution is exemplary and not exhaustive. The non-discrimination clause deploys no third-party effect (supra §1 III) nor does it confer an enforceable individual right vis-à-vis the state to establish equality in fact (*see* Decisions of the Federal Supreme Court BGE 134 I 108 paragraph 5 [refusal to pay the modification costs for a disabled person's second home]; BGE 136 I 297 paragraph 7.3 [no payment of family allowances for a child with domicile in a country, which has not concluded a social security treaty with Switzerland]).

565. Paraphrasing a formula of the Federal Supreme Court, *direct* discrimination can be understood as an unequal treatment of a person solely based upon his/her affiliation or membership to a certain group, which has historically tended to or tends in the present social reality to be marginalized or treated as inferior. Discrimination is a *qualified mode* of unequal treatment of persons in comparable situations causing a disadvantage, which results in disparagement or social exclusion, because it is based on classifications, which constitute an essential and not hardly waivable element of the identity of the persons concerned; non-discrimination is closely intertwined with the human dignity clause in Article 7 of the Constitution. An *indirect* discrimination can be affirmed if a facially neutral provision (i.e., provisions without classifications manifestly disadvantaging a specifically protected group) has an impact *in fact* disadvantaging members of such a group in a particular manner without an objective justification (*see, inter alia*, Decisions of the Federal Supreme Court BGE 141 I 250 paragraph 4.3.2 and BGE 134 I 49 paragraph 3.1).

566. According to the theory of 'blind equal protection', the State is not entitled to draw any *legal classification* based upon the grounds listed in Article 8(2) of the Constitution (*Anknüpfungsverbot*). In this respect, the non-discrimination clause grants *symmetrical* protection for everyone. The theory of 'specific equal protection' is grounded in the idea that the non-discrimination clause was introduced into the catalogue of fundamental rights to grant protection to specific groups that have suffered or are still suffering from discrimination. According to this theory, the State is entitled to draw legal classifications as long as they are objectively justified. Said classifications must be effectively in favour of the protected group. Consequently, the non-discrimination clause grants *asymmetrical* protection for the protected group only, whereas individuals not within the penumbra of Article 8(2) of the Constitution can only invoke the general equal protection clause in Article 8(1) of the Constitution.

567. In its analysis of Article 8(2) of the Constitution, the Federal Supreme Court points out that the non-discrimination clause does not exclude per se classifications based on, for example, origin, race, sex or religious convictions. Such a classification initially establishes merely a *suspicion* of an illegitimate differentiation. However, this suspicion can be reverted if the challenged government action can be upheld by a *qualified justification* (*see* Decisions of the Federal Supreme Court BGE 141 I 251 paragraph 4.3.2; BGE 135 I 49 paragraph 4.1; BGE 136 I 121 paragraph 5.2; BGE 136 I 297 paragraph 7.1). The still evolving case law of the Federal Supreme Court indicates that the question whether the government has brought forward a qualified justification is affirmed or denied according to the fact-pattern of the case (*see*, e.g., Decision of the Federal Supreme Court BGE 135 I 49, where the Court held that *in the present case – and not in general* – the denial of a naturalization request of a disabled foreign person living in Switzerland for a long period of time due to her insufficient economic funds to support herself was discriminatory). Hence, from a tactical perspective, the Court currently seems to favour holdings, which are narrowly tailored to the fact-pattern at hand; so far, it has not developed 'levels of scrutiny' and 'tests' when such levels are (not) met.

568. Since their introduction in the catalogue of fundamental rights, the importance of the classifications in Article 8(2) of the Constitution is reflected in the case law of the Federal Supreme Court (selection): *Origin and social position* cannot be invoked by children of parents receiving social welfare benefits (Decision of the Federal Supreme Court BGE 136 I 309 paragraph 4.3); *origin* is referring to unchangeable aspects of one's identity – and not to the changeable geographical, ethnical, national or cultural background of a person (*see* Decisions of the Federal Supreme Court BGE 129 I 398; BGE 129 I 227, regarding the overall rejection of naturalization request of persons from Ex-Yugoslavia in the municipality of Emmen); *race* refers to human beings (and not to dog breeds, but the general protection clause may apply *see* Decision of the Federal Supreme Court BGE 132 I 7 paragraph 4.2 *in fine*); *sex*: discrimination denied in a case of a bylaw excluding the transfer of membership of a deceased women to her descendants (Decision of the Federal Supreme Court BGE 134 I 257 paragraph 3.4; *see also* BGE 132 I 68 paragraphs 4.2–4.4); *age*: statutory provision refusing to pay a sixty years' old person the costs for a surgery to cure adipositas not discriminatory (Decision of the Federal Supreme Court BGE 136 I 121 paragraph 5); *lifestyle*: expel and removal orders of the police against groups of persons consuming alcohol in and around the Bernese railway station is not based on the classification 'lifestyle' (Decision of the Federal Supreme Court BGE 132 I 49 paragraph 8); *religious convictions*: denial of naturalization requests due to insufficient integration of the person (Decision of the Federal Supreme Court BGE 132 I 167 paragraph 4) or due to insufficient knowledge of the German language and citizenship education (Decision of the Federal Supreme Court BGE 134 I 56 paragraph 3) or due to the fact that the female is wearing a headscarf (Decision of the Federal Supreme Court BGE 134 I 49 paragraph 3.2) held not discriminatory; *corporal or mental disabilities*: an obligation for the parents of a disabled child to partially pay the costs for integrative or separative primary education is a discriminatory derogation from the principle that primary education is free of charge (Article 19 of the Constitution; Decision of the Federal Supreme Court BGE 141 I 13 paragraph 3.1); denial of a naturalization request of a disabled foreign person living in Switzerland for a long period of time due to her insufficient economic funds to support herself held discriminatory (Decision of the Federal Supreme Court BGE 135 I 49 paragraph 6.3). According to Article 7(3)(b) of the Constitution of the Canton of Bern a person shall not be naturalized if she or he is receiving social welfare benefits or has not fully paid back the benefits received. In a recent case, the Federal Supreme Court held that this provision is neither discriminatory nor arbitrary and does not violate the equal protection clause as long as the holding in BGE 135 I 49 and other federal provisions are observed (Decision of the Federal Supreme Court 1D_4/2016 of 4 May 2017).

IV. Equality Between Men and Women

569. According to the first sentence of Article 8(3) of the Constitution, men and women have equal rights, which can be directly enforced before court. This provision constitutes a *lex specialis* to the principle of relative equality and demands a nearly *absolute* equal treatment before the law. As a rule, any unequal treatment by the State cannot be grounded on gender classifications (Decisions of the Federal Supreme Court BGE 141 II 419 paragraph 6.1.2; BGE 127 III 207 paragraphs 4 and 5b-c; BGE 129 I 265 paragraphs 3.2–3.3). However, according to a formula of the Federal Supreme Court, such classifications are allowed in those rare cases of inherent necessity where 'biological or functional differences' exclude per se equal treatment (e.g., maternity, *see also* Decisions of the Federal Supreme Court BGE 108 Ia 22 [gender-based secondary school admission scheme held discriminatory]; BGE 123 I 56 [exclusion of women from municipal fire brigade operations, which are compulsory for men, and requirement to pay a municipal tax instead is discriminatory]; BGE 129 I 265 [payment of family and children income supplements only to the father held discriminatory]). Note that the Constitution itself contains gender classifications in Article 59(1), obliging Swiss male citizens to render compulsory military service, and in Article 61(3), according to which the Confederation may make the civil defence service compulsory for men.

570. Furthermore, Article 8(3) of the Constitution mandates that *equality in law and in fact* shall be granted through appropriate legislation on all levels of the State, particularly in family, education and work. Meanwhile, the Federal Parliament has enacted an important federal act in order to promote equality between men and women (Federal Gender Equality Act of 24 March 1995, GEA; SR 155). This statute aims at fostering true equality between women and men (Article 1 GEA). It envisions the effective promotion of factual equality between men and women not only within the government, but also in the private sector, e.g., by means of labour and employment law. According to Article 3 GEA, employees must not be discriminated against on the basis of their sex, whether directly or indirectly, including on the basis of their marital status, their family situation or, in the case of female employees, of pregnancy. This prohibition applies in particular to hiring, allocation of duties, setting of working conditions, pay, basic and advanced training, promotion and dismissal. Article 4 GEA states that any harassing behaviour of sexual nature or other behaviours related to the person's sex that adversely affect the dignity of women or men in the workplace is discriminatory. Such behaviour includes in particular threats, the promise of advantages, the use of coercion and the exertion of pressure in order to obtain favours of a sexual nature. Anyone who is the victim of discrimination may apply to the court or to the administrative authority for an order prohibiting or stopping threatened discrimination, requiring existing discrimination to cease, confirming that discrimination is taking place if it is continuing to have a disruptive effect, and for the payment of any salary due (Article 5(1) GEA). Note that the burden of proof is reversed in discrimination litigation procedures: In relation to the allocation of duties, setting of working conditions, pay, basic and advanced training, promotion and dismissal, discrimination is *presumed* if the person concerned can substantiate the same by prima facie evidence (Article 6 GEA). In order to fight discrimination effectively, the statute contains several procedural provisions, *inter alia*, granting standing to anti-discrimination organizations. According to Article 7 GEA, organizations that have been in existence for at least two years and that have the promotion of gender equality or safeguarding the interests of employees as their stated purpose in their articles of incorporation may in their own names have a finding of discrimination declared if the probable outcome of proceedings will have an effect on a considerable number of jobs. They must allow the employer concerned the opportunity to state his/her position before they institute conciliation proceedings or bring an action.

571. *Quotas* are a controversial issue in the promotion of equality between men and women. In the *Solothurn* case, the Court had to assess the issue of *fixed quotas* of a cantonal initiative according to which the number of representatives in all branches of the cantonal government had to correspond to the proportion of the female population in the Canton of Solothurn. The Court rejected the admissibility of fixed quotas (Decision of the Federal Supreme Court BGE 123 I 165), because the *Solothurn* scheme constituted an undue restriction of political rights (Article 34 of the Constitution). However, in the following *Uri* case, the Court distinguished that a popular initiative introducing a scheme to promote equality within the personnel of the cantonal administration and of cantonal commissions was not per se unconstitutional because these persons were not elected by the people (Decision of the Federal Supreme Court BGE 125 I 21). In the subsequent *University of Fribourg* case, which concerned a fixed quota system for female academics ('[e]n raison des critères fixes[…], seules les candidatures féminines peuvent entrer en ligne de compte pour l'occupation de ce poste'), the Court reaffirmed the importance of the principle of proportionality in the review of constitutionality of positive measures. The Court pointed out that the distinction between fixed quotas and variable quota is decisive in order to appreciate the proportionality of positive measures. Gender-based quotas are admissible regarding measures favouring women in the sense of the second sentence of Article 8(3) of the Constitution, provided that they are reasonable and constitute the least invasive measure to the achievement of the goal pursued (i.e., the realization of equality *in fact*), that they balance the interests of those who are disfavoured, and take into account their fundamental rights, which could be violated by the positive measure as well. In summary, the Court declared that fixed quotas seem to be hardly operable considering the gravity of the infringement they are causing in view of the formal prohibition of gender discrimination (Decision of the Federal Supreme Court BGE 131 II 361 paragraph 5).

572. Finally, the third sentence of Article 8(3) of the Constitution entitles men and women to equal pay for work of equal value (regarding the term 'equal value' *see* Decision of the Federal Supreme Court BGE 133 III 545 paragraph 4.3). It is one of the rare provisions of the catalogue of fundamental rights conferring a direct and enforceable right of the individual to sue not only public but also *private employers* (*see, inter alia,* Decisions of the Federal Supreme Court BGE 131 I 105 paragraph 3.6; BGE 131 II 393 paragraph 8.3; regarding the issue of direct third-party effect *see supra* §1 III of this Chapter). Thirty years after the popular vote of 14 June 1981, which led to the introduction of Article 4(2) in the Constitution of 1874 (now: Article 8(3) of the Constitution), equal pay for work of equal value for men and women is still a *constitutional desideratum* and far from being achieved in fact. According to recent studies, the average difference in salary between men and women was 24% in 2006 and 12.5% in 2014. In 2014, women with an academic degree earned on the average 19.7% less than men with a comparable education (source: Federal Statistical Office).

V. Elimination of Disadvantages Affecting Disabled Persons

573. Article 8(4) of the Constitution encourages the legislature to provide for measures to eliminate disadvantages affecting disabled persons. This mandate to the lawmaker does not confer enforceable rights to the individual (Decisions of the Federal Supreme Court BGE 131 V 9 paragraph 3.5.1.2; BGE 134 I 105 paragraph 5). On 1

January 2004, the Federal Disabilities Act (SR 151.3) entered into force aiming at the elimination of discriminations against people with disabilities, mainly in the fields of construction law (access to federal public buildings), public transport, education and employment law.

§4. Civil Liberties

I. Introduction

574. The protection from undue intrusion of the State in essential spheres of human existence falls within the penumbra of *civil liberties* (*Freiheitsrechte; libertés; libertà*). Based on the idea of the *status negativus*, the Constitution imposes upon the state an obligation to tolerate these spheres, to refrain from undue interference therein, and to safeguard legal institutions, such as marriage and property. Restrictions of civil liberties are only permitted if there is a legal basis, a public interest, if the restriction is proportional to the goal pursued and if it does not violate the essence of the civil liberty (*see* Article 36 of the Constitution; *supra* §1 IV of this Chapter). In this paragraph, the civil liberties guaranteeing personal freedom, privacy and free communication and expression will only be shortly outlined because most of these constitutional provisions are covered by the ECHR and are also interpreted by the Federal Supreme Court in the light of the ECHR. Hence, the focus of the presentation will lie on some controversial topics, such as the right to die and the right to abortion, or on civil liberties, which are – from a comparative constitutional law perspective – atypical and unknown in other constitutional systems, such as the general guarantee of economic freedom (Article 27 of the Constitution).

II. Life and Personal Freedom

Selected Bibliography: Auer, Malinverni & Hottelier, Vol. II, 143 et seq.; Biaggini. Kommentar, Articles 10, 11, and 13 (with further references); Häfelin Haller, Keller & Thurnherr, §11; Haller. 'Menschenwürde, Recht auf Leben und persönliche Freiheit'. In *Handbuch der Grundrechte*, edited by Merten & Papier, §209, Hangartner Yvo. *Schwangerschaftsabbruch und Sterbehilfe – eine grundrechtliche Standortbestimmung.* Zurich: Schulthess, 2000; Jaag Tobias & Rüssli Markus. 'Sterbehilfe in staatlichen Spitälern, Kranken- und Altersheimen', In *Schweizerisches Zentralblatt für Staats- und Verwaltungsrecht [ZBl]*. 2001, 113 et seq.; Walter Kälin. 'Death is different: the death penalty and the right to a fair trial'. In *The Right to Life*, edited by Tomuschat Christian, Lagrange Evelyne & Oeter Stefan. Leiden/Boston: Nijhoff Publ., 2010, 21 et seq.; Mahon, commentaire, Articles 10, 11, and 13; Müller & Schefer, 39 et seq. (with further references); Rhinow, Schefer & Uebersax, §14; Schweizer Rainer, J. St. Galler Kommentar, Article 10 (with further references).

A. Overview

575. The catalogue of fundamental rights codifies the elements of personal freedom, as developed by the Federal Supreme Court (*supra* §1 I of this Chapter) and influenced by international treaties, namely by Articles 2–5 and 8 of the ECHR and by Articles 6–12 and 17 of the UN-Pact II. Furthermore, Switzerland has ratified the Additional Protocol No. 6 and No. 13 to the ECHR concerning the abolition of the death penalty (SR 0.101.06). The Constitutions of 1848 and 1874 did not grant a general or encompassing protection of personal freedom, because it was primarily guaranteed by cantonal constitutional law. However in 1963, the Federal Supreme Court recognized personal freedom as an *unwritten* civil liberty of the Constitution of 1874 (Decision of the Federal Supreme Court BGE 89 I 92). The Court held that corporal integrity, the autonomy of the person and mental integrity form the core of personal freedom. The Court pointed out that the Swiss concept of personal freedom does not correspond with *general personal liberty* in Article 2 of the German Basic Law (*allgemeine Handlungsfreiheit*). However, under the influence of the ECHR and the case law of the European Court on Human Rights, the originally narrow concept of personal freedom has been continually extended (namely the right to life and the prohibition of torture). In recent cases, the Court also had to deal with issues not expressly protected by the Convention, e.g., organ transplantation and medical assistance to procreation. Public authorities shall ensure through adequate legislation in the field of private, criminal and administrative law that personal freedom shall, wherever applicable, also take effect in relationships between individuals. However, so far, an enforceable 'right to breathe fresh air' cannot be deduced from personal freedom.

B. Aspects of Personal Freedom

576. The Federal Supreme Court points out that personal freedom grants every individual a sphere of liberty, which allows him/her to develop and realize his/her potential (*see*, for example, Decision of the Federal Supreme Court BGE 136 I 254 paragraph 6.2: 'le droit de toute personne à un espace de liberté dans lequel elle puisse se développer et se réaliser').

577. The *right to life* (Article 10(1) of the Constitution) is a classic civil liberty directed against the State (Decision of the Federal Supreme Court BGE 136 I 96 paragraph 4.2; for the delicate question regarding the beginning and the end of life *see* already *supra* §1 II of this Chapter). It is, however, not absolute. Under certain restrictive conditions, the use of a gun during police operations may be constitutionally permissible (Decision of the Federal Supreme Court BGE 136 I 87 paragraph 4.2). The right to life obliges the State to guarantee security of the population and to conduct effective and independent investigations in cases of homicide (Decision of the Federal Supreme Court BGE 136 I 113 paragraph 2.1 [referring also to Article 2(1) of the ECHR]). As a minimum requirement, the provision may oblige the state to ensure through adequate procedures that the decision to assisted suicide really corresponds to the free and independent will of the concerned person; the state has no obligation to grant access to the substances or instruments required for assisted suicide (Decision of the Federal Supreme Court BGE 133 I 58 paragraph 6.2.1).

578. The *prohibition of the death penalty* (Article 10(1) of the Constitution) is absolute and even in exceptional situations, e.g., in wartime, always impermissible. Switzerland abolished the death penalty during peace in 1942 and death penalty during wartime in 1992. Recent attempts to reintroduce the death penalty for sexual offenders through a popular initiative are from a constitutional perspective clearly null and void (the initiative was withdrawn by the initiators before the collection of the required 100,000 signatures had started; *see* Federal Gazette BBl 2012 2439). Furthermore, a person may not be extradited in a country where he/she is threatened with the death penalty (*see also* Article 25(3) of the Constitution; for a case, where the Swiss Federal Supreme Court declared to extradite a person, who allegedly committed manslaughter, only under the condition that the Taiwanese Department of Justice procured sufficient guarantees to the Court that the death penalty will neither be pronounced nor executed, *see* Decision of the Federal Supreme Court BGE 130 II 217 paragraph 8.8).

579. The *right to corporal and mental integrity and to freedom of movement* (personal freedom *strictu sensu*; Article 10(2) of the Constitution) used to be an unwritten civil liberty under the Constitution of 1874. Paraphrasing a leading case of the Federal Supreme Court, personal liberty does not merely protect physical and mental integrity. As a civil liberty, it aims to guarantee in a general manner the exercise of all essential freedoms indispensable for the development of a person. As a default provision, personal freedom protects the personality and the dignity of the individual in those cases where a specific fundamental right is not at hand. The disparate character of the case law of the Court indicates that personal freedom cannot be defined in a general and abstract manner. It must be assessed from case to case taking into account the goals of personal freedom, the intensity of the interference and also of the personalities of the concerned persons. In its case law, the Federal Supreme Court held that personal freedom protects the free choice of a medical doctor in case of an abortion; the right to certain forms of assisted procreation; the right to know one's ancestors; the right to have personal relations; the right to determine the destiny of one's own corpse; the right to meet and to consume alcohol. However, the Court has held that personal freedom was not violated in the following cases: the right to gamble; the right of a detainee to choose his/her own medical doctor; the right to navigate just in designated zones of a lake. The right to work and the right to education cannot be deduced from personal freedom. The Court also denied that the consumption of illegal drugs – *in casu* cannabis – constituted an essential freedom indispensable for the development of a person (BGE 133 I 119 paragraph 5.2.1 [with further references of the case law summarized above]).

580. The *prohibition of torture and any cruel, inhumane and degrading treatment or punishment* (Article 10(3) of the Constitution): This provision is applied in accordance with the Strasbourg cases law to Article 3 of the ECHR. On 12 February 2011, George W. Bush, the former President of the United States, cancelled a visit to the city of Geneva because the Swiss criminal authorities would have been obliged to open a criminal investigation owing to criminal charges pressed by Amnesty International against Mr Bush's alleged 'criminal responsibility for acts of torture he is believed to have authorised'. The UN Commission Against Torture has criticized Switzerland's measures during forced repatriation, the fact that prisons are overcrowded as well as the use of force by the police especially against foreigners and asylum seekers (session of 11 Mai 2010 [CAT/C/SR.948]). Systematic strip-searches and full body searches of prisoners do not constitute torture (Decision of the Federal Supreme Court BGE 141 I 144 paragraph 6.3).

581. The *prohibition of deprivation of liberty except in the cases and in the forms provided by statute*: The habeas corpus clause in the meaning of Article 5 of the ECHR and Article 31 of the Constitution will be discussed in detail (*infra* §6 IV. of this Chapter).

582. The *protection of the integrity of children and young people* (Article 11(1) of the Constitution): The provision has so far played a minor role in the Federal Supreme Court's case law and should be interpreted as a concretization of personal freedom (right to special protection of their personal integrity) taking into account the vulnerability and the special needs of children and young people (as enumerated in the UN Children Right's Convention, especially the right to a hearing in divorce cases; *see also* Decision of the Federal Supreme Court BGE 141 III 340 paragraph 5.4). The 'right' to encouragement and development is not justiciable (Decision of the Federal Supreme Court BGE 129 I 12 paragraph 10.5.3). The provision does not confer the right to a residence permit (Decision of the Federal Supreme Court BGE 129 II 377 paragraph 5d).

583. *The right to aid in distress* (Article 12 of the Constitution): This provision will be discussed below in §5 of this chapter in the context of social fundamental rights.

C. The Right to Die

584. An individual's free and self-determined wish to die is constitutionally protected. In contrast to other countries, suicide attempters are not punished in Switzerland. Regarding suicide assistance, Switzerland probably has one of the most liberal regimes in Europe. However, several forms must be distinguished: Direct and active euthanasia, which is clearly prohibited (e.g., a physician intentionally injecting a lethal dose to a person; *see* Articles 111, 113 and 114 of the Criminal Code [SR 311.0]). Indirect active euthanasia (e.g., injections of morphine, which alleviate pain, but might also cause a premature death of the person) and passive euthanasia (retreat from life-sustaining measures, e.g., switching off the breathing apparatus) are not prohibited by the Criminal Code. *Suicide assistance* is only prohibited 'for selfish motives': Article 115 of the Criminal Code states that any person who for selfish motives incites or assists another to commit or attempt to commit suicide shall, if that other person thereafter commits or attempts to commit suicide, be liable to a custodial sentence not exceeding five years or to a monetary penalty.

585. Assisted suicide in Switzerland is usually performed by a non-physician of a right-to-die organization who has no vested interests in the death of the person. Physician-assisted suicide is regulated by guidelines issued by the Swiss Academy of Medical Sciences (SAMS/ASSM), which are currently – after a heated debate about the role of doctors – under revision. A recent empirical study proposes that the current guidelines regulating physician-assisted suicide in Switzerland 'should be reviewed with regard to the end-of-life criterion as a necessary condition for physician-assisted suicide' (*see* Brauer/Bollinger/Strub, 'Swiss physicians' attitude to assisted suicide.

In: Swiss Medical Weekly, May 2015, pp. 1 et seq.). The assisted suicide procedure requires an in-depth evaluation that the person wishing to die knows what she is doing (decisional capacity), does act with due consideration and not on impulse, is not under the influence of a third party and has the constant wish to die. Note that the Federal Supreme Court held in a much debated and controversial decision that the right to die also applies to mentally ill persons (BGE 133 I 58). In practice, the person will usually consume a mix of an antiemetic and a liquid lethal overdose of natrium-pentobarbiturate. Between 2008–2012, about 600 people from thirty-one countries (mostly from Germany, the United Kingdom and France) committed assisted suicide in Switzerland. On 15 May 2011, a popular referendum in the Canton of Zurich proposed to limit 'suicide tourism', by imposing a residency requirement of at least one year in the Canton of Zurich in order to qualify for the service. Some 85% opposed the ban on assisted suicide and 78% opposed outlawing it for foreigners. The size of the vote against a ban may reflect the widely held belief in the population that it is an individual and universal right to freely decide when and how to die. Nowadays, it seems that the main issue regarding the right to die in Switzerland is the NIMBY-problem (*'not in my back yard'*) because local residents object to the establishment of euthanasia facilities in their neighbourhoods owing to 'psychological nuisance' (Decision of the Federal Supreme Court 136 I 395). In a recent case, the Federal Supreme Court held that the Salvation Army must tolerate assisted suicide in their retirement facilities although it stands in contradiction to their religious beliefs (Decision 2C_66/2015 of 13 September 2016).

D. The Right to Abortion

586. The Federal Constitution contains no explicit right to or prohibition of abortion. On 2 June 2002, 72.2% of the People clearly voted for the amendment of the Criminal Code allowing abortion under certain circumstances (Articles 118–120; SR 311.0). As a federal statute, these provisions are 'immunized' from constitutional concerns (Article 190 of the Constitution; *infra* §7 of this chapter).

587. According to Article 119 of the Criminal Code, the termination of a pregnancy is exempt from penalty (so-called *legal abortion*) in the event that the termination is, in the judgment of a physician, necessary in order to be able to prevent the pregnant woman from sustaining serious physical injury or serious psychological distress. Thc risk must be greater the more advanced the pregnancy is. The termination of a pregnancy is likewise exempt from penalty if, at the written request of a pregnant woman, who claims that she is in a state of distress, it is performed within twelve weeks of the start of the pregnant woman's last period by a physician who is licensed to practice his/her profession. The physician must have a detailed consultation with the woman prior to the termination and provide her with appropriate counselling. If the woman does not have the capacity to decide, the consent of her legal representative shall be required. The cantons designate the medical practices and hospitals that may fulfil the requirements for the professional conduct of procedures to terminate pregnancy and for the provision of counselling. An abortion must be reported for statistical purposes to the competent health authority, whereby the anonymity of the woman concerned shall be guaranteed and medical confidentiality shall be preserved.

588. The Criminal Code defines in Article 118 the circumstances of *illegal abortion*: (1) Any person who terminates a pregnancy with the consent of the pregnant woman or incites or assists a pregnant woman to terminate her pregnancy without the requirements of a legal abortion being fulfilled shall be liable to a custodial sentence not exceeding five years or to a monetary penalty; (2) any person who terminates a pregnancy without the consent of the pregnant woman shall be liable to a custodial sentence of from one to ten years; (3) any woman who has her pregnancy terminated or otherwise participates in the termination of her pregnancy following the end of the twelfth week since her last period and without the requirements of legal abortions being fulfilled shall be liable to a custodial sentence not exceeding three years or to a monetary penalty. Any physician shall be fined, who terminates a pregnancy and who fails, prior to the procedure: (1) to obtain a written request from the pregnant woman; (2) to discuss the termination in detail with the pregnant woman and to counsel her, to advise her of the risks of the procedure to her health and to provide her with a written guide, the receipt of which she must acknowledge with her signature, that contains: (a) a list of agencies that provide counselling free of charge, (b) a list of associations and agencies that offer moral and material support, and (c) information on the possibility of having the child adopted; (3) to satisfy himself/herself that a pregnant woman under 16 years of age has been in contact with a counselling agency specialized in dealing with young people. According to a study of the Federal Office for Statistics there was no single condemnation for illegal abortion since the 1980s in Switzerland. Legal abortions declined for 30% between the 1970s (14–16.000) and today (10–11.000). In 2015, Switzerland was one of the countries with the lowest abortion rate worldwide of women aged between 15–44 (0.0063%).

III. Privacy

Selected Bibliography: Auer, Mainverni & Hottelier. Vol. II, 185 et seq.; Biaggini. Kommentar, Article 13 (with further references); Breitenmoser Stephan & Schweizer Rainer, J. St. Galler Kommentar, Article 13 (with further references); Caroni Martina. *Privat- und Familienleben zwischen Menschenrecht und Migration.* Berlin: Duncker & Humblot, 1999; Oliver Diggelmann. Basler Kommentar BV, Article 13; Häfelin, Haller, Keller & Thurnherr, §12; Kiener & Kälin, §13 and §14; Mahon. commentaire, Article 13; Kley Andreas. 'Unverletzlichkeit der Wohnung'. In *Handbuch der Grundrechte*, edited by Mertens & Papier, §214; Müller & Schefer, 164 et seq. (with further references); Rhinow, Schefer & Uebersax, §14.

589. The right to secrecy of mail and telecommunication constituted the only express fundamental right under the Constitution of 1874, whereas the general right to privacy formed an *unwritten element of personal freedom.* In substance, Article 13 of the Constitution corresponds with Article 8 of the ECHR (*see* recently Decision of the Federal Supreme Court BGE 136 II 178 paragraph 5.2) and contains the following elements.

590. The right to privacy in one's private life: The right to privacy is a concretization of the right to personal liberty, which is – in view of its scope of application – much broader (Article 10(2) of the Constitution). Personal freedom is defined by the Federal

Supreme Court as 'the exercise of all essential freedoms indispensable for the development of a person'. However, the right to privacy afforded by Article 13(1) of the Constitution is primarily intended to ensure the development, *without outside interference*, of the personality of each individual in his/her relations with other human beings. It includes an 'inner circle' in which the individual may live his/her own personal life as he/she chooses and to exclude therefrom entirely the outside world not encompassed within that circle. Respect for private life must also comprise to a certain degree the right to establish and develop relationships with other human beings. Hence, apart from the 'inner circle', there is also a zone of interaction of a person with others, even in a public context, which may fall within the scope of 'private life'. The question whether Article 10(2) or 13(1) will apply in a given privacy case is not always evident. In practice, a plaintiff should invoke both provisions simultaneously before the Federal Supreme Court. In a recent case, the Federal Supreme Court held that the observation by a private detective of an allegedly injured person receiving benefits from an accident insurance company was admissible and did not violate the right to privacy (Decision of the Federal Supreme Court BGE 135 I 169 paragraphs 4.4–5.7). This practice was overruled by the European Court of Human Rights in the case *Vukota-Bojic v. Switzerland* of 18 October 2016, 61838/10, where the applicant alleged that the secret surveillance of her daily activities ordered by her insurance company had violated her rights under Article 8. The Court found for a violation and pointed out that the domestic law did not indicate 'with sufficient clarity the scope and manner of exercise of the discretion conferred on insurance companies acting as public authorities in insurance disputes to conduct secret surveillance of insured persons. In particular, it did not, (…), set out sufficient safeguards against abuse'. Since the practice of secret surveillance is not 'in accordance with the law' the authorities had to suspend their activities in this field; the Swiss legislature is currently under high pressure to provide for an adequate legal basis.

591. The right to privacy in one's family life: The exercise of this civil liberty obviously requires the existence of a family, which is guaranteed as an institution in Article 14 of the Constitution (including the right to found a family and to raise children). The term 'family' in Article 13(1) of the Constitution includes not only the traditional two-parent families, but also alternative forms of relationships (e.g., single-parent families, children raised by the grandparents, etc.), as long as this relationship is effectively lived with a certain intensity and stability. However, it does not include same-sex relationships (Decision of the Federal Supreme Court BGE 126 II 425 paragraph 4b). In accordance with Article 8 of the ECHR, the constitutional provision confers the right for a minor foreign child of a Swiss citizen to live in Switzerland permanently (Decisions of the Federal Supreme Court BGE 129 II 249 paragraph 1.2; BGE 130 II 137 paragraph 2.1; but *see El Ghatet v. Switzerland* of 8 November 2016, 56971/10 [violation of Article 8 ECHR]). Regarding the right of foreign residents to be joined by their partners and/or children, international treaties may confer an enforceable right (*see*, for European Union (EU)/European Free Trade Association (EFTA)-citizens, the Agreement on the Free Movement of Persons between the Swiss Confederation and the European Union [SR 0.142.112.681]). Alternatively, an enforceable right might be directly deduced from Article 8 of the ECHR and Article 13(1) of the Constitution. The Federal Supreme Court follows the widely ramified Strasbourg case law and examines in a thorough manner the existence of an intact family bond and whether the familiar relationship is practised (*see* for a summary of the complex case law Decision of the Federal Supreme Court BGE 130 II 281); in any case, the right to live with one's family may be denied if the individual's conduct gravely threatens public order, security and health (Decision of the Federal Supreme Court BGE 129 II 215 paragraph 7 [regarding an Italian cocaine dealer]; *see also Salija v. Switzerland* of 10 January 2017, 55479/10 [gravity of the applicant's offence, the ties both the applicant and his wife have to 'the former Yugoslav Republic of Macedonia' as well as the adaptable age of their children, and considering the sovereignty of Member States to control and regulate the residence of aliens on their territory]). Several Strasbourg judgments regarding the expulsion of foreigners and the right to respect for family life, namely the case of *Udeh v. Switzerland* of 16 April 2014, 12020/09, have led to so-called counter-dynamics at the national level (*see also Hasanbasic v. Switzerland* of 11 June 2013, 52166/09). However, a recent proposal of a member of the Federal Council to terminate ECHR membership failed to gain the approval of the other members of the Federal Council.

592. The right to the respect of one's home: The German, French and Italian words in the constitutional text (*Wohnung, domicile, domicilio*) have a broader connotation than the word 'home' and may extend, for example, to a professional person's office or to rooms just for temporary abode (e.g., a hotel room). According to some constitutional scholars, vehicles should also fall under the penumbra of Article 13(1) of the Constitution.

593. The secrecy of mail and telecommunication: The guarantee comprises traditional and new forms of communication (e.g., postal letters, telephone calls, e-mails, SMS, etc.). Through federal legislation, private telecommunication companies have an obligation to confidentiality. According to Article 43 of the Federal Telecommunication Act of 30 April 1997 (SR 784.10), no person who is or has been responsible for providing a telecommunications service may disclose to a third-party information relating to subscribers' communications or give anyone else an opportunity to do so. Control and surveillance techniques (e.g., telephone tapping) require a judicial authorization (*see* Article 7 of the Federal Act regarding the Control of Mail and Telecommunication of 6 October 2000 [SR 780.1]). Furthermore, the Federal Administrative Court has stated that the Federal Ordinance regarding the Control of Mail and Telecommunication of 31 October 2001 [SR 780.11] is lacunary and needs to be improved by the legislative branch (Decision A-8267/2010 of 23 June 2011). In 2016, in a referendum, 65.5% of the voters and 23 cantons opted for the introduction of a new Act regarding the Federal Intelligence Service. The act provides for a legal basis for the surveillance of e-mails and internet activities as well as the installation of Trojans. Furthermore, the Federal Intelligence Service may penetrate on private premises and infiltrate computer systems in Switzerland and abroad.

594. The protection against the abuse of personal data: The constitutional text is too narrow and includes also the collection, processing, storage and dissemination of personal data (in this sense Decision of the Federal Supreme Court BGE 133 I 77 paragraph 3.2). It includes the right to disseminate one's own data by all legally permitted and purposive means without the interference of the authorities (Decision of the Federal Supreme Court BGE 141 I 221 paragraph 4.1). According to constitutional doctrine and to Article 3(a) of the Federal Act on Data Protection of 19 June 1992 (SR 235.1) the term 'personal data' must be understood as all information relating to an identified or identifiable person. In contrast to the Constitution, the Act protects sensitive personal data as well (e.g., data on religious, ideological, political or trade union-related views or activities, health, the intimate sphere or the racial origin, social security measures, administrative or criminal proceedings and sanctions). The Act applies to the processing of data pertaining to natural persons and legal persons by private persons and federal authorities; it does not apply to, *inter alia*, personal data that is processed by a natural person exclusively for personal use and which is not disclosed to outsiders, and pending civil proceedings, criminal proceedings, international mutual assistance proceedings (Article 2).

595. In Switzerland, the protection against the abuse of personal data is a field relatively unexplored by the courts. In 2009, the Federal Data Protection and Information Commissioner filed a complaint before the Federal Administrative Court against Google Inc. and Google Switzerland concerning the online service Google Street View. The Court held that the defendants must pixelate all faces and vehicle number plates before the pictures can be published on the Internet. In the vicinity of sensitive facilities, the anonymity of individuals must be ensured. The Court concluded that the interest of the public (the right to one's own image) clearly outweighs the commercial interests of the defendants because the pictures can be made totally or partially unrecognizable (so that pixelating them is not a disproportionate measure; *see* Decision of the Federal Administrative Court A-7040/2009 of 30 March 2011). The judgment was appealed to the Federal Supreme Court which held partially in favour for Google on the ground that a complete pixelation of all faces and licence plates is not proportional (Decision of the Federal Supreme Court 1C_230/2011 of 31 May 2012). In a recent case regarding a Swiss bank, the Federal Market Supervisory Authority (FINMA) issued an order which contained a clause that the order and the content thereof may not be made available or accessible to third parties without the consent of FINMA. The Federal Supreme Court held that this unconditional restriction imposed on the bank violated Articles 13 and 16 of the Constitution (Decision of the Federal Supreme Court BGE 141 I 204 paragraphs 4.2–4.8; *see also* 1C_33/2016 of 17 November 2016 [right to publish personal data about oneself on the Internet]).

IV. Marriage

Selected Bibliography: Auer, Malinverni & Hottelier. Vol. II, 203 et seq.; Biaggini. Kommentar, Article 14 (with further references); Breitenmoser Stephan, & Schweizer Rainer, J. St. Galler Kommentar, Article 14 (with further references); Rhinow, Schefer & Uebersax, §15; Schweizer Rainer. 'Recht auf Ehe und Familie'. In *Handbuch der Grundrechte*, edited by Mertens & Papier, §213; Peter Uebersax. Basler Kommentar BV, Article 14 (with further references).

596. The case law of the Federal Supreme Court and the preparatory materials for the Constitution indicate that the right to marry in Article 14 of the Constitution is limited to traditional, monogamous, permanent unions between human beings of the opposite sex (*see* Federal Gazette 2003 1303; Decision of the Federal Supreme Court

126 II 425 paragraph 2b). To be able to marry, the parties must have reached 18 years of age and have the capacity to consent (Article 94 of the Civil Code; SR 210). Impediments to marriage are (1) an existing and still valid marriage (a person wishing to remarry must prove that any previous marriage has been annulled or dissolved; *see* Article 96 of the Civil Code) and (2) kinship (marriage between lineal relatives and between siblings or half-siblings, whether related to each other by parentage or adoption; adoption does not remove the impediment to marriage constituted by kinship between the adopted child and his/her issue on the one hand and his/her adoptive family on the other hand; *see* Article 95 of the Civil Code).

597. Same-sex couples do not fall under the penumbra of Article 14 of the Constitution, but they are namely protected by the non-discrimination clause (Article 8(2) of the Constitution: 'life form'), personal freedom (Article 10(2) of the Constitution) and the right to privacy (Article 13(1) of the Constitution, Article 8 of the ECHR). Hence, same-sex marriages as such are excluded. However, since 1 January 2007, the Federal Act regarding Registered Partnerships of Same-Sex Couples (adopted by popular vote on 5 June 2005) allows same-sex couples to register their partnership and to establish a marriage-like relationship with mutual rights and obligations. The Act excludes the adoption of children and fertility treatments (Article 26); moreover, the partners cannot take the same surname. In 2010, a total of 720 partnerships were registered (male couples: 499; female couples: 221) and 77 partnerships were dissolved (male couples: 49; female couples: 28).

V. Communication and Expression

Bibliography (selection): Auer, Malinverni & Hottelier. Vol. II, 251 et seq.; Auer Andreas. 'D'une liberté non écrite qui n'aurait pas dû l'être: la liberté de langue'. In *Aktuelle Juristische Praxis [AJP]*. 1992, 955 et seq.; Biaggini Giovanni. 'Die schweizerische direkte Demokratie und das Völkerrecht – Gedanken aus Anlass der Volksabstimmung "Gegen den Bau von Minaretten"'. In *Zeitschrift für öffentliches Recht [ZÖR]* 2010, 325 et seq.; Biaggini. Kommentar, Articles 15–18, and Articles 20–23 (with further references); Biaggini Giovanni. 'Vereinigungsfreiheit und Koalitionsfreiheit'. In *Handbuch der Grundrechte*, edited by Mertens & Papier, §223; Brunner Stephan C. & Burkert Herbert. Basler Kommentar BV, Article 17; Cavelti Urs J. & Kley Andreas. Basler Kommentar BV, Article 15 (with further references); Ehrenzeller Bernhard. 'Glauben, Gewissen und Weltanschauung'. In *Handbuch der Grundrechte*, edited by Mertens & Papier, §212; Errass Christoph. Basler Kommentar BV, Articles 22–23; Fleiner Thomas. 'Sprachenfreiheit'. In *Handbuch der Grundrechte*, edited by Merten & Papier, §217; Häfelin, Haller, Keller & Thurnherr, §§14–19; Haller. *Swiss Constitution*, 189 et seq.; Kägi-Diener Regula. Basler Kommentar BV, Article 18 (with further references); Kley Andreas & Tophinke Esther. Basler Kommentar BV, Article 16 (with further references); Malinverni Giorgio. 'Meinungs-, Medien- und Informationsfreiheit'. In *Handbuch der Grundrechte*, edited by Mertens & Papier, §216; Müller & Schefer, 251 et seq., 345–650; Rhinow, Schefer & Uebersax, §15 (with further references); Schweizer Rainer, J. 'Wissenschaftsfreiheit und Kunstfreiheit'. In *Handbuch der Grundrechte*, edited by Mertens & Papier, §218; Zimmerli Ulrich.

'Versammlungsfreiheit'. In *Handbuch der Grundrechte*, edited by Mertens & Papier, §219.

A. Overview

598. Communication is not only an essential aspect of the personhood and autonomy of every human being, but also crucial to every democratic discourse. The freedom of opinion is – especially in a semi-direct democracy like Switzerland –'the prerequisite of a democratic society' (Decision of the European Court for Human Rights of 7 December 1976, ser. A, no. 24 §49, *Handyside*). As John Milton (1608–1674) pointed out, the independent development of the human mind is not possible without freedom of opinion. But only when people are able to freely *express* their thoughts in the 'marketplace of ideas' (Oliver W. Holmes) can they exchange, test, criticize, modify and extend their views and their knowledge. Although it might be debateable whether truth is more likely to emerge from this clash of ideas – the acceptance of competing ideas by the majority might not be the 'best test' and also be flawed by emotions, demagoguery, prejudice, corruption or favouritism, etc. – the alternative – the selection of 'facts', the determination of 'truth' and the censorship of 'falsehoods' by the state – has proven to be worse. A society that does not allow freedom of opinion destroys in the long run its historical, cultural, intellectual and political roots.

599. The catalogue of fundamental rights of the Federal Constitution does not contain a fully satisfying and coherent systematization of communication and expression rights. For example, the *specific* right to express religious beliefs is granted in Article 15 of the Constitution, whereby liberty of opinion as a more *general* civil liberty is anchored in Article 16 of the Constitution (*see also* the very questionable position of the social fundamental right to primary education [Article 19 of the Constitution] after the liberty of language [Article 18 of the Constitution] and before the freedom of science [Article 20 of the Constitution]). In the following context, the term 'communication and expression' is understood in a very large sense and includes all civil liberties of the Constitution that guarantee or protect the imparting or exchanging of information and the action of making known one's thoughts or feelings. In its political implications, the *guarantee of political rights* protects the freedom of the citizen to form an opinion and to give genuine expression to his/her will (Article 34(2) of the Constitution). The provision has already been discussed *infra* in Part II, Chapter 2, §2, in the context of the democratic principle.

600. The Constitution of 1874 only expressly protected the freedom of the press. In 1961, the Federal Supreme Court finally recognized the liberty of opinion as an *unwritten civil liberty of the Constitution* (Decision of the Federal Supreme Court BGE 87 I 117). In contrast to the general clauses in Article 10 of the ECHR or Article 19 of the UN-Pact II, the catalogue of fundamental rights of the Swiss Constitution codifies and protects communication and expression in several provisions, which shall be discussed below.

B. Freedom of Opinion and Information

601. The *freedom of opinion* in Article 16(1) and 16(2) of the Constitution guarantees that all persons shall have the right to freely form, express and disseminate their opinions. Like human dignity (Article 7 of the Constitution) and personal freedom (Article 10(2) of the Constitution), the freedom of opinion is a default civil liberty, which can be invoked by every individual, when other provisions protecting communication and expression in a more specific way do not apply (Decision of the Federal Supreme Court BGE 127 I 145). The provision does not only protect the free formation, expression and dissemination of opinions, feelings, thoughts, advertisements, etc., but includes unpopular or distasteful speech as well. However, Article 261*bis* of the Criminal Code (SR 311.0) punishes racial discrimination, e.g., the public denigration or discrimination of another person or of a group of persons on the grounds of their race, ethnic origin or religion in a manner that violates human dignity, whether verbally, in writing or pictorially, by using gestures, through acts of aggression or by other means, or any person who on any of these grounds denies, trivializes or seeks justification for genocide or other crimes against humanity. In 2007, the Federal Supreme Court dismissed an appeal in criminal matters of a Turkish politician, publicly denying on Swiss territory the genocide of the Armenian population of the Ottoman Empire during and just after World War I (Decision of the Federal Supreme Court 6B_398/2007 of 12 December 2007). This decision was overruled by the Grand Chamber of the European Court of Human Rights in the case of *Perincek v. Switzerland* of 15 October 2015, 27510/08 (selected for case reports) for breach of Article 10 of the Convention. In this very controversial (and in its reasoning not always coherent) judgment, the Grand Chamber pointed out that 'the applicant's statements bore on a matter of public interest and did not amount to a call for hatred or intolerance, that the context in which they were made was not marked by heightened tensions or special historical overtones in Switzerland, that the statements cannot be regarded as affecting the dignity of the members of the Armenian community to the point of requiring a criminal law response in Switzerland, that there is no international law obligation for Switzerland to criminalize such statements, that the Swiss courts appear to have censured the applicant for voicing an opinion that diverged from the established ones in Switzerland, and that the interference took the serious form of a criminal conviction'. The Court concluded 'that it was not necessary, in a democratic society, to subject the applicant to a criminal penalty in order to protect the rights of the Armenian community at stake in the present case'. Note that restrictions to freedom of opinion must follow the general rules of Article 36 of the Constitution (*infra* §1 IV. of this Chapter). Public servants have a duty of loyalty, which may restrict the exercise of their liberty of opinion regarding extra-professional activities as well (Decision of the Federal Supreme Court BGE 136 I 332 paragraph 3.2 [regarding the dissemination of flysheets]).

602. The *freedom of information and the Freedom of Information Act* – as a derivate of the freedom of opinion – is guaranteed in Article 16(1) and 16(3) of the Constitution and provides that all persons shall have the right to freely receive information, to gather it from generally accessible sources and to disseminate it (*see also* Decision of the Federal Supreme Court BGE 141 II 195 paragraph 6.4.1 regarding the right to radio and television reception). According to the case law of the Federal

Supreme Court, the freedom of information does not confer a right to the media to interview prisoners (a prison not being a generally accessible institution). However, in a recent case the Court re-examined this questionable holding, but left the question open, because the right of the media to interview prisoners was deduced from Article 17 of the Constitution (Decision of the Federal Supreme Court BGE 137 I 8 paragraph 2.7). With regard to the right to access federal documents, the Federal Administration is bound by the principle of transparency and contributes to informing the public by ensuring access to official documents. The Federal Act on Freedom of Information in the Administration of 12 December 2004 entered in force on 1 July 2006 (SR 152.3). It applies to the Federal Administration, public and private bodies outside the Federal Administration, insofar as they enact legislation or issue first instance rulings within the meaning of Article 5 FAPA (*see supra* Part IV, Chapter 5, §2), and the Parliamentary Services. It does not apply to the Swiss National Bank or the Swiss Financial Market Supervisory Authority (FINMA). With regard to the scope of application *ratione materiae*, access to federal documents is granted, unless the document relates to civil and criminal proceedings, international mutual and administrative assistance proceedings, international dispute settlement proceedings, judicial proceedings in the field of constitutional and administrative law, or arbitration proceedings (Article 3). An 'official document' in the sense of the Act is any information which has been recorded, regardless of the medium, retained by the authority which issued the same or to which it has been communicated, and which concerns the execution of a public function (Article 5). According to Article 6 of the Act, any person has the right to inspect official federal documents and to obtain information about the content of official federal documents. The documents may be inspected *in situ* or a copy thereof may be requested. Article 7 of the Act states, that the right of access shall be limited, deferred or refused if, *inter alia*, such access to an official document is likely to compromise the domestic and international security of Switzerland or to affect the interests of Switzerland in matters of foreign policy and international relations, or is likely to affect the economic or monetary interests of Switzerland or may reveal professional, business or manufacturing secrets. As the recent case law of the Federal Supreme Court indicates it took some time until the new possibilities of the Freedom of Information Act were 'discovered' by the public, especially by the media. In BGE 142 II 340, the Court had to examine whether the Swiss Agency for Therapeutic Products (Swissmedic) had to reveal information about the identity of the experts who had participated in the preparation of the authorization documents for a pharmaceutical product (the case was partially remanded to the Federal Administrative Court; *see also* 1C_74/2015 of 2 December 2015 [access to a study of the Swiss National Fund]). In BGE 142 II 324, the Court held that an Outlook agenda of the former director the Federal Office for Defence Procurement (armasuisse) is an official document in the sense of Article 5 of the Freedom of Information Act and must be made available to the public upon request. *See also* 1C_122/2015 of 18 May 2016 (access to information regarding the foreign partner services of the Federal Intelligence Service), or BGE 142 II 313 (access to tax information from the Federal Tax Administration). – Note that the seventeen cantons, whose cantonal (and municipal) administration is governed by the transparency principle, have each their own cantonal freedom of information act (Aargau, Basel-City, Basel-Land, Berne, Fribourg, Geneva, Jura, Neuchâtel, Schaffhausen, Schwyz,

Solothurn,, St. Gallen, Ticino, Valais, Vaud, Zug and Zurich). The cantons of Grison and Uri have anchored the transparency principle only on the cantonal level. In the canton of Appenzell Ausserrhoden, access to information is granted to persons with a 'legitimate interest'. So far, the cantons of Appenzell Innerrhoden, Glarus (the *Landsgemeinde* will decide on this matter in 2018), Lucerne, Nidwalden, Obwalden and Thurgau (signatures are collected for a popular initiative) have not undergone a paradigm shift towards transparency. Nevertheless, the air for administrative secrecy is growing thinner since the recent ECHR judgment *Magyar Helsinki Bizottság v. Hungary* of 8 November 2016, 18030/11, where the Grand Chamber held that Article 10 §1 of the Convention constitutes a basis for recognizing a right of access to information held by public authorities, and that that right can be exercised by anyone (even bloggers) who wishes to inform the public in the capacity of a public 'watchdog'. Furthermore, the UNECE Convention on Access to Information, Public Participation in Decision-making and Access to Justice in Environmental Matters (Aarhus Convention; SR 0.814.07) entered into force for Switzerland in June 2014 (*see* especially Article 4 with regard to the access to environmental information).

C. *Freedom of the Media*

603. The *freedom of the media* is guaranteed in Article 17(1) of the Constitution. The term 'media' is broad and includes, *inter alia*, the press, radio, television, and other forms of disseminating opinions and information by means of telecommunications (*see* Decision of the Federal Supreme Court BGE 141 I 214 paragraph 3.1). The provision must be read in connection with Article 93(3) of the Constitution, which guarantees the independence of radio and television and the autonomy of their programmes. The balancing between this constitutionally granted independence and the responsibility of the media as the 'fourth branch' of the State can be delicate. Therefore, due to the influence of the media on society and politics and the scarcity of available frequencies, the Constitution mandates that radio and television shall contribute to education and cultural development, to the free formation of opinion and to entertainment, thereby taking the particularities of the country and the needs of the cantons into account; events shall be presented with objectivity and reflect the diversity of opinions in an adequate manner (Article 93(2) of the Constitution). The form of how a subject is presented by the media (e.g., an interview, a written article, etc.) lies within the discretion of the journalist (Decision of the Federal Supreme Court BGE 137 I 8 paragraph 2.3.2) His/her sources of information are constitutionally protected (Article 17(3) of the Constitution). The Criminal Code provides in Article 28a that if persons who are professionally involved in the publication of information in the editorial section of a periodical medium or their auxiliary personnel refuse to give evidence as to the identity of the author or as to the content and sources of their information, they shall not be liable to any penalty nor to any procedural law enforcement measures. Exceptionally, journalistic sources are not protected if a court holds the evidence is required in order to save a person from immediate danger to life or limb or if, without the evidence, a case of homicide or another felony listed in Article 28a(b) of the Criminal Code will not be solved or the persons suspected of committing the said offence may not be apprehended. The Federal Supreme Court upheld the protection of journalistic sources in a case where a journalist claimed, with reference to well-informed sources, that a team of surgeons had intentionally implanted a heart, incompatible with the blood group of the patient, which caused the death of the patient (Decision of the Federal Supreme Court BGE 132 I 181).

604. In *Haldimann and others v. Switzerland* of 24 February 2015 (21830/09) the European Court of Human Rights examined the use of hidden cameras by investigative journalist to expose the malpractice of insurance brokers (the meeting did not take place in the broker's offices or any other business premises). On the domestic level, the Federal Supreme Court had previously held that the applicants had committed acts falling under Article 179*bis* (intercepting and recording of private conversations) and Article 179*ter* (unauthorized recording of conversation) of the Criminal Code. The journalists were convicted and ordered to pay a small fine. The European Court of Human Rights held for a violation of Article 10 of the ECHR. It first established that the report in question concerned a matter of public interest because the subject of the report, namely the poor-quality advice offered by private insurance brokers, raised an issue in terms of consumer protection and thus concerned a debate of considerable public interest. It was capable of contributing to the public debate on this issue regardless of the question whether it fully achieved that objective. Although the broker was not a public figure and filmed without his knowledge and consent (and could therefore have 'had a reasonable expectation of privacy' as regards the conversation), the report did not focus on the broker *himself* but 'on certain commercial practices employed within a particular profession'. The Court therefore considered that the interference with the broker's private life was less serious than if the report had been personally and exclusively focused on him. The recording was then broadcast as part of a report which was particularly disparaging towards the broker. Although only brief excerpts of the recording were shown, this footage was liable to entail a more significant interference with the broker's right to privacy, since it was seen by a large number of viewers. The Court acknowledged that the audiovisual media often have a much more immediate and powerful effect than the print media. Viewers of the programme were thus able to form an opinion as to the quality of the broker's advice and his lack of professionalism. Nevertheless, a decisive factor in the present case was that the applicants had pixelated the broker's face so that only his hair and skin colour could still be made out; they also distorted his voice (in contrast to *Bremner v. Turkey* of 13 October 2015, 37428/06, regarding surreptitious filming). The Court therefore considered that the interference with the private life of the broker was not so serious as to override the public interest in information about alleged malpractice in the field of insurance brokerage. With regard to the fine the Court reiterated, even relatively small fines can have a chilling effect discouraging the media from using certain journalistic methods for their reporting. The case has drawn international attention because, until *Haldimann*, conducting interviews with hidden cameras, a technique used mainly in undercover journalism, was considered unsafe due to the unforeseeable litigation risk. However, the ECHR left the question open whether it would also back the use of hidden cameras if alternative methods to obtain the information were available (this was the position of the Federal Supreme Court arguing that the journalists 'could have used different means' for their reporting, which would have been 'less damaging to the broker's private interests'.). It is just a question of time until the Court will have to assess whether the interests must be balanced differently if the footage is recorded on business premises (note that according to the case law of the ECHR, a place of work is a 'private place', *see Niemietz v. Germany*).

605. According to Article 17(2) of the Constitution, systematic preventive and repressive censorship is prohibited. Although the media are usually the first target of censorship, the provision also applies to all other fundamental rights granting free communication. Note that interim measures ordered by a court to prevent an imminent violation of one's personality (Articles 261 et seq. of the Federal Code of Civil Procedure; SR 272) or the confiscation of propaganda material (Article 13a of the Federal Act regarding the Preservation of National Security; SR 120) does not constitute preventive censorship.

D. Freedom of Language

606. Language is an essential and necessary prerequisite for the exercise of other fundamental rights (Decision of the Federal Supreme Court BGE 91 I 480 paragraph II). In a multilingual country like Switzerland, the liberty of language in Article 18 of the Constitution plays an important role in constitutional practice. Under the Constitution of 1874, it was recognized as an unwritten fundamental right by the Federal Supreme Court (Decision of the Federal Supreme Court BGE 91 I 480). The liberty of language namely guarantees the right to speak in one's mother tongue and in any other language one wishes. If the mother tongue corresponds with one of the four national languages (German, French, Italian and Romansh), its use is also protected by Article 4 of the Constitution. Furthermore, the non-discrimination clause in Article 8(2) of the Constitution prohibits discriminations based on language (*supra* §3 III of this Chapter).

607. However, most practical problems centre on conflicts between the use of one's mother tongue and the official language in public schools or in cantonal administrative and judicial proceedings. In those cases, the liberty of language must be read in connection with Article 70 of the Constitution. According to Article 70(2) of the Constitution, the cantons shall decide on their official languages. In order to preserve harmony between linguistic communities (i.e., in the bi- or trilingual cantons, *see supra* General Introduction, Chapter 4), the cantons shall respect the traditional territorial distribution of languages, and shall take indigenous linguistic minorities into account. This provision enshrines – according to the Federal Supreme Court – *the principle of territoriality*. This principle is not an individual fundamental right. It restricts the freedom of language insofar as it allows the cantons to determine the official cantonal language in order to preserve the homogeneity and the traditional borders of the linguistic regions (*see* Decision of the Federal Supreme Court BGE 136 I 149 paragraph 4.2 [with further references]).

608. Of course, *the* principle of territoriality is not undisputed (not only because Article 70(2) of the Constitution does not use that term): conflicts between the fundamental right and the principle may arise because the freedom of liberty protects the right to use one's language, whereas the principle of territoriality tries to guarantee stability and homogeneity of the linguistic regions (Decision of the Federal Supreme Court BGE 136 I 149 paragraph 4.2; but note that Article 70(2) of the Constitution does not use the term 'homogeneity'). The Federal Supreme Court states that homogeneity implies *strictu sensu* that one language corresponds with one territory; therefore, each canton, district or municipality should be able to conserve its traditional language regardless of the immigration of persons speaking another national or foreign language. However, in trying to establish a harmony between the freedom of language and the principle of territoriality, the Court points out that the peaceful coexistence of the national languages and the protection of the language of the minority must be favoured (Decisions of the Federal Supreme Court BGE 136 I 149 paragraph 4.2; BGE 122 I 236 paragraph 2e; BGE 121 I 196 paragraph 2b). In relation with public authorities, the freedom of language in Article 18 of the Constitution is limited by the principle of the official cantonal language. Outside the scope of Articles 5(2) and 6(3)(a) of the ECHR, there is generally no right to communicate with cantonal authorities in any language other than the official cantonal language (i.e., the language, which is normally spoken in the territory concerned; Decision of the Federal Supreme Court BGE 136 I 149 paragraph 4.3; BGE 122 I 236 paragraph 2c). In order to promote the understanding and exchange between the linguistic communities and to support the pluri-lingual cantons in the fulfilment of their particular tasks, the Federal Act regarding National Languages and the Understanding Between the Linguistic Communities of 5 October 2007 (in force since 1 January 2010; SR 441.1) has been created. The Act supports, *inter alia*, the measures taken by the Cantons of Grisons and Ticino to safeguard and promote Romansh and Italian.

E. Freedom of Science and Art

609. The *freedom of science and the freedom of art* in Articles 20 and 21 of the Constitution have been newly introduced in the catalogue of fundamental rights and are inspired by Article 15(3) of the UN-Pact I, Article 19(2) of the UN-Pact II and Article 5(3) of the German Basic Law. The scope of their application is still subject to the evolving Federal Supreme Court case law (*see* Decision of the Federal Supreme Court BGE 135 II 384 [authorization for the use of non-human primates in experiments]. The freedom of science guarantees scientific research and teaching, whereas the freedom of art guarantees protection of artistic expression in a broad sense, the presentation of his/her art and the piece of art as such. Although cases are rare, the protection of the liberty of art is also an issue in Switzerland (recalling, e.g., the case of the Swiss artist Thomas Hirschhorn, who urinated during an artistic performance in Paris on the picture of a former member of the Federal Council, which most likely led the Federal Parliament to shorten the budget of Pro Helvetia, a foundation under public law promoting cultural and artistic activities, and entirely funded by the federal government). While movies are not expressly mentioned as protected media in Article 17 of the Constitution, they incontestably fall under the penumbra of freedom of art.

F. Freedom of Religion

610. The *freedom of religion and conscience* guarantees the right to freely choose a religion or philosophical convictions and to practice them alone or in community with others (Article 15(2) of the Constitution; Decision of the Federal Supreme Court

BGE 134 I 51 paragraph 2.3 and 134 I 116 paragraph 2.1), the right to join or to belong to a religious community, to attend religious teachings (Article 15(3) of the Constitution) and the prohibition to be forced to join or belong to a religious community, to participate in a religious act, or to attend religious teachings (Article 15(4) of the Constitution). Freedom of religion will be also discussed *infra* in Part V, Chapter 3, in context with the relationship between the State and the church. Surprisingly, the popular initiative 'Against the Construction of Minarets' was approved by popular vote on 29 November 2009. Although the Federal Council and almost all political parties strongly recommended to vote against the initiative the outcome of the vote was clear: 57.8% of the People and twenty-three of the twenty-six cantons voted in favour of the prohibition. This came as a surprise because the previous opinion polls had predicted a rather low percentage of approval (between 30% and 40%). Article 72(3) of the Constitution now states: 'The construction of minarets is prohibited.' Note that there are around 100 mosques in Switzerland, and that the provision does not ban the construction of mosques (which would be a clear violation of the freedom of religion clause of the Constitution and the ECHR); the four already erected minarets in Switzerland are not affected by the decision. There is broad consensus among constitutional scholars that this constitutional amendment conflicts not only with the freedom of religion clause of the Constitution but also especially with Articles 9 and 14 of the ECHR. However, since a considerable number of countries do not guarantee religious freedom (or have submitted reservations to the corresponding human rights conventions) these fundamental rights are not peremptory norms of international law (*ius cogens*). That was the main reason why Parliament could not declare the initiative inadmissible *ratione materiae* because Article 139(2) of the Constitution prohibits only popular initiatives infringing with 'peremptory norms of international law'. Therefore, the initiative had to be put on a vote. The outcome of the vote triggered intense media attention far beyond the borders of Switzerland. On 28 June 2011, after the exhaustion of all available domestic remedies, the European Court on Human Rights declared two applications inadmissible. The Court held that the applicants, though offended, were not directly affected (i.e., 'victims' in any sense defined by the ECHR) and could not claim damage *from theoretical future events*. The Convention does not guarantee a remedy allowing a State's legislation to be challenged on the ground of being contrary to the Convention (*see Ouardiri v. Switzerland* [no. 665840/09]: '[...] Article 13 de la Convention ne va pas jusqu'à exiger un recours par lequel on puisse dénoncer devant une autorité nationale la législation d'un Etat comme étant contraire en tant que telle à la Convention'. *See also Ligue des Musulmans de Suisse and Others v. Switzerland* [no. 66274/09]). This outcome was foreseeable: As long as persons are not directly affected by an administrative order based on Article 72(3) of the Constitution (e.g., the denial of a construction permit by the competent local authorities) the Strasbourg Court will dismiss such cases on formal grounds. But even if standing is granted, it is an open question whether the Court will base its judgment on a broadly construed reasoning and declare the prohibition of minarets as a violation of Article 9 and/or Article 14 of the Convention. In any case, the debate regarding the supremacy of direct democracy and the 'government of *foreign* judges' is relaunched.

611. Freedom of religion and social integration: On burkas, mixed swimming lessons, and handshakes – In the canton of Ticino, over 65% of the voters voted in favour of banning the veil in 2013. Wearing the burka in public is an offence punishable (even for tourists) by a fine of a minimum of CHF 100 up to CHF 10,000. The Ticino law was inspired by a similar law in force in France, which was upheld by the European Court of Human Rights in 2014 (*S.A.S. v. France*, 43835/11). After the National Assembly narrowly accepted a parliamentary initiative for a nationwide ban on the burka, the Council of States rejected the plan in March 2017 by twenty-six votes to nine, with four abstentions. The proposal put forward by a member of the Swiss People's Party has therefore been definitively rejected. Whether the minimum of 100,000 signatures needed to launch a popular vote will be collected until September 2017 is uncertain. – In 2017, the European Court of Human Rights delivered an important judgment regarding the question whether Muslim parents must enrol their daughters in a mandatory mixed swimming class despite the parents' objections. The girls, 9 and 7 at the time, were allowed by the school authorities to wear body-covering swimsuits, known as burkinis. Since the parents, both Swiss-Turkish nationals, refused to send their daughters to the swimming lessons, a fine of CHF 1,400 was imposed. In *Osamoglu et Kocabas v. Switzerland* of 10 January 2017 (29086/12), the ECHR rejected a violation of the freedom of thought, conscience and religion. The Court held that the public interest in following the full school curriculum should prevail over the applicants' private interest in obtaining an exemption from mixed swimming lessons for their daughters. According to the Court the interference was justified by the need to protect the children from social exclusion since school plays a special role in the process of social integration, particularly where children of foreign origin were concerned. Swimming lessons are not just to learn to swim, but above all to take part in that activity with all the other pupils, the Court added. Furthermore, the fine was fair and proportional in order to ensure that the parents do send their children to compulsory lessons, which is above all in their own interest, for socialization and successful integration. – In some areas in Switzerland, shaking a teacher's hand before and after class is considered an important part of Swiss culture and a sign of politeness and respect. In 2016, the authorities in the canton of Basel-Landschaft ruled that two Syrian immigrant brothers, aged 14 and 15, who studied at a public school, could not refuse to shake their female teacher's hand on religious grounds. Their refusal to do so had provoked a national outrage and the family's request for naturalization was suspended. Meanwhile, in the Canton of Basel-Land, some politicians proposed a 'Handshake Act' or even an amendment of the cantonal constitution, however, with probably too vague formulations ('obligation to participate at local and well-established rituals' or 'religious beliefs and practices may not dispense from the fulfilment of civic obligations').

G. Assembly, Association and Freedom to Unionize

612. Like Article 11 of the ECHR, the *freedom of assembly* in Article 22 of the Constitution guarantees the right to organize meetings and to choose whether to participate in them or not. The *freedom of association* in Article 23 of the Constitution allows every person to form associations and to join, belong to or participate in their activities. However, no person can be forced either to join or belong to them (for a *tour d'horizon* over the case law of the Federal Supreme Court *see* Christoph Errass.

St. Galler Kommentar, Article 22). The *freedom to unionize* in Article 28 of the Constitution grants workers, employers and their organizations the right to form, join or remain out of unions and the right to unionize for the defence of their interest. Whenever possible, conflicts shall be resolved through negotiation and mediation. Strikes and lockouts are only permitted when they are not contrary to obligations to keep labour peace intact or to resort to conciliation. Some categories of persons, such as public officers, prisoners or members of the Army, may be prohibited from striking.

VI. Domicile, Extradition and Expulsion

613. The *freedom of domicile* in Article 24 of the Constitution grants every Swiss citizen the right to establish his/her domicile anywhere in the country and within every canton as well as the right to leave and return to Switzerland. The provision can only be invoked by Swiss natural persons (for legal persons and foreign natural and legal persons, especially EU/EFTA-nationals, *see supra* §1, II B of this Chapter). The freedom of domicile can be restricted, if the nature of the public office imperatively requires the immediate presence of the person (e.g., for police officers or members of the fire brigade, etc.) or if a close relationship with the population is important for the accomplishment of a public task (e.g., primary school teachers or democratically elected officials, etc.). In these cases, the persons can be obliged to reside at or in the vicinity of his/her place of employment (for further references *see* Kley Andreas. 'Niederlassungsfreiheit'. In *Handbuch der Grundrechte*, edited by Mertens & Papier, §215).

614. According to Article 25(1) of the Constitution, no Swiss citizen may be expelled from the country; they may only be extradited to a foreign authority with their consent. If consent is refused, the Swiss person, who committed a crime abroad, will be prosecuted in Switzerland (*aut dedere aut iudicare*; *see* Article 6 of the Criminal Code; SR 311.0). The general principle of non-refoulement is anchored in Article 25(2) of the Constitution: refugees may not be removed by force or extradited to a State in which they would be persecuted. Note, however, that the principle of non-refoulement does not exclude removal or extradition in an absolute manner. Article 5(2) of the Federal Asylum Act of 26 June 1998 (SR 142.31) provides that the ban on refoulement may not be invoked if there are substantial grounds for the assumption that, because the person invoking it has been convicted of a particularly serious felony or misdemeanour, they represent a threat to Switzerland's security or are to be considered dangerous to the public.

615. Finally, Article 25(3) of the Constitution protects everyone from being removed by force to a country where he/she is threatened by torture or any other form of cruel and inhuman treatment or punishment (*see*, *inter alia*, Article 10(3) of the Constitution, Article 3 of the ECHR, Article 7 of the UN-Pact II and Article 3 UN Convention Against Torture and Other Cruel, Inhuman or Degrading Treatment or Punishment [SR 0.105]). The prohibition is absolute and takes precedence over international extradition treaties between Switzerland and other contracting States. However, diplomatic assurances of the requesting State that the prohibition of torture will be observed may allow extradition. The assessment can be difficult and delicate (*see,* regarding an extradition to Russia, Decision of the Federal Supreme Court BGE 134 IV 156 paragraph 6 [the Court orders – also in view of the Strasbourg case law, which clearly indicates that Article 3 of the ECHR violations in Russian prisons mirror a structural problem – that the Swiss authorities must ensure that the assurance given by Russia is closely monitored by Swiss diplomacy]). In *X. v. Switzerland* of 26 January 2017 (16744/14), the European Court of Human Rights held for a violation of Article 3 ECHR with regard to the Swiss authorities' failure to properly assess the deportation of a family of Tamil origin in August 2013 to Sri Lanka regardless the fact that, in a parallel case, the deportation of another person of Tamil origins to Sri Lanka in July 2013 had resulted in detention, ill-treatment and hospitalization.

VII. Property

Bibliography (selection): Biaggini Giovanni. 'Eigentumsgarantie'. In *Handbuch der Grundrechte*, edited by Mertens & Papier, §221; Biaggini. Kommentar, Article 26 (with further references); Häfelin, Haller, Keller & Thurnherr, §22; Haller. *Swiss Constitution*, 203 et seq.; Hänni Peter. 'Eigentumsschutz, Sozialbindung und Enteignung bei der Nutzung von Boden und Umwelt'. In *Veröffentlichung der Vereinigung Deutscher Staatsrechtslehrer [VVDStRL]*. 1992 [51], 252 et seq.; Müller & Schefer, 1007 et seq.; Rhinow, Schefer & Uebersax, §17; Rhinow et al., *Öffentliches Wirtschaftsrecht.* 2nd ed. Basel: Helbing & Lichtenhahn, 2011, §6 (with further references); Riva Enrico. *Hauptfragen der materiellen Enteignung*. Berne: Stämpfli, 1990; Riva Enrico. *Wohlerworbene Rechte–Eigentum–Vertrauen.* Berne: Stämpfli, 2007; Riva Enrico & Müller-Tschumi Thomas. 'Eigentumsgarantie'. In Thürer et al., §48; Ruch Alexander. 'Die expansive Kraft der materiellen Enteignung'. In *Schweizerisches Zentralblatt für Staats- und Verwaltungsrecht [ZBl]*. 2000, 617 et seq.; Vallender Klaus, A. & Hettich Peter. St. Galler Kommentar, Article 26 (with further references); Waldmann Bernhard. Basler Kommentar BV, Article 26 (with further references); Waldmann Bernhard. 'Eigentum und Eigentumsordnung – Einige Gedanken zum Recht auf Eigentum'. In Mélanges Steinauer. Berne, 2013, 653 et seq.

A. Overview

616. Until its approval by popular vote in 1969, the Constitution of 1874 did not expressly protect a general right to property (but note that the right to full compensation in cases of expropriation was already granted in the Constitution of 1848). The need to anchor a generally formulated provision on the federal level was negligible because almost all cantonal constitutions contained corresponding guarantees. Additionally, in its earlier case law, the Federal Supreme Court deduced from the various cantonal constitutional provisions a general legal framework for the protection of property. Finally, the Court recognized in an unpublished case the right to property as an *unwritten fundamental right of the Confederation* (Decision of the Federal Supreme Court of 11 May 1960, *Municipality of Zurzach*). The Swiss Confederation has not signed the First Additional Protocol to the ECHR, which protects in Article 1 the right to property (but note that Article 26 of the Constitution has a much broader scope of application than the Protocol). Regardless that fact, in the case of *Di Trizio v. Switzerland* of 2 February 2016 (7186/09), the European Court decided that the refusal of the Swiss social security authorities to grant disability allowances to the applicant, based on the so-called combined method on the grounds that even if she had not had a disability the applicant would not have worked full-time after the birth of her children, violated Article 14 in conjunction with Article 8 of the Convention. The Court pointed out that measures enabling one parent to stay at home to look after the children promoted family life and thus had an impact on the way it was organized; such measures therefore came within the ambit of Article 8 of the Convention. The overwhelming majority of people affected by the combined method were women who wished to reduce their working hours after the birth of a child. Accordingly, the applicant could claim to be the victim of discrimination on grounds of gender. It followed that Article 14 taken in conjunction with Article 8 was also applicable. In practice, the Court stated, for the great majority of women wishing to work part time following the birth of their children, the combined method was a source of discrimination. It concluded that there had been no reasonable justification for the difference in treatment to which the applicant had been subjected. This judgment is noteworthy insofar as *purely monetary complaints* regarding discrimination are not based on Article 8, but rather on Article 1 of the Additional Protocol to the ECHR. Since Switzerland (together with Monaco) has not ratified this Protocol, it is not bound by its provisions. Such a flexible application of Article 8 would require that any grant or denial of social benefits falls under Article 8 since social benefits are always likely to have some impact on a household or even private life. The Court's interpretation – basically introducing the right to property 'through the backdoor' of Article 8 of the Convention for Swiss cases – could not only threaten to allow any measure of labour law to fall under Article 8 as well, as the dissenting judges rightly feared, but opens a much wider field of possibilities in various areas of law (e.g., does the denial of a construction permit for a family home fall within the scope of application of Article 8 of the Convention? etc.). It is probably only a question of time until the first applicants from Switzerland will start to test and challenge the Court on this issue.

617. The constitutional term 'property' is to be understood in a broad sense, including not only real property (e.g., ownership in land, condominium; Articles 655–712t of the Civil Code [SR 210]), personal property (chattel ownership; Articles 713–729 of the Civil Code), limited rights in rem (e.g., easements, usufruct, personal servitudes, mortgages; Articles 730–915 of the Civil Code), possession (Articles 919–941 of the Civil Code), personal rights (e.g., leaseholds, patents and other intellectual rights), but also rights deriving from public contracts, concessions and licences, social benefits and pensions, and certain 'pre-constitutional' rights, which already exist from time immemorial (*wohlerworbene Rechte*, e.g., the right to use public waters, pasture rights, etc.). The constitutional concept of property is based on three guarantees: *First*, it protects the individual's interests in property (in the broad sense as defined above) in the present given situation from governmental intrusion (guarantee of the status quo; *Bestandesgarantie*). *Second*, it provides full compensation in cases of expropriations and restrictions of ownership equivalent to expropriation (guarantee of full compensation; *Wertgarantie*). *Third*, Article 26 of the Constitution guarantees the right to property as an essential and inviolable feature of the Swiss legal order (*Institutsgarantie*).

B. Restrictions to Property

618. As any other fundamental right, restrictions to the right to property must fulfil the four conditions of Article 36 of the Constitution (*see also supra* §1 IV of the Chapter):

(1) Any restriction to property requires a legal basis or a clear and present danger (for recent examples *see* Decisions of the Federal Supreme Court BGE 130 I 360 paragraph 1 [the burning of confiscated cannabis plants during the investigation procedure lacks a legal basis]; BGE 133 II 220 paragraph 2.5 [cantonal ordinance protecting hedges constitutes a sufficient legal basis]; BGE 135 I 233 paragraph 2.1 [democratically legitimized municipal regulation containing quotas and contingents regarding secondary residences in the Canton of Valais]).
(2) The limitation to property must be justified by a public interest or by the need to protect the fundamental rights of others. Generally, any public interest can justify a restriction as long as the goal of the restriction is not purely fiscal in nature, and the restriction does not violate other provisions of the Constitution (*see, inter alia,* Decisions of the Federal Supreme Court BGE 107 Ia 35 [oversized industrial zones]; BGE 120 Ia 270 paragraph 6b [protection of historical buildings]; BGE 115 Ia 370 [protection of the silhouette of the historical centre of the City of Berne]; BGE 135 I 209 paragraph 3.3.1 [confiscation of weapons and parts thereof without compensation]).
(3) The limitation must be proportionate to the goal pursued (*see, inter alia,* Decisions of the Federal Supreme Court BGE 128 I 295 paragraphs 6b and 8b/cc [the prohibition of a tobacco advertisement on private ground, which could be seen from public grounds, is proportional; this kind of advertisement is also subject to authorization, which is not disproportional]; BGE 126 I 462 paragraph 5e [blocking of Mobutu's banking accounts for several years held disproportional]).
(4) The essence (*Kerngehalt*) of the right to property may not be violated. According to Federal Supreme Court, this could be the case if a legislative act ignores basic rights deriving from the right to property as an essential and inviolable feature of the Swiss legal order – e.g., the right to use or to dispose of property as provided by the rules and forms of the Civil Code – or if a legislative act has the effect to extinguish the right to property as such. The Federal Supreme Court stated that a taxation scheme, which is *confiscatory* in its effects and not limited in time, would violate the essence of the right to property (Decisions of the Federal Supreme Court BGE 106 Ia 342, 349; BGE 128 II 112, 126). So far, the Court has never held that a taxation scheme was confiscatory in nature.

C. Expropriation and Compensation

619. Even if a limitation of the right to property is *lawful* because it fulfils the requirements set out above, Article 26(2) of the Constitution provides that expropriations and restrictions equivalent to expropriation must be fully compensated. An expropriation in the meaning of Article 26(2) of the Constitution (formal expropriation) always involves a transfer of the title of ownership from the individual to the State (*see also* Article 16 of the Federal Expropriation Act of 20 June 1930 [SR 711]). In cases of restrictions equivalent to expropriation (material expropriation), the individual keeps the title of ownership, but, as a matter of fact, the State's restriction partially or totally deprives the landowner of his/her ability to use or dispose of his/her property (*see also* Article 5(2) of the Federal Land-Use Planning Act of 22 June 1979 [SR 700]). The distinction between material expropriations, which are subject to full compensation, and other restrictions to property, which are not subject to compensation, can be very difficult and delicate. In such situations, the Federal Supreme Court relies on several criteria, such as the intensity of the restriction, the equal distribution of the charges, the harm caused by the restriction and the probability of a diminished value of the restricted use of property (*see, inter alia,* Decision of the Federal Supreme Court, 91 I 329, 338 et seq.).

620. Compensation 'in full' means, that the person or the persons affected by the formal or material expropriation shall neither suffer a pecuniary loss nor take a profit from the restriction to their right to property (*see, inter alia,* Decisions of the Federal Supreme Court BGE 122 I 168 paragraph 4b/aa; BGE 127 I 185 paragraph 3). The compensation is generally paid in money and comprises the fair market value of the expropriated real property. The case law of the Federal Supreme Court, which cannot be set out here, regarding the methods of the exact calculation of the financial compensation due in cases of formal and material expropriation, is complex in practice and highly disseminated.

VIII. Economic Freedom

Bibliography (selection): Biaggini. Kommentar, Article 27 (with further references); Biaggini Giovanni 'Die Wirtschaftsfreiheit und ihre Einschränkungen'. In ius.full 2003, 2 et seq.; Biaggini et al., *Wirtschaftsverwaltungsrecht des Bundes.* 6th ed. Basel: Helbing & Lichtenhahn, 2016; Häfelin, Haller, Keller & Thurnherr, §23; Haller. *Swiss Constitution,* 205 et seq.; Grisel Etienne, *Liberté économique.* Berne: Stämpfli, 2006; Hänni Peter & Stöckli Andreas. *Schweizerisches Wirtschaftsverwaltungsrecht.* Berne: Stämpfli, 2013; Mahon. commentaire, Article 27; Müller & Schefer, 1042 et seq.; Rhinow, Schefer & Uebersax, §32; Rhinow et al., *Öffentliches Wirtschaftsrecht.* 2nd ed. Basel: Helbing & Lichtenhahn, 2011, §4 and §5 (with further references); Richli Paul. *Grundriss des Wirtschaftsverfassungsrechts.* Berne, 2007; Uhlmann Felix. Basler Kommentar BV, Article 27 (with further references); Vallender Klaus, A. St. Galler Kommentar, Article 27 (with further references); Vallender Klaus, 'Wirtschaftsfreiheit'. In *Handbuch der Grundrechte,* edited by Mertens & Papier, §222; Vallender Klaus, A. et al., *Wirtschaftsfreiheit und begrenzte Staatsverantwortung.* 4th ed. Berne: Stämpfli, 2006.

A. Overview

621. Switzerland was the first country to introduce an encompassing *general guarantee of economic freedom* as an individual right (Article 31 of the Constitution of 1874; now: Article 27, which is closely intertwined with Articles 94–107 of the Constitution). In a comparative constitutional context, only the Constitution of Liechtenstein has so far followed the Swiss example (Article 36: freedom of commerce and industry). A comparable equivalent to the Swiss guarantee of economic freedom cannot be found in international human rights treaties ratified by the Swiss Confederation. Other constitutions only grant certain aspects of economic freedom, e.g., the contracts clause in the Federal Constitution of the United States (Article I, section 10, §1) or the right to choose an occupation in the German Basic Law (Article 12(1)). In Swiss constitutional practice, the guarantee of economic freedom plays an important role, although a lot of questions regarding this atypical and enigmatic civil liberty are still unresolved.

622. The Swiss Constitution contains a threefold concept of economic liberty. *First*, economic liberty is recognized as a *civil liberty* of the individual, which includes, *inter alia*, the freedom to choose one's profession and to enjoy both free access to and free exercise of a remunerative private economic activity (Article 27 of the Constitution). *Second*, economic freedom fulfils an *institutional function* insofar as Article 94(1) of the Constitution contains the basic principles for an economy based upon free market and free competition (Decision of the Federal Supreme Court BGE 125 I 422). *Third*, according to Article 95(2) of the Constitution, the Confederation shall strive to create a unified Swiss economic area and guarantee that persons holding a university degree or a federal or cantonal education certificate or an education certificate recognized by a canton may exercise their profession throughout Switzerland; hence, by preventing cantonal protectionism, economic freedom should fulfil an important *federal function* as well. In order to strengthen and to sharpen this third (often neglected) function of the guarantee of economic freedom, the Federal Internal Market Act of 6 October 1995 (SR 943.02) was introduced. Due to the meagre outcome of the Act, Parliament party revised it in 2005 and expanded the principle of free access to the market (this time at least with some success).

B. Economic Liberty as a Civil Liberty

623. Originally a civil liberty was granted to Swiss citizens only, economic freedom can be nowadays invoked by almost all natural and legal persons. As set out in §1 of this Chapter, foreign natural persons are only beneficiaries of economic freedom if they have a permanent residence permit or if they possess a statutory or international treaty-based right to a residence permit. Consequently, Non-EU/EFTA-citizens who have a residence permit without a statutory or treaty-based right of extension may not invoke economic freedom (Decisions of the Federal Supreme Court BGE 129 II 401, 408 paragraph 4.3; BGE 123 I 19, 20 et seq. paragraph 2). Foreign legal persons are beneficiaries of economic freedom if they have a treaty-based right to exercise a private economic activity on the territory of the Swiss Confederation (Decision of the Federal

Supreme Court BGE 131 I 223, 227). For further questions regarding public and mixed corporations and municipalities *see supra* §1 III of this Chapter.

624. According to the case law of the Federal Supreme Court, economic freedom protects *every private economic activity with the objective to generate profits or income* (regardless whether the main purpose of the activity is to gain profits or whether income is actually achieved; *see also* Decision of the Federal Supreme Court BGE 141 I 127 paragraph 4.1 with regard to lawyers). Hence, whoever exercises a State function or a public office (e.g., medical doctors in public hospitals, judges, notary publics or employees of the federal or cantonal administration) is not regarded as a beneficiary of economic freedom (*supra* §1 II of this Chapter; Decisions of the Federal Supreme Court BGE 131 II 639 paragraph 6.1; BGE 133 I 259 paragraphs 2.2, 4.4; BGE 132 I 201 paragraph 7.1; BGE 132 V 6 paragraph 2.5.4) Exceptionally, public officers, who exercise secondary private economic activities, may be protected by the guarantee of economic freedom if no preponderant public interest interferes. The *independent and non-independent* character of the private economic activity is no longer of relevance (Decision of the Federal Supreme Court BGE 84 I 21). The activity may be exercised on a regular basis (main or secondary occupation) or just occasionally. It includes also activities that are legally permitted, but may be morally objectionable (e.g., gambling, prostitution). Begging is not an economic activity (Decision of the Federal Supreme Court BGE 134 I 214 paragraph 3; the Court did not have to deal with the delicate question whether charity fund-raising falls within the penumbra of economic freedom). For recent cases *see*: Decisions of the Federal Supreme Court BGE 131 II 271 paragraph 9.2.1 (disposal of special waste); BGE 135 I 130 paragraph 4.2 (sports events); BGE 136 I 1 paragraph 5.1 (breeding of dogs); BGE 136 I 17 paragraph 3.2 (prohibition of water pipe smoking in restaurants). As a principle, economic freedom does not grant the right to state benefits (Decision of the Federal Supreme Court BGE 141 V 569 paragraph 5.1).

625. Article 27(2) of the Constitution names the three most important aspects of economic freedom:

(1) The freedom to choose one's profession (*Berufswahlfreiheit*), which prohibits the State from regulating education according to its will and needs (Decision of the Federal Supreme Court BGE 103 Ia 401), but does not guarantee per se a right to access to any public education institution (Decision of the Federal Supreme Court BGE 121 I 24). In a controversial leading case, the Court affirmed the permissibility of the introduction of a *numerus clausus* to restrict admissions to medical schools (BGE 125 I 173 paragraph 3).

(2) The freedom to enjoy free access to private economic activity (*Berufszugangsfreiheit*) prohibits the State from taking measures to hinder, totally or partially, the individual's access to the market on the territory of the Swiss Confederation (Decision of the Federal Supreme Court BGE 100 Ia 169, 175).

(3) The freedom of free exercise of private economic activity within the boundaries of the law (*Berufsausübungsfreiheit*) allows the individual to choose freely the means for the exercise of the activity, the form of organization and the employment policy of the enterprise or corporation. Furthermore, within the boundaries of antitrust and other relevant regulations, economic freedom includes the right to

advertise (Decision of the Federal Supreme Court BGE 136 I 184 paragraph 3.2.4), the choice of contract partners and the choice of the content of contracts (Decision of the Federal Supreme Court BGE 136 I 197 paragraph 4.4.1).

626. Economic freedom does not protect individuals from private competition. No right to benefits, subventions, etc. from the State may be deduced from economic freedom (*see* Decision of the Federal Supreme Court BGE 130 I 26 paragraph 4). Note that economic freedom does not protect from general taxes (Decision of the Federal Supreme Court BGE 128 I 102 paragraph 5).

627. Public monopolies are generally exempt from economic freedom. Until 2009, the cantons could derogate from the principle of economic freedom in the hotel and restaurant industry; they were allowed to apply existing regulations which made the opening of new businesses in specific sectors of the hotel and restaurant industry conditional upon establishing a need for such (*see* Transitory Provision No. 7 to Article 103 of the Constitution). According to Article 94(4) of the Constitution, derogations by the cantons from economic freedom are very rare and only permissible regarding *historical* cantonal monopolies (*Regalrechte*) – e.g., in the field of mining, hunting, fishing and commerce with salt. A recent case of the Federal Supreme Court however indicates that the introduction of *new* cantonal monopolies is in conformity with the Constitution if they are sufficiently justified by a public interest and are proportional (Decision of the Federal Supreme Court BGE 124 I 18).

628. The principle of equal treatment of direct competitors – as *lex specialis* to the general equal protection clause in Article 8(1) of the Constitution (*supra* §3 II of this Chapter) – follows from the guarantee of economic freedom (Decisions of the Federal Supreme Court BGE 141 V 569 paragraph 7.2; BGE 131 II 271 paragraph 9.2.2; BGE 132 I 97 paragraph 2.1; BGE 136 I 1 paragraph 5.5.2). The principle requires that measures undertaken by the State must be neutral in effect. They are unconstitutional if *competition between direct competitors is distorted in effect.* Direct competitors are members of the same branch of business offering the same products to the same group of consumers in order to satisfy the demand of that group of consumers (Decision of the Federal Supreme Court BGE 125 I 431, 436; *see also* BGE 141 V 569 paragraph 7.2). The Federal Supreme Court tends to draw a rather narrow circle of direct competitors (*see, inter alia,* Decision of the Federal Supreme Court BGE 131 I 205, 211: regarding the sale of medical drugs, medical doctors and pharmacists are not direct competitors). In contrast to the general equal protection clause in Article 8(1) of the Constitution, the principle of equal treatment of direct competitors protects private businesses from unequal treatment by the State, which may be based on objective and serious grounds, but at the same time favours or disfavours certain other competitors, namely by regulating the access to or the exclusion from the market. However, the principle of equal treatment of direct competitors does not hinder the State from favouring certain competitors if it is justified by a preponderant public interest and as long as competition is not sensitively distorted (Decision of the Federal Supreme Court BGE 125 II 129, paragraph 10b at 150). From a procedural perspective, the principle of equal treatment of direct competitors confers to the individual the legally protected interest in the sense of Article 115(b) of the Federal Supreme Court Act; therefore, a constitutional appeal is available (in contrast to appeals merely based on Article 8(1) of the Constitution; *infra*, Part IV, Chapter V, §3 III C).

C. *Restrictions to Economic Freedom*

629. The question of whether a State activity is compatible with the guarantee of economic freedom can be complex in practice, not necessarily because general and specific rules govern restrictions of economic freedom, but because of the vagueness of the constitutional term 'principle of economic freedom' in Article 94 of the Constitution, which engages a difficult evaluation regarding the *conformity* of the State activity with that principle (*Konformität mit dem Grundsatz der Wirtschaftsfreiheit*). As every other civil liberty, restrictions to economic freedom follow the general rule of Article 36 of the Constitution. Additionally, Article 94(1) of the Constitution requires that *the principle of economic freedom* shall be respected by the Confederation and the cantons. Exceptionally, derogations from the principle are only permitted if the conditions of Article 94(4) of the Constitution are met.

630. According to the Federal Supreme Court, the principle of economic freedom generally postulates free competition. State activities which distort competition or wall off a market are prohibited. State activities in the economic domain are subject to the principle of competitive neutrality (*see*, *inter alia*, Decision of the Federal Supreme Court BGE 121 I 129 paragraph 3b). Therefore, the crucial question of whether a State activity is in conformity with the principle of economic freedom depends on the *extent* of the distortion of competition (*Ausmass der Wettbewerbsverzerrung*) that the Court is inclined to tolerate. Does the State activity merely influence competition or does it constitute a real impediment to competition? Furthermore, an analysis of the *motive of the intervention* (*Eingriffsmotiv*), which may justify the State activity, is required. Must certain side effects distorting competition be accepted? It is obvious that these (economic and political) factors involve a delicate balancing of the various interests at stake. Therefore, it does not come as a surprise that the case law of the Federal Supreme Court is highly ramified in the area of economic freedom.

631. The Court may find that a State activity is *in derogation of the principle of economic freedom*. In this event, Article 94(4) of the Constitution states that such derogations, in particular measures threatening competition, must be authorized by the Federal Constitution or be based on cantonal monopolies (*Regalrechte*). On the federal level, such authorizations are numerous, namely in stabilization policy matters (Article 100(3) of the Constitution [regarding credit and currency, foreign trade and public finance]), in foreign trade policy matters (Article 101 (2, *in fine*) of the Constitution), in the field of the national supply of essential goods and services (Article 102(2) of the Constitution), in structural policy matters (Article 103, *in fine*, of the Constitution) and in agriculture (Article 104(2) of the Constitution). The Federal Constitution also contains *implicit* authorizations to depart from the principle of economic freedom (e.g., in the areas of transportation, electricity and film). Regarding restrictions in derogation of the principle of economic freedom on the cantonal level *see supra* VIII.B of this Chapter).

632. The Court may find that a State activity is *in conformity with the principle of economic freedom*. Then, it will control whether all conditions of Article 36 of the

Constitution are met (*supra* §1 IV. of this Chapter): Restrictions of civil liberties require a legal basis, must be justified by public interests, and be proportionate to the goal pursued; furthermore, the essence of economic liberty must remain untouched. In constitutional practice, the requirement of a sufficient legal basis is rarely a problem. Not any public interest may justify a restriction of economic freedom, especially not State activities, which are motivated by economic policy (*wirtschaftspolitische Massnahmen*) to prevent free competition in order to secure or favour certain branches of industry or certain forms of management; however, restrictions for economic police reasons (*wirtschaftspolizeiliche Massnahmen*) or based on social policy (*sozialpolitische Massnahmen*) may be covered by the public interest requirement of the Constitution (*see* recently Decision of the Federal Supreme Court BGE 131 I 223 paragraph 4.2). Restrictions for 'economic police reasons' means: According to the theory of *police goods* (*Polizeigüter*), those federal and cantonal laws and regulations are considered to be in conformity with the principle of economic freedom if they are protecting *peace, order, security, public health, morality, and good faith in business relations*. Again, the Court's assessment whether a State activity may be restricted for public interest reasons is highly complex; some constitutional scholars also criticize that the Court's 'trias' is too schematic and error-prone, namely because so-called restrictions for economic police or social policy reasons may have economic-political side effects (Rhinow/Schmid/Biaggini/Uhlmann, §5 no. 111 et seq.). The proportionality test is applied from case to case and requires that a State activity must be *adequate* to achieve a legitimate public purpose; it must be suppressed if *milder means to attain the goal pursued are available*; and the public interest must *prevail over the private interest (balancing of interests)*. The essence of economic freedom may be violated in cases of forced or compulsory labour in the sense of Article 4 of the ECHR; so far, the Federal Supreme Court never rejected a case for the violation of Article 36(4) of the Constitution.

633. According to Article 95(1) of the Constitution, the Confederation may legislate the exercise of private economic activity. The cantons are free to regulate private economic activities for *police goods reasons* in conformity with the principle of economic freedom as long as the Confederation has not legislated. The Federal Labour Law (SR 822.11) has considerably diminished the competencies of the cantons to regulate for *social policy reasons*.

634. Recent cases of the Federal Supreme Court (selection): BGE 131 I 223 paragraph 4 (cantonal statute prohibiting litigation financing agreements violates economic freedom); BGE 132 I 97 paragraph 3 (municipal ordinance, which systematically attributes market stalls according to geographic provenance of the competitors, violates Article 27 of the Constitution); BGE 135 II 224 paragraph 3 (brief sports event reporting of local broadcast stations admissible, even though the Swiss public television channel possesses the exclusive rights). The Court held that economic freedom was *not* violated in BGE 133 II 136 paragraphs 6 and 7 (prohibition of television advertisement with pornographic content harmful to minors); BGE 133 I 110 paragraphs 7.4 and 7.5 (prohibition of smoking in public buildings and areas); BGE 132 II 485 paragraphs 6.3 and 8.5 (rejection, alteration and withdrawal of a broadcasting concession); BGE 134 II 223 paragraph 3.4.3 (sponsoring restrictions in television shows); BGE 136 I 1 paragraphs 5.3.2–5.5 (prohibition on breeding potentially dangerous dogs); BGE

136 I 17 paragraph 4 (protection from passive smoking); BGE 132 I 282 paragraph 3 (popular initiative for the formation of a legal monopoly for electricity supplies in the Canton of Geneva); BGE 135 I 130 paragraph 4.3 (charge fee for potentially dangerous sports events, e.g., with potential for hooliganism).

§5. Social Fundamental Rights

Bibliography (selection): Amstutz Kathrin. *Das Grundrecht auf Existenzsicherung.* Berne: Stämpfli, 2002; Gächter Thomas & Werder Gregori. Basler Kommentar BV, Article 12 (with further references); Epiney Astrid & Waldmann Bernhard. 'Soziale Grundrechte und soziale Zielsetzungen'. In *Handbuch der Grundrechte*, edited by Mertens & Papier, §224; Häfelin, Haller, Keller & Thurnherr, §§29–31; Haller. *Swiss Constitution*, 225 et seq.; Meyer-Blaser Ulrich & Gächter Thomas. 'Der Sozialstaatsgedanke'. In Thürer et al., §34; Müller & Schefer, 763 et seq.; Müller Lucien. St. Galler Kommentar, Article 12 (with further references); Plotke Herbert. *Schweizerisches Schulrecht.* 2nd ed. Berne: Haupt, 2003; Rhinow, Schefer & Uebersax, §36; Wyttenbach Judith. Basler Kommentar BV, Article 19 (with further references).

635. The so-called *social fundamental rights* (*Sozialgrundrechte*) confer to the individual a directly enforceable right to be supported by the State in certain situations or under certain conditions. The catalogue of fundamental rights contains two social fundamental rights: the right to aid in distress (Article 12 of the Constitution) and the right to primary education (Article 19 of the Constitution). There is a certain reluctance to expand the set of social fundamental rights (e.g., right to housing rejected by the People in 1970; the right to education rejected by the People in 1973). The social goals in Article 41 of the Constitution differ from social fundamental rights insofar as individuals may not derive direct subjective rights from social goals (Article 41(4) of the Constitution). The Federal Supreme Court has held that (in general) the limitation of social fundamental rights must follow the rules set out in Article 36 of the Constitution *per analogiam* (*see supra* §1 IV of this Chapter).

636. The right to secure one's existence (*Recht auf Existenzsicherung*) used to be an unwritten fundamental right under the Constitution of 1874 (Decision of the Federal Supreme Court BGE 121 I 367). Under a new name, but with the same substance, the right to aid in distress (*Recht auf Hilfe in Notlagen*) in Article 12 of the Constitution guarantees persons, who are in need and unable to provide for their living, the right to assistance and care; they have the right to the means indispensable for living in dignity. This social fundamental right does not guarantee a minimum salary. The objective of this provision is to prevent beggardom and to provide a person with the absolutely minimal and necessary means in order to survive and to exist in dignity ('ne pas être abandonné à la rue et réduit à la mendicité': Decision of the Federal Supreme Court BGE 136 I 254 paragraph 4.2; *see also* BGE 131 I 166 paragraph 3.1 [with further references], where the plaintiff received on a daily basis CHF 13 – for housing and CHF 8 – for food and hygiene). The situation of distress must be actual or imminent. The right to aid in distress is a default fundamental right (*leistungsrechtliches Auffanggrundrecht*) and conceived as transitory help (e.g., money, food, clothes, housing, basic medical care) in extreme situations. Due to the narrow ties to human dignity (Article 7 of the Constitution), the right to aid to distress is absolute – there is no room, not even *per analogiam*, for restrictions based on Article 36 of the Constitution (*supra* §1 IV of this Chapter). Hence, the provision cannot only be invoked by Swiss citizens, but also by foreigners, regardless of their immigration status (including illegal foreigners and rejected asylum seekers obliged to leave the country). Article 83a of the Federal Asylum Act of 26 June 1998 (SR 142.31) provides that the person seeking aid in distress must cooperate in the determination of whether the requirements for emergency aid are fulfilled. The question regularly arises, mainly in political debates, whether the fundamental right to aid in distress could be abolished by partially amending the Constitution. As long as the international *ius cogens* is not violated (Article 194(2) of the Constitution), the answer depends on whether fundamental rights, due to their 'fundamentality', are (not) implicitly 'immunized' from any constitutional amendment. Note that, unlike Article 79(3) of the German Basic Law, the Constitution does not explicitly exempt certain provisions, which are deemed to be fundamental, from being amended.

637. Article 19 of the Constitution guarantees to all children a sufficient and free primary school education of at least nine years' duration (*see* Concordat Regarding the Coordination of Schools of 29 October 1970; Decision of the Federal Supreme Court BGE 133 I 156 paragraph 3.1). The provision must be read in connection with Article 62 of the Constitution, which states that the system of school education is a competence of the cantons. They are therefore the addressees of the fundamental right. Furthermore, the cantons shall ensure that there is a sufficient primary school education, open to all children. This education shall be mandatory and supervised by the state. Primary school education in state schools shall be free of charge. Additionally, the cantons shall ensure that adequate special needs education is provided to all children and young people with disabilities up to the age of 20. The requirement that primary school education must be *sufficient* leaves considerable discretion to the cantons; however, it must be adequate and appropriate with the goal to prepare the student to lead an independent life, to be capable of integration into society and to face the problems of modern everyday life. The lessons shall be given in the municipality where the student resides; the spatial distance between the student's residence and the school premises may not jeopardize sufficient primary school education (Decisions of the Federal Supreme Court 129 I 12 paragraph 4.2; BGE 129 I 35 paragraph 7.3). Hence, the cantons have to bear the transportation costs if the way to school is excessively long or dangerous (Decision of the Federal Supreme Court BGE 133 I 156 paragraph 3.1). Although the fundamental right to primary school education is formulated in unconditional terms, Article 36 of the Constitution applies *per analogiam* (*supra* §1 IV of this Chapter). Hence, a suspension of twelve weeks from elementary school for disciplinary reasons was held to be in the public interest and proportional (Decision of the Federal Supreme Court BGE 129 I 12).

§6. Fundamental Procedural Guarantees

Bibliography (selection): Auer, Malinverni & Hottelier. Vol. II, 561 et seq.; Biaggini. Kommentar, Articles 29–32 (with further references); Egli, 155 et seq.; Göksu Tarkan.

Basler Kommentar BV, Article 32; Haefliger. *Alle Schweizer sind vor dem Gesetze gleich*, 115 et seq.; Haller. *Swiss Constitution*, 216 et seq.; Häfelin, Haller, Keller & Thurnherr, §26; Hänni Peter. 'Grundrechte des Angeschuldigten im Strafprozess'. In *Handbuch der Grundrechte*, edited by Mertens & Papier, §226; Hottelier Michael. 'Les garanties des procédure'. In Thürer et al., §51; Keller Helen. 'Garantien fairer Verfahren und des rechtlichen Gehörs'. In *Handbuch der Grundrechte*, edited by Mertens & Papier, §225; Kiener Regina. 'Garantie des verfassungsmässigen Richters'. In *Handbuch der Grundrechte*, edited by Mertens & Papier, §227; Kley Andreas. St. Galler Kommentar, Article 29a; Mahon. commentaire, Articles 29–32; Müller & Schefer, 817 et seq.; Reich Johannes. Basler Kommentar BV, Article 30; Rhinow et al., *Öffentliches Prozessrecht*. 2nd ed. Basel: Helbing & Lichtenhahn, 2011; Rhinow, Schefer & Uebersax, §30 (with further references); Schürmann Frank. Basler Kommentar BV, Article 31; Steinmann Gerold. St. Galler Kommentar, Articles 29 and 30 (with further references); Vest Hans. St. Galler Kommentar, Articles 31 and 32 (with further references); Waldmann Bernhard. Basler Kommentar BV, Article 29 and 29a.

I. Introduction

638. The realization and the safeguard of a fair trial for everyone is of utmost importance to the *Rechtsstaat* (*supra* General Introduction, Chapter 2, §4). The fundamental procedural guarantees of the Constitution, which will be discussed below, shall not only ensure fairness, equality of chances and respect for all parties in a proceeding before a judicial authority, but also a correct and just decision. The Constitution of 1874 did not contain written fundamental procedural guarantees. They were considered derivatives of the *Rechtsstaat* principle and have been developed subsequently by the case law of the Federal Supreme Court under Article 4 of the Constitution of 1874. Their primary function was to form a minimal procedural safeguard against missing or lacunary cantonal procedures. The case law of the Federal Supreme Court indicates that regardless of the introduction of the Federal Code of Civil Procedure and the Federal Code of Criminal Procedure on 1 January 2011, which substitute the respective cantonal civil and criminal acts, the constitutional guarantees have preserved their importance. In Articles 29–32 of the Constitution, the catalogue of fundamental rights codifies these fundamental procedural guarantees recognized by the Federal Supreme Court. Although they usually have a larger scope of application than Articles 5 and 6 of the ECHR, the impact of the Convention is paramount.

II. General Procedural Guarantees

A. *Procedural Fairness*

639. Article 29 of the Constitution constitutes a *default rule* establishing a minimal standard of procedural fairness in cases where the special guarantees of Articles 30–32 of the Constitution do not apply. According to Article 29(1), every person has the right to be treated equally and fairly in *all* proceedings before judicial and administrative authorities (regardless if civil, criminal or administrative in nature; Decision of the Federal Supreme Court BGE 131 II 169 paragraph 2.2.3) and to have their case decided within a reasonable time. The wording of the provision is too narrow insofar as it also includes proceedings before parliamentary and governmental authorities adjudicating upon rights and duties of an individual. However, Article 29 of the Constitution does not apply to the process of law-making (*see* regarding the right to be heard Decision of the Federal Supreme Court BGE 131 I 95 paragraph 3.1). The provision does not grant an absolute right to access to justice (but *see* now Article 29a of the Constitution; the Decisions of the Federal Supreme Court BGE 131 II 169 paragraph 2.2.3; BGE 133 I 49 paragraph 3.1, were issued before the introduction of the reform of the judiciary).

640. Concretizing the principle of procedural fairness, the Federal Supreme Court has deduced several principles and prohibitions from Article 4 of the Constitution of 1874 (now: Article 29 of the Constitution; *see* §1 of this Chapter), as follows.

641. The principle of equality of arms ('Waffengleichheit'): Every party must be given an adequate opportunity to present their case and to produce the relevant evidence under conditions that do not constitute a significant disadvantage vis-à-vis the opposing party (Decision of the Federal Supreme Court BGE 133 I 1 paragraph 5.3.1 [referring to civil procedures and to the judgment of the European Court of Human Rights *Ankerl v. Switzerland* of 23 October 1996, Recueil CourEDH 1996-V p. 1553, no. 38]).

642. The prohibition of formal denial of justice ('formelle Rechtsverweigerung'): Any public authority refusing to decide a case, even though it is required to do so by statute, commits a denial of justice. Even if the authority is not competent or lacking jurisdiction or if a complaint does not satisfy the formal requirements, the authority must briefly explain its motives for not handling the case. In criminal cases, the authority is required to review a res judicata if the applicant produces relevant facts and evidence, which were unavailable or impossible to bring forward in the earlier procedure (*see, inter alia,* Decision of the Federal Supreme Court BGE 127 I 133 paragraph 6).

643. The prohibition of excessive formalism: As special form of the prohibition of denial of justice, excessive formalism can be affirmed in proceedings where, without any objective justification, rigorous formal requirements or excessive hardship are imposed upon plaintiff, which impede or frustrate the realization of material justice in an untenable manner (*see, inter alia,* Decisions of the Federal Supreme Court BGE 142 V 158 paragraphs 4.2 and 4.3; BGE 127 I 31 paragraph 2a/bb; BGE 132 I 249 paragraph 5; BGE 134 II 244 paragraph 2.4.2; BGE 135 I 6 paragraph 2.1).

644. The right to be judged within reasonable time: In application of Article 6(1) of the ECHR, the European Court for Human Rights held that the following criteria are essential for determining the reasonableness of time: the complexity of the case, the behaviour of the authority and the behaviour of the party involved (for a recent overview over the ECHR case law *see* EU Agency for Fundamental Rights an Council of Europe. *Handbook on European law relating to access to justice*, Luxembourg 2016, 133 et seq.). The reasonable time requirement must be assessed from case to case. The case law of the Federal Supreme Court is widely ramified on this matter and cannot be summarized here. The Court stated for example that the requirement is violated if a case is pending for thirty-three months and could have been judged already after six months of pendency (Decision of the Federal Supreme Court, 125 V 373, 375); it is not violated in an international child abduction case before two Swiss judicial instances lasting approximately seven months (Decision of the Federal Supreme Court 131 III 334 paragraphs 2.2–2.3). For the reasonable time requirement in pre-trial detention cases *see* Article 31 of the Constitution.

B. Right to Be Heard

645. Article 29(2) of the Constitution, which constitutes the backbone of the Swiss concept of procedural fairness, contains the right to be heard *in all legal proceedings*. This guarantee fulfils a double function: On one hand, it serves for the establishment of the relevant facts, on the other hand, it constitutes a personal participatory right during the process of decision-making and issuance of a decision that affects the legal position of an individual (*see* recently Decision of the Federal Supreme Court BGE 135 I 279 paragraph 2.3). The authority must take into account the arguments brought forward by the concerned person in a careful and serious manner (Decision of the Federal Supreme Court BGE 136 I 184 paragraph 2.2.1). The right to be heard in Article 29(2) constitutes only a minimal standard, which is – first of all – defined by cantonal laws (Decision of the Federal Supreme Court BGE 135 I 279 paragraph 2.2). The Federal Supreme Court will uphold the interpretation and application of such cantonal provisions as long as they are not arbitrary (Decision of the Federal Supreme Court BGE 126 I 19 paragraph 3a). On the federal level, Articles 29–33b of the FAPA (SR 172.021) guarantee the right to be heard with a wider scope of application than Article 29(2) of the Constitution. As a rule, the violation of the constitutional right to be heard renders an administrative order or a court decision *null and void* regardless of whether the violation had an impact on the substance of the decision (so-called *formal nature* of the right to be heard; *see* Decisions of the Federal Supreme Court BGE 141 V 500 paragraph 2.2; BGE 135 I 187 paragraph 2.2; BGE 135 I 279 paragraph 2.6.1). Exceptionally, minor violations of the right to be heard can be 'healed' if the concerned person has the possibility to appeal before a higher authority, which can fully review the case *in law* and *in fact* (so-called *healing effect* of a violation of the right to be heard; *see, inter alia,* Decisions of the Federal Supreme Court BGE 131 II 200 paragraph 4.3; BGE 134 I 140 paragraph 5.5; BGE 136 III 174 paragraph 5.1.2).

646. The Federal Supreme Court has deduced several aspects of the right to be heard from Article 4 of the Constitution of 1874 (now: Article 29(2) of the Constitution), such as:

- *The right to be informed* ('Recht auf Orientierung'): The authority must inform the individual concerned about the preparation of an administrative order, which might limit rights or impose new obligations upon the person concerned (e.g., in criminal proceedings or where an authority is acting ex officio). This shall give the party concerned, for example, the chance to be informed of the arguments brought forward against the person, the disclosure of findings of relevant facts and evidence given to the authority by third parties or by civil servants.
- *The right to be heard* ('Äusserungsrecht'): The term 'heard' in Article 29(2) of the Constitution is insofar ambiguous as it generally does not imply a right to an

oral hearing. Rather, the addressee of an administrative order must usually file a written submission. As set out above, the cantonal legislation determines the precise content of the right to be heard. The FAPA generally requires a preliminary 'hearing' before an administrative order is issued (for exceptions *see* Article 30(2) FAPA). If it is probable that an administrative order will affect numerous persons or if it is not possible to identify all the parties without incurring unreasonable expense, the authority, before issuing its ruling, may publish the application or the intended order without stating the grounds in an official gazette, while at the same time making the application or the intended order with the grounds thereof available for public inspection, and giving notice of where it may be inspected. It shall hear the parties, by allowing them an appropriate period to file their opposition (Article 30a FAPA).

- *The right to access to one's records* ('Akteneinsichtsrecht'): The necessary prerequisite for the effective exercise of this right is that the records are complete (Decision of the Federal Supreme Court 129 I 88 paragraph 4.1). In the course of, but also after the termination of a proceeding, the right to be heard includes the right to view one's records in the premises of the agency or the court and to make photocopies or take notes (without causing unreasonable expenses to the authority). The constitutional right to access to one's records may be limited or denied due to either a demonstration of preponderant public interests by the relevant authority or to opposing legitimate interests of private person(s).
- *The right to produce relevant evidence*: This right includes motions to take evidence and either to participate in the taking of the relevant evidence (*Beweiserhebung*) or at least to comment on the result thereof (*Beweisergebnis*), if it may materially influence the decision (*see, inter alia,* Decision of the Federal Supreme Court BGE 141 I 64 paragraph 3.3).
- *The right to legal counsel*: The general right to be represented by a legal counsel is guaranteed by Article 29(2) of the Constitution, whereas the right to free legal counsel is granted by Article 29(3) of the Constitution.
- *The obligation to motivate a decision* ('Begründungspflicht'): According to the Federal Supreme Court the authority is not required to deal with all points of a pleading in detail; it must not expressly refute every single allegation. Rather, a limitation to all relevant aspects, which are decisive for the case, is permitted. The motivation must be formulated in a way that the person concerned realizes the consequences of the decision in order to make an appeal before a higher authority in full knowledge of the matter. In this sense, the authority must at least briefly indicate the considerations, which were guiding in the decision-making process and upon which the decision was finally based on (*see, inter alia,* Decision of the Federal Supreme Court BGE 136 I 229 paragraph 5.2; *see also* BGE 141 III 41 paragraph 3.2.4; BGE 141 IV 253 paragraph 1.3.1).

C. Right to Free Legal Assistance and Free Legal Counsel

647. The right to free legal assistance and free legal counsel in Article 29(3) of the Constitution applies to *all* proceedings before judicial and administrative authorities and constitutes a minimal standard, which is primarily defined by cantonal laws (*see*

Decisions of the Federal Supreme Court BGE 141 I 74 paragraph 5.2 and BGE 135 I 91 paragraph 2.4.2). The term 'free legal assistance' needs some explanation: To secure the costs of a proceeding before a court (*Verfahrenskosten*), the plaintiff must usually advance a sum of money (*Kostenvorschuss*); if this advance fee is not paid, the court will dismiss the case on formal grounds. In order to guarantee the principle of equality of arms and to avoid that access to justice is barred for persons solely because they lack the necessary financial means, the right of free legal assistance unburdens the plaintiff from paying the advance sum of money and also from the costs of the proceeding. However, the plaintiff is usually required to reimburse the advanced sum if his/her financial situation improves again. The right to free legal assistance does not include any compensations that the plaintiff needs to pay to the prevailing party (*Parteientschädigung*). The beneficiaries of this socially motivated constitutional right are all natural persons and (in very exceptional cases) also legal persons, if the only asset of the legal person is in dispute and if all other economic participants lack the required funds (Decision of the Federal Supreme Court BGE 131 II 306 paragraph 5.2.2).

648. The right to free legal assistance is of considerable practical importance. According to a well-established formula of the Federal Supreme Court, the courts may grant the right if two conditions are fulfilled (*see, inter alia,* Decision of the Federal Supreme Court BGE 133 III 614 paragraph 5): (1) the person lacks the necessary financial means; and (2) the case does not appear to be devoid of a chance of success, i.e., the prospects of winning the case are not considerably lower than the risks of losing it; the decisive question is whether a party of sufficient financial funds would reasonably file the lawsuit and assume the corresponding costs and risks (Decision of the Federal Supreme Court 141 I 245 paragraphs 3.3.1 and 4.2.5).

649. The right to *free legal counsel* is available if the above-mentioned conditions (1) and (2) are fulfilled, and (3) if legal representation is necessary to protect the person's rights (third sentence of Article 29(3) of the Constitution). The necessity must be assessed from case to case. Again, this provision constitutes a minimal standard that must be concretized by cantonal legislation. But note that with the introduction of the Federal Code of Civil Procedure on 1 January 2011 the cantons can no longer exclude the representation of a party by a lawyer in minor employment cases before cantonal district courts (Article 343 of the Code of Obligations is abolished; hence, the holding in Decision of the Federal Supreme Court BGE 105 Ia 288 no longer applies).

III. Access to Justice

650. According to Article 29a of the Constitution, everyone has the right to have legal disputes judged by a judicial authority. In exceptional cases, the Confederation and the Cantons may by law exclude the access. This relatively new provision was introduced in the catalogue of fundamental rights with the entry into force of the reform of the judiciary on 1 January 2007 (*supra* General Introduction, Chapter 2, §4). The scope of application of and the exceptions to this procedural fundamental right have already been discussed *supra* in Part II, Chapter 5, §2). For an interesting overview over the case law of the Federal Supreme Court *see* the decision 1C_517/2016 of 12 April 2017 (publication in BGE 143 pending). Limitations must not restrict the exercise of the right of access to justice to such an extent the very essence of the right is impaired. This is an important lesson to be drawn from *Howald Moor and others v. Switzerland* of 11 March 2014 (52067/10 and 41072/11), where the European Court of Human Rights held for a violation of Article 6 §1 of the Convention. The case concerned a worker who was diagnosed in May 2004 with malignant pleural mesothelioma (a highly aggressive malignant tumour) caused by his exposure to asbestos in the course of his work in the 1960s and 1970s. He died in 2005. The Swiss courts dismissed the claims for damages brought by his wife and two children against Mr Moor's employer and the Swiss authorities, on the grounds that they were time-barred. The Court held that the rules on limitation periods infringed the rights of persons suffering from diseases which, like asbestos-related diseases, could not be diagnosed until many years after the events. Under the law in force, claims by asbestos victims were invariably time-barred. The Court considered that in cases where it was scientifically proven that an individual could not know that he or she was suffering from a particular disease, that fact should be taken into account in calculating the limitation period. In view of the *exceptional circumstances* in the present case it considered that the application of the periods in question had restricted the applicants' access to a court to the point of breaching Article 6 §1 of the Convention.

IV. Guarantees in Judicial Proceedings

651. In order to strengthen the institutional aspects of the independence of the judiciary (Article 191c of the Constitution; *supra* Part II, Chapter 5, §1) and the separation of powers principle, the most important guarantees in judicial proceedings were anchored as fundamental rights in Article 30 of the Constitution. These guarantees were mostly developed under the Constitution of 1874 and influenced by the Strasbourg case law regarding Article 6(1) of the ECHR and Article 14(1) of the UN-Pact II. Whereas Article 29 of the Constitution applies to *all* proceedings before judicial and administrative authorities, the scope of application is narrower, entailing only procedures before a court.

652. According to Article 30(1) of the Constitution, in judicial proceedings, every person has the right to be judged by a court established by law, which has jurisdiction, and is independent and impartial. Exceptional tribunals ('ad hoc-tribunals') acting outside the constitutional framework are prohibited. However, specialized tribunals granted with special jurisdiction are constitutional (e.g., cantonal commercial courts, cantonal district courts in employment law or landlord and tenant law cases). The terms 'court', 'established by law' and 'jurisdiction' are interpreted by the Federal Supreme Court according to Article 6(1) of the ECHR and the respective Strasbourg case law. The fundamental right to an independent and impartial court has already been discussed *supra* in Part II, Chapter 5, §1.

653. For civil actions, Article 30(2) of the Constitution grants the person against whom a civil action is brought the right to have the case heard before the court *in the canton of the defendant's domicile*. However, federal and cantonal legislation and international treaties may provide for another *locus standi*, e.g., the Federal Code of Civil Procedure (SR 272), the Federal Bankruptcy Act of 1889 (SR 281.1), the Lugano Convention on Jurisdiction and the Enforcement of Civil and Commercial Matters of 1988 (SR 0.275.11), or the Federal Civil Jurisdiction Act of 2000 (SR 272).

654. 'Sunshine is the best disinfectant.' (Justice Brandeis) – Finally, Article 6(1) of the ECHR, Article 14(1) of the UN-Pact II and Article 30(3) of the Constitution provide that court hearings shall be public and the judgment shall be publicly proclaimed. The Constitution of 1874 did not contain a similar provision. Rather, the question was regulated on the statutory level (e.g., Article 17 of the former Federal Judiciary Act of 1943). The Federal Supreme Court's oral *deliberations* of a case (and not only the proclamation of the judgment) are traditionally public, unless there is unanimity among the Federal Supreme Court judges (Article 58 of the Federal Supreme Court Act). The Federal Supreme Court underlines the central importance of transparency of the judiciary in the democratic *Rechtsstaat* (Decision of the Federal Supreme Court BGE 137 I 16 paragraph 2.2), which eradicates secrecy and corruption and allows the media and the public to monitor the consistency of the performance of the courts. Note that Article 30(3) of the Constitution is broader in its scope of application: The provision applies to all judicial proceedings and is – in contrast to Article 6(1) of the ECHR – not restricted to cases involving 'civil rights and obligations' and 'criminal charges'. However, the Federal Supreme Court favours a narrow reading of Article 30(3) of the Constitution in the sense that the provision does not grant an enforceable right to a public court hearing in every case; it only guarantees that in those cases when a court hearing must be held (i.e., when Article 6(1) of the ECHR is applicable) and no statutory exception provides otherwise that this court hearing must be public (Decision of the Federal Supreme Court BGE 128 I 288). For a case regarding the complete exclusion of the public and accredited journalists from a criminal procedure on appeal as well as from the proclamation of the judgment on the grounds that a public court hearing could re-traumatise the victims (here: children) *see* Decisions of the Federal Supreme Court 1B_349/2016 and 1B_350/2016 of 22 February 2017 (violation of Articles 30, 16 and 17 of the Constitution; publication in Volume 1 of BGE 142 pending).

V. Habeas Corpus

655. According to the principle of Habeas Corpus, which mainly corresponds with the more detailed Article 5 of the ECHR and Article 9 of the UN-Pact II, no person may be deprived of liberty except in situations and in the forms provided by the law (Article 31(1) of the Constitution). As deprivations of liberty always are grave restrictions to personal freedom (*see* the second sentence in Article 36(1) and Article 10(2) of the Constitution), a formal statutory basis is required (*supra* §1 IV of this Chapter). A deprivation of liberty can only be ordered in the circumstances enumerated in Article 5(1) of the ECHR. According to Article 221 of the Federal Code of Criminal Procedure, detention on remand or security detention shall only be legitimized if the accused person is strongly suspected of having committed a crime or an offence and there is a serious risk that he or she will evade the criminal proceedings or the punishment expected to be imposed by absconding (letter a), or will manipulate people or interfere with evidence in order to compromise the establishment of the truth (letter b), or will commit serious crimes or offences which substantially endanger the safety of others, after having already committed similar types of criminal offences (letter c). Furthermore, detention shall also be legitimatized if there are serious reasons to fear that a person will act on his or her threats to commit a serious crime (Article 221(2) of the Federal Code of Criminal Procedure).

656. Strengthening the general right to be heard, Article 31(2) of the Constitution contains the right of the party concerned to be *informed immediately*. The term 'immediately' means: within a reasonable period of time in order to allow the detainee to assert his/her rights (in contrast to US criminal procedure, where the detainee must be informed of his/her rights 'prior to any questioning', *see Miranda v. Arizona*, 384 U.S. 436 [1966]). The party must be informed in a language he/she understands for the reasons of the detention (Article 31(2) of the Constitution). Note that the Constitution does not prescribe how the detainee must be informed. Furthermore, all persons deprived of their liberty must be informed of their rights. Apart from the right that the detainee is entitled to inform his/her next of kin, Article 31(2) of the Constitution does not explicitly enumerate further rights. However, with regard to Articles 29 and 31(3) of the Constitution and Articles 5 and 6 of the ECHR, the detainee has the right to remain silent and the right to judicial review of the legality of the detention. Note that the right to immediate legal council does not fall within the penumbra of Article 31(2) of the Constitution, but is guaranteed in Articles 158 and 159 of the Federal Code of Criminal Procedure (the right to a lawyer 'of the first hour').

657. According to Article 31(3) of the Constitution and Article 5(3) of the ECHR, in cases of *preventive detention* (also: *detention on remand*; *Untersuchungshaft*, i.e., detention while awaiting trial), every person shall have the right to be brought before an impartial and independent judge without delay. The judge, who has to hold a personal and oral hearing within twenty-four to forty-eight hours after the detention (Decision of the Federal Supreme Court BGE 131 I 36 paragraph 2.6), shall decide whether the arrested person must remain in detention or be released. The judgment must be delivered within a reasonable time. Regarding the reasonableness requirement, the Federal Supreme Court follows the case law of the European Court of Human Rights; decisive elements are the circumstances and the complexity of the case, the behaviour of the accused person and of the competent authorities (for a recent summary of the ECHR case law *see* Decision 1B_283/2016 of 26 August 2016 consid. 5.5; *see also* Decisions of the Federal Supreme Court BGE 132 I 21 paragraph 4.1; BGE 133 I 168 paragraph 4.1; BGE 133 I 274 paragraph 3.4.2).

658. Finally, Article 31(4) of the Constitution guarantees every person whose deprivation of liberty has not been ordered by a court the access to a judge at any time. It is a *lex specialis* to Article 29a of the Constitution (Decision of the Federal Supreme Court BGE 137 I 23 paragraph 2.4.2: *'besondere Rechtsweggarantie'*). The court decides as soon as possible whether the detention is legal. Note that Article 31(4) of the Constitution does not say that the court must review the legality of the detention 'immediately', but only 'as soon as possible'. There is no right to a personal and oral hearing. The Federal Supreme Court held that a waiting period of one month to present a case before court was in accordance with Article 5(4) of the ECHR. However, the

Court has regarded the period of forty-one days to deliver a judgment as excessive, possibly subject to tort claims (Article 5(5) of the ECHR).

VI. Guarantees in Criminal Procedures

659. Article 32 contains guarantees in criminal procedures that were developed by the Federal Supreme Court under Article 4 of the Constitution of 1874. The provision only applies in cases where the 'criminal charges' requirement in the sense of Article 6(1) of the ECHR is fulfilled, which includes, *inter alia*, criminal tax proceedings. The Federal Supreme Court has ruled in a case regarding a Zurich statute against domestic violence that the measures to protect the victim contained therein (e.g., restraining orders), which were imposed upon defendant, do not fall within the penumbra of Article 32 of the Constitution (Decision of the Federal Supreme Court 134 145 paragraph 4.3). With the entry into force of the Federal Code of Criminal Procedure on 1 January 2011, which contains detailed provisions regarding the practical implementation of procedural fairness in criminal proceedings, the minimal guarantees of Article 32 of the Constitution are most likely to lose their importance. Note that Article 32 of the Constitution is incomplete: Neither the principle of double jeopardy (*ne bis in idem*) as enacted in the Additional Protocol No. 7 of the ECHR and in Article 14(6) of the UN-Pact II, nor the right to be recompensed in cases of illegal detention or error in court as provided by Article 5(5) of the ECHR and Article 9(4) of the UN-Pact II is mentioned.

660. In accordance with Article 6(2) of the ECHR and Article 14(2) of the UN-Pact II, every person shall be presumed innocent until formally and validly convicted (Article 32(1) of the Constitution). The presumption incorporates the principle *in dubio pro reo*, according to which the criminal court judge may not declare himself/herself convinced of the existence of facts, which are not favourable for the accused, if there are objective and apparent doubts, which cannot be ignored. However, the margin of appreciation for the judge is considerable. The Federal Supreme Court will only intervene when an accused is found guilty, even though manifestly relevant doubts, which cannot be ignored, persist. The presumption of innocence in Article 32(1) of the Constitution contains also a rule of burden of proof: It is incumbent upon the competent authority to prove the guilt of the accused; the accused must not prove his/her innocence (*see* Decision of the Federal Supreme Court BGE 127 I 38 et seq.).

661. Concretizing the general right to be heard in Article 29 and the right to be informed in Article 31 of the Constitution, Article 32(2) of the Constitution states that every accused person has the right to be informed as quickly and as completely as possible of the charges against them. Furthermore, the person must be given the opportunity to assert their rights to a proper defence – e.g., the right to sufficient time to prepare a case, the right to communicate freely and unguarded with the legal counsel, the right to cross-examination, and eventually the right to free assistance of an interpreter. The constitutional guarantee also includes the right of the defendant *not* to appear personally before the criminal Court of Appeal (Decision of the Federal Supreme Court BGE 133 I 12 paragraph 8).

662. Finally, according to Article 32(3) of the Constitution, every convicted person has the right to have the sentence reviewed by a superior court that satisfies the requirements of Article 30 of the Constitution. In accordance with international public law, the court of appeal must review the case only for *errors of law* (*see* Article 2(1) Additional Protocol No. 7 to the ECHR of 22 November 1984 and Article 14(5) of the UN-Pact II). The second sentence of Article 32(3) of the Constitution points out that the right to review by a superior court does not apply to cases where the Federal Supreme Court has original jurisdiction. This constitutional guarantee no longer applies, because with the entry into force of the reform of the judiciary on 1 January 2011 and the creation of a Federal Criminal Court, the Federal Supreme Court does not possess original jurisdiction in criminal matters anymore.

§7. Constitutional Jurisdiction and Fundamental Rights

Selected Bibliography: Andreas Auer. *Die schweizerische Verfassungsgerichtsbarkeit.* Basel/Frankfurt a.M.: Helbing & Lichtenhahn, 1984; Biaggini Giovanni. 'Abstrakte und konkrete Normenkontrolle'. In *ius.full* 2006, 164 et seq.; Biaggini. Kommentar, Article 190; Biaggini Giovanni. *Verfassung und Richterrecht.* Basel/Frankfurt a.M.: Helbing & Lichtenhahn, 1991; Chiariello Elisabeth. *Der Richter als Verfassungsgeber?.* Zurich/St. Gallen: Dike, 2009; Häfelin, Haller, Keller & Thurnherr, §64–§66 (with further references); Haller. *Swiss Constitution*, 255 et seq.; Haller. 'Das schweizerische Bundesgericht als Verfassungsgericht'. In *Verfassungsgerichtsbarkeit in Westeuropa*, edited by Starck Christian & Weber Albrecht. 2nd ed. Vol. 1. Baden-Baden: Nomos 2007, 91 et seq.; Haller. 'Verfassungsfortbildung durch Richterrecht'. In *Zeitschrift für Schweizerisches Recht [ZSR].* 2005, 5 et seq.; Hangartner Yvo. 'La protection des droits constitutionnels en Suisse'. In *Les droits individuels et le juge en Europe*, edited by Constance Grewe. Strasbourg: Mélanges en l'honneur de Michel Fromont, Presses univ. de Strasbourg, 2001, 267 et seq.; Hangartner Yvo. 'Ausbau der Verfassungsgerichtsbarkeit'. In *Aktuelle Juristische Praxis [AJP].* 1995, 1013 et seq.; Hertig Randall Maja. 'L'internationalisation de la juridiction constitutionnelle: défis et perspectives'. In *Zeitschrift für Schweizerisches Recht [ZSR].* 2011 II, Referate zum Schweizerischen Juristentag 2010, 221 et seq.; Kälin Walter. 'Verfassungsgerichtsbarkeit'. In Thürer et al., §74; Kälin Walter. *Das Verfahren der staatsrechtlichen Beschwerde.* 2nd ed. Berne: Stämpfli, 1994; Misic. *Verfassungsbeschwerde*, passim; Seiler Hansjörg. 'Verfassungsgerichtsbarkeit'. In *Zeitschrift für Schweizerisches Recht [ZSR].* 2011 II, Referate zum Schweizerischen Juristentag 2010, 381 et seq.; Zimmerli Ulrich. 'Verfassungsgerichtsbarkeit'. In *Zeitschrift für Schweizerisches Recht [ZSR].* 2002, 445 et seq.; Zünd Andreas. 'Grundrechtsverwirklichung ohne Verfassungsgerichtsbarkeit'. In *Aktuelle Juristische Praxis [AJP].* 2013, 1349 et seq.

I. Definition and Types of Constitutional Jurisdiction

663. Constitutional jurisdiction (*Verfassungsgerichtsbarkeit; jurisdiction constitutionnelle; giurisdizione costituzionale*) can be defined as control over the constitutionality of government action by a law-applying authority. The main function of this control over compatibility with the constitution is to protect the individual (subjective function) and to ensure and safeguard the uniformity of law-application (objective function). Different types of constitutional jurisdiction can be distinguished:

- Abstract judicial review (*abstrakte* or *prinzipale Normenkontrolle*): In Switzerland, within thirty days of the publication of a *new cantonal statute*, the plaintiff can challenge the constitutionality of the cantonal statute before the Federal Supreme Court for the violation of constitutional rights (*supra*, §1 I of this Chapter). In an appeal in public law matters (Article 82 of the Federal Supreme Court Act), the Federal Supreme Court will grant *virtual standing* only if plaintiff plausibly claims that he/she could be (with a minimum of probability) a future addressee of the provision, which is in his/her view unconstitutional (Decision of the Federal Supreme Court BGE 130 I 174 paragraph 1.2; BGE 133 I 206 paragraph 2.1 [Zisyadis]). If the Court reviews a cantonal statute in the abstract mode, the statute will only be declared unconstitutional if an interpretation in conformity with the Constitution is highly unlikely or impossible (Decision of the Federal Supreme Court BGE 130 I 82 paragraph 2.1). The abstract review of constitutionality includes all possible reasons and circumstances (and is not only limited to the special fact-pattern of the case presented to the Court). If the Federal Supreme Court finally holds that the cantonal statute is unconstitutional it will declare the whole statute or parts thereof null and void (the so-called *nature cassatoire* of the appeal); the Court will not confine its attention to the gratifying task of writing new law (although Article 107(1) of the Federal Supreme Court Act would allow reformatory judgments).
- Concrete judicial review (*konkrete* or *inzidente Normenkontrolle*): Here, plaintiff can challenge an administrative order or a decision before any law-applying authority on the grounds that it derives from an unconstitutional cantonal statute or an unconstitutional ordinance of the Federal Council (*control of the individual act with preliminary control of the norm*). As a preliminary matter, the court will first review the constitutionality of the underlying cantonal statute, but – in contrast to abstract judicial review – without the possibility of going beyond the particular circumstances of the case. If the cantonal statute is found unconstitutional, the decision or the administrative order will be declared null and void (but not the underlying cantonal statute; this task is left to the cantonal legislator).
- Judicial review (without preliminary control of a normative act): Here, plaintiff merely argues that an administrative order or a judicial decision violates fundamental rights as such without the claim that the cantonal statute upon which the order or the decision are based upon are unconstitutional as well. This judicial control of constitutionality will be discussed in detail *infra* in the context of Part IV, Chapter 5.

664. Despite its proximity to the spheres of politics, constitutional jurisdiction in Switzerland is predominantly a *typical judicial activity*; the Federal Assembly – the legislative branch – controls the constitutionality only in a few cases, such of cantonal constitutions (Articles 51 and 172 of the Constitution), international treaties between a canton and a foreign country (Article 172(2) of the Constitution) or the validity of federal popular initiatives (Article 173(1)(b) of the Constitution). The Swiss model of constitutional jurisdiction is based on the so-called diffuse system of judicial review, which allows plaintiff to contest the constitutionality of a given state or governmental action before any judicial authority – unless it is 'immunized' by Article 190 of the Constitution. Therefore, in contrast to a concentrated system of judicial review, there is no 'specialized' constitutional court (e.g., the German *Bundesverfassungsgericht* or the Italian *Corte Costituzionale*), which would be – on the national level – hierarchically superior to the Federal Supreme Court and exclusively competent in constitutional review. Rather, comparable to the US Supreme Court, the Federal Supreme Court, as 'the highest judicial authority of the Confederation' (Article 188(1) of the Constitution and Article 1(1) of the Federal Supreme Court Act), has general jurisdiction in all branches of the law. Article 113(1)(3) of the Constitution of 1874 and (until 1 January 2007) Article 189(1)(a) of the Constitution both stated that the Federal Supreme Court had jurisdiction over complaints regarding the violation of *constitutional rights* of citizens (*see supra* §1 I of this Chapter). The new Article 189(1)(a) of the Constitution generally refers to the Federal Supreme Court jurisdiction concerning the violation of *federal law*. Although it may appear that the Federal Constitution has limited the Court's jurisdiction, it is undisputed that the term 'federal law' must be interpreted in a very large sense, including federal constitutional law in general and constitutional rights in particular.

II. Constitutional Jurisdiction and Article 190 of the Constitution

665. According to Article 190 of the Constitution, federal statutes and international law are binding on the Federal Supreme Court and all other law-applying authorities (*see* already General Introduction, Chapter 2, §4). This means that the courts must apply federal statutes (Article 163 of the Constitution), including federal emergency legislation (Article 165) and binding international law (especially treaties) regardless of their constitutionality (*see*, e.g., Decision of the Federal Administrative Court BVGE 2010/7 paragraph 3.1.1). *E contrario* the following legislative acts are not 'immunized' by Article 190 of the Constitution and can be the object of judicial review: cantonal statutes (except cantonal constitutions, *see* above); federal ordinances of the Federal Assembly, federal ordinances of the Federal Council including emergency ordinances, *see* Articles 173(1)(c), 184(3), 185(3) of the Constitution.

666. The Federal Supreme Court may fully review the constitutionality of ordinances of the Federal Council based upon a direct constitutional delegation of authority (independent ordinances of the Federal Council). However, the Court gives particular weight to the political leeway granted to the Federal Council by the constitutional delegation of authority. Ordinances of the Federal Council based upon a delegation in a federal statute (dependent regulations) are only subject to a restricted judicial review of constitutionality. The Court will only invalidate the constitutionality of a dependent ordinance of the Federal Council if the federal statute contains no clause authorizing the Federal Council to derogate from the Constitution. Quite often in practice, very broad discretion is granted to the Federal Council by federal statutory delegations. This leeway binds the Court and it may not intervene by substituting its own discretion for the one of the Federal Council. In reviewing the constitutionality of the ordinance of the Federal Council, the Court will control, whether the ordinance manifestly breaches ('*offensichtlich sprengt*') the boundaries of the delegation granted to the Federal Council by the federal statute or whether the ordinance is unconstitutional or illegal for other reasons (*see*, *inter alia*, Decision of the Federal Supreme Court BGE 131 II 162 paragraph 2.1).

667. Switzerland is one of a number of countries that introduced constitutional review in the nineteenth century. The Federal Supreme Court had jurisdiction to fully invalidate the constitutionality of cantonal statutes. At that time, due to the few competences of the still weak Confederation and the paucity of federal statutes, it was beyond imagination to extend constitutional review to federal statutes. In the twentieth century, however, the distribution of competences changed considerably in favour of the Confederation. But Article 190 of the Constitution (respectively Article 191 of the Constitution of 1874) remained untouched by that evolution. Note, however, that in order to avoid conflicts with the European Court of Human Rights, the Federal Supreme Court has also held in an important case that provisions of federal laws, which violate the ECHR shall not be applied (*see* the so-called PKK decision of the Federal Supreme Court BGE 125 II 417 paragraph 4d). Whether this case has created two classes of fundamental rights – the 'first class' of the fundamental rights of the Constitution which are also covered by the ECHR, and the 'second class' of purely national fundamental rights not covered by the ECHR (such as economic freedom or the guarantee of property) – is a widely disputed question among Swiss constitutional scholars. Although there have been initiatives in Swiss constitutional history to introduce constitutional review of federal statutes, all those proposals have been ultimately rejected. In February 2011, the majority of the Legal Commission of the National Council voted for the complete abolition of Article 190 of the Constitution. This proposal would allow all law-applying authorities to control in a given case (concrete judicial review) not only the constitutionality of (inter-) cantonal laws and federal ordinances, but of federal laws as well. Unfortunately, from a realistic perspective, it is unlikely that this proposal will get the required majority in Parliament (and it has not so far).

668. Nevertheless, it appears that the scepticism towards a government of judges (*Richterstaat*) and the commitment to the *supremacy of the democratic principle* (*see* General Introduction, Chapter 2, §2 and §4) are still deeply rooted in the population. In this view, the Federal Parliament is the highest representative of the People, embodying the *volonté générale*, which cannot be questioned, let alone nullified, for constitutional reasons by a court. Of course, this does not confer to Parliament a free pass to ignore the issue of the constitutionality of its laws; on the contrary, Article 141(2)(a) of the Federal Parliamentary Act (SR 171.10) obliges the lawmaker to ensure the constitutionality of its legislative drafts. This *preventive control* is usually made by the Federal Office of Justice, which is not a judicial authority, but whose results may (and in fact often do) have a great impact on the outcome of parliamentary debates. But this preventive control of constitutionality is not the key argument for the maintenance of Article 190 of the Constitution: As all statutes passed by Federal Parliament are subject to an optional referendum (Article 141 of the Constitution), they are considered to be ratified either implicitly by the People when they do not invoke the right of referendum, or explicitly because they have been approved in a referendum by the majority of the People. Accordingly, there is no judicial body that would have the legitimacy to call into question that which has been expressly or tacitly ratified by the sovereign. So far, this argument has proved to be more convincing than the traditional Common Law argument that society should be governed by laws and not by men.

Chapter 3. Constitutional Problems of Minorities

Selected Bibliography: Basta Fleiner Lidija, R. 'Minority and Legitimacy of a Federal State: An Outsider Perception of the Swiss Model'. In Basta Fleiner & Fleiner, 99 et seq.; Borghi Marco. 'Sprachenfreiheit und ihre Schranken'. In Thürer et al., §38; Fleiner Thomas. 'Switzerland: Constitution of the Federal State and the Cantons'. In Basta Fleiner & Fleiner, 126–143; Fleiner Thomas & Misic Alexander. 'Föderalismus als Ordnungsprinzip der Verfassung'. In Thürer et al., §27; Schindler Dietrich. 'Schweizerischer Föderalismus – Europäischer Föderalismus'. In Daniel Thürer & Elmar Ledergerber. Regional und sicherheitspolitische Aspekte Europas. Zurich: Schulthess Polygraphischer Verlag, 1995; Töpperwien Nicole. *Nation-state and Normative Diversity.* Basel: Helbing & Lichtenhahn, 2001.

§1. Overview

669. The title 'constitutional problems of minorities' raises two questions: what is considered a minority and what is considered a problem. Countries have very varied ways of approaching minorities. Switzerland developed its very own approach to deal with Swiss diversity.

I. Definition of the Term Minority

670. If the meaning of minority is to be interpreted from its linguistic origin, then a minority is a group that does not form a majority. Under this definition, a minority is distinguished based on the numerical importance of the group. However, minority status is not solely meant to express the numerical relevance of a group, as it also includes the assumption that there is difference that distinguishes the minority from the majority, and that this difference leads to inequality and tends to render the group and its members vulnerable. A numerical minority can in fact dominate the country, and sometimes the numerical majority might form the vulnerable part of the population. Therefore, inequality and/or vulnerability are core criteria for the distinction of minorities.

II. Minorities and the Constitution

671. A group will be especially vulnerable when the differences are based on criteria that cannot easily be adopted or relinquished, such as race, ethnicity, religion or culture. Inequality can find expression in open or hidden, legal or social negative discrimination. In general, there is consensus that legal negative discrimination of persons belonging to minorities is problematic and that the Constitution should prevent such discrimination. More complicated is the issue of social discrimination. In how far shall the state intervene to alleviate social discrimination of persons belonging to minorities? Shall the state use affirmative action or even positive discrimination in support of persons belonging to minorities?

672. Inequality already starts at state building level if the state is defined as the state of and for one group. This unequal status can be particularly problematic when the state has as one of its aims to maintain and promote the interests of this one group – or nation – as is the case in many western nation-states. Does a minority group have the right to be equal at the state building level? Put differently and perhaps even more provocatively, does the majority nation have the right to claim the state as its nation-state though it shares the territory with other groups?

673. The adequate constitutional status of minority ethnicity, religion, culture, or language in comparison to the status of the majority ethnicity, religion, culture, or language are of further dispute. For instance, is it discrimination if the Constitution does not provide the same official status to the minority language as the majority language?

674. Many countries avoid the minority question from the very outset. They assume, based on concepts of individual equality, that they have no minorities. Does the minority have a right to be recognized as such? Does it have the right to be recognized as a group distinct from the majority?

III. Minorities in Switzerland

675. As described above, Switzerland has a multicultural population (as illustrated by Figure 2, General Introduction, Chapter 4, §3). While the majority of the Swiss population is German-speaking, nonetheless, Switzerland is not regarded as the state of and for the German-speaking group. Switzerland accords an equal status to the different pre-existing linguistic, religious and cultural groups on the state building level as well as in respect to constitutional design. Further, Switzerland does not rely on the 'melting pot' or 'colour blindness' idea like the United states, but expects and accepts that the 'Swiss People' is composed of different groups thus making the Swiss nation a composed nation.

676. Due to their equal status, it is more adequate to speak of different groups than to phrase the debate in minority/majority terms. At the federal level, among the traditional groups, only the Romansh-speaking community is, to some extent, in a minority position because their status is slightly different than that of the other linguistic groups, and because of their vulnerability due to their very small number (less than 1% of the population). In addition, new diversity is not accepted and expected in the same way as traditional diversity; therefore, it can be argued that the immigrants in Switzerland form a minority, or numerous minorities.

677. Historically, religious diversity was the main reason for tensions in Switzerland. It can be argued that religious tensions again are on the rise, however, this time not between the Protestants and the Catholic as previously. Immigration increased religious diversity. In respect to the pre-existing Swiss diversity, today, linguistic diversity creates more tensions than religious diversity. Therefore, the Swiss way to accommodate linguistic diversity will be regarded. Developments in relation to religion will be addressed in the chapter on new minorities (*infra*, §3).

§2. Accommodation of Linguistic Groups at the Federal Level

678. The *promotion of (pre-existing) diversity* is a fundamental state principle (*see supra* Part II, Chapter I, §1). The promotion of diversity is mainly realized through the mechanisms of self- and shared rule.

679. *Self-rule* is accorded to cantons and by the cantons to the municipalities. When different groups are concentrated in a specific area, territorially based self-rule can favour (internal) self-determination. Through self-rule, decisions on sensitive and dividing issues can be left to the decision-making process of the concerned community. Settled at the local level, these issues are less likely to lead to fragmentation at the higher level (for more specific information on self-rule, *see supra* Part II, Chapter I, §2 II). Based on self-rule, each canton can designate the official language for its territory.

680. *Shared rule* leads to a political institutionalization of diversity. Through participation rights, different groups are accorded a special influence in the decision-making process of the federal level. Shared rule favours the generation of compromises and promises that the essential interests of the different communities will be respected (for more specific information on the shared rule arrangement, *see supra* Part II, Chapter 1, §2 II). The different linguistic groups are represented proportionally – with smaller groups sometimes represented in an over-proportional manner – in all federal institutions.

681. In accordance with the value of diversity, Article 4 of the Constitution declared German, French, Italian and Romansh as *national languages*, thus highlighting the equal value of all four languages.

682. The four national languages are also considered *official languages* (Article 70(1) of the Constitution). All Swiss who are German-, French-, Italian- or Romansh-speaking can address the federal authorities in their mother tongue and will receive answers in their language (*see also* for the freedom of language as a fundamental right *infra* Part IV, Chapter 2, §4 V D).

683. German, French and Italian speakers have a slightly better status than the Romansh. While individual acts, orders and decisions will be prepared in Romansh, general ones will in most cases only be published in German, French and Italian. Only important texts are translated into Romansh. These texts are selected by the Federal Chancery in consultation with the Canton of Grisons (as the canton of origin of the Romansh-speaking community in Switzerland). In addition, federal authorities must provide forms, the main page of their homepage and signalization of their buildings in the four languages.

684. Thus, all federal legal texts are at least published in German, French and Italian. All three language versions have the same validity. When the three versions suggest different interpretation, the judge or civil servant who is interpreting or applying the law cannot just rely on the language version in which the legal text was drafted but has to use the most convincing of the three versions (*see supra* Part I, Chapter 7, §1).

685. While the Romansh language is to some extent disfavoured, the Romansh and the Italian are also favoured by the Constitution. According to Article 70(5) of the

Constitution, the Confederation must support the measures taken by the cantons of Grisons and Ticino to maintain and to promote Romansh and Italian.

686. These two languages were accorded a *preferential status* because they are regarded as more vulnerable than the two dominant languages – German and French. Thus, the Confederation is supposed to support the two concerned cantons, which have Switzerland's largest Italian- and Romansh-speaking populations.

687. Based on a similar logic, the Constitution mandates the Confederation to support the bilingual cantons and the trilingual canton. According to Article 70(4) of the Constitution, the Confederation shall support the pluri-lingual cantons in the fulfilment of their particular tasks.

688. In addition, the Confederation shall take measures to encourage better understanding between the different language groups (Article 70(3) of the Constitution). Even though Switzerland as such is pluri-lingual, most Swiss citizens are monolingual. The Confederation and the cantons shall therefore take measures so that a true exchange and understanding between different groups can develop. In this respect, language instruction in schools is heatedly debated, particularly the importance of English compared to national languages.

689. Finally, the Constitution accommodates linguistic groups by guaranteeing the freedom of language in Article 18 (*see infra* Part IV, Chapter 2, §4 V D).

690. Within the Swiss parliament, the general rules applies that everyone speaks his/her own language. In the National Council, simultaneous interpretation is provided. In the Council of States, parliamentarians are expected to have passive knowledge of the other national languages – though in effect this is not always the case. All documents must be translated into German, French and Italian before they are debated in Parliament.

691. In the Federal Council and the administration, Federal Councillors and public employees have the choice to work either in German, French or Italian.

692. It might come as a surprise that for more than 160 years federal Switzerland did not have a language law (*see* for the Federal Act regarding National Languages and the Understanding Between the Linguistic Communities of 5 October 2007 [in force since 1 January 2010; SR 441.1] also *infra* Part IV, Chapter 2, §4 V D). Switzerland enacted its first language law on 5 October 2007. This law incorporates language provisions that previously have been scattered in different legal acts or had developed over time without being included in any legal act. For a long time, the Swiss population and politicians did not see the need to consolidate the Swiss language law.

§3. Linguistic Accommodation on the Cantonal and Municipal Level

693. Of the twenty-six Swiss cantons and half-cantons, seventeen are German-speaking (Zurich, Lucerne, Uri, Schwyz, Obwalden and Nidwalden, Glarus, Zug, Solothurn, Basel-City and Basel-Land, Schaffhausen, Appenzell Ausserrhoden and Appenzell Innerrhoden, St. Gallen, Aargau and Thurgau), four are French-speaking (Vaud, Neuchâtel, Geneva and Jura), one is Italian-speaking (Ticino), three are bilingual (German/French; Valais with a German-speaking minority, Fribourg with a German-speaking minority and Berne with a French-speaking minority),and one canton is trilingual (German, Italian, Romansh, Grisons).

694. Problems most often arise in the bilingual and trilingual cantons. The cantons have the right to regulate which languages shall be the official languages in their territory for communication with cantonal and municipal authorities. For the designation of official languages, the cantons are requested to abide by the territoriality principle and to take indigenous linguistic minorities into account (Article 70(2) of the Constitution). Both requests are introduced in order to *preserve peaceful relations* among the different linguistic groups. Smaller linguistic groups shall not have to fear that they or their territory will become dominated by another linguistic community.

695. In order to take *indigenous linguistic minorities* into account, bilingual and trilingual cantons designate all languages that are indigenous to their territory as official languages for the purpose of communicating with cantonal authorities.

696. Article 70(5) implies that the cantons of Ticino and Grisons can adopt *special measures* (positive discrimination) for the protection of the Italian and the Romansh (e.g., prohibition to advertise other than in the vulnerable language, Decision of the Federal Supreme Court BGE 116 Ia 345).

697. The Canton of Grisons is the only canton that adopted a language law. In the law, the canton made use of the right to adopt special measures for vulnerable language groups (Article 70(5) of the Constitution). For instance, the canton provides that if a linguistic community (Romansh or Italian) who historically have been in a majority in a certain area still form at least 40% of the population their language can be designated as only official language. If the linguistic community forms more than 20% of the population the municipality can be considered bilingual.

698. For purposes of communication with municipal authorities, the *territoriality principle* is of prime importance (*see infra* Part IV, Chapter 2, §4 V D). The territoriality principle maintains the territorial linguistic *status quo*, meaning the language that is traditionally spoken by the population of the territory is designated as official language. Only when there is a high and stable influx of persons from another language group the language status of the territory is adjusted. In an obiter dictum, the Federal Supreme Court suggested that only when the newly immigrated language group forms about one-half of the population they will have the right to have their language designated as an official language (Decision of the Federal Supreme Court BGE 106 Ia 345).

699. For instance, German-speaking Swiss who take up residence in a French-speaking municipality will have to address the municipal authorities in French and will normally have to send their German-speaking children into French-speaking schools. As example, a municipality in the Canton of Grisons with a minority of Romansh-speakers (20%) did not offer school instruction in Romansh and was not willing to pay for the costs of sending the children to a Romansh-speaking school. The Federal Supreme Court upheld the municipality's actions as constitutional (Decision of the Federal Supreme Court BGE 100 Ia 462). However, according to a somewhat newer decision concerning the Canton of Fribourg, when parents are willing to send their children to private schools in a different municipality or another municipality accepts the children and the parents cover the additional costs, the canton must not intervene (Decision of the Federal Supreme Court BGE 122 I 236). The canton can even restrict the use of another national language for instruction in private schools (Decision of the Federal Supreme Court BGE 91 I 480).

700. Therefore, the territoriality principle, like some measures of positive discrimination, is in conflict with the freedom of language. In most cases the Federal Supreme Court gave precedence to the aim of harmonious relationships between the different linguistic groups and therefore to the territoriality principle over the freedom of language.

701. International law restricts the territoriality principle to some extent. For example, according to the ECHR all arrested and accused persons must be informed of the reasons for their arrest or accusation in a language that they understand (Articles 5(2) and 6(3) of the ECHR; *infra* Part IV, Chapter 2, §6 V and VI).

§4. New Minorities

702. One of the main purposes of the Swiss state is to maintain and promote diversity (*see supra* Part II Chapter 1, §1). This promotion of diversity, however, is limited to traditional or indigenous diversity. The understanding what kind of diversity merits promotion is relatively static.

703. As was shown above, immigrants are supposed to assimilate in order to receive Swiss citizenship. For instance, persons who want to receive Swiss citizenship must show that they can master one of the official languages. In addition, also after naturalization, a Portuguese-speaking Swiss does not enjoy the same institutionalization of diversity, as do the German-, French-, Italian-, or Romansh-speaking Swiss, even though Portuguese-speaking Swiss outnumber the Romansh-speaking Swiss. For instance, representation of this language group is not considered when filling positions for the Federal Supreme Court or when proposing members for the Federal Council.

704. Immigration led to an increase in diversity of the population of Switzerland not only in respect to linguistic diversity. For instance, 5.1% of the population in Switzerland are Muslims (2015). On 29 November 2009, Switzerland made international news. In a popular vote, a majority of the Swiss People and of the cantons decided to introduce a provision into the Swiss Constitution: 'The construction of minarets is prohibited' (Article 72(3) of the Constitution). The popular debate before and after the popular vote was highly polarized. The initiators of the constitutional amendment pointed out that their initiative was not to be understood as opposition towards Islam but concerned mainly 'construction issues' and would not violate the freedom of religion of Muslims. At the same time however, proponents made strong allusions to the in their view 'insufficient' integration of Muslims in Switzerland. Opponents argued in favour of a violation of the freedom of religion and understood the initiative as discriminatory and xenophobe. In addition, opponents pointed out that there are hardly any minarets in Switzerland as most mosques in Switzerland do not have one. The broad acceptance of the initiative in the popular vote however shows that the population is concerned about integration and expects assimilation. There are only very few instances, in which a redefinition of what kind of diversity shall be promoted has taken place:

- With the foundation of the Canton of Jura in 1978, the people of the canton received a state building status like the people of the other cantons.
- The voting right for women that was accorded at the federal level only in 1971 led to the inclusion of women into the political body. The Swiss tradition of unofficial quota led to a comparably quick representation of women in political institutions. However, they remain under-represented in politics and high level positions in business.
- On the cantonal level, some cantons granted Jewish religious communities public law status, like that of Christian communities. This is a particularly noteworthy example because although Switzerland granted Jews equal rights as individuals in 1874, it took another one hundred years for Jewish communities to be granted equality as a group.

705. The inequality in status which is not expressed in unequal rights but in a missing institutionalization of diversity could only be eradicated when either the new diversity would be equally institutionalized (e.g., through representation based on informal quotas, recognition of languages), or when the Swiss state would cease to maintain and promote diversity. This issue of how to best deal with new diversity is still unsolved.

Chapter 4. Legal Position of Aliens

Selected Bibliography: Achermann Alberto & Hausammann Christine. *Handbuch des Asylrechts.* Bern/Stuttgart, 1991; Caroni Martina, Gächter Thomas & Thurnherr Daniela (eds). *Bundesgesetz über die Ausländerinnen und Ausländer (AuG), Stämpflis Handkommentar.* Berne, 2010; Caroni Martina et al., *Migrationsrecht.* 3rd ed. Berne: Stämpfli, 2014; Fleiner Thomas. 'Rechtsstaatsdefizite für Ausländerinnen und Ausländer im schweizerischen Verwaltungsrecht'. In *Mélanges Morand.* Basel 2001, 231 et seq.; Epiney Astrid. 'Freizügigkeit Schweiz-EU: status quo, Perspektiven und offene Fragen'. In *Jahrbuch für Migrationsrecht* 2015/2016, 3 et seq.; Kälin Walter. 'Die Bedeutung des Freizügigkeitsabkommens für das Ausländerrecht'. In *Die sektoriellen Abkommen Schweiz-EG, Ausgewählte Fragen zur Rezeption und Umsetzung der Verträge vom 21. Juni 1999 im schweizerischen Recht*, edited by Cottier & Oesch. Berne, 2002, 11 et seq.; Mahon. 49 et seq.; Malinverni Giorgio. 'Le droit des étrangers'. In Thürer et al., §63, 979–991; Rhinow, Schefer & Uebersax. 69 et seq. (with further references); Spescha Marc et al., *Migrationsrecht: Kommentar.* 4th ed. Zurich: Orell Füssli 2015; Spescha Marc, Antonia Kerland & Bolzli Peter. *Handbuch zum Migrationsrecht.* 2nd ed. Zurich: Orell Füssli 2015; Uebersax Peter et al., *Ausländerrecht.* 2nd ed. Basel: Helbing & Lichtenhahn, 2009.

§1. Legal Sources

706. Today about one-fifth of the Swiss population does not have Swiss citizenship ('four-fifths democracy', Thomas Fleiner). Until 1925, regulation concerning foreigners was a cantonal matter. However, in 1848 the federal level attained the power to order the expulsion of foreigners for political reasons, and between 1910 and 1925 the Federal Government restricted immigration by decrees without relying on a constitutional basis. In 1925, the Federal Constitution of 1874 was amended so as to establish a federal competence concerning immigration, emigration, residence, domicile of foreigners and asylum. The main aim of federal laws concerning foreigners is to limit the number of foreigners as well as to protect the security and economic interests of the country.

I. Provisions in the Federal Constitution

707. The Federal Constitution outlines only the distribution of powers concerning legislation on foreigners and establishes the mandatory loss of the right to stay and return to Switzerland in the case of certain offences. According to Article 121 of the Constitution, legislation on immigration, emigration, residence and domicile of foreigners, and on granting asylum are federal matters. Foreigners who endanger Switzerland's security may be removed from Switzerland by force (*see infra* Part IV, Chapter 2, §4 VI). However, no person shall be removed by force to a state where he/she is threatened by torture, or other means of cruel and inhuman treatment or punishment

(Article 25(3) of the Constitution). Refugees are additionally protected against extradition to states in which they are persecuted (Article 25(2) of the Constitution; *see infra* Part IV, Chapter 2, §4 VI).

708. Furthermore, in 2014 a constitutional amendment was adopted that establishes that Switzerland shall steer the immigration of foreigners independently (read: and not in conjunction with the EU). For this, the Confederation shall determine the maximum number of persons per year to enter and settle in Switzerland. According to the constitutional provision, all immigrants shall be included in the count, including asylum seekers. For immigrants seeking gainful employment, economic interests of Switzerland and preference for Swiss employment-seekers shall be considered. The Constitution bars the Confederation from concluding international treaties that run counter to this provision (Article 121a of the Constitution). Negotiations with the EU on this matter are ongoing. The Federal Council is aiming at arriving at an interpretation of the provision that is compatible with current and future agreements with the EU.

II. Further Federal Provisions

709. The Federal Foreigners Act of 16 December 2005 (SR 142.20) is the main legal text concerning foreigners. It replaced the *Residence and Domicile of Foreigners Act of 26 March 1931.* In large parts the Act of 2005 is more restrictive than the previous one, in particular concerning the access of foreigners to Switzerland. The focus is on highly qualified foreigners. On the other hand, the Act provides amongst others for measures to promote the integration of foreigners and provides greater flexibility for foreigners to change domicile or job.

III. International Law

710. International law remains a very important source for Swiss immigration law. Most parts of the Federal Foreigners Act do not apply to EU/EFTA citizens because there are specific treaties on the Freedom of movement of persons, amongst others the treaty between Switzerland, the European Community, and the members of the EU (FZA) of 1999 which entered into force in 2002. Based on this treaty, citizens of EU member countries have the right to freely choose their place of gainful employment and of residence. The Federal Foreigners Act only applies if the FZA does not include differing provisions or the law is more generous than the treaty. Since June 2002, the same rules apply for citizens of EFTA. More than half of the foreigners in Switzerland are citizens of EU or EFTA. The stepwise introduction of the freedom of movement is regulated in a decree (SR 142.203). These agreements remain in force despite of Article 121a of the Constitution. In addition, Switzerland has concluded treaties granting a *right* to domicile after a certain time of residence and to facilitate the obtaining of domicile. Most of these were concluded with EU or EFTA countries. In addition, treaties that regulate the return of foreigners to their home country are being concluded. Further, international multilateral treaties – e.g., concerning the dispensation of visa obligations, or for the protection of human rights – are gaining importance. The ECHR is in this respect the most important international document (regarding Article 8 *see infra* Part IV, Chapter 2, §4 III).

§2. Access to Swiss Territory

711. Unless exceptions are granted, every foreigner needs a valid identification document (e.g., passport) and a visa to enter Switzerland. Furthermore, they must have the necessary financial means, must not present a safety hazard to Switzerland, and must not have been subjected to a prohibition to enter Switzerland or a measure of expulsion from Switzerland (Article 5(1) of the Federal Foreigners Act). In addition, they have to credibly assure that they will leave the country in case the person is admitted to Switzerland for a limited time period (Article 5(2) of the Federal Foreigners Act).

§3. Residence and Domicile

712. Foreigners need an authorization in order to receive the right to reside or to establish domicile on Swiss territory. Unless specially provided by law or international treaty, there is no right to receive such authorization. The authorizations are issued by the cantons. The Federal Government can grant permits to asylum seekers or can allow in some cases provisional admission. Federal law, however, binds the cantons by establishing quantitative (contingents) and qualitative (mainly labour related) limits. Additionally, for most authorizations concerning foreigners who are not citizens of the EU, the cantons need the approbation of the Federal Government for rendering the authorization valid.

713. The Federal Foreigners Act gives a clear preference to highly skilled foreigners. For instance, Article 23 of the Federal Foreigners Act provides that, as a rule, authorizations for short time stays and for the right to reside in Switzerland can only be given to management cadres, specialists and skilled workers. In addition, the professional qualifications, professional and social flexibility as well as language skills and age have to be such that it can be expected that the person will integrate professionally and socially in a sustainable way. Prospective employers must demonstrate that there are no equally qualified Swiss or EU applicants for the job position. Persons in retirement will only be admitted if they have a minimum age, as defined by the Federal Council, if they have personal links to Switzerland and the necessary financial means (Article 28 of the Federal Foreigners Act).

714. In addition, persons will be permitted based on international obligations, humanitarian reasons, or to enable the unification of families (Article 3 of the Federal Foreigners Act). Article 30 of the Federal Foreigners Act provides a list of situations in which authorizations in line with Article 3 can be provided even if the overall (economic) conditions are not fulfilled, e.g., to allow the residency of victims and witnesses of human trafficking, to promote cultural and scientific exchange, or to facilitate the re-entry of foreigners who in the past already once had a residency or domicile permit.

715. Those who request a working permit are normally issued a single authorization combining the residency and working authorization. In this case, as a first step, the cantonal labour department has to give its approval based on the labour market situation. Following approval, the cantonal immigration bureau considers non-economic grounds, e.g. can refuse the authorization based on safety concerns.

716. Swiss law distinguishes between residency and domicile. The *residence permit* is always limited in time. The *domicile authorization* gives an unlimited and unconditioned right to establish domicile in the canton that issued the authorization as well as on request in other cantons (Article 37 of the Federal Foreigners Act). A domicile authorization is normally granted after five to ten years of residency, and it includes a work permit. Minor children and the spouse of a person who was issued a domicile authorization have a right to a residency permit and after five years to a domicile permit if they live in the same household.

§4. Removal from Swiss Territory

717. As a rule, everyone who does not have a valid authorization to stay in Switzerland and who is not in danger of suffering persecution, cruel and inhumane treatment or punishment in the country to which they should return to, can be removed from the territory. The authorization either has ceased to be valid or the persons never obtained an authorization. Authorizations of residence are limited in time and therefore *expire* unless they are prolonged.

718. In November 2010, the People and the cantons have adopted a popular initiative which amended Article 121 of the Constitutions. Based on the revised Article, foreign nationals can be expelled from Switzerland if they pose a risk to the security of the country and irrespective of their status under the law on foreigners, they shall lose their right of residence and all other legal rights to remain in Switzerland if they are convicted with legal binding effect of an offence of intentional homicide, rape or any other serious sexual offence, any other violent offence such as robbery, the offences of trafficking in human beings or in drugs, or a burglary offence; or have improperly claimed social insurance or social assistance benefits. This constitutional provision is in clear tension with the prohibition to remove anyone to a country where he/she is in danger of suffering persecution, cruel and inhumane treatment or punishment.

719. According to the Federal Foreigners Act, both authorizations of domicile and of residence can be *revoked* when the person, at the time of applying for the authorization made false declarations or was convicted to long-term imprisonment or a special measure based on criminal law. Based on the Federal Foreigners Act, authorizations of residence can also be revoked when the person's conduct in Switzerland repeatedly disturbed public peace or when a person in his/her care depends on social services. Authorizations of domicile can be revoked when the foreigner seriously disturbed public peace or when he/she or a person in his/her care depends on social services continuously or in an extensive way. The domicile permit of a person living orderly for more than fifteen years in Switzerland can only be revoked in very limited cases (Article 63 of the Federal Foreigners Act).

720. Previously, criminal courts could order the expulsion of a foreigner as a supplementary sentence. This possibility was abolished in 2007. Now it is within the authority (and in certain cases obligation) of the administration to revoke the domicile or residency permit, and the Federal Office of Migration can (or in some cases must) impose prohibitions to re-enter Switzerland. There have been several court decisions considering the relation between the revocation of domicile or residency permits and Article 8 of the ECHR, establishing a right to family life. In the case of a Nigerian citizen, the ECHR deemed the expulsion due to criminal conviction as in violation of Article 8. The Court considered the right of his children to family life as more important than the public interest in an expulsion (Decision of the European Court on Human Rights, 6 April 2013). Shortly afterwards, in a case concerning a person from Kosovo, the Federal Supreme Court upheld the revocation of a residence permit because of criminal conviction because – in the view of the court – the whole family could relocate to Kosovo (Decision of the Federal Supreme Court 2C_365/2013 of 30 August 2013).

721. Authorizations of residence and domicile will *cease* when the person receives an authorization in a different canton. Authorizations of residence and domicile also cease when the person leaves the country for more than six months (in the case of a domicile permit, this period can be extended to four years upon demand).

722. When the foreigner does not have a valid authorization – either because it was never issued, has expired, was revoked, ceased to be valid, or because the person was ordered expelled – the authorities will set a deadline for the person to leave the canton and/or the country, depending on which authorities – cantonal and/or federal – are setting the deadline.

723. When the person does not leave the country voluntarily or is expected to plan to stay illegally, authorities can adopt coercive measures, including detention. When extradition is not possible, illicit, or not reasonable due to practicality considerations, the foreigner will receive a provisionary authorization.

724. Except in specific cases and if so ordered, extradition does not include a legal prohibition or restriction for a future return to Switzerland – though in practical terms it tends to prejudice authorities against issuing a visa or a new permit.

§5. Freedom of Movement Between Switzerland and the European Community and Their Member Countries

725. The above-mentioned Federal Foreigners Act mainly applies to persons who are not from EU or EFTA countries. For citizens of EU and EFTA countries as well as their family members, bilateral treaties apply. Agreements between Switzerland and the EU envisage a step-by-step enlargement of the freedom of movement between Switzerland and the EU. The Agreement allows for transitional periods during which restrictions on immigrant workers, such as priority for the country's own citizens or prior control of wage and employment conditions, can be maintained and the number of residence permits issued can be limited (quotas). After expiry of these restrictions, the number of permits can again be limited on a temporary basis in the event of a very high influx of foreigners into Switzerland. Switzerland established such a limitation for citizens of Bulgaria and Romania, starting from June 2017 and lasting for a twelve-month period. For persons from other EU and EFTA countries no quotas apply anymore and they are treated equally on the job market. They receive a domicile permit if they have a valid employment contract or are self-employed and have a health insurance. Persons can also enter Switzerland for a period of three months to look for a job (which can be prolonged up to a year) or can stay in Switzerland without employment if they have the necessary financial means.

§6. Status of Foreigners

726. International law fixes minimal standards upon Switzerland, such as a prohibition on imposing military service on foreigners, or arbitrarily expulsion of foreigners. International law also calls for the recognition of certain fundamental rights.

727. According to Swiss law, foreigners have an equal or similar status as Swiss citizens in nearly all fields of law. For instance, they have equal access to services, e.g. the access to health services or the possibility to go to school does not depend on citizenship. To ensure that illegal foreigners dare to send their children to school, the status of the parents is not checked. Restrictions or difference in treatment are only admissible when they are justified by objective reasons.

728. On the federal level, *political rights* are limited to Swiss citizens. However, the cantons can grant political rights for elections and popular referenda in cantonal and communal matters. Two cantons accord the right to vote and elect to foreigners at the cantonal level. So far, for cantonal elections, no canton provides the right to foreigners to stand for election. Four cantons provide foreigners the right to vote, elect and to be elected at municipal level. In one canton, foreigners have the right to vote at the municipal level but not to stand for elections. Cantons can also leave some autonomy in this respect to the municipalities so that municipalities can decide whether they attribute the right to vote, elect and be elected.

729. As mentioned above, foreigners do not have an unlimited right to choose a place of domicile; however, under the current law of 2005, it has become easier to change the place of residency from one canton to another. For persons with a residence permit, economic freedom is limited insofar as the working permit can be granted with conditions. Some professions that demand a special loyalty to and understanding of Switzerland are restricted to Swiss citizens, for instance, in most cantons the profession of police, or judges. Today – although not historically – the freedom of expression, assembly and association are guaranteed to foreigners to the same degree they are guaranteed to Swiss citizens. Until 1998, political speech received only limited freedom of expression protection. It was allowed only with prior authorization.

730. To give further examples of differences in treatment: a foreigner cannot hold bonds of the Swiss National Bank. Additionally, there are some limits with respect to the acquisition of real estate (authorization requirement according to the Federal Act concerning the acquisition of real estate by foreigners (SR 211.412.4)).

731. As a general rule, foreigners with a domicile permit and, in some cases, persons with a residence permit can invoke the right to reunion of the family. This right is anchored both in Article 42 of the Federal Foreigners Act (and in Article 8 of the ECHR).

Chapter 5. Judicial Control of Administrative Action

Bibliography (selection): Aemisegger Heinz. 'Der Beschwerdegang in öffentlichrechtlichen Angelegenheiten'. In Ehrenzeller & Schweizer (eds), 103 et seq.; Aemisegger Heinz. 'Öffentlichkeit der Justiz'. In Tschannen (ed.), 375 et seq.; Auer Andreas. 'Le recours constitutionnel – terra incognita'. In Foëx, Hottelier & Jeandin (eds), 157 et seq.; Auer Andreas. *Die schweizerische Verfassungsgerichtsbarkeit.* Basel/Frankfurt a.M.: Helbing & Lichtenhahn, 1984; Auer Christoph, Müller Markus & Schindler Benjamin (eds), *Kommentar zum Bundesgesetz über das Verwaltungsverfahren (VwVG).* Zurich/St. Gallen: Dike, 2008; Bellanger François & Tanquerel Thierry (eds). *Les nouveaux recours fédéraux en droit public.* Zurich: Schulthess, 2006; Besson Michel. 'Die Beschwerde in Stimmrechtssachen'. In Ehrenzeller & Schweizer (eds), 403 et seq.; Corboz Bernard et al., *Commentaire de la LTF (Loi sur le Tribunal fédéral).* 2nd ed. Berne: Stämpfli, 2014; Donzallaz Yves. *Loi sur le Tribunal fédéral.* Berne: Stämpfli, 2008; Ehrenzeller Bernhard & J. Schweizer Rainer (eds). *Die Reorganisation der Bundesrechtspflege – Neuerungen und Auswirkungen in der Praxis.* Schriftenreihe des Instituts für Rechtswissenschaft und Rechtspraxis, St. Gallen, 2006; Gygi Fritz. *Bundesverwaltungsrechtspflege.* 2nd ed. Berne: Stämpfli, 1983; Häfelin Ulrich, Müller Georg & Uhlmann Felix. *Allgemeines Verwaltungsrecht.* 7th ed. Zurich/St. Gallen: Schulthess/Dike, 2016; Häner Isabelle. *Die Beteiligten im Verwaltungsverfahren und Verwaltungsprozess*, Schulthess. Zurich, 2000; Hottelier Michel. 'Entre tradition et modernité: le recours constitutionnel subsidiaire'. In Bellanger & Tanquerel (eds), 71 et seq.; Kälin Walter. *Das Verfahren der staatsrechtlichen Beschwerde.* 2nd ed. Berne: Stämpfli, 1994; Karlen Peter. *Das neue Bundesgerichtsgesetz: die wesentlichen Neuerungen und was sie bedeuten.* Basel: Helbing & Lichtenhahn, 2006; Kiener Regina, Rütsche Bernhard & Kuhn Mathias. Öffentliches Verfahrensrecht. 2nd ed. Zürich: Dike, 2015; Kley-Struller Andreas. *Der richterliche Rechtsschutz gegen die öffentliche Verwaltung.* Zurich: Schulthess, 1995; Kölz Alfred. *Prozessmaximen im schweizerischen Verwaltungsprozess.* 2nd ed. Zurich: Schulthess, 1974; Kölz Alfred, Häner Isabelle & Martin Bertschi. *Verwaltungsverfahren und Verwaltungsrechtspflege des Bundes.* 3rd ed. Zurich, 2013. Mächler August. *Vertrag und Verwaltungsrechtspflege.* Zurich/Basel/Genf: Schulthess, 2005; Marti Arnold. 'Aktueller Stand und neue Fragen in der scheizerischen Verwaltungsrechtspflege'. In *Schweizerisches Zentralblatt für Staats- und Verwaltungsrecht [ZBl].* 2009, 405 et seq.; Misic Alexander. *Verfassungsbeschwerde – Das Bundesgericht und der subsidiäre Schutz verfassungsmässiger Rechte (Art. 113–119 BGG).* Zurich: Schulthess, 2011; Moor Pierre. 'De l'accès au juge et de l'unification des recours'. In Bellanger & Tanquerel (Hrsg.), 153 et seq.; Moor Pierre & Poltier Etienne. Droit administratif. Vol. II. Les actes administratifs et leur contrôle. 3rd ed. Berne: Stämpfli, 2011; Moser André, Beusch Michael & Kneubühler Lorenz. *Prozessieren vor Bundesverwaltungsgericht.* 2nd ed. Basel: Helbing & Lichtenhahn, 2013; Müller Markus. 'Rechtsschutz gegen Verwaltungsrealakte'. In Tschannen (ed.), 313 et seq. Niggli Marcel Alexander, Uebersax Peter & Wiprächtiger Hans (eds). *Basler Kommentar zum Bundesgerichtsgesetz (BGG).* 2nd ed. Basel: Helbing & Lichtenhahn, 2011; Rhinow René et al., *Öffentliches Prozessrecht.* 3rd ed. Basel, 2014; Schinder Benjamin. *Verwaltungsermessen.* Zurich: Dike/Schulthess, 2010; Seiler

Hansjörg, von Werdt Nicolas, Güngerich Andreas & Niklaus Oberholzer. *Stämpflis Handkommentar, Bundesgerichtsgesetz (BGG)*. Berne: Stämpfli, Bundesgesetz über das Bundesgericht, 2nd ed. Berne, 2007; Tornay Schaller Bénédicte, 'Le recours au Tribunal fédéral en matière d'élections fédérales'. In *Aktuelle Juristische Praxis [AJP]*. 3/2017, 351 et seq.; Tschannen Pierre (ed.). *Neue Bundesrechtspflege – Auswirkungen der Totalrevision auf den kantonalen und eidgenössischen Rechtsschutz. Berner Tage für die juristische Praxis (BTJP) 2006*. Berne: Stämpfli, 2007; Tschannen Pierre, Zimmerli Ulrich & Müller Markus. *Allgemeines Verwaltungsrecht*. 3rd ed. Berne: Stämpfli, 2015; Waldmann Bernhard et al. (eds). *VwVG – Praxiskommentar zum Bundesgesetz über das Verwaltungsverfahren*. 2nd. ed. Zurich: Schulthess, 2016.

§1. INTRODUCTION

732. The purpose of this chapter is to discuss administrative orders (*Verfügung; décision administrative; decisione amministrativa*), the most important form of administrative action subject to control by judicial authorities (*infra*, §2 of this Chapter). The second part of the chapter will deal with the judicial control of administrative action by the Federal Administrative Court (*infra*, §3 I. of this Chapter), the Federal Supreme Court (*infra*, §3 II. of this Chapter), and – in very rare cases, which will not be analysed here – by the Federal Council and the Federal Assembly. The organizational structure of the federal and cantonal judiciary has already been depicted *supra* in Part II, Chapter 5, §2 II C. Taking into account that cantonal administrative procedures and procedures before cantonal judicial authorities are governed by a multitude of cantonal acts, the following chapter will mainly focus on their adjudication at the *federal level*.

733. On the federal level, the process of *adjudication* is governed by Articles 1–43 of the FAPA of 20 December 1968 (FAPA; SR 172.021). The substance of the most important provisions of the FAPA, which also apply *per analogiam* to procedures before the Federal Administrative Court (Article 37 of the Federal Administrative Court Act; SR 173.32) shall be briefly outlined.

734. (1) The preliminary stage of adjudication: Article 1(2) of the FAPA determines which *federal authorities* are subject to this statute, e.g., the Federal Council, its Departments, the Federal Chancery, the Federal Administrative Court, independent federal enterprises, or other authorities or organizations outside the Federal Administration implementing delegated federal public law duties. During this stage of adjudication, the agency must examine its competence ex officio for the matter concerned. An agreement of competency (prorogation) between the agency and the party is inadmissible (Article 7 of the FAPA). Furthermore, the agency must examine possible personal conflicts (Article 10 of the FAPA) and verify the capacity of the individual as a party as well as a participant in the process of adjudication (Article 6 of the FAPA). Provisions of federal law that regulate a procedure in greater detail apply, provided that they are not contradictory to the provisions of the FAPA.

735. (2) Fact-finding process: During the investigatory phase of the process of adjudication the agency must establish the relevant facts (Articles 12–19 of the FAPA). It is a distinctive feature of European continental administrative law that the process of adjudication is characterized by the *inquisitory principle* (*Untersuchungsgrundsatz*), which holds that the agency is not bound by the facts brought forward by the parties. In theory, the agency must find the relevant facts itself and prove their existence (so-called principle of substantive truth). Admissible evidence includes official documents, statements made by the parties or by a third party, inspection reports and expert testimony (Article 12 of the FAPA). However, the inquisitory principle does not imply that the parties are completely dispensed from the *obligation to participate* in the fact-finding process. A party may even be statutorily obliged to participate in the process of investigation, as a violation of duty to participate can result in the agency not deciding the matter (Article 13 of the FAPA). The authority shall admit the evidence offered if it appears *reliable* for determining the facts of the case (Article 33(1) of the FAPA). Furthermore, by granting a *hearing* (Article 29 of the FAPA), the agency has to determine the parties' legal position and establish the applicable law.

736. (3) The decision (order): An administrative order resulting from the agencies' investigatory process must contain a description of the relevant facts as well as an explanation of the legal grounds for the decision. According to Article 34(1) of the FAPA, an administrative order must be notified *in writing* as a prerequisite for its validity. According to Article 70 of the Constitution, the *official languages* of the Confederation are German, French and Italian. Romansh is one of the official languages of communication with Romansh-speaking people. Consequently, federal administrative orders have to be written in the official language of the party who has made the request (or who could possibly have made a request). Administrative orders issued by the last cantonal instance must be written in the official language of the canton (Article 37 of the FAPA). A non-observance of the language provisions affects the *validity* of the administrative order insofar as the material legal effect of the order and the running of the statute of limitations are suspended (Article 38 of the FAPA). Moreover, the order must inform the addressee of the existence of legal remedies, the competent authority for appeal, and the running of the statute of limitations (Article 35 of the FAPA). According to the Federal Supreme Court, however, even if the agency gives *inadequate or even wrong information about the available remedy*, the principle of good faith would not protect an addressee who might have found the error with due diligence (*see*, *inter alia*, Decisions of the Federal Supreme Court BGE 124 I 255 paragraph 1; BGE 112 Ib 417 paragraph 2d). Conversely, good faith does protect the addressee of an administrative order against the *wrong indication of the statute of limitations*. Nonetheless, the protection of good faith cannot be invoked if the addressee is a lawyer or represented by a lawyer, who could have easily found the error by studying the relevant legal provisions (Decision of the Federal Supreme Court BGE 117 Ia 421 paragraph 2).

737. (4) Enforcement: As a rule, a person must appeal against the order within thirty days after its issuance. After the thirty-day period has elapsed, it can be enforced like a judgment. Therefore, it is possible for an order to be enforced even though the order itself or its preparation procedure was unlawful. According to Article 39 of the FAPA, the authority may enforce its administrative orders provided: (a) the administrative order may no longer be contested through legal remedies; (b) the administrative order may still be contested, but the permitted legal remedy does not have a suspensive effect; or (c) the suspensive effect of the legal remedy has been revoked. Article 40 of the FAPA states that administrative orders on the payment of money or the provision of a security must be enforced by means of debt collection proceedings in accordance with the Federal Act of 11 April 1889 on Debt Collection and Bankruptcy of 11 April 1889 (SR 281.1). According to Article 41 of the FAPA, to enforce other administrative orders, the authority shall take the following measures: (a) substitute performance by the authority issuing the administrative order itself or by a third-party instructed at the expense of the party liable; the costs to be determined by special administrative order; (b) direct enforcement against the party liable in person or against his/her property; (c) prosecution in the event that another federal act provides for a penalty; or (d) prosecution for contempt under Article 292 of the Criminal Code (SR 311.0), if no other criminal law provision applies. Before the authority takes any enforcement measure, it shall give notice thereof to the party liable and allow him/her a suitable period in which to comply, indicating the statutory penalties in the cases referred to in paragraph 1 letters c and d. In the cases referred to in paragraph 1 letters a and b, it may dispense with giving notice of the enforcement measure and allowing a period for compliance if there is any risk in a delay. As a general rule in enforcement proceedings, the authority must not use a more rigorous enforcement measure than the circumstances require (principle of proportionality; Article 42 of the FAPA). The cantons shall provide the federal authorities with mutual legal assistance in enforcing administrative orders (Article 43 of the FAPA).

§2. The Administrative Order: The Prototype Form of Administrative Action

738. *Action* is usually regarded as one of the main features of the administration and one of the legitimizing elements of its existence. The implementation of multiple and complex administrative tasks, prescribed by law, must often follow *standardized types* of procedures and forms. According to the Swiss concept, agency action can only be reviewed by a court in cases where the administrative procedure has been terminated, in substance as in form, followed by the issuance of an administrative order (*Verfügung*). Hence, on both the federal and on the cantonal level, the *administrative order* is the most important form and instrument of administrative action, which is influenced by French and German administrative law, especially by the theory of the *acte administratif*. The FAPA focuses exclusively on *administrative orders as a prototype form of administrative action* (Article 5 of the Administrative Procedure Act). An appeal before the Federal Administrative Court is only available against administrative orders based upon federal public law (Article 31 of the Federal Administrative Court Act).

739. Hence, the definition of an administrative order is crucial to Swiss administrative law – as it was in Germany in the late 1960s before the introduction of the theory of subjective public rights (*subjektive öffentliche Rechte*). According to Article 5 of the FAPA, administrative orders are decisions of the authorities in individual cases that are based on the public law of the Confederation and have as their subject matter the following: (a) the establishment, amendment or withdrawal of rights or obligations; (b) a finding of the existence, non-existence or extent of rights or obligations; or (c) the rejection of applications for the establishment, amendment, withdrawal or finding of rights or obligations, or the dismissal of such applications without entering into the substance of the case. Article 5(2) of the FAPA places the following forms of administrative actions on equal footing with administrative orders: enforcement measures (Article 41(1)(a) and (b) FAPA), interim orders (Article 45 FAPA), decisions on objections (Articles 30(2)(b), 46(b) and 74(b) FAPA), appeal decisions (Articles 61 and 70 FAPA), decisions in a review (Article 68 FAPA) and on explanatory statements (Article 69 FAPA). According to Article 5(3) of the Administrative Procedure Act, an administrative order is not required if (a) it is *excluded* by statute; or (b) the statute entitles the agency to *act in another form*, e.g., in the form of a public contract (Article 49(c) of the Federal Expropriation Act [SR 511] or Articles 16(2) and 19 of the Federal Subsidy Act [SR 616.1]).

740. The administrative order as defined above is a *final and unilateral decision.* The requirement that the agency give its order unilaterally does not imply that the agency can take its decision without the participation of the concerned individual(s). On the contrary, the parties have a set of multiple participatory rights at hand (Articles 18, 26, 29, 31 and 33(1) of the FAPA). However, the power to make a unilateral decision means that the agency is authorized to issue an administrative order regardless of the parties' approval. Furthermore, the unilateral decision-making power is dogmatically necessary to distinguish the administrative order from contracts based upon public or private law.

741. The administrative order is a unilateral decision in *an individual and concrete case.* From a dogmatic perspective, this element is necessary to distinguish the administrative order from *rules*. The administrative order determines the rights and duties of a single addressee or a determined and limited number of addressees, whereas rules are *general*, binding on everyone. Furthermore, the administrative order deals with a *concrete* set of facts that has already occurred in a determined place and in a determined time, whereas rules are abstract, applying to an indeterminable, and yet virtually limitless number of facts.

742. The administrative order determines the *legal relationship* between the addressee(s) and the administration with binding (i.e., executory) force. The content of the legal relationship determines the creation, modification or termination of rights and duties. The *element of binding legal force* of administrative orders is dogmatically necessary to distinguish the administrative order from the *actus realis*, which is *merely factual*, lacking a legal relationship between the addressee(s) and the administration (e.g., recommendations, cautions, declarations of intent, reports and other administrative forms of communication and information).

743. Of course, the administration also has the possibility to act in other forms, such as by concluding public contracts, which are bilateral agreements between at least two legal subjects in order to create a concrete administrative relationship based upon public law. The provisions concerning the creation of contracts of the Code of Obligations are applicable *per analogiam*; there are no special or formal requirements and the FAPA is not applicable. However, public contracts are only admissible in cases where the use of an administrative order is inadequate. Hence, public contracts are *subsidiary* to administrative orders and – in comparison to administrative orders – rather rare in practice. Other forms of administrative action, such as an *administrative plan* or an *actus realis*, are not mentioned by the FAPA (although they are important in practice). The emergence of new forms of administrative action, such as *cooperative informal action* as a particularly important derivate and form of the *actus realis,* e.g., gentlemen's agreements or arrangements between the administration and the addressee(s), is still a dogmatically unexplored area in administrative law (*see* for such cooperative agreements, e.g., Articles 29–30 and 37 of the Federal Antitrust Act [SR 251] or Article 41a of the Federal Environmental Protection Act [SR 814.01]). One main problem of practical importance connected with the emergence of new forms of administrative action is the inadequacy of judicial protection. Nevertheless, note that the addressee of an administrative action, e.g., an *actus realis* (which is not an administrative order), can always demand the issuance of an administrative declaration, which is analogous to an administrative order and thus appealable before judicial authorities. Article 25a of the FAPA, in force since 1 January 2007, states that anyone who has an interest that is worthy of protection may request from the authority (i.e., responsible for acts that are based on federal public law and which affect rights or obligations) that it: (a) refrains from, discontinues or revokes unlawful acts; (b) rectifies the consequences of unlawful acts; or (c) confirms the illegality of such acts. In these cases, the authority shall decide by way of an administrative order.

§3. Judicial Control of Administrative Action

I. Introduction

744. As a rule, *federal* administrative orders are reviewed by the Federal Administrative Court as Court of First Instance and by the Federal Supreme Court as Court of Appeal and last resort on the domestic level (so-called principle of 'double instance').

745. Derogations from this institutional two-tier model of judicial review must have a clear legal basis in a federal statute. These exceptions are mostly listed in the Federal Administrative Court Act and the Federal Supreme Court Act and are the following:

- *Federal Administrative Court as court of first and last resort*: Matters for which the Federal Administrative Court is exclusively competent, cannot be appealed before the Federal Supreme Court (*see*, e.g., in the area of asylum law Article 83(d) of the Federal Supreme Court Act). It should be noted however, that a revision of the Federal Supreme Court Act is currently underway circumcising the exclusive competence of the Federal Administrative Court in most fields of law considerably. This revision allows an appeal before the Federal Supreme Court against decisions of the Federal Administrative Court in cases which raise a legal question of fundamental significance ('Rechtsfrage von grundsätzlicher Bedeutung') or which are of particular importance ('besonders bedeutsam').
- *Federal Criminal Court as Court of First Instance*: Federal administrative orders in the field of mutual legal assistance in criminal matters must be appealed before the Federal Criminal Court (Article 37(2)(2) of the Federal Act of 19 March 2010 concerning the Organization of the Criminal Authorities of the Confederation

[SR 173.71]) and subsequently – but only if a question of considerable importance is at stake – before the Federal Supreme Court (Article 84 of the Federal Supreme Court Act).

- *Requirement of a preliminary appeal procedure before an administrative body*: In some branches of the federal administration, namely where a great number of administrative orders are issued (so-called mass procedures), e.g., in the area of taxation, the federal statutes may prescribe that the addressee of an administrative order must file an objection (*Einsprache*) before the agency that has issued the decision. Alternatively, the law may also prescribe that the addressee files an appeal before the directly superior administrative body (*verwaltungsinterne Beschwerde*), e.g., in the field of custom duties. In both cases, after the termination of the preliminary procedure, the matter may be appealed to the Federal Administrative Court and subsequently (if not excluded by law) to the Federal Supreme Court.
- *Administrative orders of the Federal Council*: These orders are generally final (Article 32 (1)(d–f) and (h) of the Federal Administrative Court Act).
- *Political character of the case*: In some rare cases (Article 32(1)(a) and (c) of the Federal Administrative Court Act), mostly regarding external affairs, the order must be appealed before the Federal Council who decides as last instance. Federal administrative orders regarding political participation, popular elections and popular votations (Article 32(1)(b) of the Federal Administrative Court Act) must be directly appealed to the Federal Supreme Court.
- *Judicial authorities as Court of First Instance replacing the Federal Administrative Court*: In some cases, namely in the field of social security law, a federal administrative order must be appealed to a cantonal judicial authority, which replaces the Federal Administrative Court (Article 32(2)(b) of the Federal Administrative Court). The cantonal decision can be appealed to the Federal Supreme Court. The same principle applies in the field of broadcast and telecommunication law, where the Independent Instance of Appeal replaces the Federal Administrative Court (Article 32(1)(g) of the Federal Administrative Court Act).

746. On the *cantonal level*, the principle of 'double instance' applies as well. The cantons are free to go beyond that minimum requirement in order to optimize their system of judicial protection against administrative actions and create preliminary appeal procedures before an administrative body (which are common in most cantons) or further judicial authorities. However, since all cantonal decisions usually can be appealed to the Federal Supreme Court, the cantonal authority of last resort must be a court in the meaning of Article 6(1) of the ECHR (Article 191b of the Constitution and Article 86(2) of the Federal Supreme Court Act). The remedies of the Federal Supreme Court – i.e., the appeal in public law matters and the constitutional appeal – are only available against decisions of judicial authorities. Exceptionally, the cantons may derogate from that requirement and create non-judicial bodies for cases with a preponderant political character (*supra* Part II, Chapter 5, §2 II C 3; Article 86(2) of the Federal Supreme Court Act). These cases are very rare – and must be kept rare – because they place the Federal Supreme Court in the uncomfortable position of

reviewing a case in which no previous judicial authority has determined and reviewed the facts of the case. Such situations are hardly compatible with the principle aim of the reform of the judiciary: To discharge the highest court of Switzerland from tasks which are usually fulfilled by lower courts. Note that in some very rare cases, cantonal decisions of last resort must be appealed before the Federal Administrative Court (instead of the Federal Supreme Court), e.g., in the area of agricultural subventions (Article 166(2) of the Federal Agriculture Act; SR 910.1).

747. The following section will focus only on the most important remedies against administrative action in daily Swiss constitutional and administrative practices: Appeal to the Federal Administrative Court, appeal in public law matters and the constitutional appeal to the Federal Supreme Court. In Swiss administrative law, these remedies are called 'formal remedies' (*förmliche Rechtsmittel*) because they confer to the individual a right to have his/her case be decided by a judicial authority if certain forms, conditions and the relevant statute of limitation are observed. Alternatively, the cantonal administrative procedure acts and the Federal Procedure Act foresee 'informal legal instruments' (*Rechtsbehelfe*) as well, which usually do not oblige the authorities to decide and which are not bound to certain forms, conditions or to a statute of limitation. With a *supervisory complaint* (*Aufsichtsanzeige/Aufsichtsbeschwerde*) an individual notifies to the hierarchically superior administrative authority that some action, omission, practice or behaviour of the deciding agency must be controlled or supervised. With the *request for reconsideration* (*Wiedererwägung*), an addressee of an administrative order petitions the agency in writing to reconsider ('have second thoughts on') its decision and to change it or to declare it null and void. In practice, the request for reconsideration plays a considerable role in situations where an administrative order has already entered into force but suffers from an original or subsequent error (e.g., relevant evidence has not been observed at the issuance of the administrative order or plaintiff produces new relevant evidence that was not available at the issuance of the administrative order). Here, the request for reconsideration switches from an informal legal instrument to a so-called extraordinary remedy and confers to the individual the right to have his/her administrative order revised.

II. The Control of Administrative Action Before the Federal Administrative Court

A. Overview

748. The Federal Administrative Court Act of 17 June 2005 (SR 173.32) contains the relevant provisions regarding the organizational structure of the Federal Administrative Court, the position of the judges, the jurisdiction of the Court, and the available remedies. Unless the Act provides otherwise, the procedure before the Court is mainly governed by the FAPA (Article 37 of the Federal Administrative Court Act). The plaintiff has the possibility to appeal an administrative order (Articles 44 et seq. FAPA), to file a complaint (Article 44 of the Federal Administrative Court Act), to ask for a revision (Articles 45 et seq. of the Federal Administrative Court Act) or to ask for an explanation or correction of the Court's ruling (Article 48 of the Federal Administrative

Court Act). The appeal is by far the most important and common remedy: According to the statistical report, in 2015, the Federal Administrative Court decided 7,625 appeals, 3 complaints and 116 revisions. Therefore, the following short presentation will focus on appeals only.

B. The Appeal

749. The appeal before the Federal Administrative Court can be characterized as a formal remedy with suspensive effect directed against administrative orders issued by a federal authority that have not entered into force yet. The appeal is also called a 'complete' remedy, because the Federal Administrative Court may review all factual, legal and discretionary aspects of the administrative order for violations of *federal law* (e.g., false or incomplete findings of fact; false, incomplete or invalid conclusions of substantive law or procedural rules; the excess, abuse, or omission of administrative discretion). The appeal proceeding is governed by several principles:

- The inquisitory principle (*Untersuchungsmaxime*) is set out in Article 12 FAPA, according to which the authority shall establish the relevant facts ex officio. Of course, owing to the broad and heterogeneous jurisdiction *ratione materiae* of the Federal Administrative Court (e.g., cases concerning asylum, custom duties, taxation, social security, agriculture, antitrust, etc.), it is impossible to define a qualitative and quantitative common standard regarding the extent of judicial fact-finding. However, as a rule of thumb, it could be observed that the Federal Administrative Court will usually not review the facts de novo, unless particular circumstances call for an independent judicial fact-finding; rather, the Court will correct or complete the factual record. The judicial exercise of this power may vary in intensity, depending largely on the nature of the case and whether the Federal Administrative Court acts as the court of last resort. The consequence of this 'relativisation' of the inquisitory principle is that the parties must take an active role in the appeal proceeding by collaborating in the establishment of the relevant facts (Article 13 FAPA). At any stage of the appeal proceeding, relevant evidence may be brought forward by the parties and be considered by the Court (Article 32(2) FAPA). Furthermore, in their own interest, the parties must motivate their appeal petition 'with details of the evidence' (Article 52(1) FAPA).
- The principle of party disposition (*Dispositionsmaxime*) confers to the parties (i.e., the concerned individual or the agency) the right to determine the matter in dispute (*Streitgegenstand*) before the Federal Administrative Court. According to Article 62 FAPA, the Court may amend the contested administrative order in favour of a party. But it may also amend the contested administrative order *to the prejudice of a party* (*ire ultra petitum*), provided the administrative order violates federal law or is based on an incorrect or incomplete determination of the facts of the case (the contested administrative order may not be amended to the prejudice of a party on the grounds that it is inappropriate, other than in the case of an amendment in favour of a respondent). If the Federal Administrative Court intends to amend the contested administrative order to the prejudice of a party, it must

notify the party of this intention and grant the right to be heard (*supra* Part IV, Chapter 2, §6 II B).

- The procedure before the Federal Administrative Court is characterized by the principle of *iura novit curia* ('the court knows the law'). In contrast to Anglo-Saxon tradition, the parties do not need to plead or prove the law that applies to their case. It is the Court's sole responsibility to interpret and apply knowledgeably and correctly the legal provision(s) to a particular case. Hence, in no event is the Federal Administrative Court bound by the party's legal arguments (Article 64(4) FAPA). The principle of *iura novit curia* does not oblige the Federal Administrative Court to take into account all imaginable legal arguments, which have not been expressly raised by the parties or by the lower federal instance. In practice, the Court will raise new legal questions on its own initiative if the factual record of a case obviously requires it (or – paraphrasing a Decision of the Federal Supreme Court BGE 119 V 349 paragraph 1a – if the necessity to examine the new legal question 'catches one's eye' ['in die Augen springen']).
- In appeal proceedings before the Federal Administrative Court, the official language used in the contested administrative order determines the language before the Court. If the parties use a different official language, the proceedings may be conducted in this language (Article 33a(2) FAPA).

750. As a general principle, any administrative order may be subject to an appeal before the Federal Administrative Court (Article 31 of the Federal Administrative Court Act in conjunction with Article 44 FAPA). The Federal Administrative Act contains procedural restrictions regarding separately notified interim administrative orders: An appeal is permitted against separately notified interim administrative orders *on jurisdiction and on requests for recusal*. However, these court rulings may not be contested at a later date (Article 45 FAPA). An appeal is permitted against *other* separately notified interim administrative orders (1) if they may cause a non-redressable prejudice; or (2) if granting the appeal would immediately bring about a final decision and thus would obviate significant expenditure in time or money. If an appeal under point (1) is not permitted or if such right of appeal has not been exercised, the interim orders concerned shall be contestable by appeal together with the final administrative order, provided they have an effect on the content of the final ruling of the Court (Article 45 FAPA). Finally, an appeal before the Federal Administrative Court may be filed against the unlawful refusal of or delay in issuing an administrative order (Article 46a FAPA).

751. General standing is accorded to anyone who (1) has participated or has been refused the opportunity to participate in proceedings before the lower instance; (2) has been specifically affected by the contested administrative order; and (3) has an interest that is worthy of protection in the revocation or amendment of the administrative order (*see* Article 48(1) FAPA). Furthermore, persons, organizations and authorities who are explicitly granted standing by another federal act shall also be entitled to appeal (*see* Article 48(2) FAPA).

752. According to Article 49 FAPA, in the appeal, the appellant may contend that (1) there has been a violation of federal law (including the excess or abuse of discretionary powers); (2) there has been an incorrect or incomplete determination of the legally relevant facts of the case; or (3) the administrative order is inappropriate (however, in very rare cases, a plea of inappropriateness is inadmissible if a cantonal authority has already reviewed the order as the appellate authority).

753. As a general rule, an appeal must be filed with the Federal Administrative Court within thirty days after the issuance of an administrative order. However, an appeal may be filed at any time against the unlawful refusal of or delay in issuing an administrative order (Article 50 FAPA).

754. The content and form of the appeal petition must fulfil the requirements set out in Article 52 FAPA: The appeal petition must contain the application, the grounds for appeal with details of the evidence and the signature of the appellant or his/her legal counsel; the official copy of the contested administrative order and documents cited as evidence must be attached, provided they are in the appellant's possession. If the appeal fails to satisfy these requirements, or if the application made by the appellant lacks the required clarity (but the appeal is not clearly inadmissible), the Federal Administrative Court shall grant the appellant a short additional period to revise the appeal petition. It shall at the same time notify the appellant that if there is no response within the additional period, it shall be decided on the basis of the case files or, in the absence of an application, grounds or a signature, to declare the appeal inadmissible.

755. As a general rule, an appeal before the Federal Administrative Court has a suspensive effect on the administrative order (Article 55(1) FAPA). This aspect of the appeal can be crucial because the administrative order cannot be executed during the suspension period. However, if the administrative order does *not* relate to the payment of money, the lower administrative instance may revoke the suspensive effect (Article 55(2) FAPA). It is in the discretion of the president or the instructing judge of the Federal Administrative Court to reinstate the suspensive effect revoked by the lower instance; an application for the reinstatement of the suspensive effect must be decided immediately (Article 55(3) FAPA). If the suspensive effect is revoked in an arbitrary manner (*supra* Part IV, Chapter 2, §2 II) or an application for the reinstatement of the suspensive effect is arbitrarily not granted or granted late, the public corporation or autonomous institution on whose behalf the authority has issued the administrative order shall be liable for any loss or damage incurred thereby (Article 55(4) FAPA). Note that provisions of other federal acts under which an appeal does not have a suspensive effect may apply (Article 55(5) FAPA).

III. The Control of Administrative Action Before the Federal Supreme Court

A. *Overview*

756. With the entry into force of the Reform of the Judiciary on 1 January 2007 (*supra* General Introduction, Chapter 2, §4), the system of judicial protection against administrative action before the Federal Supreme Court has been radically simplified. In a nutshell, the plaintiff has the following options: to appeal a case, to file a complaint, to demand a revision, or to ask for an explanation or correction of the Court's ruling.

757. In public law matters, the Federal Supreme Court Act distinguishes between situations, where an inferior cantonal or federal instance, which in the majority of cases is a judicial authority in the sense of Article 6 of the ECHR, *has issued a decision* against which the plaintiff wishes to appeal to the Federal Supreme Court (*Beschwerdeverfahren*) in the form of an appeal in public law matters (as the principle remedy; Articles 82 et seq. of the Federal Supreme Court) and/or a constitutional appeal (as the subsidiary remedy; Articles 113–119 of the Federal Supreme Court). However, appeals are excluded in circumstances where an authority *has not decided yet* (e.g., because of conflicts of competence between federal and cantonal authorities); here, the relevant remedy for the resolution of these controversies is the complaint (*Klageverfahren*; Article 120 of the Federal Supreme Court Act). Apart from these formal remedies – the appeal and the complaint – the plaintiff may also demand a revision of his/her case, which has been already decided by the Federal Supreme Court (e.g., in the event that the European Court for Human Rights has overruled the case and held for appellant, or if new facts are discovered, which would change the outcome of the Federal Supreme Court's ruling; Articles 121 et seq. of the Federal Supreme Court Act). Finally, if the ruling (*Dispositiv*) of the Court is, for example, unclear, incomplete, ambiguous or contains calculation errors, the plaintiff may demand an explanation (*Erläuterung*) and correction (*Berichtigung*) of the ruling (Article 129 of the Federal Supreme Court Act).

758. In constitutional litigation, appeals in public law matters are by far the most important and common remedy before the Federal Supreme Court, followed by constitutional appeals. It should be noted that Federal Parliament is currently discussing the possibility to abolish the constitutional appeal as well. However, since no decision has been taken so far (and some important scholars strongly disagree with the project), this monograph will continue to present this remedy. According to the annual report of the Federal Supreme Court, in 2016, approximately 3,513 appeals in public law matters, 379 constitutional appeals, 2 complaints and 186 revisions were lodged with the Court. Due to their practical importance, the following presentation will exclusively focus on appeals.

B. The Distinction Between Appeals in Public Law Matters and Constitutional Appeals

759. Appeal in public law matters and constitutional appeals have a lot of features in common:

- In cases before the Federal Supreme Court, where the appellant claims a violation of fundamental rights (and constitutional rights), the principle of *iura novit curia* is restricted insofar as the appellant must explicitly name the fundamental rights at stake and set forth in a concise and thorough manner *to what extent* they have been violated by the decision of the previous instance (so-called *Rügeprinzip*, *see* Article 106(2) of the Federal Supreme Court Act). In most appeals regarding the violation of fundamental rights this strict standard of pleading, as required by the Federal Supreme Court, is difficult to meet.

- Appeals in public law matters and constitutional appeals generally do not have suspensive effect (Article 103 of the Federal Supreme Court Act) in order to make frivolous appeals less attractive (Decision of the Federal Supreme Court 4A_116/2007 of 26 June 2007 paragraph 2). This implies that the decision of the lower court appealed to the Federal Supreme Court, may be executed unless the presiding judge orders the suspensive effect (this order is final, *see* Article 32(3) of the Federal Supreme Court Act, but may be reconsidered by the presiding judge in the event that the circumstances have changed in relevant aspects).
- In both forms of appeal, the Federal Supreme Court has not only the power to quash the decision of the previous instance but also to decide the case on the merits (Article 107(2) of the Federal Supreme Court Act). In practice, however, the Court will usually quash the decision and remand it to the previous instance for reappraisal.
- Finally, the rules of procedure regarding appeals in public law matters are applicable *per analogiam* to constitutional appeals (Article 117 of the Federal Supreme Court Act), e.g., concerning the type of decisions subject to appeal (Articles 90–94 of the Federal Supreme Court Act), the statute of limitation (Article 100 of the Federal Supreme Court Act), other forms of interim relief (Article 104 of the Federal Supreme Court Act), simplified procedures (Article 108–109 of the Federal Supreme Court Act), and the miscellaneous procedural prerequisites, which the cantons must fulfil (Articles 110–112 of the Federal Supreme Court Act).

760. Appeals in public law matters and constitutional appeals also differ in various ways:

- If the requirements are met, a constitutional appeal is only available against *certain cantonal decisions* of previous cantonal instances (Article 113 of the Federal Supreme Court Act). All other decisions and legislative acts must be challenged with an appeal in public law matters.
- A constitutional appeal can only be invoked for the violation of *constitutional rights* (*supra* Part IV, Chapter 2, §1 I). Errors in the determinations of the relevant facts committed by the lower court can only be corrected before the Federal Supreme Court if (and only if) fundamental rights have been violated (Article 118 of the Federal Supreme Court Act). In contrast, the appeal in public law matters is available against *any violation of federal (constitutional) law* (Article 95(a) of the Federal Supreme Court Act), of international public law (Article 95(b) of the Federal Supreme Court Act), of cantonal constitutional rights (Article 95(c) of the Federal Supreme Court Act), of cantonal provisions regarding the citizens' political right to vote and regarding popular elections and votes (Article 95(d) of the Federal Supreme Court Act) and of inter-cantonal law (Article 95(e) of the Federal Supreme Court Act).
- As set out below, the rules regarding standing for appeals in public law matters and constitutional appeals differ fundamentally from each other.
- Finally, an appeal in public law matters is generally available for authorities; here, standing is granted by another federal act (Article 89(2)(d) of the Federal

Supreme Court Act). In contrast, authorities usually have no general standing to invoke constitutional appeals.

761. The distinction between the scope of application of appeals in public law matters and of constitutional appeals can be very complex in practice (and cannot be depicted here in full detail). However, many problems can be avoided if the following guidelines are observed:

(1) A constitutional appeal is never available against decisions of a *federal* lower court; furthermore, an abstract control of *legislative acts* is excluded. In both cases, an appeal in public law matters might be available, if the other procedural requirements are fulfilled. Note that an appeal in public law matters is also excluded against certain federal decisions, mainly in the area of asylum and international mutual administrative assistance (Article 83(d) and 83(h) of the Federal Supreme Court Act).
(2) Hence, the distinction between the scope of application of appeals in public law matters and constitutional appeals only poses problems regarding *cantonal decisions in public law matters* of lower cantonal instances (usually a court in the sense of Article 6 of the ECHR). If the cantonal decision does not concern *public law*, an appeal in civil law matters (Articles 72 et seq. of the Federal Supreme Court Act) or in criminal law matters (Articles 78 et seq. of the Federal Supreme Court Act) might be available.
(3) In a further step, it must be analysed whether the cantonal decision concerns an issue regarding public procurement law, public employment law or public torts law. In these three areas, the Federal Supreme Court Act sets a minimum level on the amount in dispute (e.g., CHF 8.7 million for works in public procurement cases). If in a given case the amount in dispute exceeds those limits (*see* Articles 83(f) and 85(1) of the Federal Supreme Court Act), an appeal in public law matters is available, provided that all other procedural requirements are met. If the amount in dispute is below those minimum levels, it must be examined whether the case raises a fundamental question of law (*see* Articles 83(f)(2) and 85(2) of the Federal Supreme Court Act). The Court usually admits the presence of a fundamental question of law only under very restricted conditions (e.g., if the resolution of the question contributes to the uniform application of the law throughout the Confederation).
(4) The appellant must anticipate and conclusively detail why his/her cases raises a fundamental question of law. In doing so, the plaintiff must appeal in the forms of both available remedies. If the Court affirms the presence of a fundamental question of law, it will admit the appeal in public law matters. However, the chances of success are relatively low (*see*, *inter alia*, Decision of the Federal Supreme Court BGE 133 III 493 paragraph 1.1 ['de manière restrictive']). If the Court denies a fundamental question of law, which is very likely in practice, it will permit a constitutional appeal.
(5) Article 83 of the Federal Supreme Court Act contains an exemption list, which excludes appeals in public law matters (but not constitutional appeals). As set out above, certain decisions – mainly of the Federal Administrative Court – cannot

be appealed to the Federal Supreme Court. However, if international public law confers an entitlement, an appeal in public law matters may again be available, for example, in cases regarding national security and residence permits for foreigners (Articles 83(a) and 83(b)(2) of the Federal Supreme Court Act). Certain areas of law listed in Article 83 of the Federal Supreme Court Act may also concern *cantonal decisions*, especially regarding the ordinary procedure for the naturalization of foreigners, gender equality cases without pecuniary interest, exams, etc. Here, a constitutional appeal may be available, if the other procedural requirements are fulfilled.

C. *Procedural Requirements and Effects of the Appeals*

1. Objects of Litigation

762. According to Article 82 of the Federal Supreme Court Act, the following decisions, acts or actions, based on public law, can be the object of litigation for an appeal in public law matters.

763. Final, partial or interim decisions based on public law (Article 82(a) of the Federal Supreme Court Act). The term 'decision' is usually understood as the authoritative and unilateral result of law-application in an individual and concrete case. For the definition of the various types of decisions *see* Articles 90–93 of the Federal Supreme Court Act, whereby Article 94 of the Federal Supreme Court Act states that the illegal refusal or delaying of a decision by the lower court is analogous to a 'decision' and can be appealed before the Federal Supreme Court. Use zoning plans (*Nutzungsplan*) are subject to appeals in public law matters (Article 34(1) of the Federal Spatial Planning Act (SR 700). In contrast, development plans (*Richtplan*) do not confer rights and duties to individuals and are thereby generally excluded from the scope of application of appeals in public law matters. Municipalities though have standing to defend their autonomy against development plans. However, individuals may, by challenging a use zoning plan, demand that the Court rules in a preliminary preceding on the conformity with regard to federal law of regional development plans (Decision of the Federal Supreme Court BGE 107 Ia 77 paragraph 3). In the majority of cases, the decision being challenged before the Federal Supreme Court is a judgment of a lower court. The question whether a decision is based upon public, private or criminal law can be complex. The decisive factor is which area of law *prevails* in the concrete case. Additionally, the Federal Supreme Court Act contains in Article 72(2)(b) a list of decisions, which are – from a strictly dogmatic perspective – based upon public law, but which are – owing to their close nexus to private law and for reasons of practicability – classified as appeals in civil law matters.

764. Acts of the cantons (Article 82(b) of the Federal Supreme Court Act). In this context, the term 'act' means general and abstract, infra-constitutional rules, based on cantonal law, usually in the form of a statute, ordinance, decree or regulation, which confer rights and/or duties to an indeterminable number of individuals and apply to a multitude of fact-patterns. Hence, the appeal in public law matters is not available against cantonal acts, which do not cause external effects by directly affecting the legal position of the citizens (e.g., internal administrative ordinances). Acts are not decisions; thus the exemption list in Article 83 of the Federal Supreme Court Act does not apply. If a cantonal act is challenged before the Federal Supreme Court, the act will be reviewed in the abstract mode (*abstrakte Normenkontrolle; supra* Part IV, Chapter 2, §7). In the event that the act at stake has been totally amended, all provisions thereof may be reviewed by the Court. Following to partial amendments, the newly introduced provisions are subject to judicial review including those provisions, which have not been altered by the amendment, but may have changed their meaning in the new context (Decision of the Federal Supreme Court BGE 135 I 28 paragraph 3.1.1). In an appeal in public law matters, the Federal Supreme Court will grant *virtual standing* only if appellant can make plausible case that he/she could be (with a minimum of probability) a future addressee of the provision, which is in his/her view unconstitutional (Decision of the Federal Supreme Court BGE 133 I 206 paragraph 2.1). If the Court reviews a cantonal statute in the abstract mode, the statute will only be declared unconstitutional if an interpretation in conformity with the Constitution is hardly imaginable (Decision of the Federal Supreme Court BGE 130 I 82 paragraph 2.1). The abstract review of constitutionality includes all possible reasons and circumstances (and is not only limited to the special fact-pattern of the case presented to the Court). Note that the abstract control of cantonal acts is not a back door for a preliminary control of federal laws. Federal laws are immunized from judicial control (Article 190 of the Constitution). Cantonal act may also be immunized from judicial review if they merely and purely implement federal laws (Decision of the Federal Supreme Court BGE 136 I 49 paragraph 3).

765. Actions concerning political rights (Article 82(c) of the Federal Supreme Court Act). Here, the object of litigation includes any action – regardless if authoritative (e.g., administrative orders) or informal (e.g., an *actus realis* in the preparation of an election or vote) – regarding any possible violation of the citizens' political right to vote and regarding popular elections and votes. According to Article 88(1)(b) of the Federal Supreme Court Act, only administrative orders of the Federal Chancellery and decisions of cantonal governments can be appealed before the Federal Supreme Court. This rule is specified by the Federal Act on Political Rights of 17 December 1976 (FAPR; SR 161.1), according to which the Federal Chancellery can issue the following administrative orders: (1) whether a request for a popular referendum or for a referendum requested by the cantons has been successful (Articles 66 and 67b FAPR); (2) whether the preliminary control of a popular initiative has shown that the initiative corresponds to the forms prescribed by the law (Article 69 FAPR); (3) whether a new political party fulfils the requirements to enter the Register of Political Parties (Article 76a FAPR). Regarding decisions of cantonal governments, the Federal Act on Political Rights states in Article 77 that an appeal may be filed with the cantonal government for (1) a violation of the provisions on voting rights (appeal on a matter related to voting rights); (2) irregularities at popular votes (appeal on a matter related to popular votes); (3) irregularities in the preparation for and conduct of elections to the National Council (appeal on a matter related to elections). The appeal must be filed by registered mail within three days of the grounds for appeal being ascertained, and at the latest on the third day following publication of the results in the official cantonal gazette. Subsequently, the cantonal government shall issue a decision on an appeal within ten days of receipt of the appeal petition. If the cantonal government establishes, whether on the basis of the appeal or in the course of its own duties, that there have been irregularities, it shall issue the orders required to remedy the deficiencies established, if possible prior to the conclusion of the election or popular vote procedure. Furthermore, the cantonal government shall reject any appeals on matters relating to popular votes or elections without conducting a detailed investigation if the irregularities complained of are not sufficient either in their nature or in their extent to have a material influence on the result of the vote as a whole. As set out above, the decision of the cantonal government can be appealed to the Federal Supreme Court (Article 80 FAPR). The Federal Act on Political Rights contains a lacuna regarding the question whether appellants can challenge the regularity of *results* of *national* votes. The Federal Supreme Court held that such appeals must be directly lodged in with the Court (based on Articles 29a and 34 of the Constitution). Finally, note that political acts and actions of the Federal Assembly and the Federal Council cannot be appealed before the Federal Supreme Court (Article 189(4) of the Federal Constitution).

766. Constitutional appeals are only available against final, partial or interim decisions based on public law issued by a lower *cantonal* instance (usually a court in the sense of Article 6 of the ECHR).

2. Grounds for Action

767. As set out above, an appeal in public law matters is available against *any violation of federal (constitutional) law* (Article 95(a) of the Federal Supreme Court Act) and the violation of international public law (Article 95(b) of the Federal Supreme Court Act). Note that the term 'federal law' includes federal constitutional law as well.

768. As a general rule, in order to preserve cantonal autonomy, a violation of the correct application of cantonal law cannot be appealed before the Federal Supreme Court, unless a violation of federal law and international public law can be demonstrated by the appellant. However, the Federal Supreme Court Act contains three exceptions: The appeal in public law matters is nevertheless available against the violation of cantonal constitutional rights (Article 95(c) of the Federal Supreme Court Act), the violation of cantonal provisions regarding the citizens' political right to vote and regarding popular elections and votes (Article 95(d) of the Federal Supreme Court Act) and the violation of inter-cantonal law (Article 95(e) of the Federal Supreme Court Act).

769. The grounds for constitutional appeals are narrowly defined. A constitutional appeal can only be filed for the violation of *constitutional rights* (*supra* Part IV, Chapter 2, §1 I; Article 116 of the Federal Supreme Court Act).

3. General Standing

770. Standing is of significant importance in constitutional litigation before the Federal Supreme Court because it addresses the question of whether a party has a sufficient interest to obtain judicial resolution of his/her case. If not, the Court will dismiss the case on formal grounds. A distinction must be drawn between general standing and special standing. Whereas general standing is only granted by the Court if the appellant can demonstrate a sufficiently grounded interest as defined by the Federal Supreme Court Act, special standing confers per se a right to appeal.

771. According to Article 89(1) of the Federal Supreme Court Act, a party has standing to appeal in public law matters if the party (1) has participated in or has been refused the opportunity to participate in proceedings before the lower instance, (2) has been *specifically affected* by the challenged decision or legislative act; and (3) has an *interest that is worthy of protection* in the revocation or amendment of the decision or the legislative act. The interest to be protected by the Court may be based upon *legal* grounds or – contrary to the standing requirement for a constitutional appeal – be merely *factual* (e.g., economic or ideal interests). The appeal in public law matters is not an *actio popularis*; therefore, a general public interest is not sufficient (Decisions of the Federal Supreme Court BGE 136 II 281 paragraph 2.3.1; BGE 137 II 40 paragraph 2.3).

772. Since the presence of a legitimate factual interest to be protected by the Court is sufficient for standing, third parties may take action against an administrative order as well, if their relationship to the administrative order at stake is *special, remarkable, and sufficiently close* (*besondere Beziehungsnähe*). As usual in such situations, questions regarding the standing of third parties with interests adverse to those of the addressee of an administrative order can be very complex in practice, especially in the field of spatial planning and construction law or appeals of competitors (*Konkurrentenbeschwerden*); the case law of the Federal Supreme Court cannot be depicted here without a thorough presentation of the infra-constitutional provisions of the areas of law concerned (for leading cases *see* the Decisions of the Federal Supreme Court BGE 125 I 7 paragraph 3d-g; BGE 127 II 264 paragraph 2).

773. In an appeal in public law matters against a cantonal act (Article 82(b) of the Federal Supreme Court Act), *virtual standing* is sufficient and available if the appellant can demonstrate that he/she might be (with a minimum of probability) a future addressee of the provision that is in his/her view unconstitutional.

774. Any person, who is eligible to vote, may lodge an appeal in public law matters regarding the violation of political rights with the Federal Supreme Court (Article 82(c) of the Federal Supreme Court Act), even if a specific personal interest in the outcome of the case is lacking (Article 89(3) of the Federal Supreme Court Act; Decisions of the Federal Supreme Court BGE 134 I 172 paragraph 1.3.3; BGE 136 I 404 paragraph 1.1.1).

775. Associations may have standing as a party directly affected by an administrative order. In that case, the requirements listed above apply. Alternatively, associations may also have standing to appeal in the interest of their members (so-called egoistic standing). This is the case if the association possesses legal personality, the interests of all members or a considerable number of members are affected and if the preservation of the interests of the members are incorporated in the by-laws of the associations.

776. In contrast to appeals in public law matters, constitutional appeals have a much stricter standing regime because they require a *legally protected interest* (Article 115(b) of the Federal Supreme Court Act). As shown above, according to the case law of the Federal Supreme Court, *general fundamental rights* (such as the equal protection clause or the prohibition of arbitrariness) do not confer per se a legally protected interest because they are not linked to a specific scope of protection (e.g., economic freedom or the right to property). Consequently, the Court refuses to consider constitutional appeals that are solely grounded on these general fundamental rights for lack of standing, unless the party can demonstrate an entitlement derived from international public law (especially and above all the ECHR) or from sub-constitutional provisions. In public law, however, such provisions are rare. Hence, and not surprisingly, this case law of the Federal Supreme Court (reaffirmed in BGE 133 I 185), which has been established to avoid a congestion of the Court in the mid-1960s, is highly controversial among constitutional scholars. Since 2009, the newly introduced Article 15b of the Swiss Citizenship Act (SCA; SR 141.0) demands that reasons must be given in order to reject an application for naturalization. This provision led the Federal Supreme Court to modify its case law regarding standing in constitutional appeals in the field of ordinary naturalizations (Decision of the Federal Supreme Court BGE 138 I 305). The Court held that standing shall be granted to plaintiffs to invoke the violation of Articles 9 and 8(1) of the Constitution if the naturalization eligibility requirements according to federal and cantonal law are obviously met and the rejection of their applications is clearly untenable ('unhaltbar') and violates the equal protection clause ('rechtsungleich').

4. Special Standing

777. According to Article 89(2) of the Federal Supreme Court Act, some entities have the per se right to lodge in the public interest an appeal in public law matters (regardless of whether they have participated in or have been refused the opportunity to participate in proceedings before the lower instance, and whether they are *specifically affected* by the challenged decision or the act). Special standing is conferred to:

- *Federal authorities* (Article 89(2)(a) of the Federal Supreme Court Act; such as the Federal Chancellery or the competent federal department). Here, special standing before the Federal Supreme Court is granted in order to secure the uniform and correct application of federal law (Decision of the Federal Supreme Court BGE 135 II 338 paragraph 1.2.1).
- *Municipalities* (Article 89(2)(c) of the Federal Supreme Court Act). Here, special standing is conferred in order to allow the municipalities to defend their constitutional right to autonomy (Article 50 of the Constitution as a minimal standard or based on the respective cantonal constitution; *see* in tax matter, *inter alia*, Decision of the Federal Supreme Court BGE 134 I 303 paragraph 1.2).
- *Certain persons, organisations and authorities if granted by another federal statute* (Article 89(2)(d) of the Federal Supreme Court Act). In practice, special standing conferred to organizations (so-called ideal standing) plays an important role in Swiss constitutional litigation. Such organizations are, for example, national environmental organization, national cultural heritage organizations, national organizations regarding the rights of disabled persons, consumer protection organizations, etc.

778. In constitutional appeals, special standing is scarcely ever an issue. So far, Article 9(2*bis*) of the Federal Internal Market Act of 6 October 1995 (SR 943.02) confers to the Federal Competition Commission the right to challenge decisions of a lower cantonal court in cases regarding cantonal public procurement law that do not raise a fundamental question of law.

5. Statute of Limitation

779. As a general rule, an appeal in public law matters and/or a constitutional appeal against a decision of a court of lower instance must be filed before the Federal Supreme Court within thirty days (Article 100(1) and Article 117 of the Federal Supreme Court Act). The statute of limitations starts to run after the delivery of the complete official copy of the judgment to the parties. In some special cases, where a decision of a lower instance must be executed in a speedy manner, an appeal in public law matters must be filed within ten days (e.g., in the area of mutual legal assistance in criminal matters or in child abduction cases), within five days (e.g., against decisions of cantonal governments regarding federal votes), or even within three days (against decisions of cantonal governments regarding elections to the National Council). An appeal against the illegal refusal or delaying of a decision by a lower court can be filed to the Federal Supreme Court at any time (Article 100(7) of the Federal Supreme Court Act).

6. Effects of the Appeal

780. On the national level, the judgments of the Federal Supreme Court as the highest court of the Confederation are final and immediately enforceable (formal and material res judicata; Article 61 of the Federal Supreme Court Act). A revision of the judgment is only possible under very strict and narrowly defined circumstances (*see* Articles 121–122 of the Federal Supreme Court Act). Alternatively, on the international level, the plaintiff will most likely decide to appeal against the decision of the Federal Supreme Court to the European Court of Human Rights.

Part V. Specific Problems

Chapter 1. Neutrality and War, Treaty and Foreign Affairs Powers

§1. Neutrality

Selected Bibliography: Biaggini. Kommentar, Articles 54, 58, and 197 no. 1; Federal Department of Defence, Civil Protection and Sports (DDPS) in conjunction with the Federal Department of Foreign Affairs (DFA). *Swiss Neutrality*. 4th revised ed. Berne: 2004; Haller. *Swiss Constitution*, 71–73; Hottelier Michel. 'L'adhésion de la Suisse à l'Organisation des Nations-Unies: aspects constitutionnels'. In *Revue française de droit constitutionnel* 2002, 485 et seq.; Rhinow & Schefer, 706 (note 3533); Riklin Alois. Article 'Neutralität'. In *Historisches Lexikon der Schweiz* (online version of 9 November 2010 on: www.hls-dhs-dss.ch/textes/d/D16572.php); Riklin Alois. 'Die Neutralität der Schweiz'. In *Neues Handbuch der schweizerisches Aussenpolitik*, edited by Riklin Alois, Haug Hans & Probst Raymond. Bern/Stuttgart/Wien: Paul Haupt Publ., 1992; Riklin Alois. 'Funktionen der schweizerischen Neutralität'. In *Passé pluriel – Mélanges Ruffieux*. Fribourg: Editions universitaires, 1991, 361–394 et seq.; Unabhängige Expertenkommission Schweiz – Zweiter Weltkrieg (eds). *Die Schweiz, der Nationalsozialismus und der Zweite Weltkrieg*. Pendo: Zürich 2002.

781. Neutrality (from the Latin expression 'ne uter' – neither one nor the other) commonly denominates the non-participation in a war or wars between other states. The rights and duties of a neutral state are governed by the *law* of neutrality as laid down in the Hague Conventions of 1907. Beyond these obligations under international public law, neutrality *policy* encompasses all measures taken by a state in order to safeguard the effectiveness and credibility of its neutrality. The concept of neutrality dictates that Switzerland will not initiate a war or participate in any military aggression. Additionally, Switzerland shall remain neutral in all wars, independent of the parties involved, the place and time, and will not support any of the parties in the conflict. Through an adequately equipped army, Switzerland ensures its defence and aims to prevent a vacuum of power on its territory. The Constitution does not confine a special provision to neutrality, which is only referred to in Articles 173(1)(a) and 185(1) of the Constitution, according to which the Federal Parliament and the Federal Council shall take measures to safeguard the neutrality of Switzerland. For foreign scholars this might come as a surprise since Switzerland is so closely associated with neutrality. However, from a historical and constitutional perspective, permanent and armed neutrality, although an essential *maxim* of Swiss foreign and security policy, has never been a constitutional goal as such, but rather a pragmatic instrument (and not an unassailable dogma) among others enabling Switzerland to maintain the highest possible degree of liberty and independence. Hence, the Federal Diet of 1847 unequivocally refused to include maintenance of neutrality among the purposes of the Confederation on the grounds that 'neutrality is a means to an end; it is a political rule that appears at this time to be the most appropriate for ensuring Switzerland's independence', and that no one could know whether neutrality 'might not at some time have to be abandoned for the sake of that independence'. This is the reason why the drafters of the new Constitution – again and intentionally – refrained from mentioning neutrality in the General Provisions of the Constitution.

782. Neutrality is closely linked to the history of Switzerland and developed over the course of time. After a long tradition of warfare and mercenary service rendered to other countries and guided by the commonly shared idea of liberty and independence, Switzerland gradually adopted a policy of neutrality in order to avoid fragmentation and conflicting loyalties of its highly diverse population (for the historical background *see supra* General Introduction, Chapter 1, §2). Neutrality therefore served as a shield to take a reserved stance in foreign policy matters and to concentrate almost exclusively on domestic policy. According to Article 84 of the Vienna Final Act of 9 June 1815, the principle of a Swiss permanent neutrality received the approval and guarantee of the Powers. On 20 November 1815, Switzerland's perpetual neutrality was internationally recognized and guaranteed in the Treaty of Paris ('Déclaration des Puissances portant reconnaissance et garantie de la neutralité perpétuelle de la Suisse et de l'inviolabilité de son territoire'). Owing to Switzerland's geostrategic position between the North and South of the Continent and its function as a buffer zone between the Powers, the Treaty points out that Switzerland's 'neutrality and inviolability and independence of any foreign influence are to be considered as in the true interest of European policy'. Swiss neutrality was internationally reconfirmed several times after that, for example in the Treaty of Versailles on 28 June 1919, in the aftermath of World War I and in the London Declaration of 13 February 1920, where the League of Nations formally recognized it. During the Second Word War, neutral Switzerland was surrounded on all sides by the Axis ('the encircled hedgehog') and threatened in its territorial existence by a potential German invasion ('Operation Tannenbaum'). It managed to stay out of the war owing to its policy of integral neutrality, its deterrence strategy and resistance (the so-called National Redoubt, i.e., a nearly impregnable complex of fortifications cutting in case of an invasion the crucial north-to-south connection through the Swiss Alps; the mobilization of up to 450,000 men and women for national service) and the population's willingness to remain free and independent (by 1939, the National Front, a radical right-wing party, had only 2,300 members before it was banned in the following year). However, it is also true that Switzerland engaged, like other neutral states (e.g., Portugal and Sweden), in considerable economic cooperation with the Axis (e.g., raw materials, petroleum products and food for Switzerland, gold deals with the Reich and other trade with Holocaust assets), and the Allies as well. In their study of Swiss history, Clive H. Church and Randolph C. Head pointed out that 'outside opinion viewed the

Confederation's economic relations with the Reich not as necessary compromises to ensure survival, but as profiteering from cooperation with evil. Despite Churchill's praise, Allied opinion generally had little sympathy for neutrality'. By a unanimously approved resolution of the Federal Assembly, an international commission of experts (so-called Bergier commission) was established in 1996 in order to investigate the volume and fate of assets moved to Switzerland before, during and immediately after the Second Wold War from a historical and legal point of view. The Bergier commission examined the gold trading and foreign currency transactions conducted by the Swiss National Bank and by private commercial banks, the assets moved to Switzerland, both of the victims of the Nazi regime as well as of its perpetrators and collaborators, the relations of Swiss industrial and commercial companies with the National-Socialist economy, Swiss refugee policy in connection with Switzerland's economic and financial relations with the Axis powers and the Allies, and government measures for the return of unlawfully acquired assets (Washington Accord 1946, Resolution the reporting of dormant accounts 1962). Based on an extensive study (25 volumes containing more than 11,000 pages), the final report of the Bergier commission was published in 2002. This report leaves no doubt that the period of WWII constituted a dark hour in the history of Switzerland. – During the Cold War (1945–1989), the *Leitmotif* of Swiss foreign relations was 'neutrality and solidarity'. Switzerland presented itself as a locking 'device' between the East and the West. It stayed out of the NATO and hosted several UN agencies in Geneva. It also provided (and still provides) mediation, good services in several conflicts and participated in peacekeeping missions abroad (beginning in 1953 by sending Swiss observers to the Demarcation Line in Korea). With the fall of the Berlin Wall, in an era of transition and manifold changes, the defence of Switzerland's interests calls for active, comprehensive solidarity, and both global and regional cooperation and participation. Hence, neutrality as an instrument has lost some of its efficiency and importance.

783. Today, Switzerland combines perpetual armed neutrality with security and foreign policy. In a nutshell, Switzerland's *security policy* in international relations include the implementation of economic sanctions (as adopted by the UN or other international actors, namely the EU), peace support (transit rights for peace-support operations, participation in peace-support operations) and international cooperation (training and armament cooperation with foreign partners). As a neutral country Switzerland cannot become a member of a military alliance such as NATO. Regarding the participation of members of the Swiss army in international peacekeeping operations the Federal Council has declared that such operations are compatible with the neutrality principle insofar as the operation corresponds (1) with the principles of Switzerland's foreign affairs and security policy and is (2) based upon a mandate by the UN or the OSCE. Furthermore, the participation of members of the Swiss Army in international peacekeeping operations is (3) optional and (4) does not include military involvement in combat situations in order to appease a party of the conflict by force (*see* Article 66 and 66a of the Federal Military Act (SR 510.10), as effective since 1 September 2001 and 1 January 2004). According to Article 66b of the Federal Military Act, the Federal Council has the competency to order a peacekeeping operation and may, if necessary, conclude international treaties. Since October 1999, the Swiss Armed Forces have been involved in Kosovo in the international Kosovo Force (KFOR) peace-support mission with SWISSCOY composed of up to 235 voluntary military persons. In 2004, Swiss Parliament authorized the ministry of defence to deploy military personnel – armed for self-defence – to the multinational European Union Force (EUFOR) for the ALTHEA mission in Bosnia-Herzegovina. Furthermore, neutrality is not only seen as part of security policy but also as an instrument for its foreign policy. The *concept of an active foreign policy* (*see infra* §4) is designed to prevent isolation as well as to promote cooperation and solidarity internationally in order to enhance security within the Swiss territory, while also fulfilling Switzerland's responsibility towards the world. These goals are enumerated in the Constitution: Article 2(4) of the Constitution states that Switzerland shall be committed to a just and peaceful international order. Article 54(3) of the Constitution adds that Switzerland's foreign policy shall be directed at enhancing respect for human rights, democracy and the peaceful coexistence of nations. Switzerland participates in international programmes and is a member of international organizations (UN, OSCE, Council of Europe, etc.) and provides a wide range of 'good offices' (such as protecting power mandates, mediation and facilitation services). As a neutral, non-aligned country it is often perceived as particularly apt to provide such services.

784. Before its accession to the United Nations (UN), Switzerland was already a member of special organizations of the UN (such as the WHO, the FAO or the ILO) and a contracting party to several UN conventions (such as the UN-Pacts I and II). The UN Office at Geneva is also the second largest site of the UN. After a first attempt failed in 1986, the Swiss people and the cantons voted in favour of joining the UN on 3 March 2002 (54.6% of the population, twelve of the twenty-three cantons; *see* Article 197 no. 1 of the Constitution). Switzerland was the first country whose membership of the UN was decided directly by its people. On 18 July 2002, Switzerland was accepted as the 190th member of the UN. According to the Federal Council accession statement, Swiss neutrality is compatible with the UN Charter and thus will not be affected by the adhesion to the UN. The UN membership does not demand Switzerland's active participation in armed conflicts. Even without being a full member, Switzerland has already participated in coercive measures adopted by the UN Security Council since 1990 under Chapter VII of the UN Charter. Switzerland's contributions to the core UN accounts for 1.14% of the regular budget for the period 2016–2018. It currently ranks 17th among contributors to the UN's regular budget and 14th among contributors to the budget for peacekeeping operations. In the last five years, Switzerland has made the following contributions (in Swiss francs): 129,969,400 (in 2011), 68,221,644 (in 2012), 125,658,846 (in 2013), 92,174,986 (in 2014) and 74,000,583 (in 2015). As the report of the Federal Council in response to the Parliamentary postulate 13.3005 of 5 June 2015 points out: 'Switzerland has gained a reputation at the UN as a partner that is impartial and ready at all times to help find solutions.' Switzerland has registered its candidature for one of the two seats available to the Western European and Other States Group (WEOG) in the Security Council for the 2023–2024 term (the voting will be held in 2022).

§2. War and National Security

Selected Bibliography: Biaggini. Kommentar, Articles 58 and 59 (with further references); Diggelmann Oliver & Altwicker Tilmann. Basler Kommentar BV, Articles 58–61 (with further references); Ruch Alexander. 'Äussere und innere Sicherheit'. In Thürer et al., §56; Schweizer Rainer J. & Mohler Markus H.F. St. Galler Kommentar, Vorbemerkungen zur Sicherheitsverfassung, 1181 et seq. (with further references).

I. The Swiss Army as Militia

785. According to Article 58(2) of the Constitution, the army shall contribute to the prevention of wars and to maintaining peace. The army also has to support civil authorities in their efforts to maintain order, to repel serious threats to internal security or to support them in cases of emergencies. Switzerland has no professional standing army but instead has organized armed forces in case of war as a militia army. The militia principle as set forth in Article 58(1) of the Constitution means that citizens fulfil a state task (here: the defence of the country) in person, in addition to their other professional duties and for a limited period of time. In time of peace the army is guided by an administrative chief of the army nominated by the Federal Council and accountable to the Federal Councillor who is also head of the defence department. The administration of the army, the education and training of soldiers and officers are organized and decided by the defence department. As far as the deployment of the armed forces is concerned it is noteworthy that originally the cantons decided almost exclusively on the army. The federal army, e.g., in the war between Germany and France in 1870, was composed of the contingents of the cantonal armed forces (Article 19 of the Constitution of 1848). Today the deployment of the army is an exclusive federal matter (Article 60 of the Constitution).

786. According to Article 168(1) of the Constitution, in cases of external threats to national security, if a larger contingent of troops is assigned or ordered to combat, the Federal Parliament must elect the General of the Swiss army (*see also* Article 85(1) of the Federal Military Act, SR 510.10), who is then the Commander-in-Chief of the army. His main duties are to ensure the defence of the independence of the country, the protection of the population and for the sake of neutrality the maintenance of the integrity of the territory including the defence of the air-space. Until the election of the General, the control of the military remains in the hands of the Federal Council who uses its powers on a temporary basis (Article 85(2) of the Federal Military Act). After the General's election, the Federal Council remains the supreme organ of the executive branch giving the General his/her commission (Article 86 of the Federal Military Act). The General is elected only in the event of, and only in case of a major external threat to national security. In Swiss history, only four officers have been formally designated as General, the last being Henri Guisan, elected in 30 August 1939. However, as history has shown, once a General is elected conflicts between the General and the Federal Council can easily arise and the Constitution does not regulate any conflict of competences between the powerful General and the seven members of the Federal Council.

787. After the German reunification in 1989, the Swiss army with its potential 650,000 militiamen was the largest one in Europe. In November 1989, the 'Group for a Switzerland without an Army' lost the votation, however 36% of the voters were in favour of abolishing the army. Since then, the Federal Council initiated a military reform ('Army 95') limiting the army to 370,000 and cutting the length of time served. In 2001, a second attempt to abolish the army failed as well. This time, 79% of the voters rejected abolition and 78% rejected proposals to replace the army with a civilian force to assist peacekeeping operations. The reform 'Army XXI' was adopted by popular vote in 2003 and further reduces manpower to about 200,000 (120,000 receiving periodic military training and 80,000 reservists who have completed their total military training requirements). The current reform (WEA) foresees a further reduction in size but increased funding in order to modernize the army and enhance its flexibility in view to new threats (especially cyberattacks).

788. According to Article 59(1) of the Constitution, every Swiss male must render military service. At the age of majority a military conscription eligibility screening is held whereby about two-thirds of the men are found suitable for service. Conscripts who do not wish to carry a weapon on moral grounds may apply for weaponless service. In general, at the age of 20, approximately 20,000 persons receive basic training in boot camps lasting eighteen to twenty-one weeks. They may also choose so-called long service fulfilling their entire military service in a continuous 300-day service. During military service an income-loss insurance is paid to the personnel and they receive a basic compensation ranging from CHF 4 a day for a recruit to 30 for a Lieutenant General. After boot camp, the soldiers keep their own personal equipment, including weapons, at home (until 2007 this also included ammunition). Up to the age of 34, soldiers have to attend 6–7 refresher courses each lasting nineteen days (for higher military ranks the military obligations last longer). The end of military obligations depends on the military rank. In the case of non-observation of the obligation to serve in the army, Article 81 of the Federal Military Criminal Code (SR 321.0) allows for imprisonment of up to eighteen months or a fine. Alternative service is possible (second sentence of Article 59(1) of the Constitution); it lasts longer than the military service. Military service is voluntary for Swiss women (Article 59(2) of the Constitution). Swiss males who perform neither military nor alternative service must pay a military service exemption tax. The tax is levied by the Confederation but is assessed and collected by the cantons (Article 59(3) of the Constitution). In the case *Glor v. Switzerland* of 30 April 2009, 13444/04, Reports of Judgments and Decisions 2009-III, the applicant complained before the European Court of Human Rights that he had been required to pay the tax in order to be exempted from compulsory military service despite the fact that he had been willing to do any form of national service, military or otherwise, compatible with his minor disability. The ECHR unanimously held that the Swiss authorities' practice in the matter amounted to discrimination within the meaning of Article 14 of the Convention.

II. Threats to National Security

789. Unlike many modern constitutions, the Swiss Federal Constitution has no specific provision regulating emergency situations. Historically, in cases of emergency (in particular in situations of war), the Federal Assembly unanimously vested the Federal Council with special competences to regulate by ordinances the emergency situation. Even today, the Constitution declares the Federal Assembly *as well as* the Federal Council responsible to take the necessary measures to uphold external as well as internal security (Articles 173(1) and 185 of the Constitution). Due to the lack of special competences in cases of emergency the Federal Council had decided to provide the Swiss bank UBS with CHF 6 billion during the financial crisis, owing to its relevance to the banking system and to the Swiss economy (*see* Ordinance regarding the Recapitalisation of UBS of 15 October 2008; Official Compilation of Federal Law [AS; RO] 2008 4741–4742; no longer in force since 25 August 2009). In addition, the National Bank of Switzerland agreed to take over problematic assets from the UBS of up to CHF 54 billion. Those measures were politically contested because they lacked democratic legitimacy and it was considered doubtful whether the constitutional power provided for security (Article 184(3) and Article 185(3) of the Constitution) would also cover such measures. Thus, in contrast to most cantonal constitutions, the Federal Constitution has no provision that would regulate emergency cases to overcome financial crises, terrorism or natural catastrophes.

790. According to Article 57(1) of the Constitution, the Confederation and the cantons shall provide, within the framework of their powers, for the security of the country and the protection of its population. There has never been in Swiss history a clear competence of the Confederation to provide for internal security. Neither does the new Constitution transfer to the Confederation such a competence. Therefore, according to Article 3 of the Constitution, the cantons are the main bearers of this responsibility. On the other hand, nobody would deny that the Confederation holds the responsibility to guarantee security for its own authorities and institutions including foreign diplomats and international organizations (such as all UN organizations seated in Geneva). Some authors also claim that by definition and by its nature states must possess the power to guarantee its own security. Based on these considerations, the legislature has adopted the Federal Act on Internal Security of 21 March 1997 (BWIS; SR 120), which aims to guarantee the security of the rule of law of the state, its democracy and its freedom. Explicitly, this Act considers in Article 5 that the cantons are primarily responsible for internal security and that the cantons are obliged to support federal authorities as far as they have specific responsibility according to international and constitutional law. In actual fact, the Confederation has no proper police force. There is only a federal police administration. In 1978, the People rejected a proposal of the federal government to introduce a special act which would oblige the cantons to give the federal government part of their police force so as to enable the federal government to guarantee internal security. However, the cantons have concluded an inter-cantonal treaty to cooperate in case they need an inter-cantonal assignment of a common police force (IKAPOL), which has been in force since 2006. This treaty also provides for police forces which are temporarily assigned for security issues of the Confederation. According to Article 2 paragraph 1 of the law on the organization of the federal penal authorities, the authority to prosecute is allocated to the police and the federal prosecutor elected by the parliament (Article 20 paragraph 1 of this law).

791. Federal criminal law is principally prosecuted by cantonal authorities which are not subordinated to the Federal Office of the Attorney General who holds no supervisory powers over them. According to Articles 23 and 24 of the Code of Criminal Procedure the Attorney General of the Confederation (*Bundesanwalt*) is for example competent in the prosecution of the following criminal offences: certain offences against property to the extent that they involve the premises. archives or papers of embassies and consulates, hostage-taking for the purpose of coercing federal or foreign authorities, felonies and misdemeanours constituting a public danger (misuse of explosives and toxic gases with or without criminal intent or through negligence, causing danger by means of nuclear energy, radioactivity or ionizing radiation, causing a flood, collapse or landslide, etc.), counterfeiting of money, official stamps and other symbols of the Confederation, weights and measurements, felonies and misdemeanours against public order, offences detrimental to foreign relations, political crimes and offences which cause or are caused by civil unrest and which result in armed federal intervention, etc. Furthermore, the Office of the Attorney General is responsible for the implementation of requests for mutual legal assistance in crime matters. His activities are supervised by a supervisory authority appointed by the Federal Assembly.

§3. Treaty Powers

Selected Bibliography: *See* Bibliography in Part I, Chapter 1, and Häfelin, Haller, Keller & Thurnherr, §63 (with further references); Haller. *Swiss Constitution*, 249 et seq.; Müller Georg. 'Rechtssetzung und Staatsverträge'. In Thürer et al., §70; Epiney Astrid. 'Beziehungen zum Ausland'. In Thürer et al., §55; Rhinow, Schefer & Uebersax, §39 II. and III.; Wildhaber Luzius. 'Aussenpolitische Kompetenzordnung im schweizerischen Bundesstaat'. In *Neues Handbuch der schweizerisches Aussenpolitik*, edited by Riklin Alois, Haug Hans & Probst Raymond. Bern/Stuttgart/Wien: Paul Haupt Publ., 1992, 121 et seq.; Wildhaber Luzius. *Treaty-Making Power and Constitution*. Basel: Helbing & Lichtenhahn, 1971.

I. Overview

792. According to Article 54 of the Constitution, treaty powers are principally a *federal matter*. Due to this extensive competency, the Confederation has always been and is also with the new Constitution entitled to conclude treaties – based upon international public law – concerning even for matters that would normally fall within the competencies of the cantons, such as taxation, police, or education. However, the cantons may participate in the decisions of foreign policy that concern their powers or their essential interests. This implies that the Confederation must inform the concerned cantons in a full and timely manner, as well as consult them (Article 55 of the Constitution). The position of the cantons has particular weight when the treaty concerns their powers. Whenever appropriate, the cantons are entitled to participate in international negotiations.

793. Switzerland follows with regard to the implementation of treaties the monistic system (*see supra* Part I, Chapter 1, §2). Treaties concluded by the Confederation falling into the competences of the cantons are according to this system still implemented. Unlike other federal states with a dualistic system, Switzerland has no lack of competences on the international level.

II. Procedure for the Conclusion of Treaties

A. Negotiation and Approval

794. According to Article 184 of the Constitution, the Federal Council represents Switzerland abroad. With respect to the participatory rights of Federal Parliament (Article 166(1) of the Constitution), the Federal Council conducts foreign relations, nominates and instructs the Swiss delegation, and grants authorization to the members of the delegation to sign the negotiated treaty.

795. Treaties based upon international public law are subject to approval by the Federal Parliament, which has the authority to accept or reject the treaty (Articles 166(2) and 184(2) of the Constitution). Although the approval by Federal Parliament is a necessary prerequisite for the ratification of the treaty, it does not constitute a binding commission for the Federal Council to ratify it. The Federal Council may refrain from ratifying the treaty, even after approval by Federal Parliament.

B. Optional and Mandatory Referendum for International Treaties

796. International treaties are subject to an *optional referendum* if they are:

(1) of unlimited duration and may not be terminated;
(2) provide for accession to an international organization; or
(3) contain important legislative provisions or whose implementation requires the enactment of federal legislation (Article 141(1)(d)(1)–(3) of the Constitution).

797. These types of international treaties are submitted to the vote of the People, at the request of either 50,000 Swiss citizens entitled to vote or of eight cantons (Article 141(1) of the Constitution).

798. Furthermore, the Federal Parliament may submit additional international treaties outside of the scope of Article 141(1)(d) of the Constitution to an optional referendum.

799. The main difference between an optional and a *mandatory referendum* is that the latter is *decided by the majority of the People and the cantons*. According to Article 140(1)(b) of the Constitution, the People and the cantons must decide on the entry of the Swiss Confederation into organizations for collective security, such as the UN, or into supranational communities, such as the EU.

800. On 16 March 1986, the Swiss People and the cantons rejected the entry of the Swiss Confederation into the UN. But in a second mandatory referendum, on 3 March 2002, Switzerland became the 190th member of the UN.

801. On 6 December 1992, a small majority of the People (50.3%), but a big majority of the cantons (fourteen full cantons and four half-cantons) rejected a proposal of the Federal Council and the Federal Parliament to access the European Economic Area and, based on this treaty, a cooperation with the EU. Although this agreement did not constitute an international organization within the meaning of Article 140(1)(d) of the Constitution, the question was submitted to the People and the cantons as a mandatory referendum due to its significant impact upon the Swiss economy and political system. The Swiss economy however depends largely on international export and import, especially to and from the EU. The Swiss earn each second Swiss Franc in a foreign country. The trade with countries from the EU is greater than 60%. For this reason, instead of joining the economic area, Switzerland concluded bilateral treaties (*see supra* Part I, Chapter 1, §4). These bilateral treaties have a considerable impact on the Swiss legal system and are for this reason politically often controversial.

C. *Ratification and Publication*

802. Upon ratification, the international treaty gains binding force under international public law. Ratification is within the powers of the Federal Council (Article 184(2) of the Constitution).

803. Since Switzerland has adopted the monistic system, further transformation is not required. As a rule, federal decrees on the approval of international treaties must be published in the Compilation of Federal Legislation (Article 2 of the Federal Act of 18 June 2004 on the Compilations of Federal Legislation and the Federal Gazette; Publications Act, SR 170.512). Furthermore, Article 3 of the Publication Act states that the following international treaties and decrees must be published: (a) international treaties that are subject to a referendum under Articles 140 paragraph 1 letter b and 141 paragraph 1 letter d of the Federal Constitution; (b) other international treaties that enact law or confer legislative powers; and (c) decrees of organizations and bodies established under international treaties that enact law or confer legislative powers. Treaties of no more than six months in duration, and treaties of limited scope shall not be published. The Federal Council shall regulate the exceptions. Upon publication in the Official Compilation of Federal Legislation, the self-executing provisions of the international treaty gain binding force for the individual (Article 8(1) of the Federal Publication Act).

III. The Relationship Between Treaties and National Law

804. *See* discussion *supra* in Part I, §1, III.

§4. Foreign Affairs Powers

Selected Bibliography: Biaggini. Kommentar, Articles 54–56 (with further references); Goetschel Laurent et al., *Schweizerische Aussenpolitik.* NZZ Verlag: Zurich 2002; Kley Roland Portmann Roland. St. Galler Kommentar, Vorbemerkungen *ad* Articles 54–56 (with further references); Rhinow, Schefer & Uebersax, §40 (with further references).

805. In Switzerland, foreign policy is a task shared between the Federal Council and the Federal Assembly (Articles 166 and 184 of the Constitution).

806. The provisions of the Federal Constitution concerning foreign policy reflect a fundamental change of paradigm from Switzerland's nineteenth century position as an 'introverted nation-state' (Rhinow) to a modern and open constitutional state. In the Preamble of the Constitution, the Swiss People and the cantons renew their alliance to strengthen liberty and democracy, independence and peace in solidarity, and openness towards the world. National and foreign policy have become highly interdependent. As a result, the basic purpose of the Confederation is not only the protection of the liberty and the rights of the People, as well as the independence and security of the country (Article 2(1) of the Constitution), but also the promotion of a just and peaceful international order (Article 2(4) of the Constitution).

807. The importance of foreign policy is also systematically highlighted in Title 3, Chapter 2 of the Constitution, which immediately follows the chapter regarding the relationship between the Confederation and the cantons. The foreign policy of Switzerland's aim is to contribute to the alleviation of the needs and poverty of the world, and promoting respect for human rights, democracy, the peaceful coexistence of nations, and the preservation of natural resources (Article 54(2) of the Constitution).

808. The provision outlines the various pillars of Swiss foreign policy, which are:

(1) the policy concerning the relationship between Switzerland and Europe;
(2) the peace and security policy; and
(3) the development policy.

Surprisingly, considering the importance of trade with foreign countries for Switzerland, the Constitution does not expressly mention foreign trade policy, except for Article 101(1) of the Constitution, which grants the Confederation the power to safeguard the interests of the Swiss economy abroad.

809. The concept of Swiss federalism as an equilibrium between self-rule and a constitutionally guaranteed shared rule has already been set out (*supra*, Part III, Chapter 1, §2). The same concept is evident in the *traditional instruments* of the cantons to influence foreign policy, such as consultation procedure, initiatives by the cantons, representation in the Council of States, the double majority requirement for important treaties, and the cantonal referendum.

810. In the Constitution of 1999, the element of *cooperation*, also included in the shared rule principle, has gained importance as a compensation for diminished cantonal autonomy (*supra*, Part III, Chapter 1, §3 III). In the context of foreign affairs, the Constitution underlines the role of the cantons in the decision-making process of foreign policy, and the relations between the cantons and foreign countries. Furthermore, although foreign relationships are a federal matter (Article 54(1) of the Constitution), the Confederation has to take into consideration the powers of the cantons as well as the protection of their interests (Article 54(3) of the Constitution).

811. According to the concept of cooperative federalism, Article 55(1) of the Constitution integrates the cantons into the *decision-making process of the preparation of foreign policy*, which concern the powers and the essential interests of the cantons. In order to avoid centralization through foreign policy, the Federal Act of 22 December 1999 regarding the Participation of the Cantons in the Foreign Policy of the Confederation (SR 138.1) also reconfirms the role of the cantons in the foreign policy process of the Confederation, but without adding new substance to Article 55 of the Constitution. In addition to the right of the cantons to be *timely and fully informed*, and the possibility of the Confederation to *consult* the cantons (Article 55(2) of the Constitution), the Constitution grants to the cantons *further appropriate participatory rights in international negotiations* (Article 55(3) of the Constitution). Furthermore, the position of the cantons shall have particular weight when their powers are concerned.

812. From an institutional perspective, as a result of the inadequate flow of information during the negotiations regarding the accession to the European Economic Community in the 1990s, the *Conference of the Cantonal Governments* (*Konferenz der Kantonsregierungen*) was created in 1993. The Conference is not focused exclusively on foreign or EU policy, but rather, it aims at coordinating the decision-making process among cantons in order to exercise joint influence on the federal level. All twenty-six cantons are members of the Conference, of which the vote of eighteen cantons is sufficient to make a decision. Additionally, the Conference sends a delegate to the EU in Brussels, who serves for informational purposes for the Conference and also to augment the Conference's influence on the EU.

813. Furthermore, the Constitution regulates the *relationship between the cantons and foreign countries*. According to Article 56(1) of the Constitution, the cantons are entitled to conclude treaties with foreign countries. The Constitution requires that:

(1) the matter is within the scope of cantonal powers cantons (Article 56(1) of the Constitution);
(2) the treaty between one or more cantons and the foreign country is not contrary to the law or the interests of the Confederation or to the laws of other cantons (Article 56(2) of the Constitution); and
(3) the cantons inform the Confederation before concluding a treaty (Article 56(2) *in fine* of the Constitution).

814. The cantons are allowed to deal *directly* with lower ranking foreign authorities (Article 56(3) of the Constitution), while in all other cases, the Confederation will act on their behalf.

Chapter 2. Taxing Power, Financial Equalization and Spending Power

Selected Bibliography: Auer, Malinverni & Hottelier. Vol. I, 395 et seq.; Behnisch Urs. Basler Kommentar BV, Article 127; Blumenstein Ernst & Locher Peter. *System des Steuerrechts*. 7th ed. Zurich: Schulthess, 2016 (with further references); Biaggini. Kommentar, Articles 127–135; De Vries Reilingh Daniel. *La double imposition intercantonale*. 2nd ed. Berne: Stämpfli, 2013; Häfelin, Haller, Keller & Thurnherr, § 27; Kocher Martin. 'Die Kriegssteuer von 1915'. In *Archiv für schweizerisches Abgaberecht [ASA]*. 2015/2016, 421 et seq.; Lienhard Andreas et al., *Öffentliches Finanzrecht*. Berne: Stämpfli, 2017; Locher Peter. 'Finanzordnung des Bundes'. In Thürer et al., §77; Oberson Xavier & Guillaume Pierre-Alain. 'Le régime financier dans le droit constitutionnel des cantons'. In Thürer et al., §78: Oberson Xavier & Hull Howard R. *Switzerland in International Tax Law*. 2nd ed. IBFD: Amsterdam, 2006; Vallender Klaus A. & Wiederkehr René. St. Galler Kommentar, Article 127; Zweifel Martin, Beusch Michael & Mäusli-Allenspach Peter (eds). *Interkantonales Steuerrecht*. Basel: Helbing & Lichtenhahn, 2011; Zweifel Martin & Beusch Michael (eds), *Bundesgesetz über die direkte Bundessteuer (DBG)*. 3rd ed. Basel: Helbing & Lichtenhahn, 2017; *id.* (eds). *Bundesgesetz über die Harmonisierung der direkten Steuern der Kantone und Gemeinden (StHG)*. 3rd ed. Basel: Helbing & Lichtenhahn, 2017; Zweifel Martin, Beusch Michael & Matteotti René (eds). *Internationales Steuerrecht*. Basel: Helbing & Lichtenhahn, 2015; Zweifel Martin et al. (eds). *Bundesgesetz über die Mehrwertsteuer (MWSTG)/Loi fédérale régissant la taxe sur la veleur ajoutée (LTVA)*. Basel: Helbing & Lichtenhahn, 2015.

§1. Taxing Power

I. Overview

815. Before the creation of the federal state, the Confederacy was a weak body because it lacked tax-based income. It only had a temporary power to levy taxes during wartime and in case of emergency situations. In 1848, the taxation authority to levy customs duties was passed over from the cantons to the Confederation. Furthermore, it could collect taxes from the income generated by the Swiss Post, from concessions for gunpowder, and later by other indirect taxes, such as taxes on alcohol and tobacco. However, the authority to levy income and net wealth taxes remained with the cantons. Until the First World War, the revenue deriving from customs duties was sufficient to cover the expenses of the Confederation. However, since the army was a federal matter, federal expenditure rose exponentially during that time and could no longer by covered by the traditional tax revenues. Consequently, in 1915, the Federal Parliament introduced a one-off war tax (*Kriegssteuer*), which was approved by popular vote in the same year. Later, a tax on war earnings for undertakings was levied (*Kriegsgewinnsteuer*;

for the period between 1916–1920) and stamp taxes were introduced. During World War II, the federal government needed additional financial means. With the authorization of the Federal Parliament (*Vollmachten-Beschluss* of 30 August 1939), the Federal Council introduced for the period of five years the so-called national defence tax (*Wehrsteuer*) in 1940, and a turnover tax (*Warenumsatzsteuer*) in 1941. Owing to the turmoil of the war, no popular votes were held. In 1958, after two negative popular votes (which led to the first and, so far, last resignation of a Federal Councillor in Swiss history), a constitutional basis entitling the Confederation to levy direct taxes was finally anchored in Article 41*bis* of the Constitution of 1874, but, again, limited in duration and extent. A renewal of that competency required (and still requires) a constitutional amendment, which must be approved by the People and the majority of the cantons. In 1982, the federal direct tax replaced the national defence tax. It is the second most important source of revenue after the value added tax (VAT), which replaced the turnover tax in 1995. All attempts to provide for a permanent federal power to levy taxes have been rejected by the People and the cantons, most recently in 1991. In a recent proposal (*Finanzordnung 2021*), the Federal Council aims at a renewal of the competency to levy the federal direct tax and the VAT until 31 December 2035 by amending Article 196 no. 13 and no. 14(1) of the Transitional Provisions of the Constitution. It is interesting to note that the initial proposal of the Federal Council to levy these taxes on a permanent basis found support in most cantons during the consultation procedure, but was thwarted by the resistance of the political parties.

816. The Federal Constitution enumerates the general principles to be observed by the federal, cantonal and also municipal legislatures to enact obligations for taxation. Article 127(1) aims at harmonizing tax statutes formally. Taxes need to be enacted by the legislature, which includes also the participation of citizens either by mandatory or optional referendum. In order to foresee the consequences of the legislation, citizens and their representatives in Parliament need to know who will have to pay taxes, on what grounds taxes can be levied and how much taxes he or she might have to pay. For this reason, the statute must determine the taxpayers, the object of the tax and its calculation. In addition, the Constitution provides also some important features to improve fiscal justice and procedural due process. As a consequence, Article 127(2) of the Constitution requires that, wherever it is possible, to apply taxes universally taking into account uniformity. Moreover the citizens' ability to pay taxes should be taken into account (*iustitia distributiva*). The Federal Supreme Court held in 2007 that a cantonal statute introducing a regressive tax system with flat-decreasing tax rates violated not only the equal protection clause but also redistributive justice in the sense of Article 127(2) of the Constitution. Insofar, the Obwalden tax statute was declared null and void by the Federal Supreme Court (Decision of the Federal Supreme Court BGE 133 I 206).

817. In addition, Article 129 of the Constitution transfers to the Confederation the obligation to introduce in its legislation the basic principles to be observed by all cantons providing for direct taxation: They shall define the object of taxation, the procedure applicable and the period of taxation. The federal legislature has also the power to determine the law for tax offences. Explicitly excluded from any federal legislation are the tax scales, the tax rates and the tax allowances. A popular initiative aiming at obligating taxpayers with very high fortune and income to pay in all cantons a minimum rate has been rejected in November 2010 with the argument not to touch on the autonomy of the cantons and not to disturb for financial reasons the cantonal fiscal competition. In recent years, the attitude of Switzerland with regard to the bank secrecy has been strongly criticized by the OECD, most of the Member States of the EU and the United States for its traditional privilege to consider tax evasion only as a contravention in the sense of Article 103 of the Criminal Code (hence, a criminal punishment is not possible and the competence for sanctions remains with the tax authority which may impose an administrative sanction), but not as a criminal offence (such as tax fraud). On the other hand, tax avoidance is not a fiscal offence under Swiss domestic law. In March 2009, a proposition for a popular initiative to embed the bank secrecy as a constitutional right failed due to the requirements of Article 139(1) of the Constitution. Considering that an initiative against the misuse of the bank secrecy has already been clearly rejected in 1984 by the People and the cantons, the chances of success of the initiative 'For the Protection of Privacy', launched in 2014, are relatively low. In order to respond to this critique, Switzerland has changed its position and in order not to profit economically from tax evasion of foreigners. In principle, it does not further protect foreign taxpayers from their countries asking Switzerland for mutual administrative assistance (for a case where mutual administrative assistance was denied to France owing to the fact that the bank data was stolen in Geneva and the French authorities had given assurances to Switzerland not to use the data *see* Decision of the Federal Supreme Court 2C_1000/2015 of 17 March 2017). The 2014 OECD global standard for the automatic exchange of information in tax matters (AEOI) provides that predominantly financial institutions and insurance companies collect financial information on their clients, so long as they are resident abroad for tax purposes. This information covers all types of investment income and account balances. As a rule, this information is automatically transmitted once a year to the tax authority, which transmits the data for the client to the respective tax authority abroad. This transparency seeks to prevent cross-border tax evasion. The AEOI does not affect domestic bank client confidentiality in Switzerland. With regard to the introduction of the AEOI standard, the Federal Parliament adopted the Multilateral Convention on Mutual Administrative Assistance in Tax Matters and the Multilateral Competent Authority Agreement, together with the AEOI Act, on 18 December 2015 (SR 653.1). The Federal Council adopted the AEOI ordinance on 23 November 2016 (SR 653.11), which entered into force on 1 January 2017. Data can be gathered from 2017, and the first exchange will take place in 2018. Switzerland has signed a corresponding agreement with the EU and further declarations have been signed with various other countries.

818. Most of state expenditures need to be paid by taxes. Considering that today's public debts have finally to be financed by later generations (e.g., with the introduction of new taxes), Article 126(1) of the Constitution requires that – in the long run – income and expenditures need to be in balance. Consequently, in case the expenditures exceed the income, later budgets need to provide for compensation. This principle has also been introduced into most of the cantonal constitutions. The constitutional provisions also require special majorities for exceptional expenditures, which surmount the income. In some cantons, the cantonal parliament is obliged in this case to raise the taxes, which is only possible with the consent of the people in a referendum. On the federal level, the proposal must be adopted with an absolute majority of both Councils (Article 159(3) of the Constitution).

II. Exclusive and Concurrent Powers

819. The federal level may only levy taxes that are explicitly enumerated in the Constitution. Federal taxing power is exclusive in the fields of VAT, special consumption taxes, as well as stamp and withholding tax (Article 134 of the Constitution). With regard to the latter taxes, the federal government is constitutionally required to give the cantons a certain percentage of its income based on these taxes (*see*, e.g., Articles 131(3) and 132(2) of the Constitution). Finally, the power of the Confederation to impose customs is exclusive. In the areas of personal and corporate income tax, as well as corporate capital tax, the Confederation and the cantons have concurrent powers. These taxes can be levied at all three levels of the Confederation. Furthermore, the cantons can introduce additional taxes (*see* table below).

Federal Taxes on Income and Other Direct Taxes	*Federal Consumption Taxes and Other Indirect Taxes*
Income Tax Corporate Income tax Federal Casino Tax Military and Civil Service Exemption Tax	VAT Withholding Tax Stamp Duties Tobacco Tax Beer Tax Tax on Distilled Spirits Mineral Oil Tax Vehicle Tax

III. Federal Taxes

820. As already shown above, the constitutional federal power to levy direct taxes is limited in duration. Additionally, the Confederation is bound by maximum tax rates (Article 128(1) and Article 130(1) and (2) of the Constitution). For example, the federal direct tax shall not exceed a maximum of 11.5% on the income of private individuals and of 8.5% of the net profit of legal entities. Until the end of 2017 (*see* Article 25 of the Value Added Tax Act (VATA) of 12 June 2009; VATA; SR 641.20), the normal VAT rate of 8% applies to the supply of goods, to services, including goods and services for personal use, and to imports. Overnight stays at a hotel (incl. breakfast) are taxed at a special rate of 3.8%. A reduced rate of 2.5% applies to certain everyday consumer goods such as foodstuffs, non-alcoholic beverages, books, newspapers, magazines, medicines, but also to tickets for sports and cultural events. As a result of the rejection of the popular vote concerning the 'Old-age pension reform 2020' on 24

September 2017 the VAT rates for 2018 will be partially reduced (7.7/3.7/2.5%). Apart from the requirement that tax increases always need a constitutional amendment, tax scales shall be established by taking the burden of direct cantonal and municipal taxes into account (Article 128 of the Constitution). This constitutional framework is the main reason for the relatively low level of fiscal centralization in Switzerland.

821. On the federal level, the most important taxes are the federal direct tax (*see* Federal Direct Tax Act (FDTA) of 14 December 1990; SR 642.11) and the VAT (*see* VATA of 12 June 2009; SR 641.20). Since it is impossible to go into details here the following outline of these two taxes is based on the very useful publication of the Federal Tax Administration 'Federal, Cantonal and Communal Taxes' (Berne 2016):

- The federal direct tax is based on Article 128 of the Constitution and on the FDTA. With regard to the *personal income tax*, residents or temporary residents in Switzerland are subject to unlimited tax liability (Articles 3 and 6(1) FDTA). Limited tax liability applies to non-resident individuals having economic relations with Switzerland; in these cases the tax is levied only on specific items of income that have their sources in Switzerland (Articles 4–5 and 6(2) FDTA). Subject to the federal direct tax is the total income from all sources (e.g., income from gainful employment and self-employment; annuities and pensions; secondary income; income from movable and immovable property; etc.; *see* Articles 16–23 FDTA). Generally, expenses related to the earning of income (e.g., professional expenses) are deductible from gross income (*see* Articles 25–33a FDTA). Furthermore, general and social deductions are granted (*see* Article 35 FDTA). The tax scale for the federal direct tax on the income of individuals is *progressive* (Article 36 FDTA). – *Legal entities* having either their registered office or their actual administration in Switzerland are subject to unlimited tax liability (for details *see* Articles 49–52 FDTA). Corporations (joint stock companies, limited partnerships, limited liability companies) and cooperative societies are subject to the federal corporate income tax, which is levied at a flat rate of 8.5% (Article 68 FDTA). The Confederation does not levy a federal tax on capital. Associations, foundations and other legal entities (public and ecclesiastical corporations and institutions as well as collective investment schemes with direct real estate ownership) are subject to the federal corporate income tax according to the general regulations for legal entities, provided they are not exempt from taxation due to their charitable, social or similar purpose. Their profit is taxed at a special flat rate of 4.25%, subject to a tax threshold of CHF 5,000 – (Article 71 FDTA). For individuals, the federal direct tax is generally assessed annually based on the actual income earned during the tax year. For legal entities, the corporate income tax is assessed for each tax period (corresponding to the entity's business year). Tax collection occurs annually by the cantons on behalf and under the supervision of the Confederation.
- According to Article 1(1) of the VATA, the Confederation shall levy a general consumption tax based on the system of net all-phase taxation with input tax deduction (VAT). The purpose of the tax is to tax non-business end use on Swiss territory. As VAT, the Confederation levies pursuant to Article 1(2) VATA: a tax on goods and services supplied for consideration by taxable persons on Swiss

territory (domestic tax); a tax on the acquisition by recipients on Swiss territory of supplies from businesses domiciled abroad (acquisition tax); and a tax on the import of goods (import tax). The tax is levied on the principles of competitive neutrality, efficiency of payment and imposition and transferability (Article 1(3) VATA). In general, any person, irrespective of legal form, objects and intention to make a profit, is liable to the VAT if that person carries on a business (an independent occupation or a commercial activity the purpose of which is to generate income), as long as the sum of its deliveries, services and its private domestic consumption exceeds CHF 100,000 per year (Article 10 VATA). Additionally, tax liability applies, *inter alia*, to importers of goods (import tax; *see* Articles 50–64 VATA). Persons who are taxable must register with the Federal Tax Administration of their own accord in writing within thirty days of the commencement of their tax liability (for further procedural questions *see* Articles 65–80 VATA). Within the tax period (the calendar year), the tax is reported, as a rule, quarterly (Articles 34–35 VATA). The basis for calculation of the tax on domestic deliveries and services is the agreed upon or alternatively the collected gross payment. Each taxable entity can deduct VAT paid on inputs (including imports). This input tax deductibility (or recovery) avoids multiple taxation (taxable purchase and taxation of the turnover). Since the VAT is intended to be borne by the consumer, it will generally be shifted to him by way of its inclusion in the sale price or as a separate item on the bill.

IV. Cantonal and Municipal Taxes

822. Direct taxes form the most important part of *cantonal and municipal tax revenue*. According to Article 127(3) of the Constitution, inter-cantonal double taxation is prohibited and the Confederation shall take the necessary measures to prevent it. Cantonal income tax is levied at the place of residence. For corporate taxes, the tax base is allocated to the branches where it has been generated in order to prevent inter-cantonal double taxation. This tax splitting favours fiscal competition. Within the limits of the Federal Constitution, the cantons can decide on the tax base, the tax scale, the tax rate and the exempt amounts. Direct taxes, including the federal taxes are assessed and collected by the cantons (Article 128(4) of the Constitution). In some cases (*see infra* Part V, Chapter III), religious communities also have the right to levy taxes, which are then equally assessed and collected by the cantons. Note: Not all taxes in the tables below are levied in all cantons and municipalities:

Cantonal Taxes on Income and Other Direct Taxes	*Cantonal Consumption Taxes and Other Indirect Taxes*
Income and Net Wealth Taxes Poll Tax and Household Tax Corporate Income Tax and Capital Tax Inheritance and Gift Taxes Lottery Income Tax Immovable Property Tax Real Estate Tax (Incl. Transfer Tax) Capital Gain Tax on Immovable Property Cantonal Casino Tax	Motor Vehicle Tax Entertainment Tax Cantonal Stamp Duties Lottery Tax Water Duty Sundry Taxes

Municipal Taxes on Income and Other Direct Taxes	*Municipal Consumption Taxes and Other Indirect Taxes*
Income and Net Wealth Taxes Poll Tax or Household Tax Corporate Income Tax and Capital Tax Inheritance and Gift Taxes Lottery Income Tax Immovable Property Tax Real Estate Tax (Incl. Transfer Tax) Capital Gain Tax on Immovable Property Trade Tax	Dog Tax Entertainment Tax Sundry Taxes

V. Harmonization of Taxes

823. Owing to increased mobility, the variety of the cantonal and municipal tax systems has reinforced tax competition between the cantons (and, within cantons, between the municipalities). The Swiss taxing system is characterized by an extensive autonomy of the subnational units. This has, *inter alia,* consequences with regard to inequalities of taxes among cantons and municipalities. The average tax burden of a representative tax payer differs decisively from one canton to the other (in the year 2014, from 50.6 index points in the canton of Zug up to 132.1 index points in the canton of Geneva by a mean of 100). For example, in 2014, a single person earning CHF 50,000 paid 3.1% of his income in the municipality of Baar (in the canton of Zug), while the taxes were four times higher in Les Verrières (in the canton of Neuchâtel). The Constitution provides only a limited federal competence to harmonize the cantonal taxation system (Article 129(2) of the Constitution). This provision basically aims at a formal and not material tax harmonization. Tax scales, tax rates and tax-exempt amounts are decided either by a cantonal parliament or by popular cantonal referendum without intervention of the federal level. The Federal Act on the Harmonisation of the Direct Taxes of Cantons and Municipalities of 14 December 1990 (SR 642.14) only prescribes the direct taxes to be levied by the cantons and is limited to set the principles, according to which the cantonal legislation is to be designed. According to Article 2 of the Act the cantons have to levy an income tax and a wealth tax from individuals, a profit tax and a capital tax from legal entities, a withholding tax from certain individuals and legal entities and a real estate gains tax. The mandatory harmonization only concerns tax liability, tax object and the taxation period. Furthermore, the Act contains provisions regarding fiscal offences (such as tax evasion in Articles 56–58, tax fraud in Article 59).

§2. Financial Equalization

824. In order to alleviate the cantonal inequalities with regard to access to financial resources due to their very different economic and population structures, Switzerland, as most other federal countries (except the United States), has set upon elaborated and complex system of equalization among the different cantons. Up to 2004, the Confederation was only allowed to promote financial equalization among the different cantons. Article 135(1) of the Constitution mandates that the Confederation regulates not only equalization among the cantons, but also between the Confederation and the cantons. Additionally, the Constitution provides for basic principles regarding financial resources and burdens, which have to be taken into account by the federal legislature when regulating financial equalization. Moreover Article 135(2) of the Constitution defines the aims which should be achieved by the financial equalization. Those goals are: to reduce the differences in financial capacities among the cantons, to guarantee to each canton a minimum level of financial resources, to compensate for excessive financial burdens on certain cantons due to geo-topographical or socio-demography factors, to encourage inter-cantonal cooperation on the burden equalization and to maintain the tax competitiveness of the cantons by national and international comparison. Based on Article 135 of the Constitution, the federal legislature has issued the Federal Act of 3 October 2003 on Equalisation of Finances and Burden-Sharing (SR 613.2).

825. One of the reasons for cantonal autonomy in tax matters is to maintain competition between the cantons on the fiscal level in order to reduce the general tax burden on the citizens. For this reason the Constitution advises the legislature to maintain the competitiveness of the cantons and not to eliminate this important economic factor by the system of equalization. The funds for fiscal equalization shall not only be supplied by the Confederation (as was the case earlier) but also by the funds from cantons with higher level of resources. Here, the solidarity between rich and poor cantons is evident, but not unlimited (and in the political arena also not undisputed). According to Article 135(3) of the Constitution payments made by the cantons with a higher level of resources shall amount to a minimum of two-thirds and a maximum of 80% of the payments made by the Confederation.

826. In order to achieve the goals set out in Article 135(2) of the Constitution, the Confederation provides for an amount of financial means to be funded by the wealthier cantons and the Confederation in order to reduce the financial differences between the wealthier and the financially weaker cantons. The amount of means available for financially weak cantons is decided every four years by the federal legislature based on a report on the evaluation of the effectiveness of this system. The financial means allocated to the financially weak cantons are not earmarked. The cantons decide on the expenditures according to their constitutional autonomy.

827. With regard to burden-sharing it is only the Confederation which provides the necessary means based on a decision of the federal legislature valid for four years. According to Articles 7–8 of the Federal Act on Equalisation of Finances and Burden-Sharing, the Confederation has to take into account the following burdens: Geographical burdens such as mountainous areas and areas with low population density. Socio-demographic burdens such as poverty within the population, the number of the elderly, adolescents with special needs for education, jobless persons, persons addicted to drugs and foreigners. In addition, the Confederation has to take into account the specific burdens of cities with large agglomerations.

828. The equalization system entered into force on January 2008. During the transitory period, the Confederation may support cantons with a hardship compensation (*see* Article 19 of the relevant Federal Act). Equalisation payments cover three equalization mechanisms, i.e., resource equalization, the cohesion fund and federal cost compensation. According to the Federal Department of Finance the total amount for all three mechanisms was almost CHF 5 billion in 2017, with CHF 3,949 million going into resource equalization, CHF 323 million into the cohesion fund and CHF 715 million into federal cost compensation. The money was redistributed vertically from the Confederation to the cantons and horizontally between the cantons. The Confederation paid CHF 2,350 million for resource equalization, and the financially strong cantons (Basel-City, Geneva, Nidwalden, Schwyz, Vaud, Zug and Zurich) contributed CHF 1,599 million. In the case of the cohesion fund, the Confederation paid CHF 215 million and the cantons CHF 108 million. Cost compensation is borne entirely by the Confederation.

§3. Spending Power

829. In Switzerland, spending power is limited by the Constitution and the relevant legislation. As set out above, national fiscal equalization and the resulting new division of tasks between the cantons and the Confederation came into effect in 2008. With this the Confederation also changed its basic concept of spending power. Spending should in general not anymore be input-oriented but rather aimed at the output (outcome, effect). In addition, a great part of federal grants will not be earmarked anymore. Cantons should rather get global federal grants which strengthen their financial autonomy. Furthermore, cooperation between the cantons and the Confederation should be developed by new common development planning in special areas where the Confederation restricts its legislative powers to general framework legislation. Earmarked grants should thus not be designed to alleviate the costs anymore (the higher the costs the higher the grants) and instead of redistributing income, incentives for cooperation and better performances (output) should be provided.

830. According to Article 183 of the Federal Constitution, the Federal Council shall prepare the financing plan, draft the budget and establish the federal accounts. Federal Parliament decides on federal spending, adopts the budget and approves the federal accounts (Article 167 of the Constitution). These decisions can be taken by simple federal decree, which are not submitted to a referendum. There is no financial referendum at the federal level. For decisions granting subsidies, authorizing credit lines, and establishing spending ceilings, which cause new one-time expenditures exceeding CHF 20 million, or new recurrent expenditures exceeding CHF 2 million, a special quorum is required. In order to reduce the general debts of the Confederation an increase of the overall expenditures according to Article 126(3) of the Constitution needs a special approval as well. In all these cases, not only a majority of those voting but a majority of the members of both Chambers of Parliaments are required (Article 159(3)(b) of the Constitution).

831. On 2 December 2001, in order to counteract the mounting deficit, the People and the cantons accepted an amendment of the Constitution that aimed to establish a balanced budget. According to Article 126(1) of the Constitution, the Confederation shall in the long term keep its expenditures and receipts in balance. This mandate is further solidified in Article 126(2). Taking into account the economic situation, the maximum of the total expenditures which may be budgeted shall be determined by the expected receipts; for extraordinary expenses the maximum amount may be increased based on receipts and the economic situation (Article 126(3) of the Constitution). The increase can only be decided by a majority of the members of both Chambers of Federal Parliament (Articles 126(3) and 159(3)(c) of the Constitution). An excess of expenditures must be compensated in the following years (Article 126(4) of the Constitution).

Chapter 3. The Constitutional Relationship Between Religion and State

Selected Bibliography: Belser Eva Maria. Basler Kommentar BV, Präambel (with further references); Carlen Louis. *Trennung von Kirche und Staat*, Ed. universitaires, Fribourg, 1994; Cavelti Urs Josef & Kley Andreas. St. Galler Kommentar, Article 72 (with further references); Ehrenzeller Bernhard. St. Galler Kommentar, Präambel; Haller. *Swiss Constitution*, 184 et seq.; Karlen Peter. *Das Grundrecht der Religionsfreiheit in der Schweiz*. Zürich: Schulthess, 1988; Kraus Dieter. *Schweizerisches Staatskirchenrecht*. Tübingen: Mohr Siebeck Publ., 1993; Mahon. commentaire. Article 72; Pahud de Mortanges René et al. (eds). *Die Zukunft der öffentlich-rechtlichen Anerkennung von Religionsgemeinschaften*. Fribourg, 2000; Pahud de Mortanges René (ed.). *Religion und Integration aus der Sicht des Rechts*. Zurich: Schulthess, 2010; Winzeler Christoph. Basler Kommentar BV, Article 72 (with further references).

§1. Historical Background

832. As already set out in the General Introduction, 38% of the population are Roman Catholic, 26.2% Protestant, 5% Muslim, 2.2% Christian Orthodox, 0.2% Jewish and 22.2% do not adhere to a religious group. Originally, Switzerland was divided into two religious groups: Protestant (Zwingli and Calvin) and Roman Catholic. In the first half of the sixteenth century this division has caused first religious wars, which ended in a peace treaty conferring to the cantons and in particular to the municipalities the right to keep their official religion. Since then, religion has become a municipal and cantonal matter. While Switzerland managed to avoid European religious conflicts, the short civil war of 1847 (*Sonderbundskrieg*) was partially attributed to religious tensions because religious divisions overlapped with political ones (*supra* General Introduction, Chapter 1): Essentially, the liberal and Protestant parts of Switzerland opted for a stronger centralization and democratization, while, in violation of the Confederate Treaty, the conservative Catholic cantons, supported by ancient European monarchies, formed a secret union (*Sonderbund*) in order to protect their ancient governmental systems. When the union was revealed, the Diet ordered the dissolution of the union. The conservative Catholic cantons resisted and left the Diet. As a consequence, the progressive Protestant cantons decided to dissolve the union by force. The *Sonderbundskrieg* led to the defeat of the Catholic cantons.

833. One of the main challenges faced during constitution-making in 1848 was to assure the loyalty of both religious communities. On the federal level, any regulation of the relationship between religion and the state threatened to lead to an unbridgeable cleavage between the Catholic and Protestant parts of Switzerland. The Federal Constitution of 1848, as well as the other federal constitutions tried to find mechanisms in order to maintain peace and to avoid alienating either of the two religious groups, as well as to provide protection to the individual. Nevertheless, traces of the Catholic Church's defeat in the *Sonderbundskrieg* were still detectable up until 1973 in Articles

51 and 52 of the Constitution of 1874, which banned the Jesuit order from any activity in churches and schools, and prohibited the establishment of new monasteries and religious orders. As a prerequisite for its accession to the European Convention of Human Rights, Switzerland had to abolish these constitutional articles.

§2. Provisions in the Federal Constitution

834. The Preamble of the Constitution starts with the proclamation 'In the name of Almighty God'. This traditional invocation of God does not imply that Switzerland is a religious State. With this invocation of God, the Constitution recognizes the limited powers of the People.

835. According to the Swiss Federal Constitution of 1999, as had been already the case under previous constitutions, it is within the powers of the cantons to regulate the relationship between religion and the state (Article 72(1) of the Constitution). It is a question of debate among constitutional scholars whether with the approval of the popular initiative prohibiting minarets (*see supra* Part IV, Chapter 2, §4 V) the Federal Constitution has introduced a paragraph which contradicts this principle.

836. However, the cantons are not completely free in their power. The federal level maintains a peacekeeping or mediating function in order to promote peace between the different communities and to protect the individual from intrusions by the state:

(a) The federal level can adopt measures to maintain or achieve peace between different religious groups (Article 72(2) of the Constitution).
(b) The Federal Constitution guarantees the freedom of religion and philosophy, including the right to enter and leave a religious community free from State coercion and to practice the religion alone and in communities (Article 15 of the Constitution; *see supra* Part IV, Chapter 2, §4 V F).
(c) The Federal Constitution prohibits mandatory religious instruction at schools and guarantees the access of all children to public schools. In addition it guarantees that schools must be controlled by public authorities (Article 62 of the Constitution). Many cantons however consider that children should be educated with the respect of traditional Christian values. The Federal Supreme Court held on several occasions that the confessional neutrality at public schools had been violated (*see* Decision of the Federal Supreme Court 116 Ia 252 [crucifix in a class room], 123 I 296 [Islamic primary school teacher wearing a headscarf during lessons; prohibition affirmed by the Court]; 125 I 347 [access to a public school may not be limited to Protestant students only]; 142 I 49 [prohibition for students to wear a headscarf violates freedom of religion]; regarding the question whether Muslim juveniles must shake the hand of their female teacher *see* already *supra* Part IV, Chapter 2, §4 V F).
(d) Further provisions that can have an impact on the rights and duties of the state and of religious communities are, for instance, the right to a decent burial (Article 7 of the Constitution; *see also* Decision of the Federal Supreme Court BGE 125 I 300) as well as provisions of criminal law (e.g., prohibition of drugs), safety regulations (e.g., duty to wear a helmet when driving a motorcycle), and the law

for animal protection (e.g., prohibition of slaughtering by bleeding without previous narcotization). A constitutional provision that provided for the need for a federal approval for the institution of new bishoprics was repealed in 2001.

§3. Cantonal Solutions

837. There are four different models regulating the relationship between the state and church, or more appropriately stated, between the state and religion. (1) A state can be a theocracy, where the authority of the state is supposed to derive directly from a divine source. (2) There can be a state religion, although state religions and their influence can vary decisively. In all cases, however, the state religion must have an exclusive, official status in the state. (3) The third model is characterized by the recognition of a special status for more than one religion, i.e., it is possible within this system that one religion has a preferential status. And (4), there can be a separation between the state and religion, or state neutrality regarding religion based on the concept of privatizing religion.

838. None of the cantons are organized as theocracies. All cantons have chosen either the secular model or pluralistic forms of recognition of a special status for several religious communities.

839. The Canton of Geneva (since 1907) and the Canton of Neuchâtel (since 1941) have opted for a separation between religion and state. Religious communities must rely on the forms of private law for their organization. The separation is relative insofar as the religious communities can raise voluntary taxes and the state collects the taxes either free of charge (Neuchâtel) or against an emolument (Geneva). In 1980, a federal initiative aiming at the complete separation of church and state was rejected with 78.9% of the voters.

840. Today, most cantons allow for a public law status for the Protestant and Roman Catholic Church, although some cantons also grant public law status to other religious communities, such as the Jewish community (Berne, Basel-City, Fribourg) and the Christ-Catholic Church (Berne). Even though the Muslim population greatly outnumbers the Jewish and Christ-Catholic communities, the Muslim community has not yet achieved a public law status in any of the cantons. According to the provisions of the Canton of Fribourg, a religious community can achieve public law status when it:

(a) is a traditional religious movement in Switzerland or of universal importance;
(b) is a member of the ecumenical council of churches or has been represented in the canton for thirty years; and
(c) respects the fundamental principles of the Swiss legal order.

841. Some cantons accord equal rights to the religious communities with public law status (Glarus, Aargau, Grisons, St. Gallen, Thurgau), while others privilege one or two of the communities, which are sometimes called state church (*Staatskirche*).

842. Religious communities with a public law status normally have the right to raise taxes that are then collected by the state. These taxes are only mandatory for the adherents of the religious communities. In cantons that denominate a so-called state church, adherence to this religious belief is normally expected, based on the territoriality principle. Any person who does not want to belong to the community must revoke his/her membership. Enterprises are mandated to pay church taxes in most of the cantons. According to the Federal Supreme Court, they cannot claim the right to religious freedom in order to leave a religious community, and therefore cannot be exempted from taxes (Decisions of the Federal Supreme Court BGE 138 I 55 and 126 I 122). Several attempts to lodge an application with the ECHR already failed at the admissibility criteria.

843. In addition, religious communities with a public law status can receive state subsidies in particular for their services in the public interest such as health, education and social aid.

Selected Bibliography

Note: Further references for in-depth research are indicated at the beginning of the relevant paragraph.

Aubert Jean-François. *Traité de droit constitutionnel suisse.* 2 vol. Paris/Neuchâtel: Edition Ides et Calendes, 1967. *Supplément 1967–1982.* Neuchâtel: Edition Ides et Calendes, 1982.

Aubert Jean-François et al. (eds). *Kommentar zur Bundesverfassung der Schweizerischen Eidgenossenschaft* vom 29. Mai 1874. Zurich/Berne, 1987–1996 (cited as Author. Kommentar BV 1874).

Aubert Jean-François & Mahon Pascal. *Petit commentaire de la Constitution fédérale de la Confédération suisse* du 18 avril 1999. Zurich: Schulthess, 2003 (cited as Author. commentaire. Article …).

Auer Andreas, Malinverni Giorgio & Hottelier Michel. *Droit constitutionnel suisse.* 2 vol. 3rd ed. Berne: Stämpfli, 2013.

Auer Andreas. *Staatsrecht der schweizerischen Kantone.* Berne: Stämpfli, 2016.

Basler Kommentar BV. See Waldmann et al.

Basta Fleiner Lidija R. & Fleiner Thomas (eds). *Federalism and Multiethnic States: The Case of Switzerland,* PIFF 16. 2nd ed. Basel: Helbing & Lichtenhahn, 2000.

Biaggini Giovanni. *Bundesverfassung der Schweizerischen Eidgenossenschaft.* Zurich: Orell Füssli, 2007 (cited as: Biaggini. Kommentar, Article …).

Biaggini Giovanni. 'Switzerland'. In *How Constitutions Change,* edited by Dawn Oliver & Carlo Fusaro Hart Publishing. Chapter 14. Oxford, 2011.

Biaggini Giovanni, Gächter Thomas & Kiener Regina (eds). Staatsrecht. 2nd ed. Zürich/St. Gallen: Dike, 2015.

Bundeskanzlei. *The Swiss Confederation: A Brief Guide.* Berne, 2016.

Burckhardt Walther. *Kommentar der schweizerischen Bundesverfassung* vom 29. Mai 1874. 3rd ed. Berne: Stämpfli, 1931.

Buser Denise. *Kantonales Staatsrecht.* 2nd ed. Basel: Helbing & Lichtenhahn, 2011.

Dessemontet François & Ansay Tuğrul (eds). *Introduction to Swiss Law.* 3rd ed. The Hague/Zurich: Kluwer/Schulthess, 2004.

Egli Patricia. *Introduction to Swiss Constitutional Law.* Zurich/St. Gallen: Dike, 2016.

Ehrenzeller Bernhard et al. (eds). *Die schweizerische Bundesverfassung: Kommentar.* 2 vol. 3rd ed. Zurich/St. Gallen: Dike & Schulthess, 2014 (cited as Author. St. Galler Kommentar, Article …).

Fleiner Fritz & Giacometti Zaccaria. *Schweizerisches Bundesstaatsrecht.* Zurich: Polygraphischer Verlag, 1949.

Fleiner Thomas & Basta Fleiner Lidija. *Constitutional Democracy in a Multicultural World.* Berlin/Heidelberg: Springer, 2009 (cited as Fleiner & Basta Fleiner. Constitutional Democracy).

Fleiner Thomas et al. (eds). *BV 2000: Die neue schweizerische Bundesverfassung: Föderalismus, Grundrechte, Wirtschaftsrecht und Staatsstruktur.* PIFF 26. Basel/Geneva/Munich: Helbing & Lichtenhahn, 2000 (cited as Author. In Fleiner et al.).

Gächter Thomas & Bertschi Martin (eds). *Neue Akzente in der 'nachgeführten' Bundesverfassung.* Zurich: Schulthess, 2000.

Giacometti Zaccaria. *Allgemeine Lehren des rechtsstaatlichen Verwaltungsrechts.* Vol. 1. Zurich: Schulthess, 1960.

Grisel Etienne. *Droits fondamentaux: Libertés idéales.* Berne: Stämpfli, 2008.

Gygi Fritz. *Bundesverwaltungsrechtspflege.* 2nd ed. Berne: Stämpfli, 1983.

Häfelin Ulrich, Haller Walter, Keller Helen & Daniela Thurnherr. *Schweizerisches Bundesstaatsrecht.* 9th ed. Zurich: Schulthess, 2016.

Häfelin Ulrich, Müller Georg & Uhlmann Felix. *Allgemeines Verwaltungsrecht.* 7th ed. Zurich: Schulthess, 2016.

Haller Walter. *The Swiss Constitution in a Comparative Context.* 2nd ed. Zurich/St. Gallen: Dike, 2016 (cited as Haller. *Swiss Constitution*).

Hangartner Yvo. *Grundzüge des schweizerischen Staatsrechts.* Vol. 1: *Organisation.* Zurich: Schulthess, 1980. Vol. 2: *Grundrechte.* Zurich: Schulthess, 1982.

Hangartner Yvo & Kley Andreas. *Die demokratischen Rechte in Bund und Kantonen der Schweizerischen Eidgenossenschaft.* Zurich: Schulthess, 2000.

Jaag Tobias, Bucher Laura & Häggi Furrer Reto. *Staatsrecht der Schweiz in a nutshell.* 2nd ed. Zurich/St. Gallen: Dike 2016.

Kälin Walter & Künzli Jörg. *Universeller Menschenrechtsschutz.* 3rd ed. Basel: Helbing & Lichtenhahn, 2013.

Kiener Regina & Kälin Walter. *Grundrechte.* 2nd ed. Berne: Stämpfli, 2013.

Kley Andreas. Geschichte des öffentlichen Rechts der Schweiz. 2nd ed. Zurich/St. Gallen: Dike, 2015.

Knoepfel Peter et al. (eds). *Handbuch der Schweizer Politik.* 5th ed. Zurich: NZZ Verlag, 2015 (cited as Knoepfel et al.).

Kölz Alfred, Häner Isabelle & Bertschi Martin. *Verwaltungsverfahren und Verwaltungsrechtspflege des Bundes.* 3rd ed. Zurich: Schulthess, 2013.

Linder Wolf. *Swiss Democracy: Possible Solutions to Conflict in Multicultural Societies.* 3rd ed. London: Pan Books Ltd., 2010.

Mahon Pascal. *Droit constitutionnel.* 2 vol. 3rd ed. Basel: Helbing & Lichtenhahn, 2014 and 2015.

Selected Bibliography

Merten Detlef & Papier Hans-Jürgen (eds). *Handbuch der Grundrechte. Grundrechte in der Schweiz und Liechtenstein.* Vol. VII/2. C.F. Müller/Dike: Heidelberg/Zürich/ St. Gallen, 2007 (cited as Author, in Merten/Papier).

Misic Alexander. *Verfassungsbeschwerde – Das Bundesgericht und der subsidiäre Schutz verfassungsmässiger Rechte.* Zurich: Schulthess, 2011.

Moor Pierre et al., *Droit administratif.* 3 vol. 3rd ed. Berne: Stämpfli, 2011/2012.

Müller Jörg Paul. *Elemente einer schweizerischen Grundrechtstheorie.* Berne: Stämpfli, 1982.

Müller Jörg Paul & Schefer Markus. *Grundrechte in der Schweiz.* 4th ed. Berne: Stämpfli, 2008.

Niggli Marcel A., Uebersax Peter & Wiprächtiger Hans (eds). *Bundesgerichtsgesetz.* 2nd ed. Helbing & Lichtenhahn, Basel: Basler Kommentar, 2011.

Rhinow René. *Die Bundesverfassung* 2000. Basel/Geneva/Munich: Helbing & Lichtenhahn, 2000 (cited as Rhinow, BV 2000).

Rhinow René, Schefer Markus & Uebersax Peter. *Schweizerisches Verfassungsrecht.* 3rd ed. Basel: Helbing & Lichtenhahn, 2016.

Rhinow René et al., *Öffentliches Wirtschaftsrecht.* 3rd ed. Basel: Helbing & Lichtenhahn, 2014.

Rhinow René A. et al., *Öffentliches Prozessrecht.* 3rd ed. Basel: Helbing & Lichtenhahn, 2014.

St. Galler Kommentar. *See* Ehrenzeller et al.

Sitter-Liver Beat (ed.). *Herausgeforderte Verfassung: Die Schweiz im globalen Kontext.* Freiburg i.Ue.: Universitätsverlag Freiburg, 1999.

Steinberg Jonathan. *Why Switzerland?.* 3rd ed. New York: Cambridge University Press, 2015.

Thürer Daniel, Aubert Jean-François & Müller Jörg Paul (eds). *Verfassungsrecht der Schweiz – Droit constitutionnel suisse.* Zurich: Schulthess, 2001 (cited as Author. In Thürer et al.).

Tschannen Pierre. *Staatsrecht der schweizerischen Eidgenossenschaft.* 4th ed. Berne: Stämpfli, 2016.

Tschannen Pierre, Zimmerli Ulrich & Müller Markus. *Allgemeines Verwaltungsrecht.* 4th ed. Berne: Stämpfli, 2014.

Tschentscher Axel & Lienhard Andreas. *Öffentliches Recht – Ein Grundriss.* Zurich/ St. Gallen: Dike, 2011.

Waldmann Bernhard, Belser Eva Maria & Epiney Astrid (eds). Bundesverfassung. Basler Kommentar. Basel: Helbing & Lichtenhahn, 2015 (cited as Author. Basler Kommentar, Article …).

Zimmerli Ulrich (ed.). *Die neue Bundesverfassung, Konsequenzen für Praxis und Wissenschaft.* Berne: Stämpfli, 2000.

Selected Bibliography

Index

The numbers here refer to paragraph numbers.

Index

Index

Index

Index

www.ingramcontent.com/pod-product-compliance
Ingram Content Group UK Ltd.
Pitfield, Milton Keynes, MK11 3LW, UK
UKHW020134290926
15471UKWH00003B/469